Vol. 4

Story & Art by
Ao Mimori

Contents

The Story Thus Far...

Ryoko falls hard for Ryunosuke, the quiet, bespectacled cutie who sits next to her in class. Then she learns that he moonlights as a host—a guy who dates women for money! Soft-spoken bookworm by day, aggressive ladies' man by night, Ryu may be more than the inexperienced Ryoko can handle. But she can't seem to get him out of her head...or her heart...

Ryu and Ryoko confront Jin, the president of Ryu's host club, and convince him to cancel Ryu's contract. Ryu promises to stop working as a host and begin a new life as Ryoko's full-time—and unpaid—boyfriend. But, as Ryoko is about to discover, not everyone wants to leave Ryu's hosting career in the past...

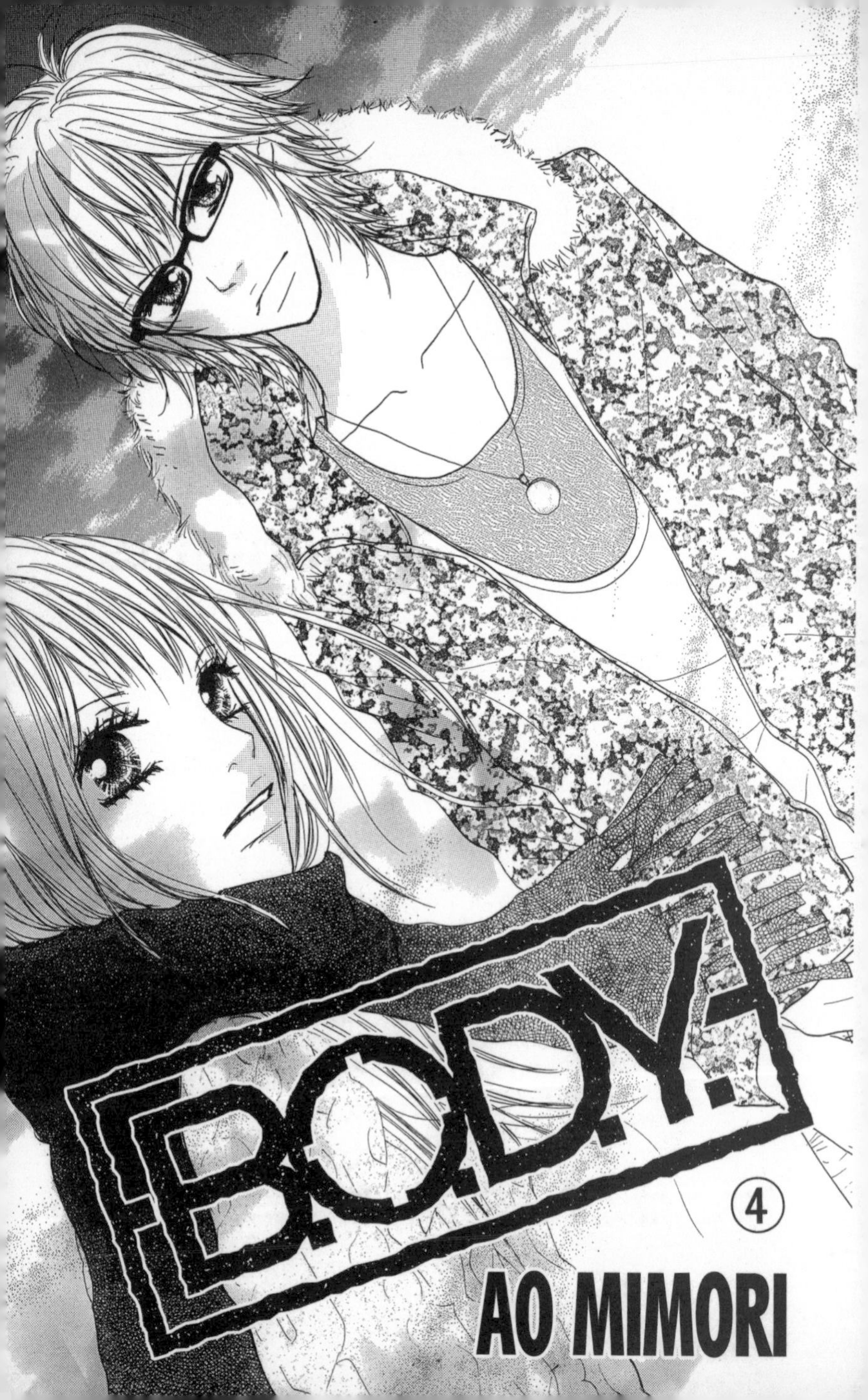
B.O.D.Y.
4
AO MIMORI

Hello—!
It's Volume 4!

Cherry Blossoms

How're you all doing? It's getting warmer, isn't it? Spring would be such a great time of year if it weren't for the pollen...
Anyway, here's B.O.D.Y. Volume 4. Ha ha ha...I've got to laugh...

A new story arc starts from this volume. What'll happen?
I hope you'll be patient with my characters.

There's more bonus stuff at the end of the volume, too.

Okay, let's get this show on the road! See ya.

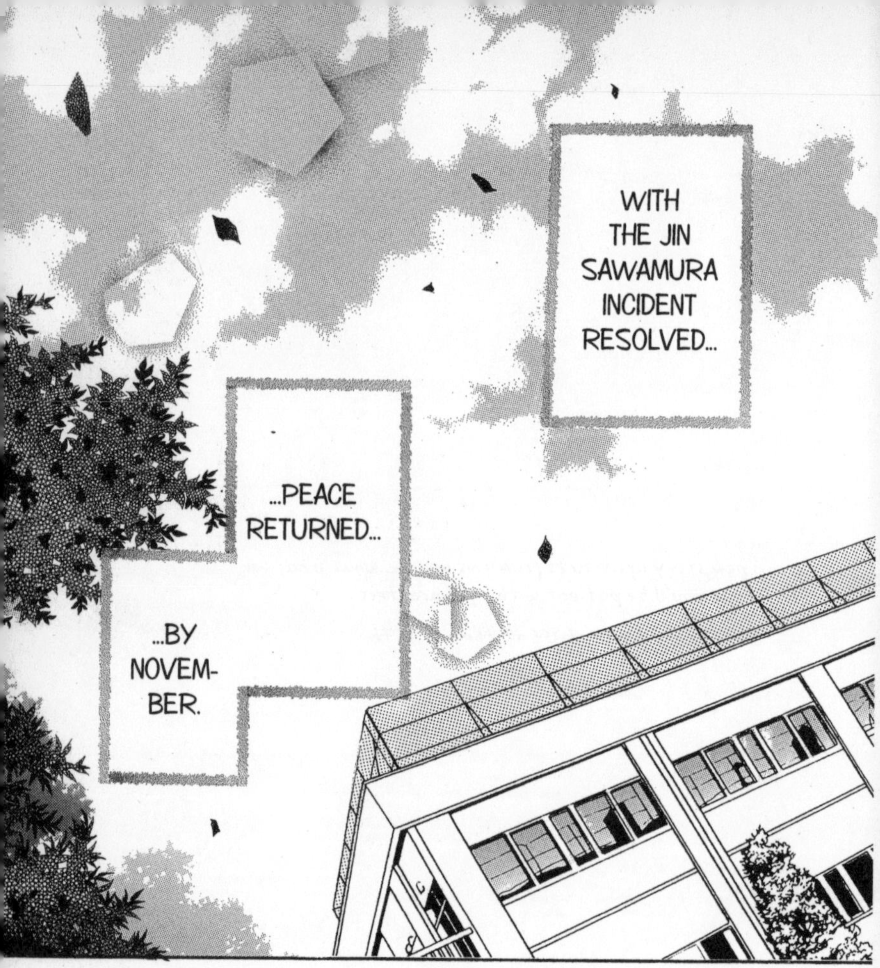
WITH THE JIN SAWAMURA INCIDENT RESOLVED...
...PEACE RETURNED...
...BY NOVEMBER.
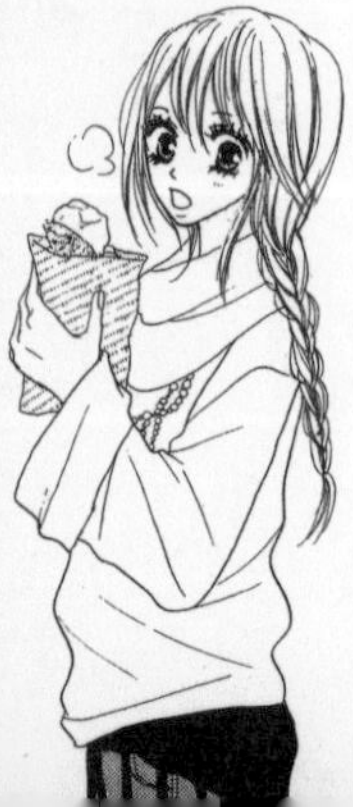

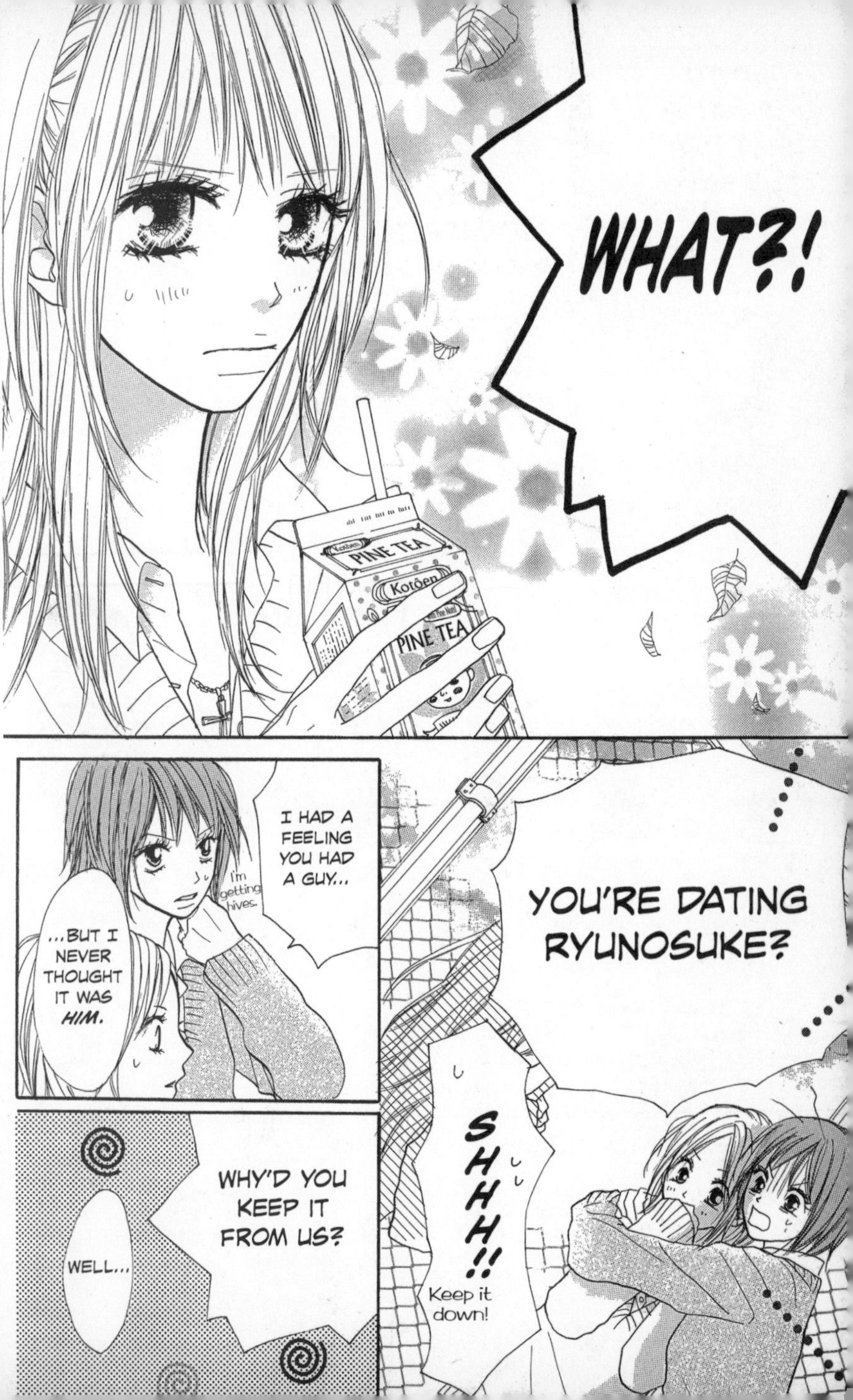
WHAT?!
YOU'RE DATING RYUNOSUKE?
SHHH!!
Keep it down!
I HAD A FEELING YOU HAD A GUY...
I'm getting hives.
...BUT I NEVER THOUGHT IT WAS *HIM*.
WHY'D YOU KEEP IT FROM US?
WELL...

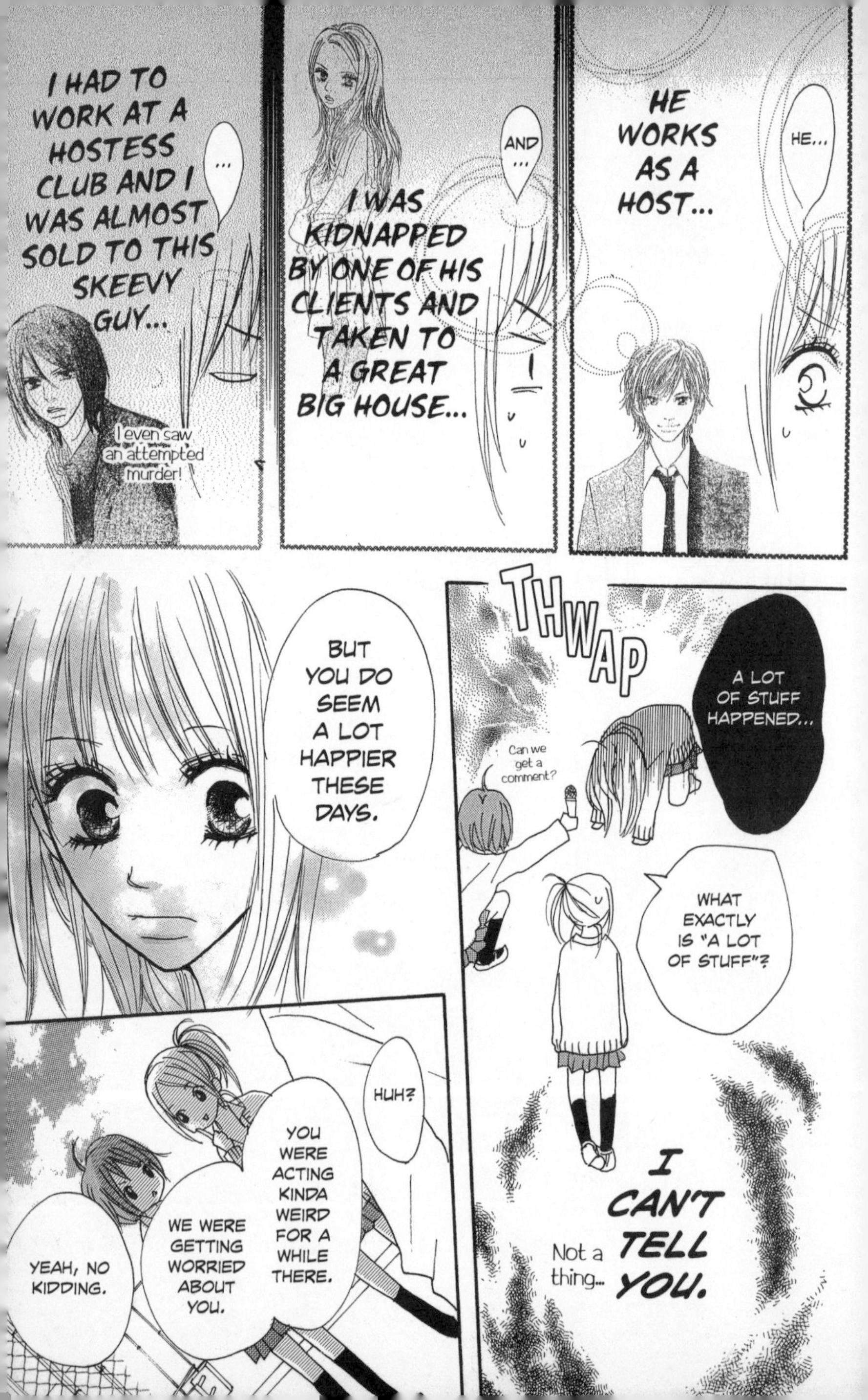
HE...
HE WORKS AS A HOST...
AND...
I WAS KIDNAPPED BY ONE OF HIS CLIENTS AND TAKEN TO A GREAT BIG HOUSE...
I HAD TO WORK AT A HOSTESS CLUB AND I WAS ALMOST SOLD TO THIS SKEEVY GUY...
...
I even saw an attempted murder!
THWAP
A LOT OF STUFF HAPPENED...
Can we get a comment?
WHAT EXACTLY IS "A LOT OF STUFF"?
I CAN'T TELL YOU.
Not a thing...
BUT YOU DO SEEM A LOT HAPPIER THESE DAYS.
HUH?
YOU WERE ACTING KINDA WEIRD FOR A WHILE THERE.
WE WERE GETTING WORRIED ABOUT YOU.
YEAH, NO KIDDING.

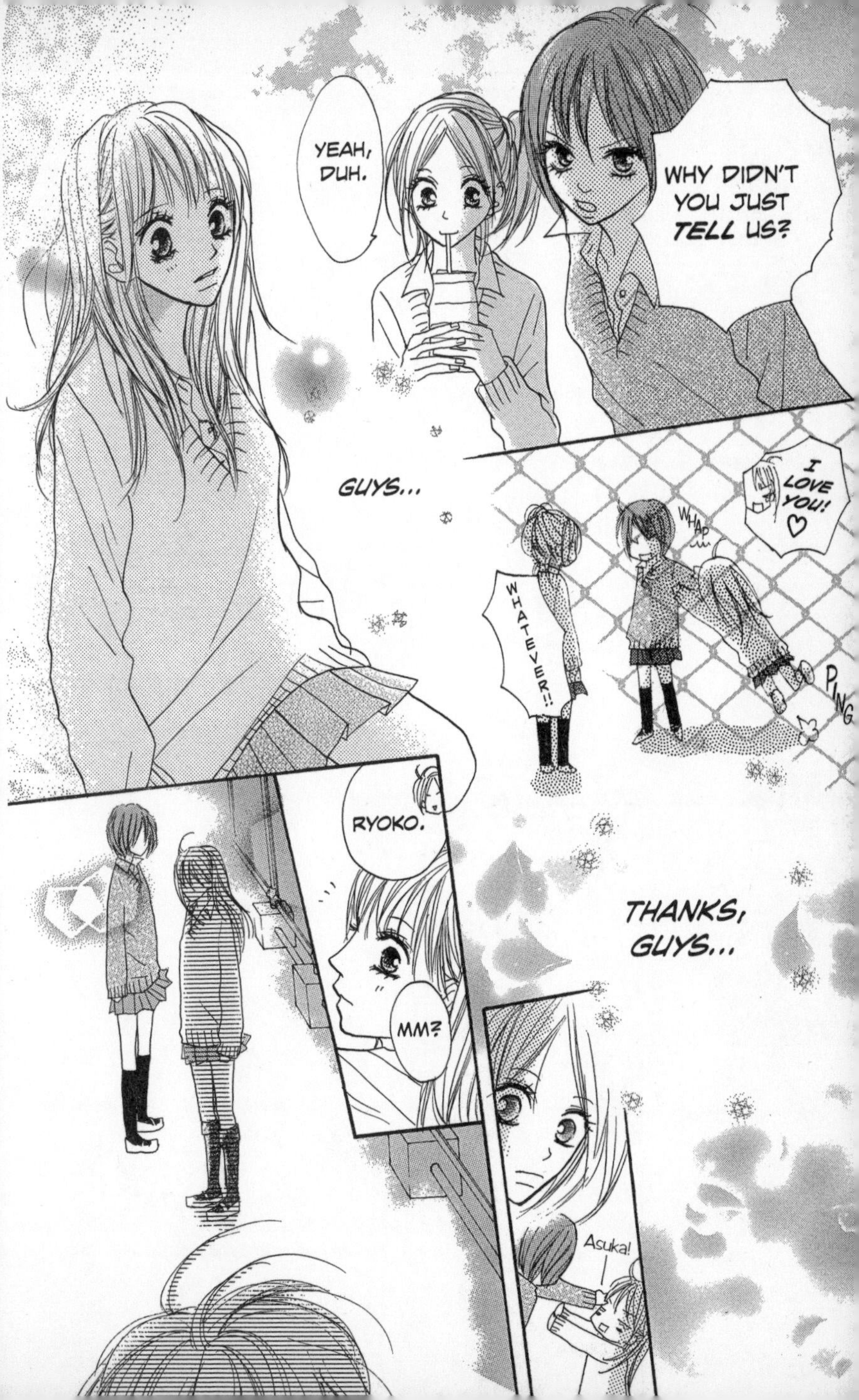
WHY DIDN'T YOU JUST TELL US?
YEAH, DUH.
I LOVE YOU! ♡
WHAP
PING
WHATEVER!!
GUYS...
THANKS, GUYS...
RYOKO.
MM?
Asuka!

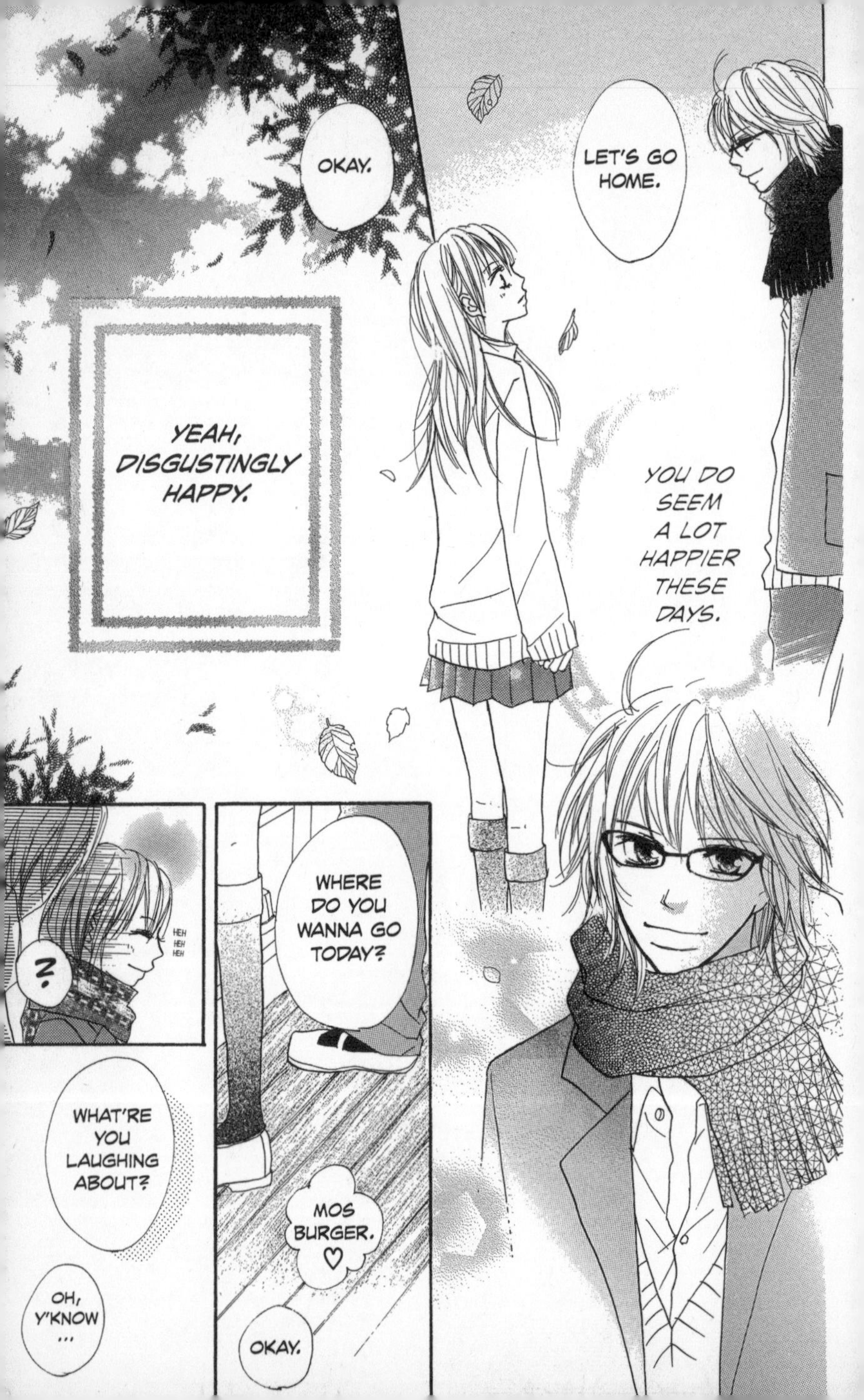
LET'S GO HOME.
OKAY.
YOU DO SEEM A LOT HAPPIER THESE DAYS.
YEAH, DISGUSTINGLY HAPPY.
WHERE DO YOU WANNA GO TODAY?
MOS BURGER. ♡
OKAY.
HEH HEH HEH
?
WHAT'RE YOU LAUGHING ABOUT?
OH, Y'KNOW ...

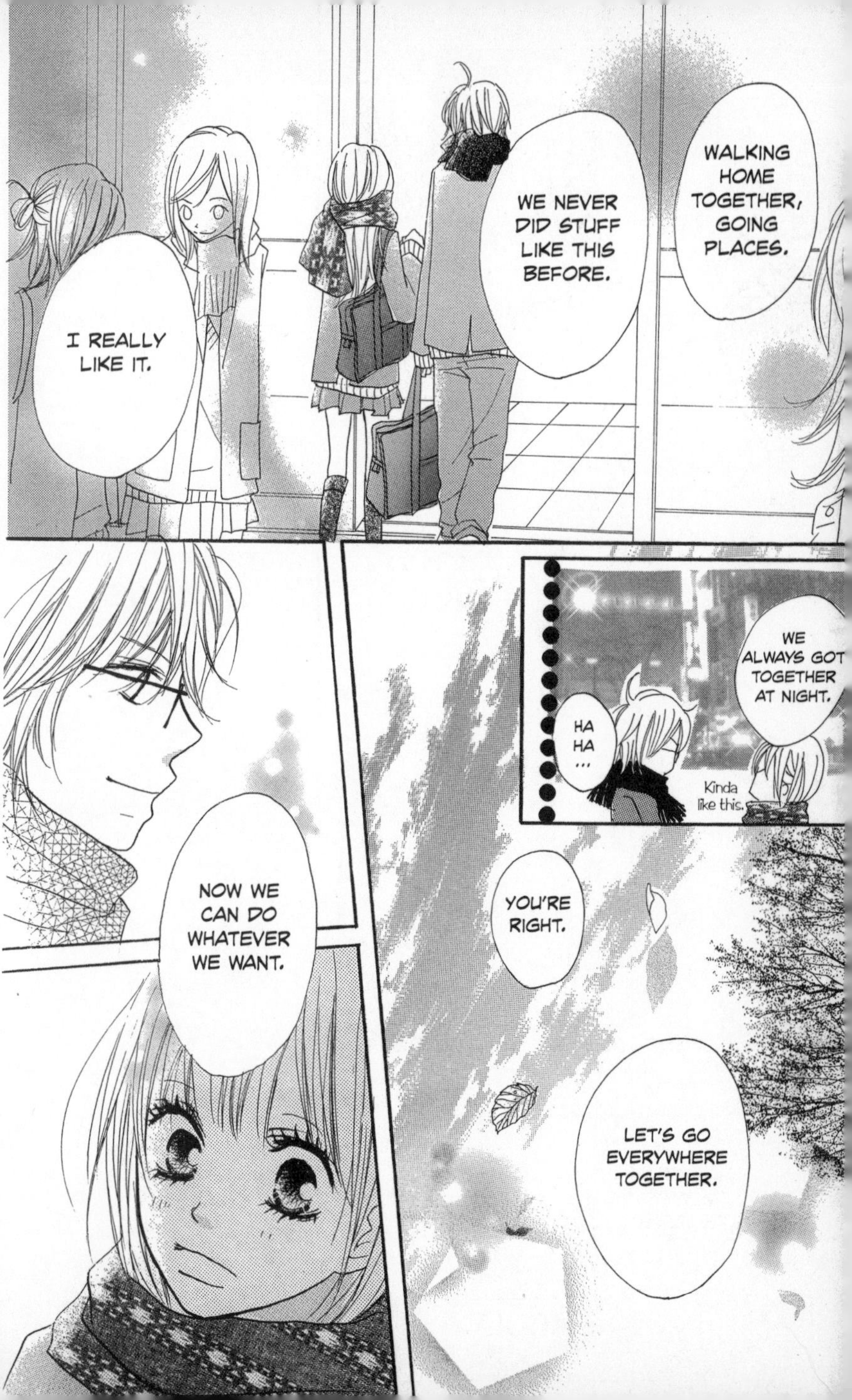
WALKING HOME TOGETHER, GOING PLACES.
WE NEVER DID STUFF LIKE THIS BEFORE.
I REALLY LIKE IT.
WE ALWAYS GOT TOGETHER AT NIGHT.
HA HA ...
Kinda like this.
YOU'RE RIGHT.
LET'S GO EVERYWHERE TOGETHER.
NOW WE CAN DO WHATEVER WE WANT.

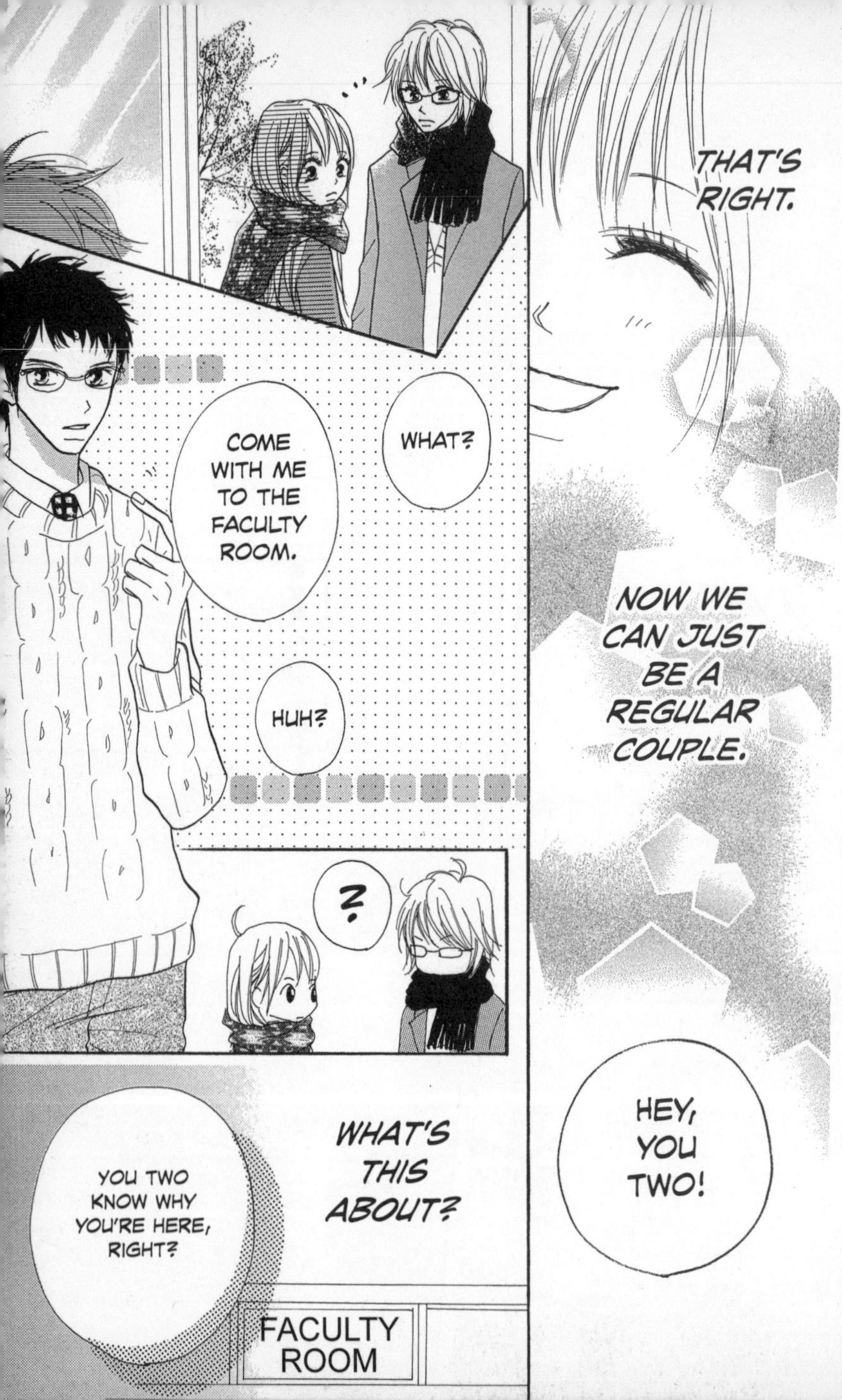
THAT'S RIGHT.
NOW WE CAN JUST BE A REGULAR COUPLE.
HEY, YOU TWO!
WHAT?
COME WITH ME TO THE FACULTY ROOM.
HUH?
?
WHAT'S THIS ABOUT?
YOU TWO KNOW WHY YOU'RE HERE, RIGHT?
FACULTY ROOM

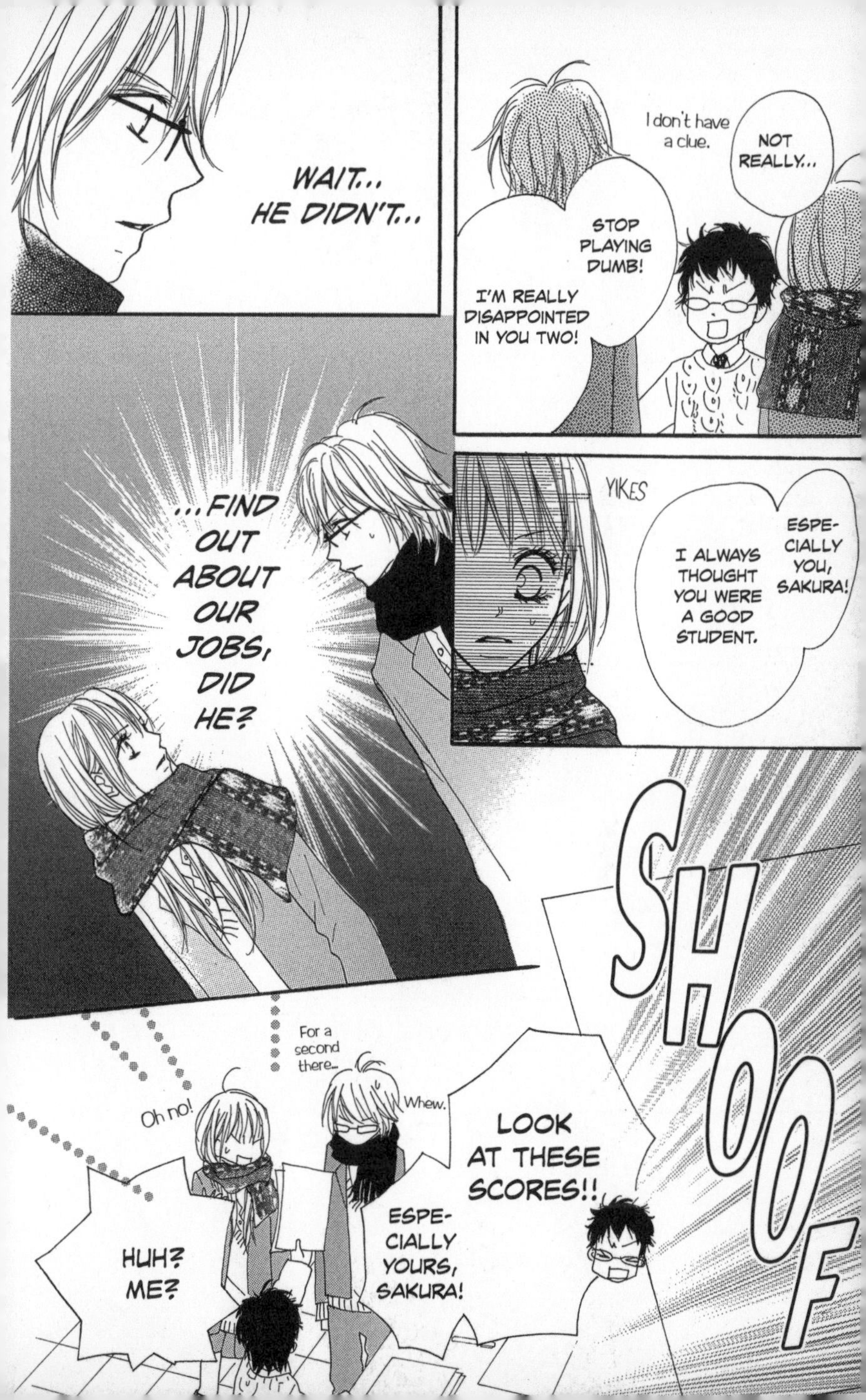
NOT REALLY...
I don't have a clue.
STOP PLAYING DUMB!
I'M REALLY DISAPPOINTED IN YOU TWO!
WAIT... HE DIDN'T...
ESPE-CIALLY YOU, SAKURA!
I ALWAYS THOUGHT YOU WERE A GOOD STUDENT.
YIKES
...FIND OUT ABOUT OUR JOBS, DID HE?
SHOOOF
LOOK AT THESE SCORES!!
ESPE-CIALLY YOURS, SAKURA!
For a second there...
Whew.
Oh no!
HUH? ME?

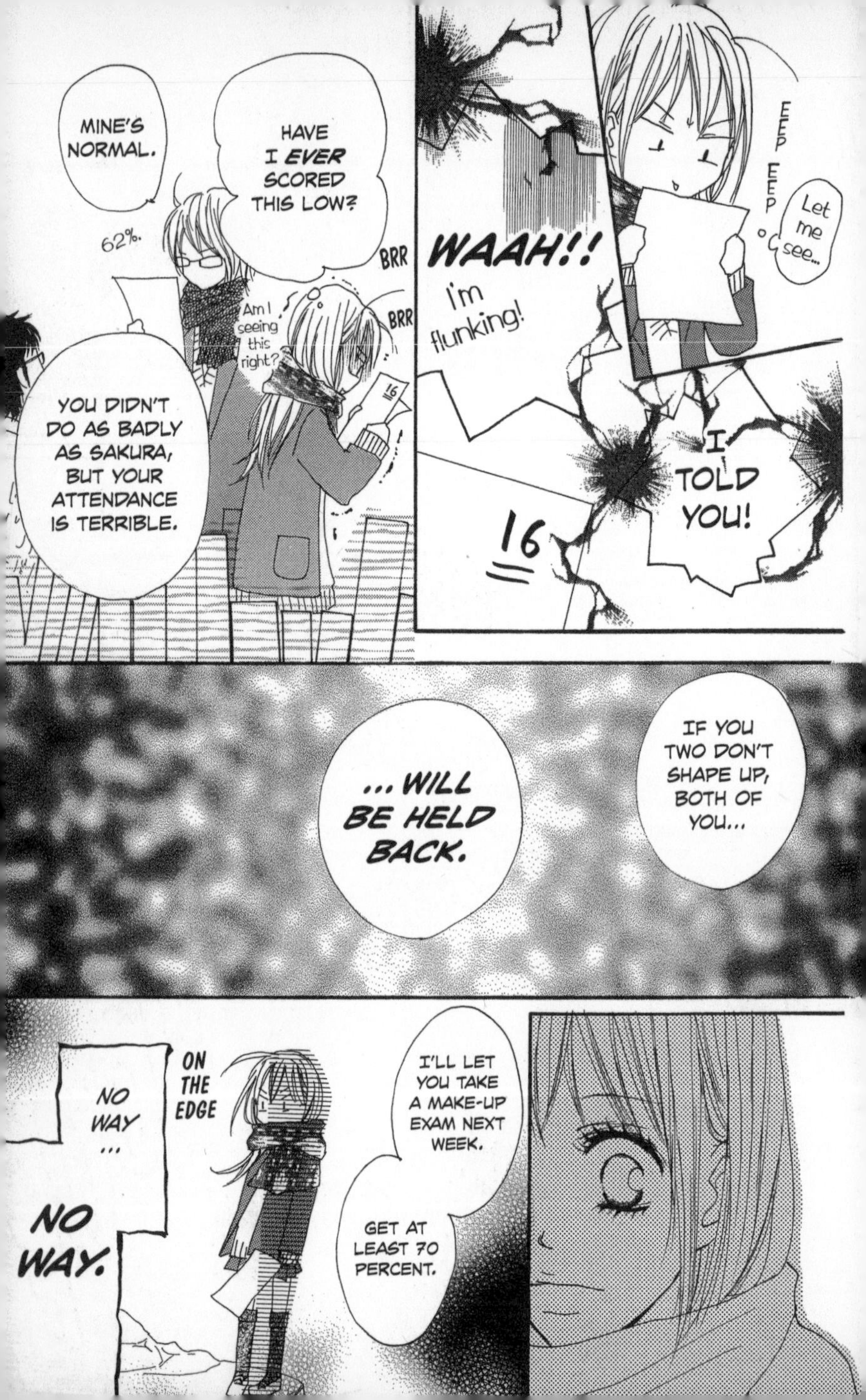
Let me see...
EEP EEP
WAAH!!
I'm flunking!
I TOLD YOU!
16
HAVE I EVER SCORED THIS LOW?
MINE'S NORMAL.
62%.
BRR BRR
Am I seeing this right?
16
YOU DIDN'T DO AS BADLY AS SAKURA, BUT YOUR ATTENDANCE IS TERRIBLE.
IF YOU TWO DON'T SHAPE UP, BOTH OF YOU...
...WILL BE HELD BACK.
I'LL LET YOU TAKE A MAKE-UP EXAM NEXT WEEK.
GET AT LEAST 70 PERCENT.
ON THE EDGE
NO WAY...
NO WAY.

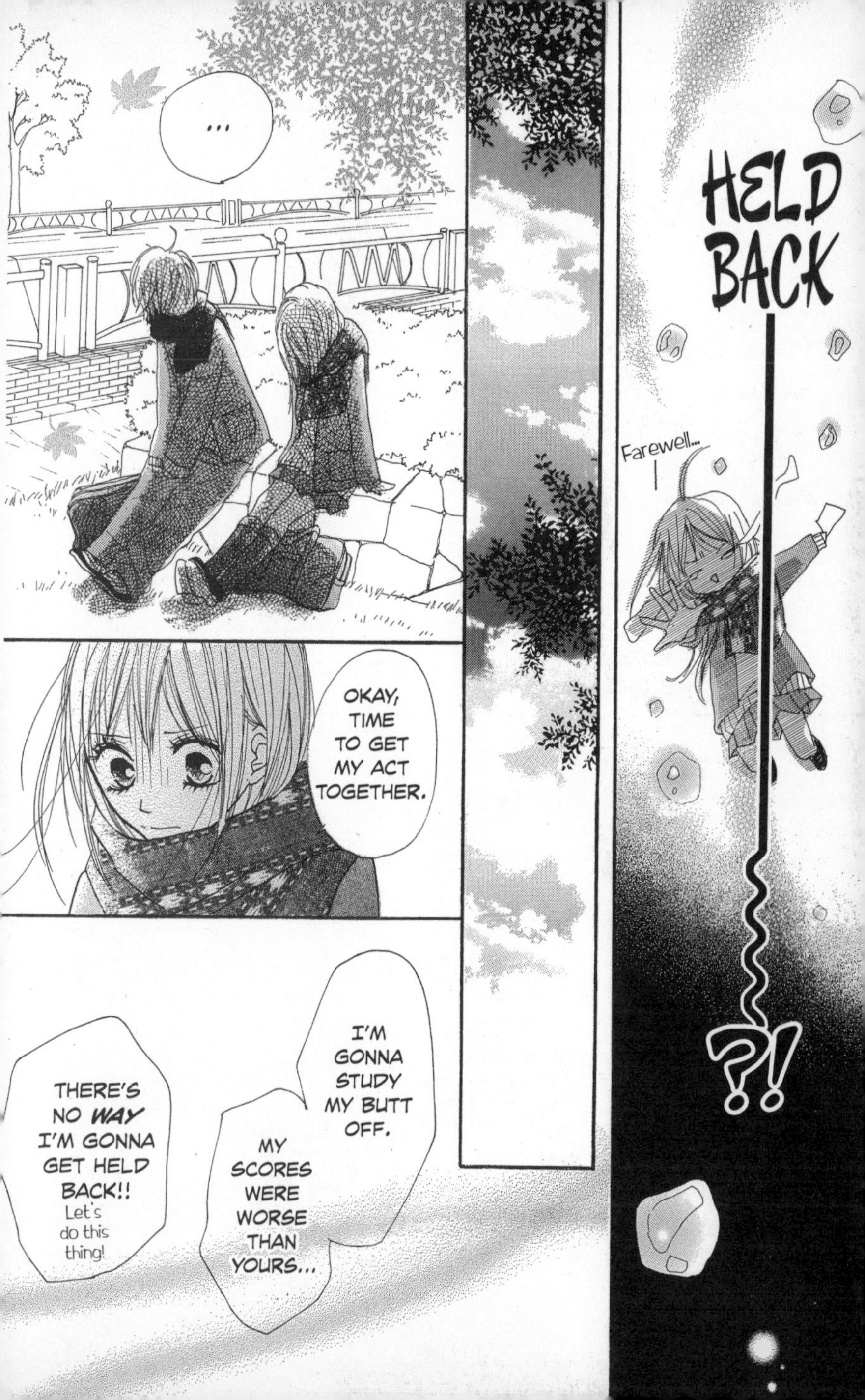
HELD BACK
Farewell...
?!
...
OKAY, TIME TO GET MY ACT TOGETHER.
I'M GONNA STUDY MY BUTT OFF.
MY SCORES WERE WORSE THAN YOURS...
THERE'S NO *WAY* I'M GONNA GET HELD BACK!! Let's do this thing!

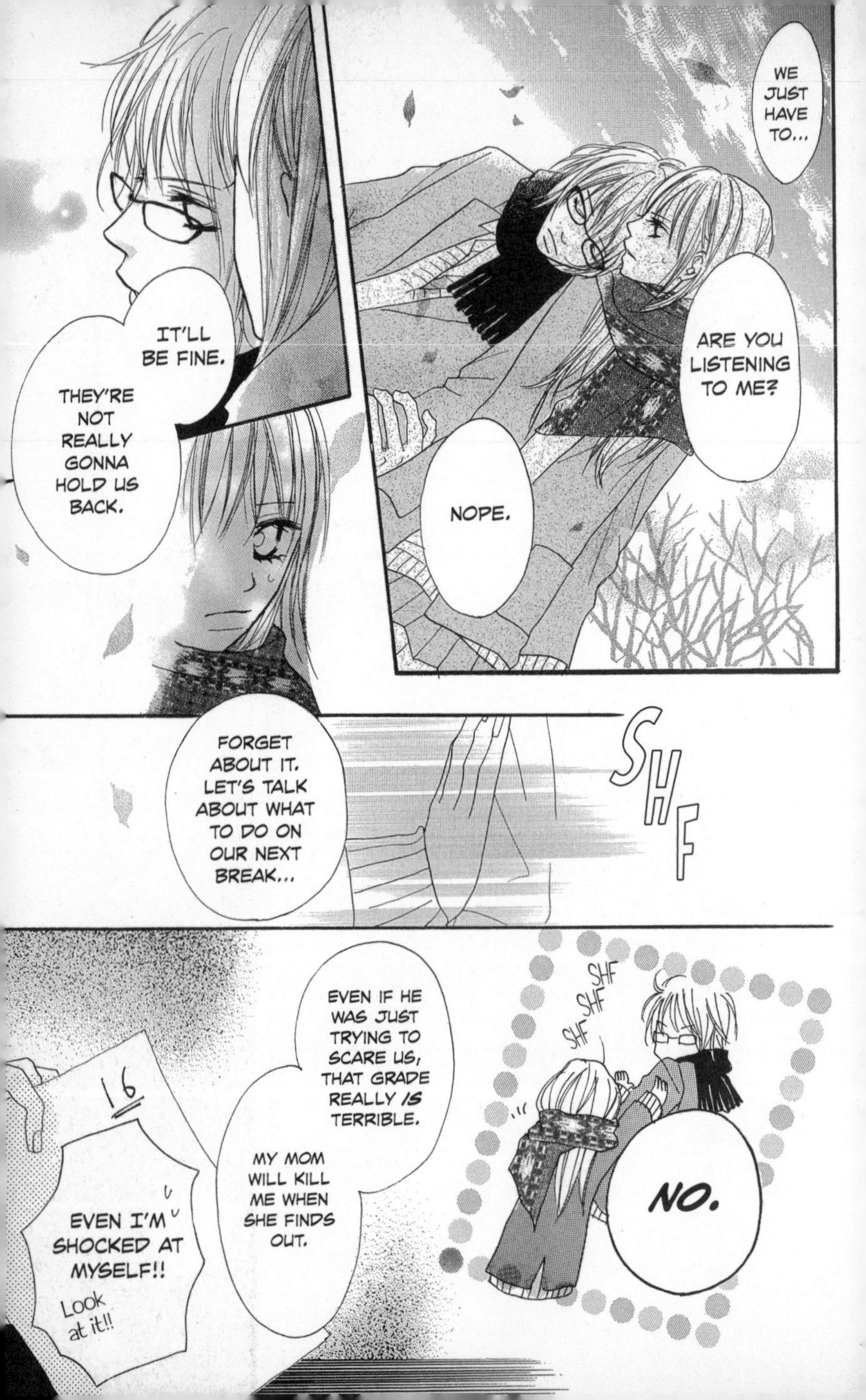
WE JUST HAVE TO...
ARE YOU LISTENING TO ME?
NOPE.
IT'LL BE FINE.
THEY'RE NOT REALLY GONNA HOLD US BACK.
SHF
FORGET ABOUT IT. LET'S TALK ABOUT WHAT TO DO ON OUR NEXT BREAK...
SHF SHF SHF
NO.
EVEN IF HE WAS JUST TRYING TO SCARE US, THAT GRADE REALLY *IS* TERRIBLE.
MY MOM WILL KILL ME WHEN SHE FINDS OUT.
16
EVEN I'M SHOCKED AT MYSELF!!
Look at it!!

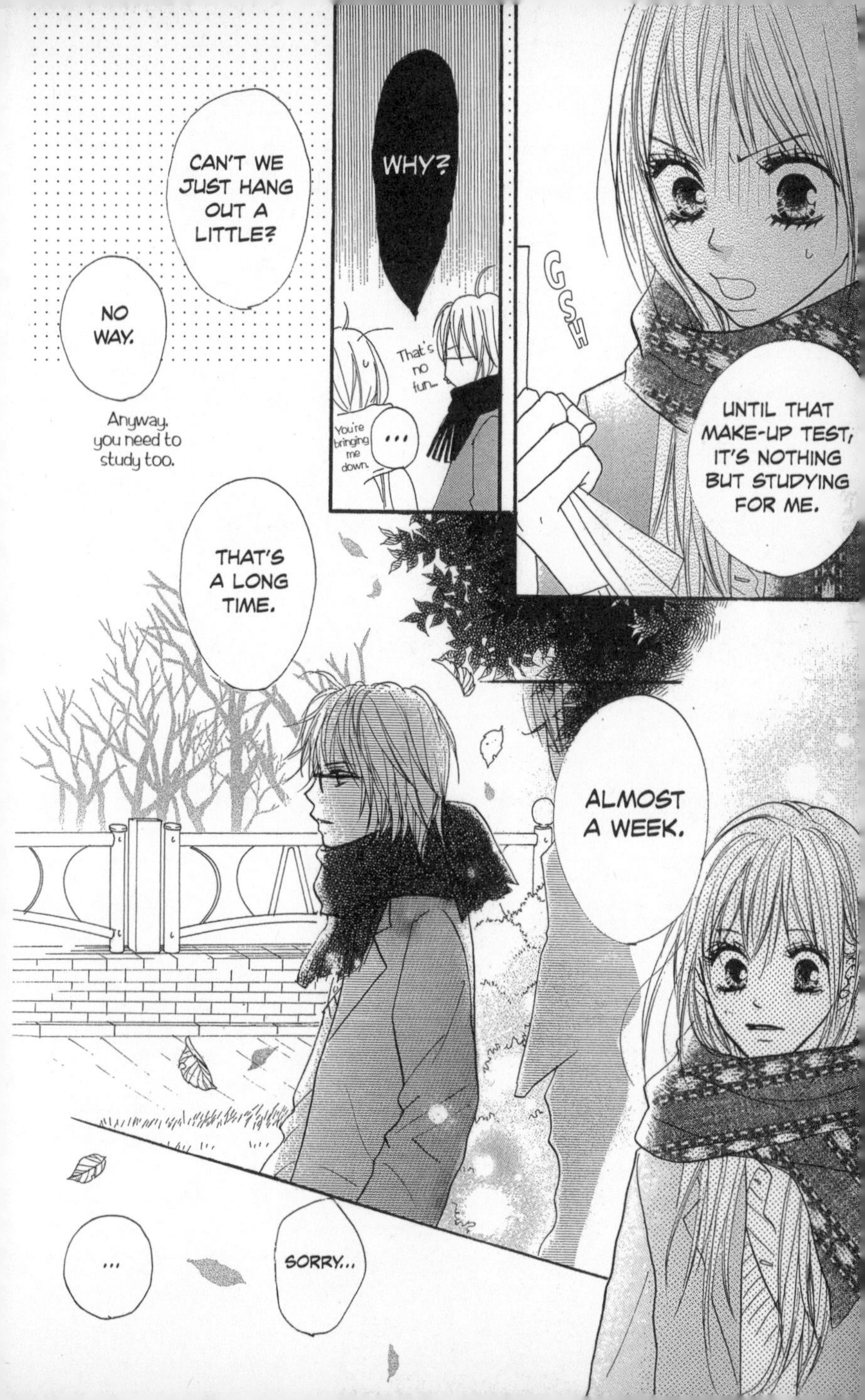
GSH
UNTIL THAT MAKE-UP TEST, IT'S NOTHING BUT STUDYING FOR ME.
WHY?
That's no fun...
You're bringing me down.
...
CAN'T WE JUST HANG OUT A LITTLE?
NO WAY.
Anyway, you need to study too.
ALMOST A WEEK.
THAT'S A LONG TIME.
SORRY...
...

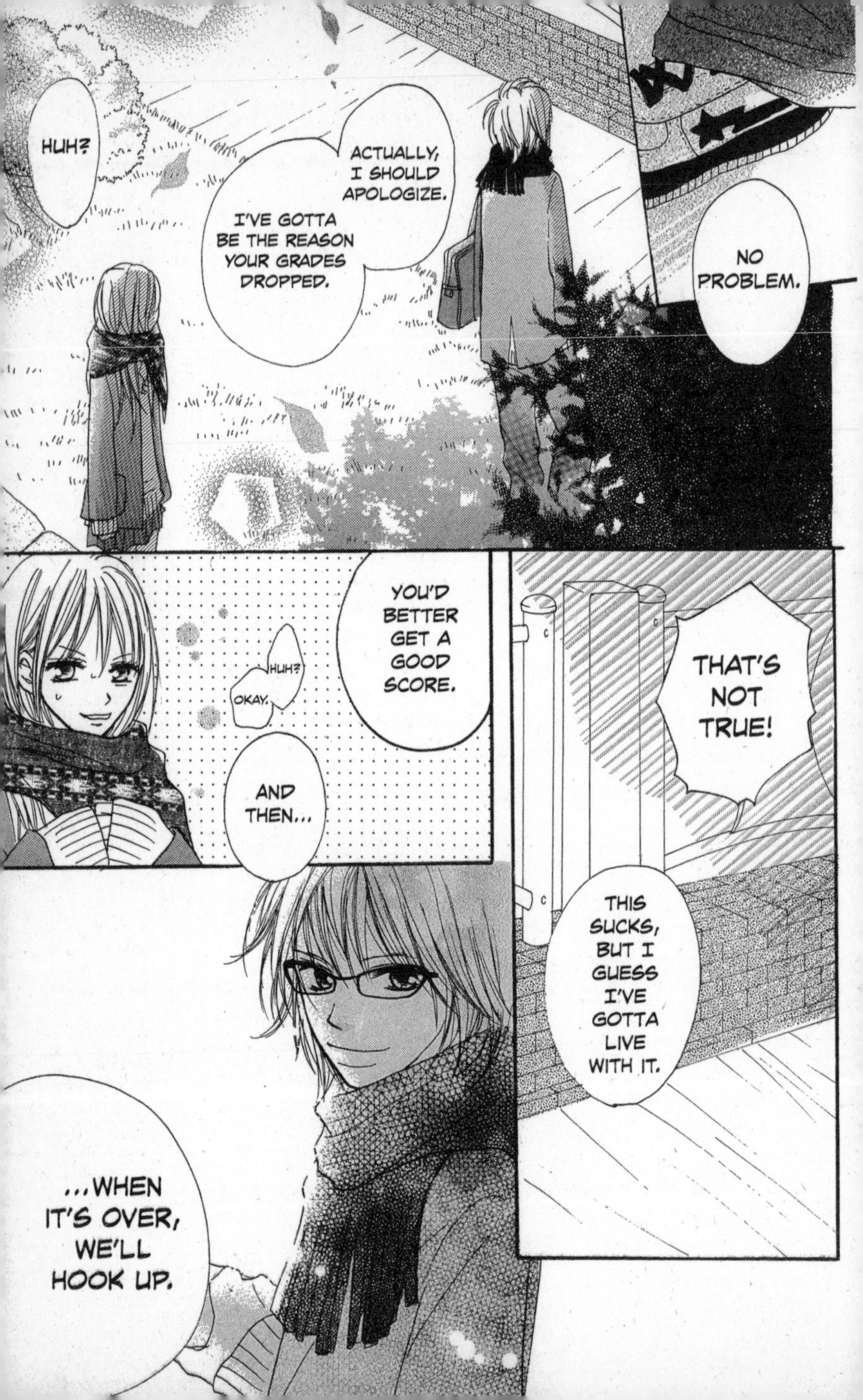
NO PROBLEM.
ACTUALLY, I SHOULD APOLOGIZE.
I'VE GOTTA BE THE REASON YOUR GRADES DROPPED.
HUH?
THAT'S NOT TRUE!
THIS SUCKS, BUT I GUESS I'VE GOTTA LIVE WITH IT.
YOU'D BETTER GET A GOOD SCORE.
HUH?
OKAY.
AND THEN...
...WHEN IT'S OVER, WE'LL HOOK UP.

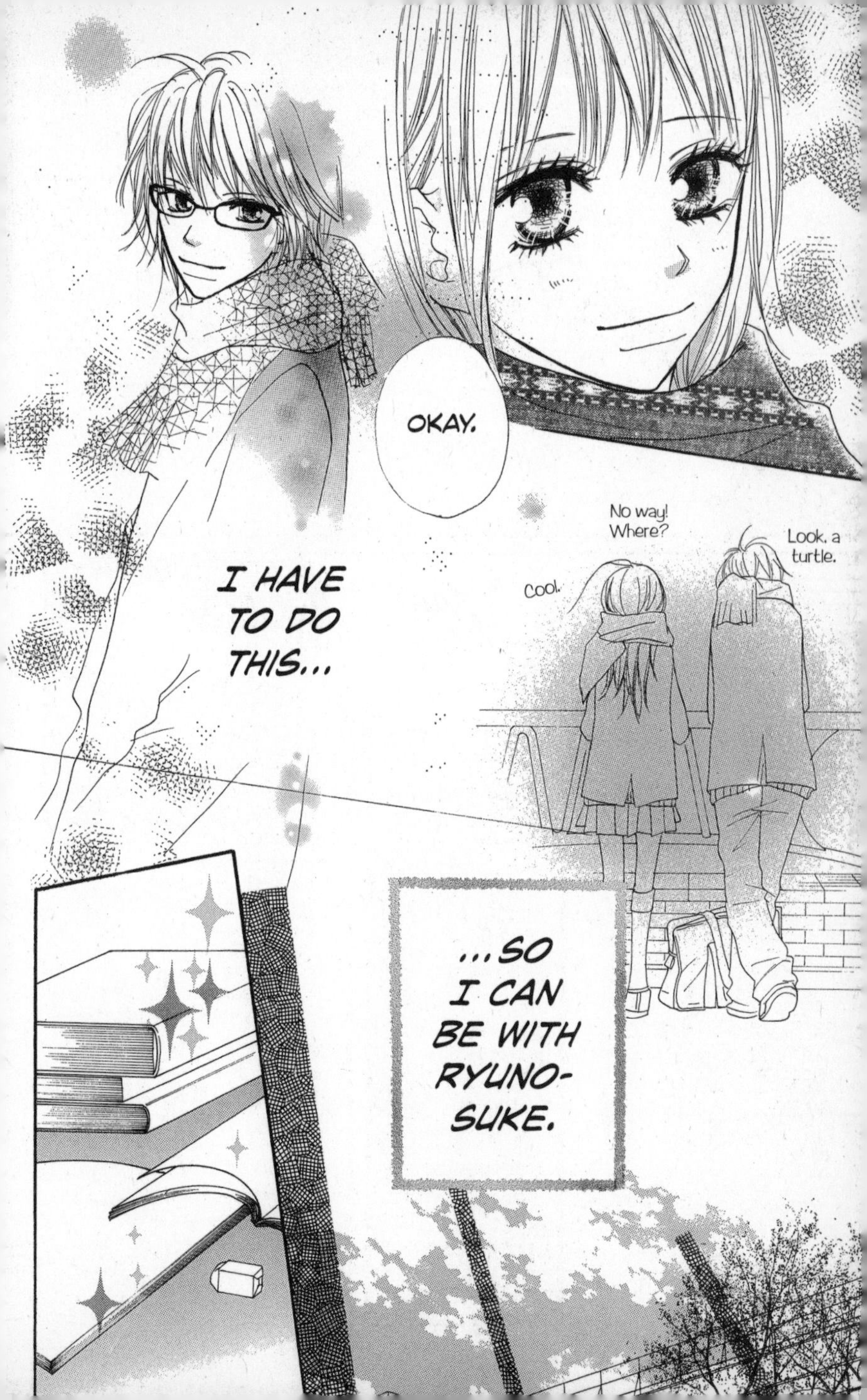
OKAY.
I HAVE TO DO THIS...
Look, a turtle.
No way! Where?
Cool.
...SO I CAN BE WITH RYUNO-SUKE.

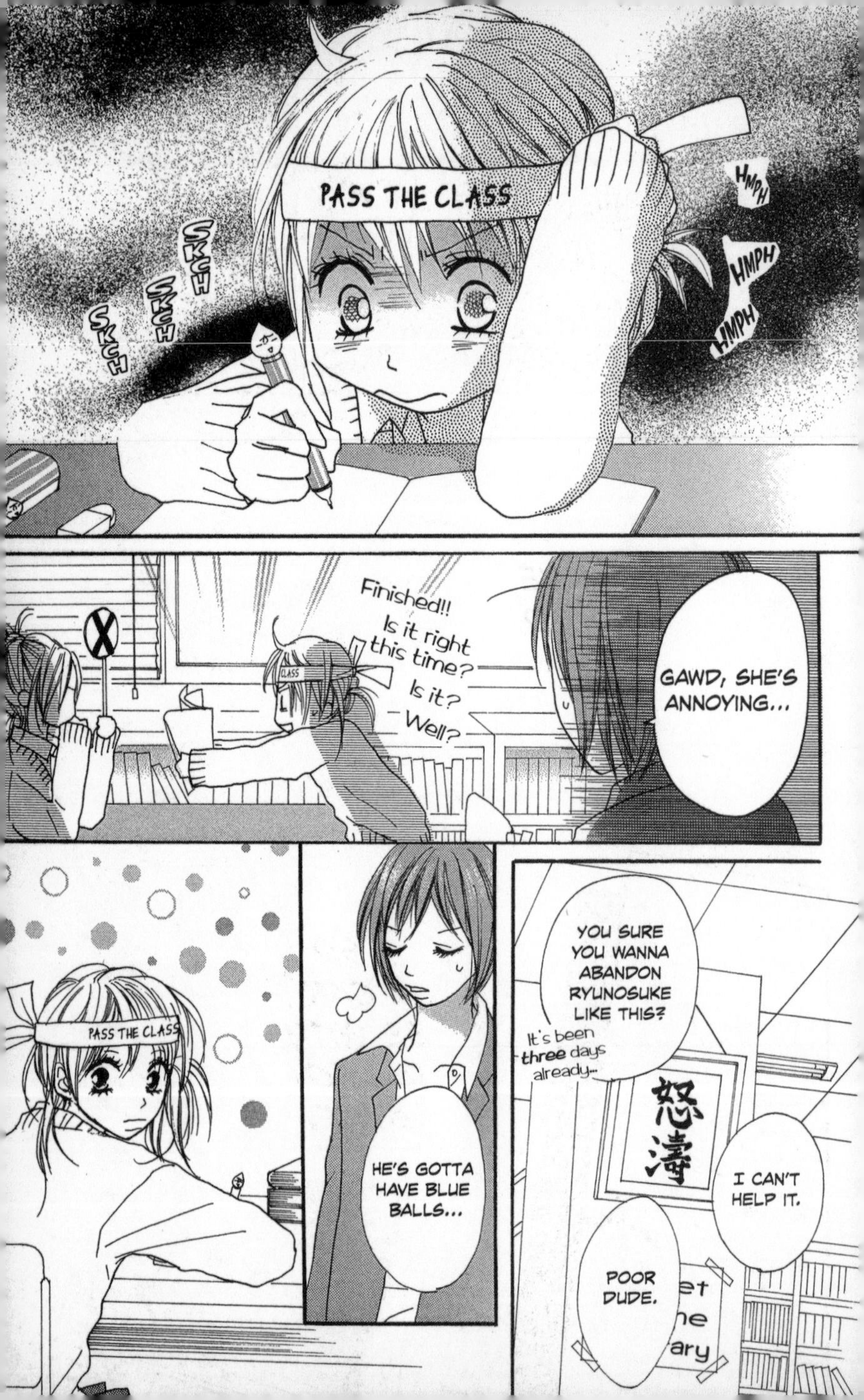
HMPH
HMPH
HMPH
PASS THE CLASS
SKCH
SKCH
SKCH
GAWD, SHE'S ANNOYING...
Finished!!
Is it right this time?
Is it?
Well?
CLASS
YOU SURE YOU WANNA ABANDON RYUNOSUKE LIKE THIS?
It's been three days already...
怒濤
I CAN'T HELP IT.
POOR DUDE.
HE'S GOTTA HAVE BLUE BALLS...
PASS THE CLASS

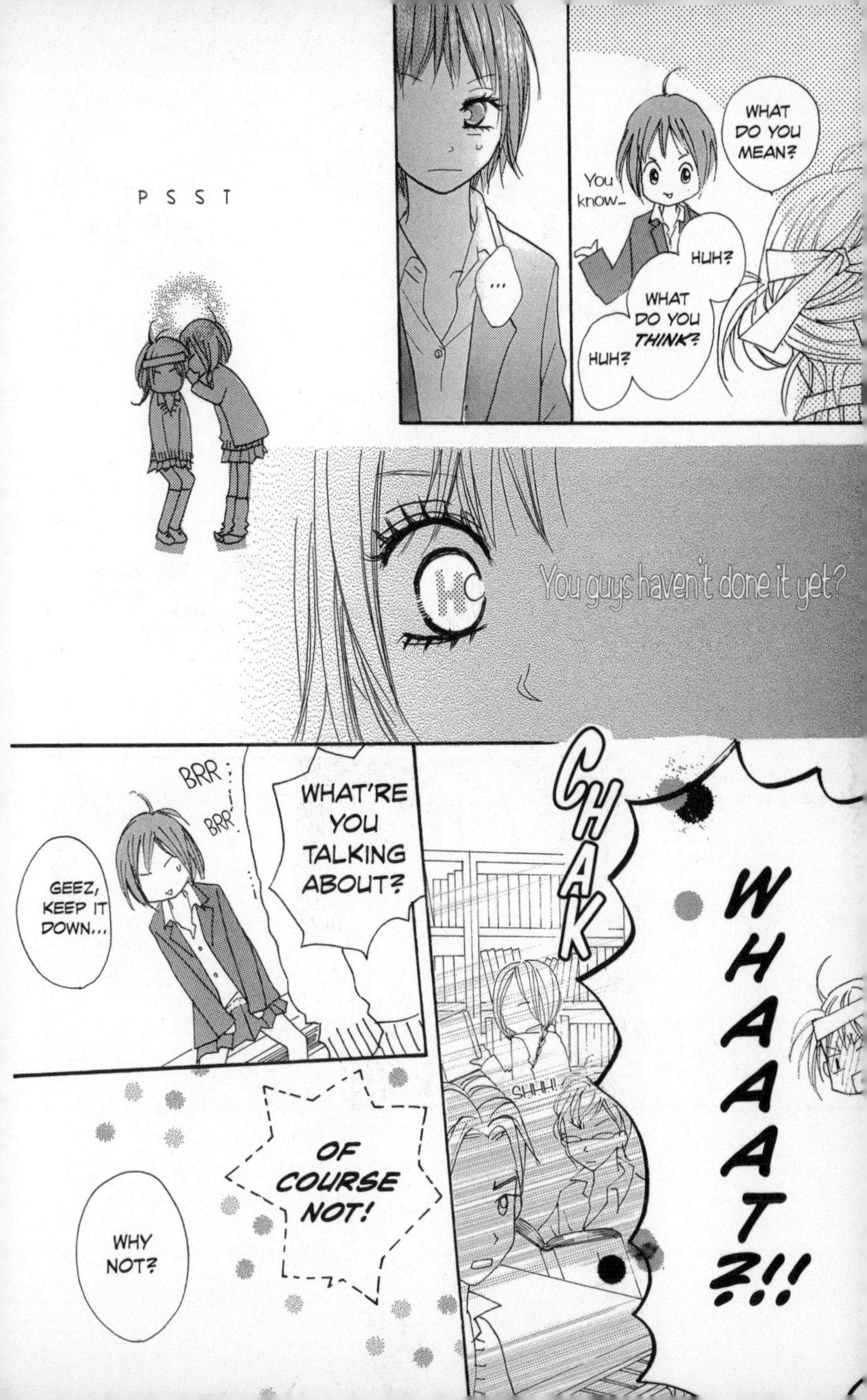
WHAT DO YOU MEAN?
You know...
HUH?
WHAT DO YOU THINK?
HUH?
...
You guys haven't done it yet?
P S S T
CHAK
WHAAAAT?!!
SHHH!
WHAT'RE YOU TALKING ABOUT?
BRR
BRR
GEEZ, KEEP IT DOWN...
OF COURSE NOT!
WHY NOT?

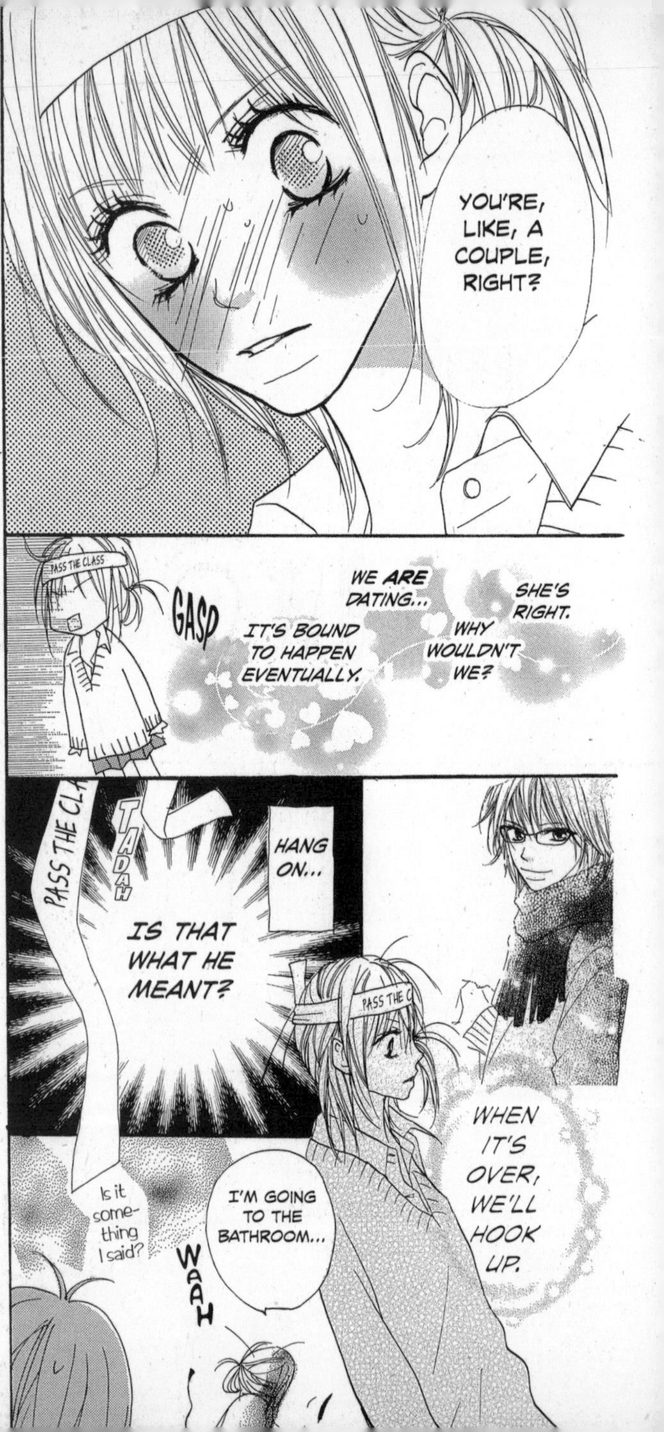
YOU'RE, LIKE, A COUPLE, RIGHT?
SHE'S RIGHT.
WHY WOULDN'T WE?
WE ARE DATING...
IT'S BOUND TO HAPPEN EVENTUALLY.
PASS THE CLASS
GASP
WHEN IT'S OVER, WE'LL HOOK UP.
PASS THE C
I'M GOING TO THE BATHROOM...
WAAH
Is it something I said?
HANG ON...
TADAH
PASS THE CLA
IS THAT WHAT HE MEANT?

① Hey there.

I think I'll just write whatever pops into my head.
Sigh...Boy, writing these notes is relaxing. I wonder why...maybe I just don't know how to really relax. Ha ha!

Anyway...I gained weight!! I gained a lot of weight!! I've never been this chubby. It's obviously because I don't exercise...I wrote in one of the previous volumes that I went jogging along the river, but it's too cold in the winter and I almost die during pollen season, so I stopped. And so...

BALANCE BALL

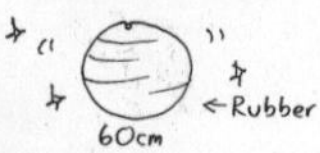
60cm
←Rubber

980 Yen at Donki...

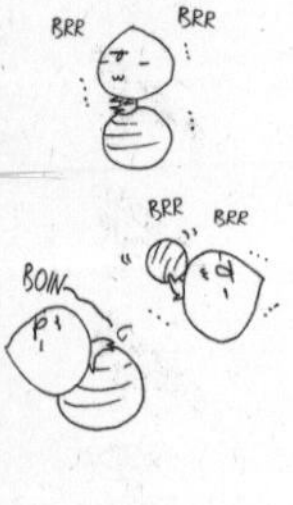
BRR
BRR
BRR
BRR
BOING

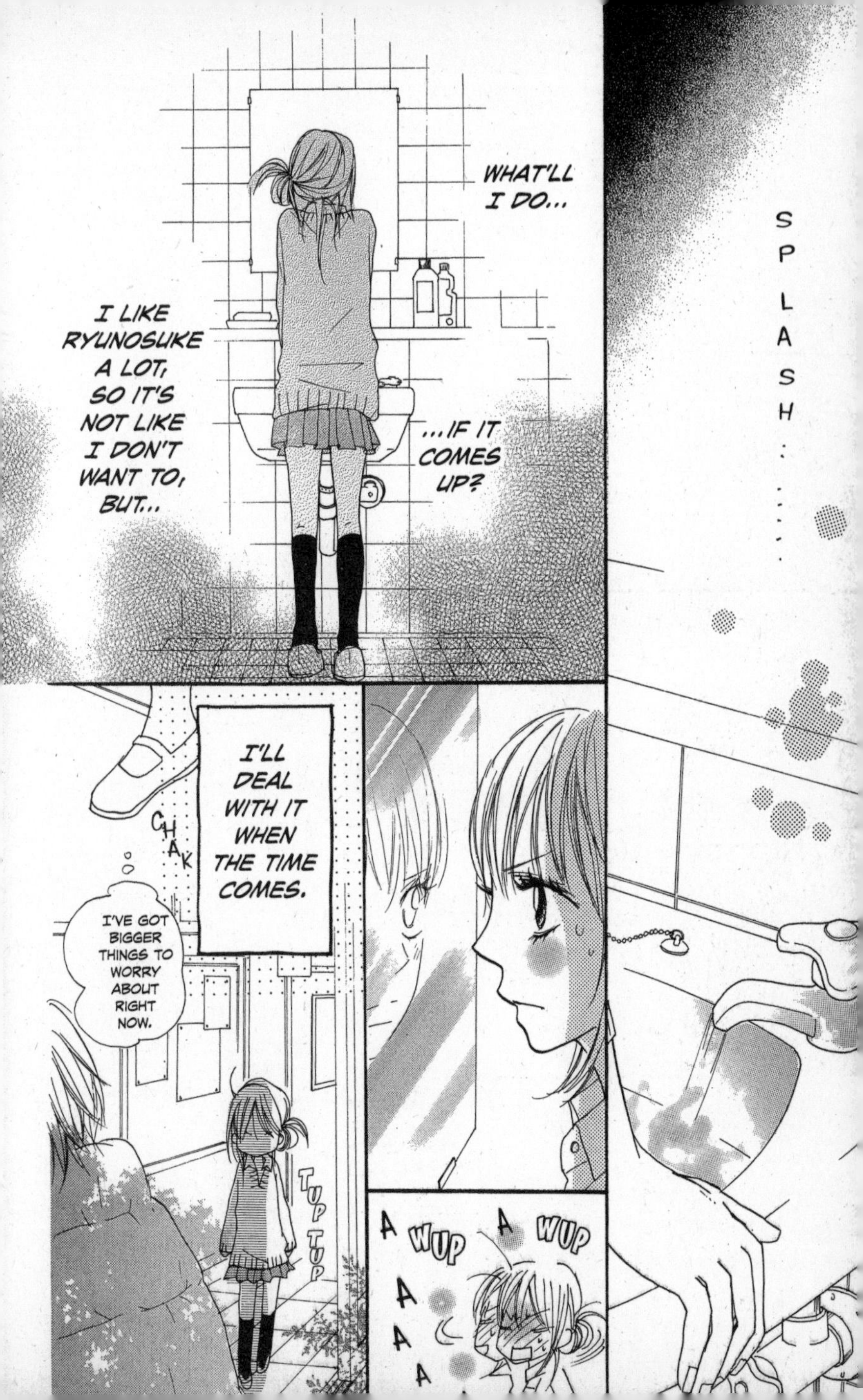
SPLASH.....
WHAT'LL I DO...
I LIKE RYUNOSUKE A LOT, SO IT'S NOT LIKE I DON'T WANT TO, BUT...
...IF IT COMES UP?
A WUP
A WUP
A A A A
CHAK
I'LL DEAL WITH IT WHEN THE TIME COMES.
I'VE GOT BIGGER THINGS TO WORRY ABOUT RIGHT NOW.
TUP TUP

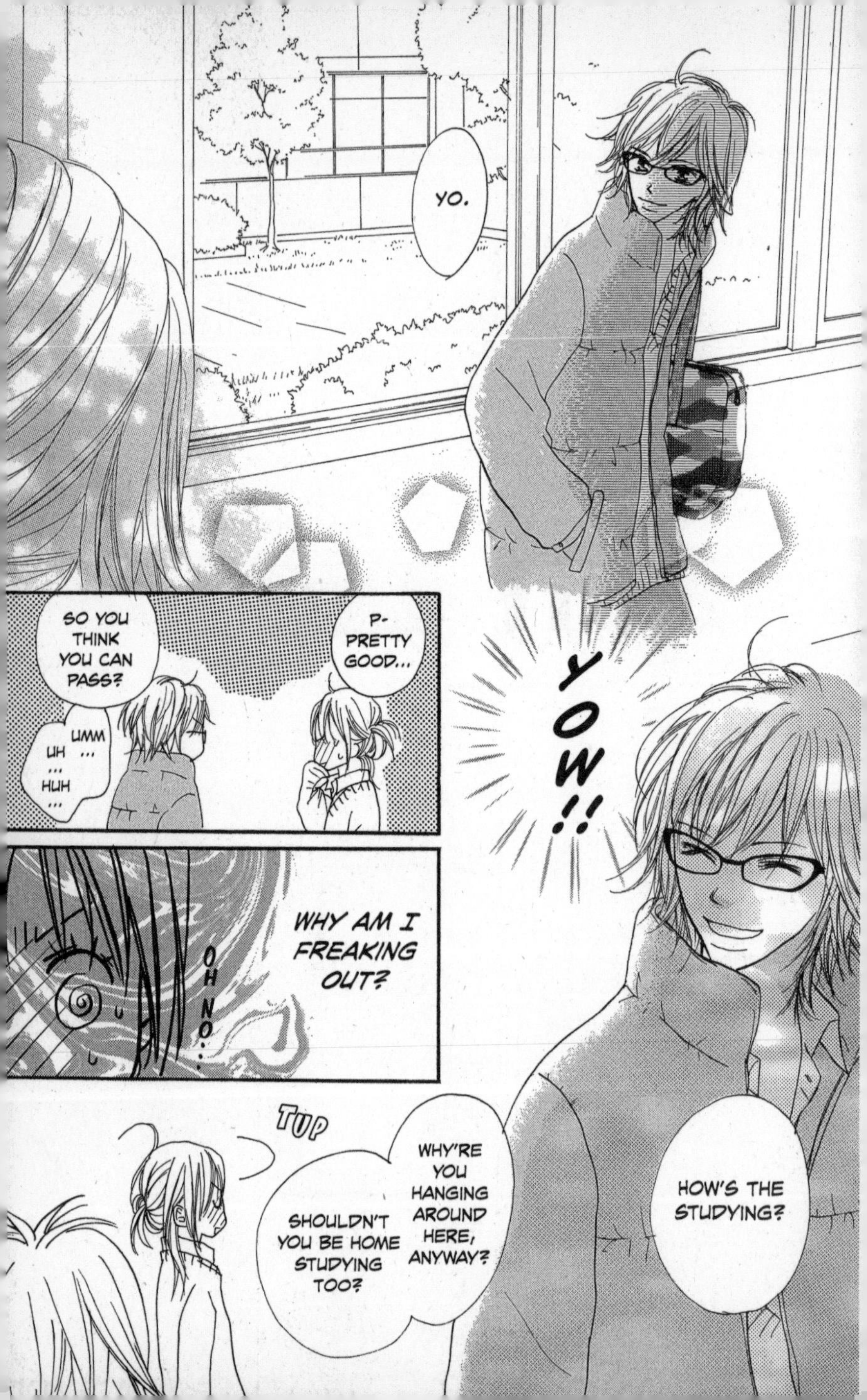
YO.
YOW!!
HOW'S THE STUDYING?
P- PRETTY GOOD...
SO YOU THINK YOU CAN PASS?
UMM ... UH ... HUH ...
WHY AM I FREAKING OUT?
OH NO...
TUP
WHY'RE YOU HANGING AROUND HERE, ANYWAY?
SHOULDN'T YOU BE HOME STUDYING TOO?

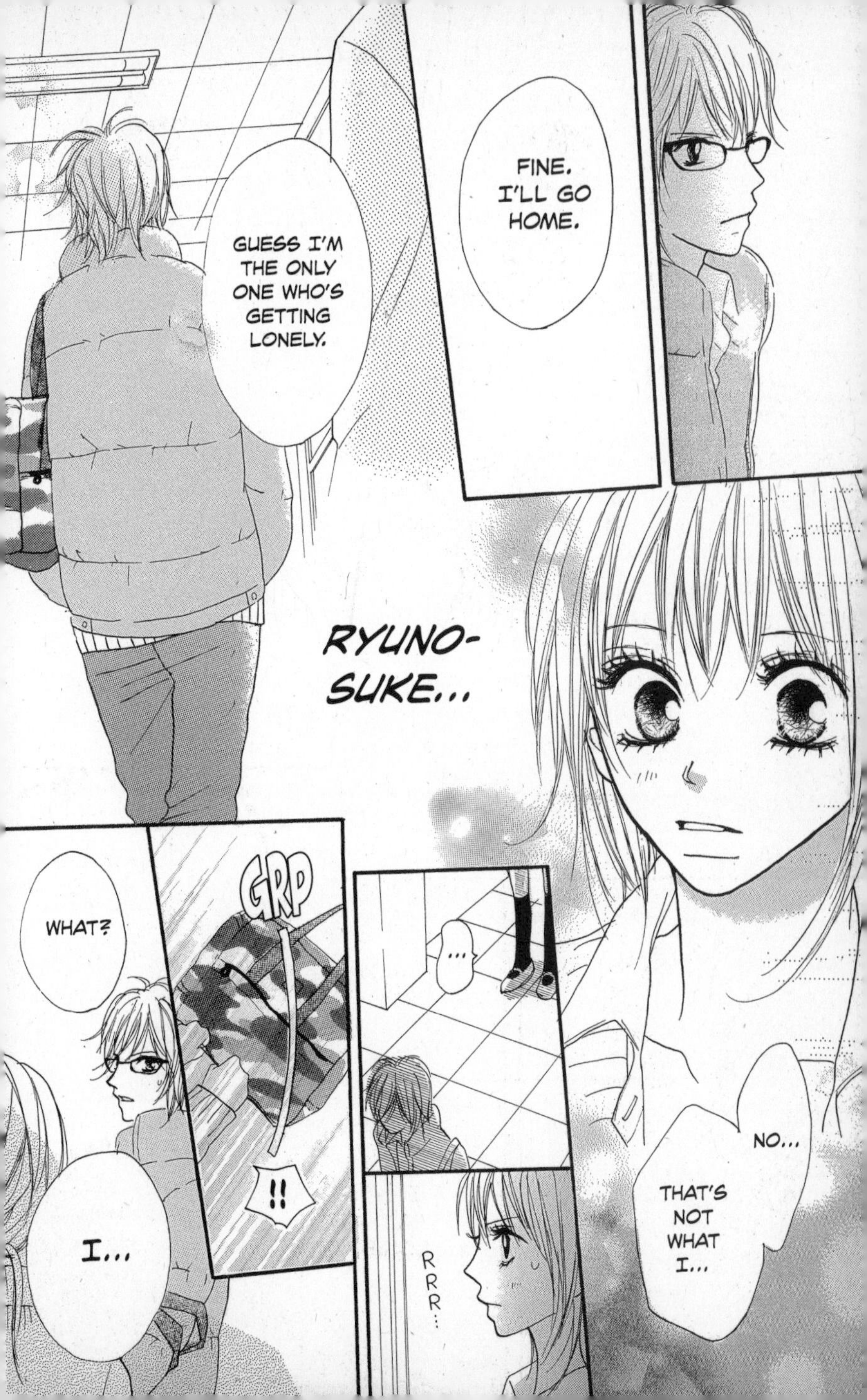
FINE. I'LL GO HOME.
GUESS I'M THE ONLY ONE WHO'S GETTING LONELY.
RYUNO-SUKE...
NO...
THAT'S NOT WHAT I...
...
RRR..
GRP
!!
WHAT?
I...

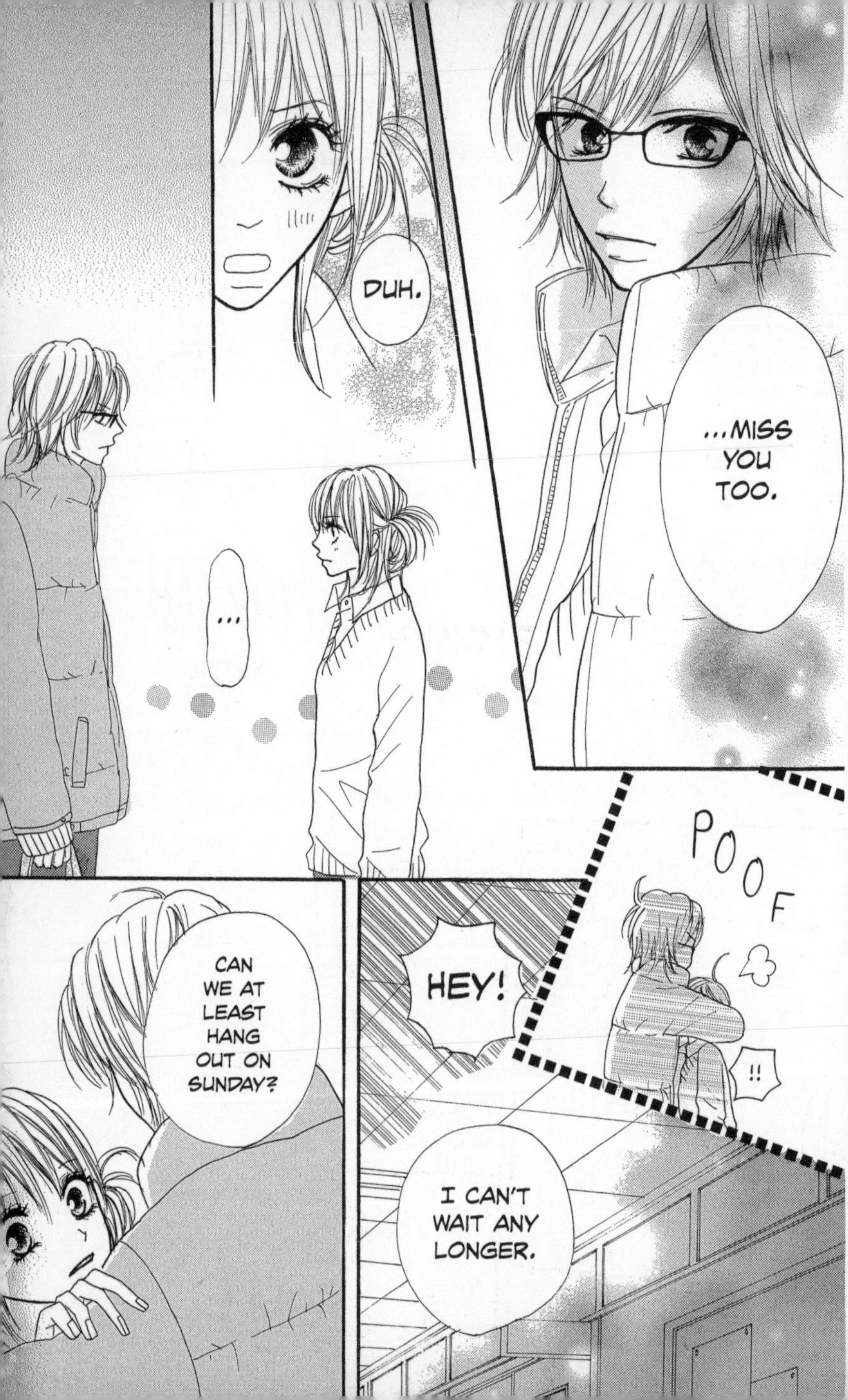
...MISS YOU TOO.
DUH.
...
POOF
!!
HEY!
I CAN'T WAIT ANY LONGER.
CAN WE AT LEAST HANG OUT ON SUNDAY?

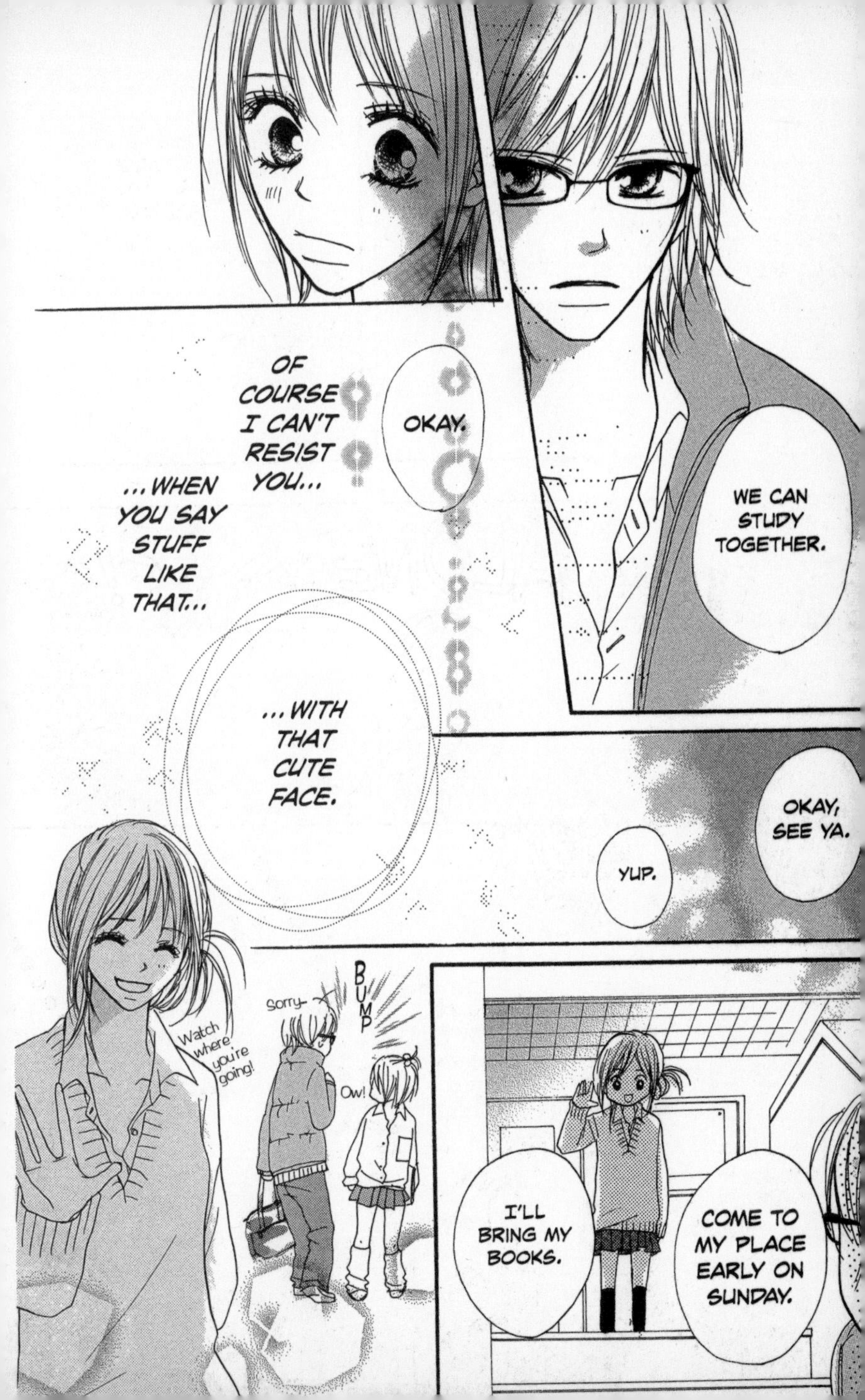
WE CAN STUDY TOGETHER.
OKAY.
OF COURSE I CAN'T RESIST YOU...
...WHEN YOU SAY STUFF LIKE THAT...
...WITH THAT CUTE FACE.
OKAY, SEE YA.
YUP.
COME TO MY PLACE EARLY ON SUNDAY.
I'LL BRING MY BOOKS.
BUMP
Sorry-
Ow!
Watch where you're going!

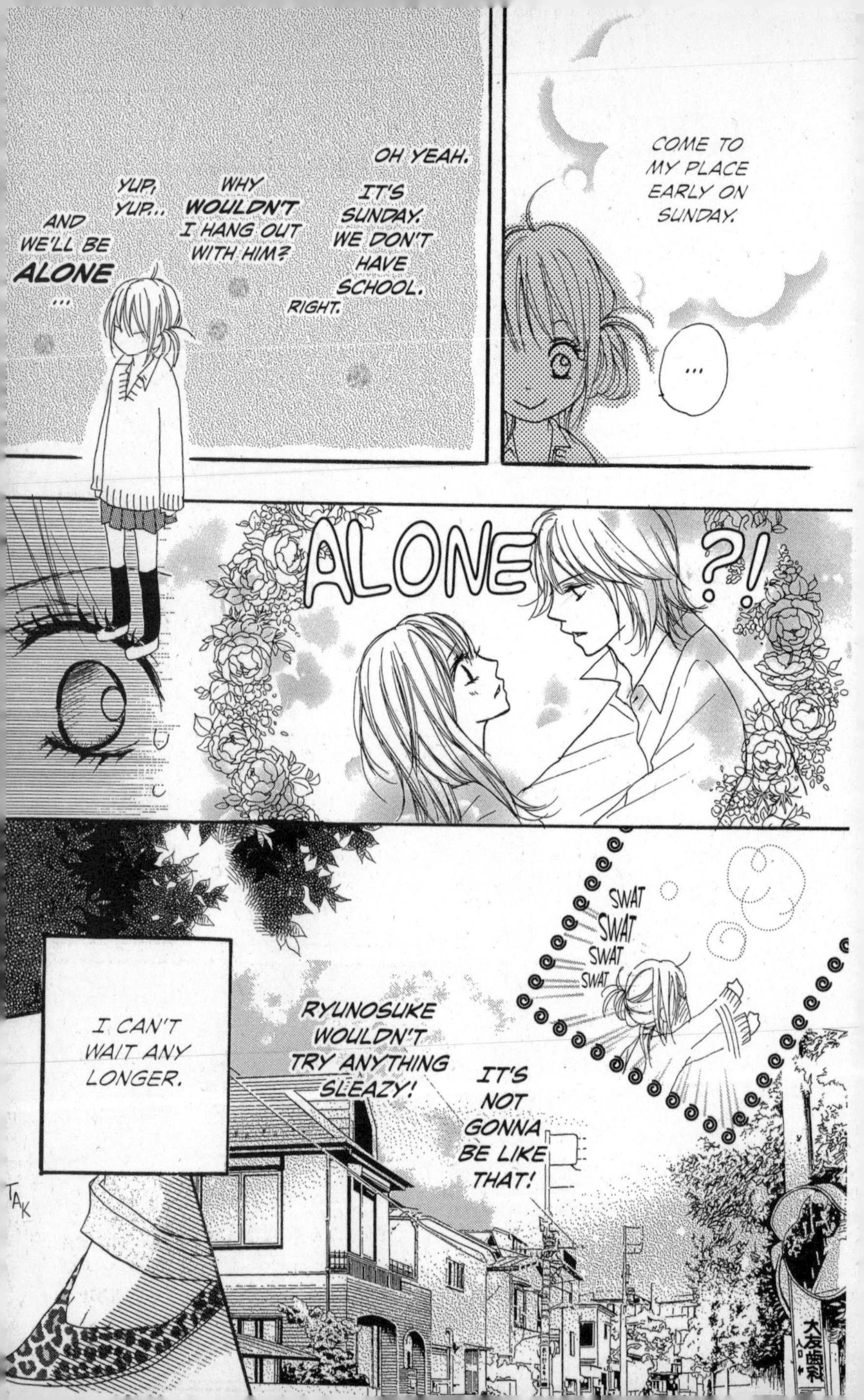
COME TO MY PLACE EARLY ON SUNDAY.
...
OH YEAH.
IT'S SUNDAY. WE DON'T HAVE SCHOOL.
RIGHT.
WHY WOULDN'T I HANG OUT WITH HIM?
YUP, YUP...
AND WE'LL BE ALONE ...
ALONE ?!
SWAT SWAT SWAT SWAT
IT'S NOT GONNA BE LIKE THAT!
RYUNOSUKE WOULDN'T TRY ANYTHING SLEAZY!
I CAN'T WAIT ANY LONGER.
TAK

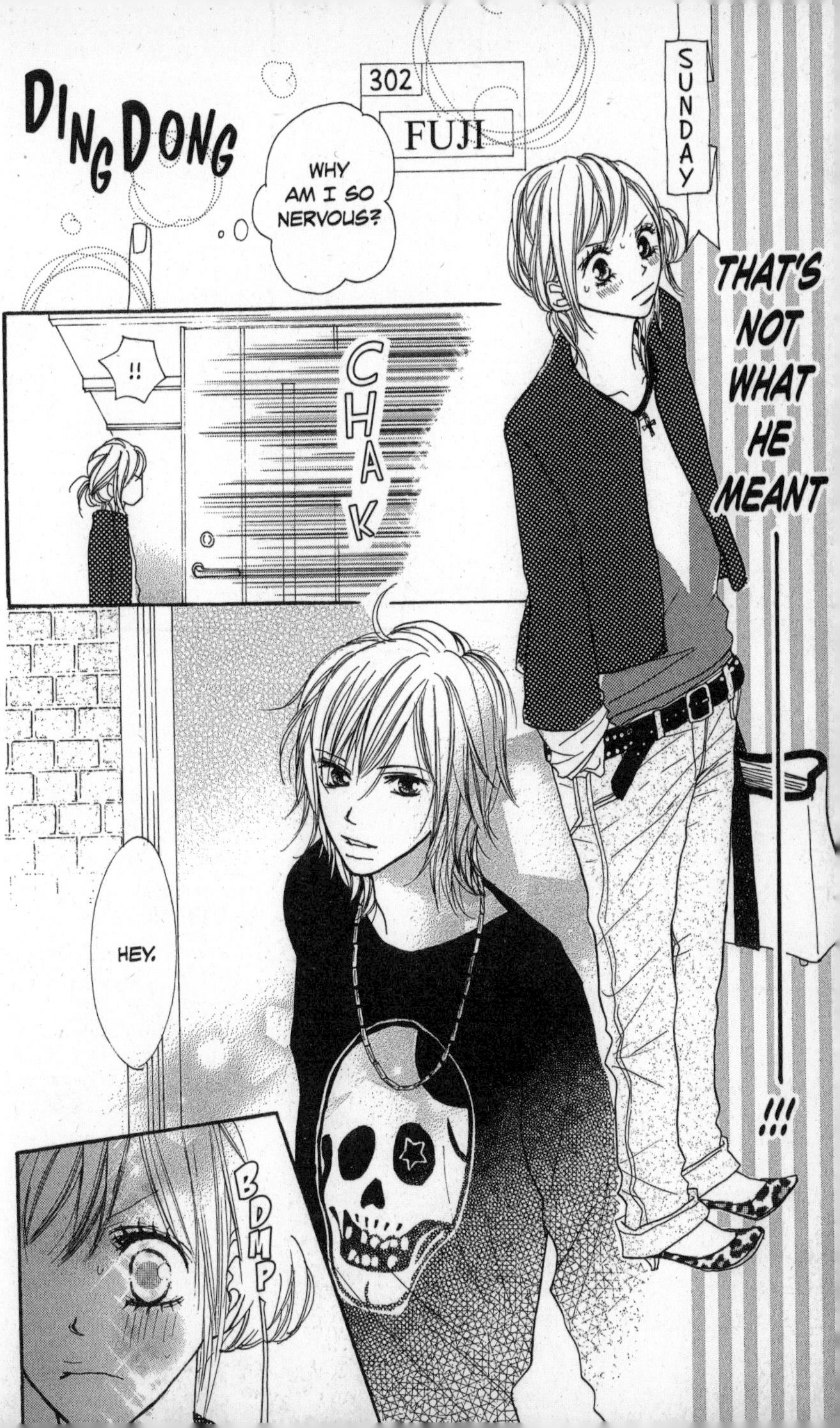
SUNDAY
302
FUJI
WHY AM I SO NERVOUS?
DING DONG
CHAK
!!
THAT'S NOT WHAT HE MEANT—!!!
HEY.
BDMP

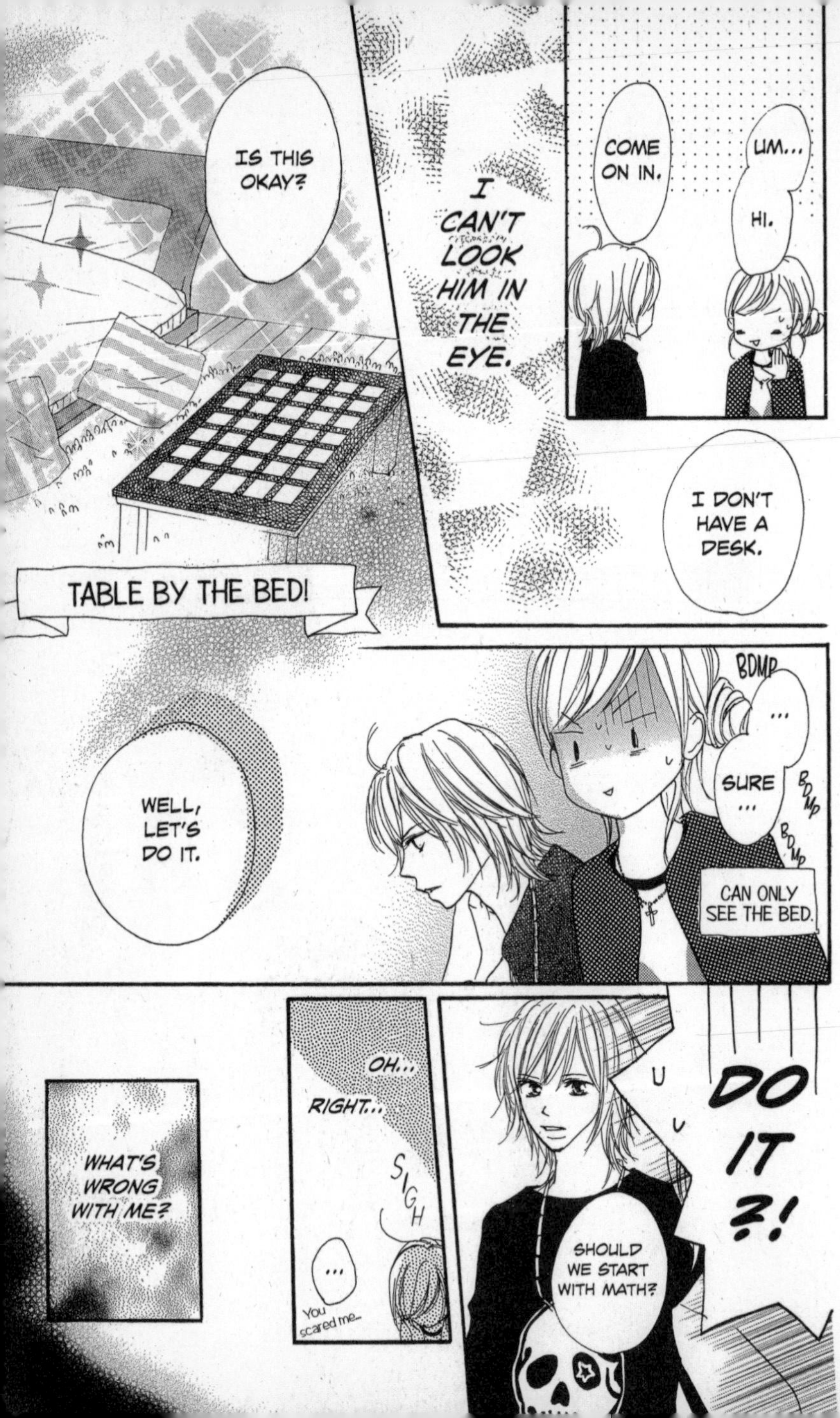
UM...
HI.
COME ON IN.
I DON'T HAVE A DESK.
I CAN'T LOOK HIM IN THE EYE.
IS THIS OKAY?
TABLE BY THE BED!
BDMP
...
SURE...
BDMP
BDMP
CAN ONLY SEE THE BED.
WELL, LET'S DO IT.
DO IT?!
SHOULD WE START WITH MATH?
OH...
RIGHT...
SIGH
...
You scared me...
WHAT'S WRONG WITH ME?

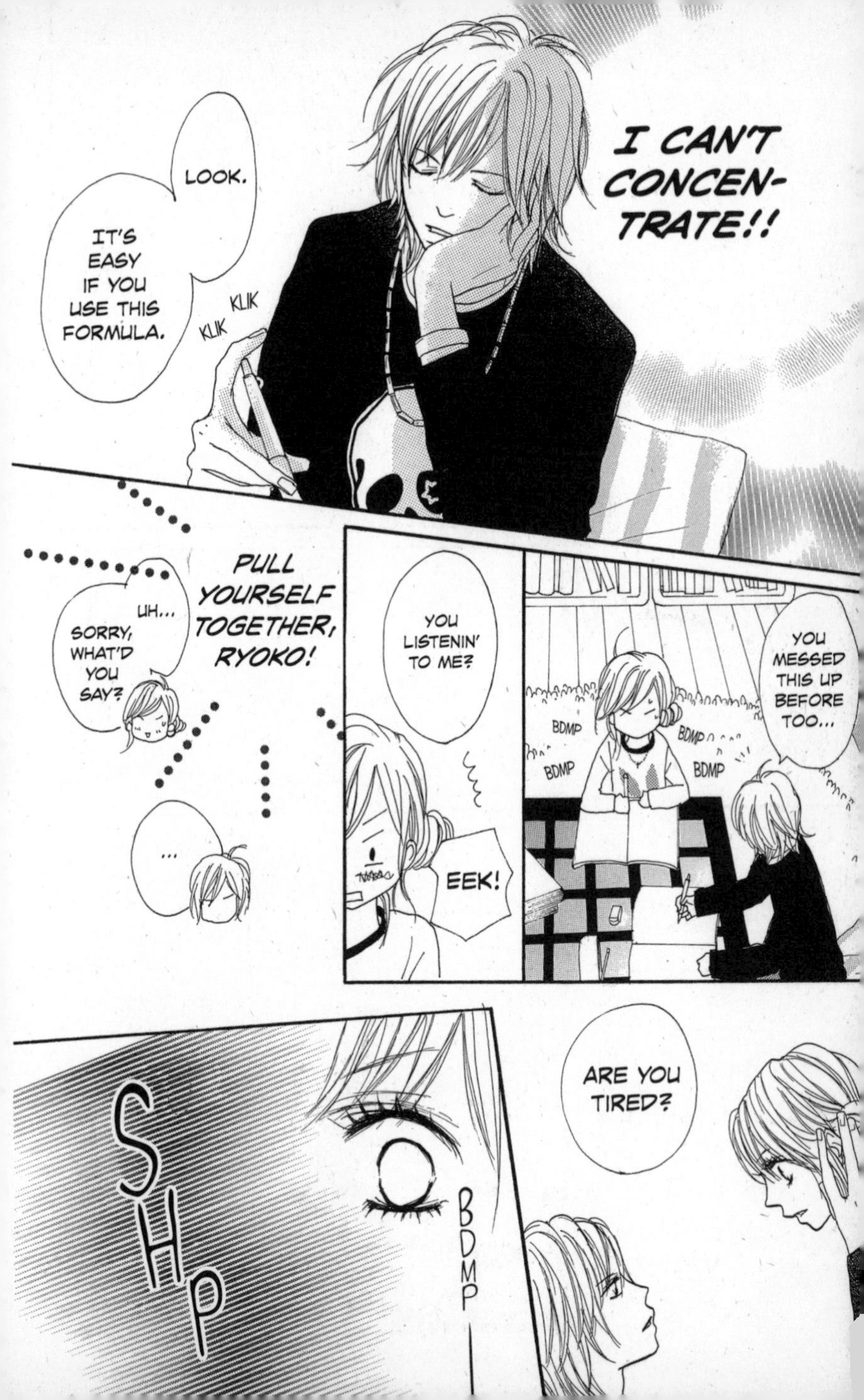
I CAN'T CONCENTRATE!!
LOOK.
IT'S EASY IF YOU USE THIS FORMULA.
KLIK KLIK
YOU MESSED THIS UP BEFORE TOO...
BDMP BDMP BDMP BDMP
YOU LISTENIN' TO ME?
EEK!
PULL YOURSELF TOGETHER, RYOKO!
......
UH... SORRY, WHAT'D YOU SAY?
...
ARE YOU TIRED?
BDMP
SHP

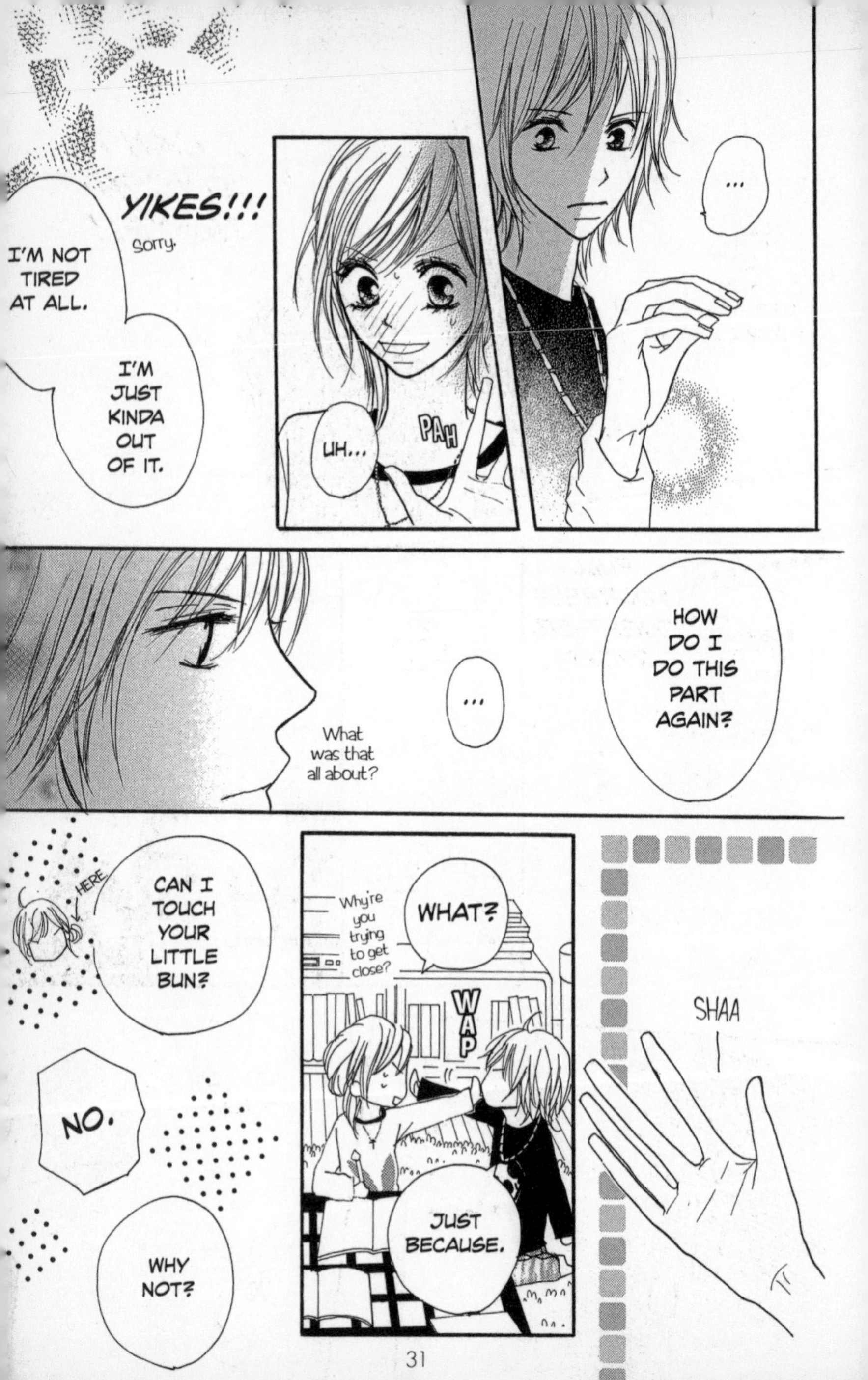
...
UH...
PAH
YIKES!!!
Sorry.
I'M NOT TIRED AT ALL.
I'M JUST KINDA OUT OF IT.
HOW DO I DO THIS PART AGAIN?
...
What was that all about?
SHAA
WHAT?
Why're you trying to get close?
WAP
JUST BECAUSE.
CAN I TOUCH YOUR LITTLE BUN?
HERE
NO.
WHY NOT?

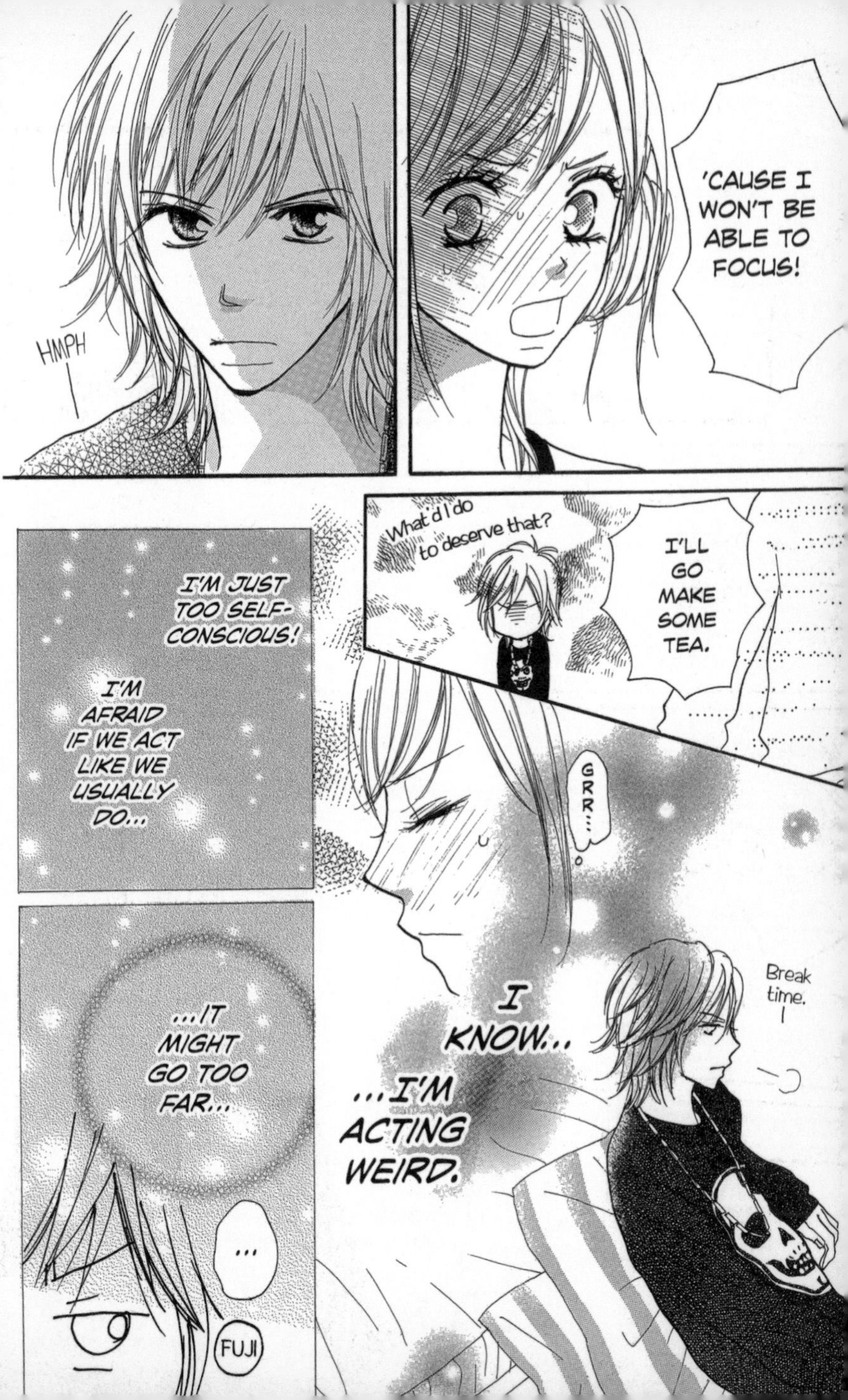
'CAUSE I WON'T BE ABLE TO FOCUS!
HMPH
......
I'LL GO MAKE SOME TEA.
What'd I do to deserve that?
GRR...
Break time.
I KNOW...
...I'M ACTING WEIRD.
I'M JUST TOO SELF-CONSCIOUS!
I'M AFRAID IF WE ACT LIKE WE USUALLY DO...
...IT MIGHT GO TOO FAR...
...
FUJI

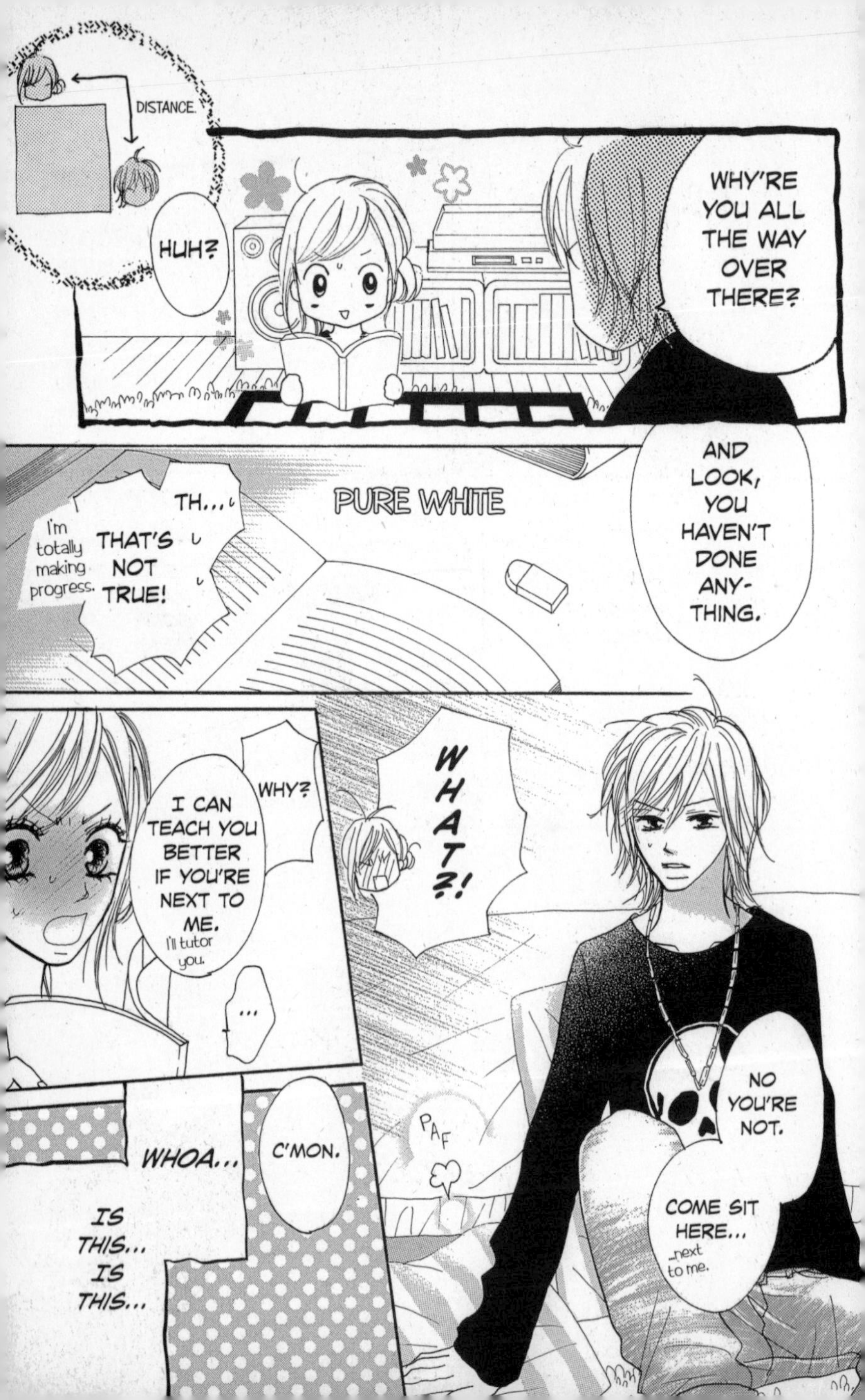
WHY'RE YOU ALL THE WAY OVER THERE?
HUH?
DISTANCE.
AND LOOK, YOU HAVEN'T DONE ANY-THING.
PURE WHITE
TH...
THAT'S NOT TRUE!
I'm totally making progress.
NO YOU'RE NOT.
COME SIT HERE...
...next to me.
WHAT?!
PAF
WHY?
I CAN TEACH YOU BETTER IF YOU'RE NEXT TO ME.
I'll tutor you.
...
C'MON.
WHOA...
IS THIS... IS THIS...

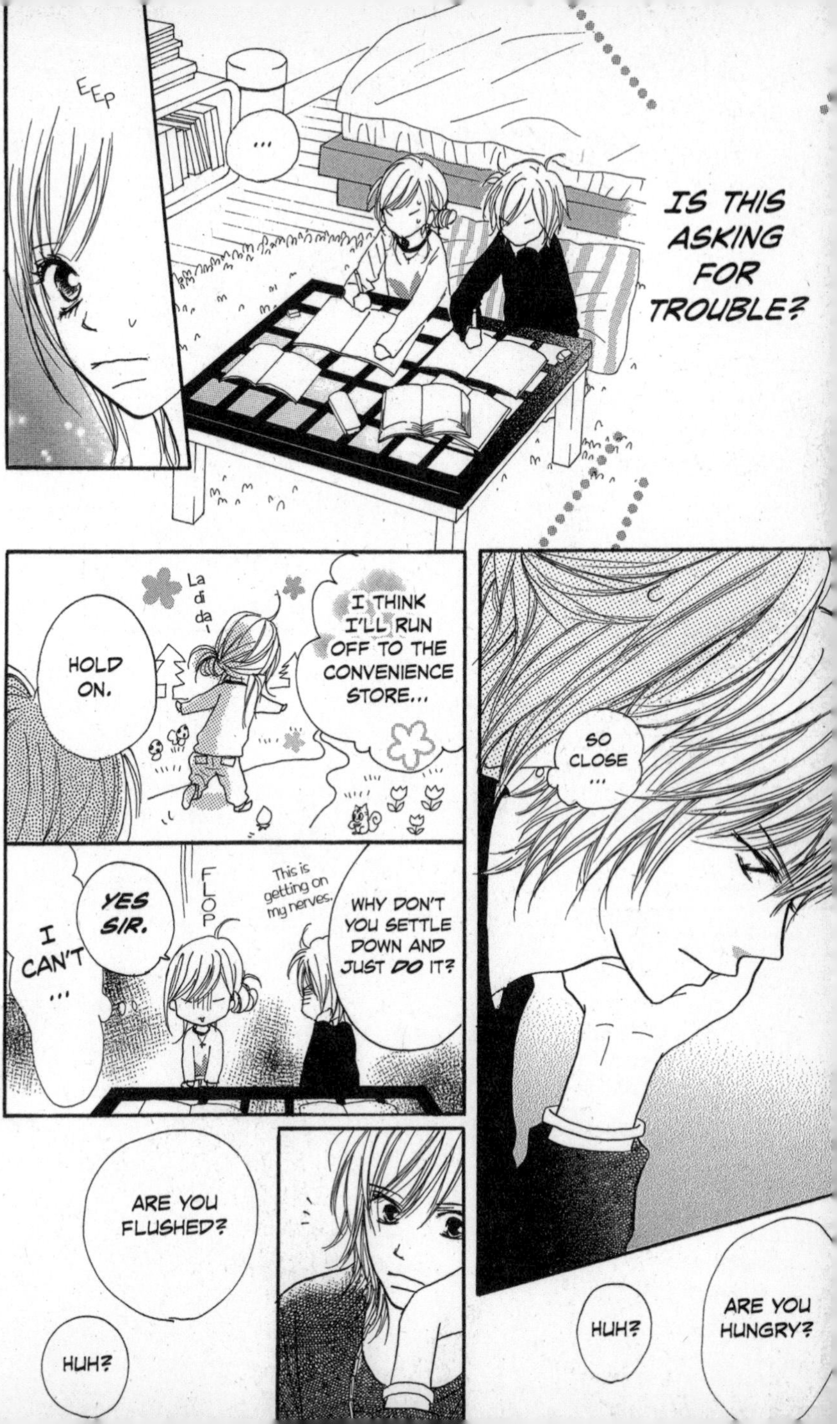

IS THIS ASKING FOR TROUBLE?
...
EEP
SO CLOSE ...
I THINK I'LL RUN OFF TO THE CONVENIENCE STORE...
La di da
HOLD ON.
WHY DON'T YOU SETTLE DOWN AND JUST *DO* IT?
This is getting on my nerves.
FLOP
YES SIR.
I CAN'T ...
ARE YOU HUNGRY?
HUH?
ARE YOU FLUSHED?
HUH?

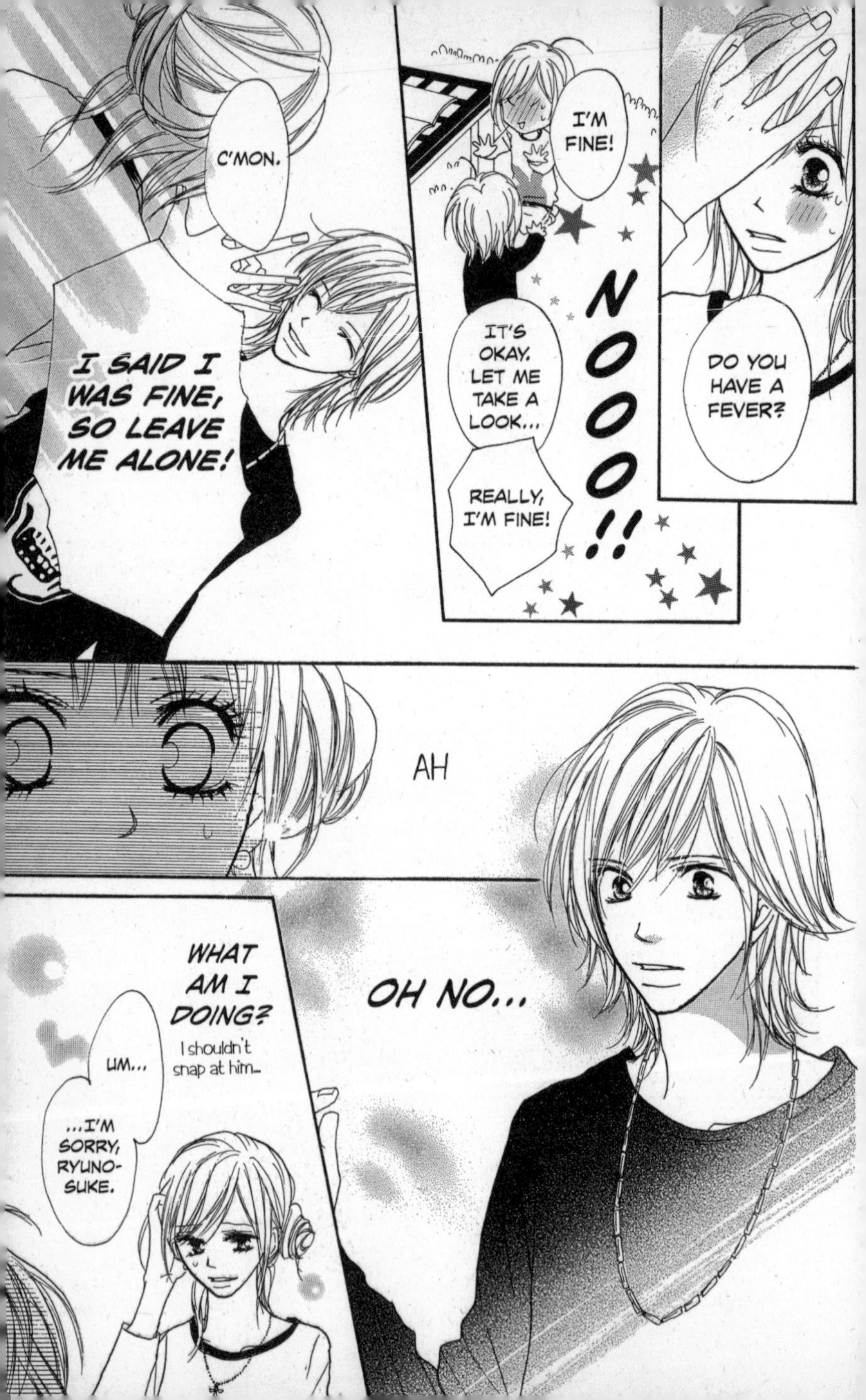
DO YOU HAVE A FEVER?
I'M FINE!
NOOOO!!
IT'S OKAY. LET ME TAKE A LOOK...
REALLY, I'M FINE!
C'MON.
I SAID I WAS FINE, SO LEAVE ME ALONE!
AH
OH NO...
WHAT AM I DOING?
I shouldn't snap at him...
UM...
...I'M SORRY, RYUNOSUKE.

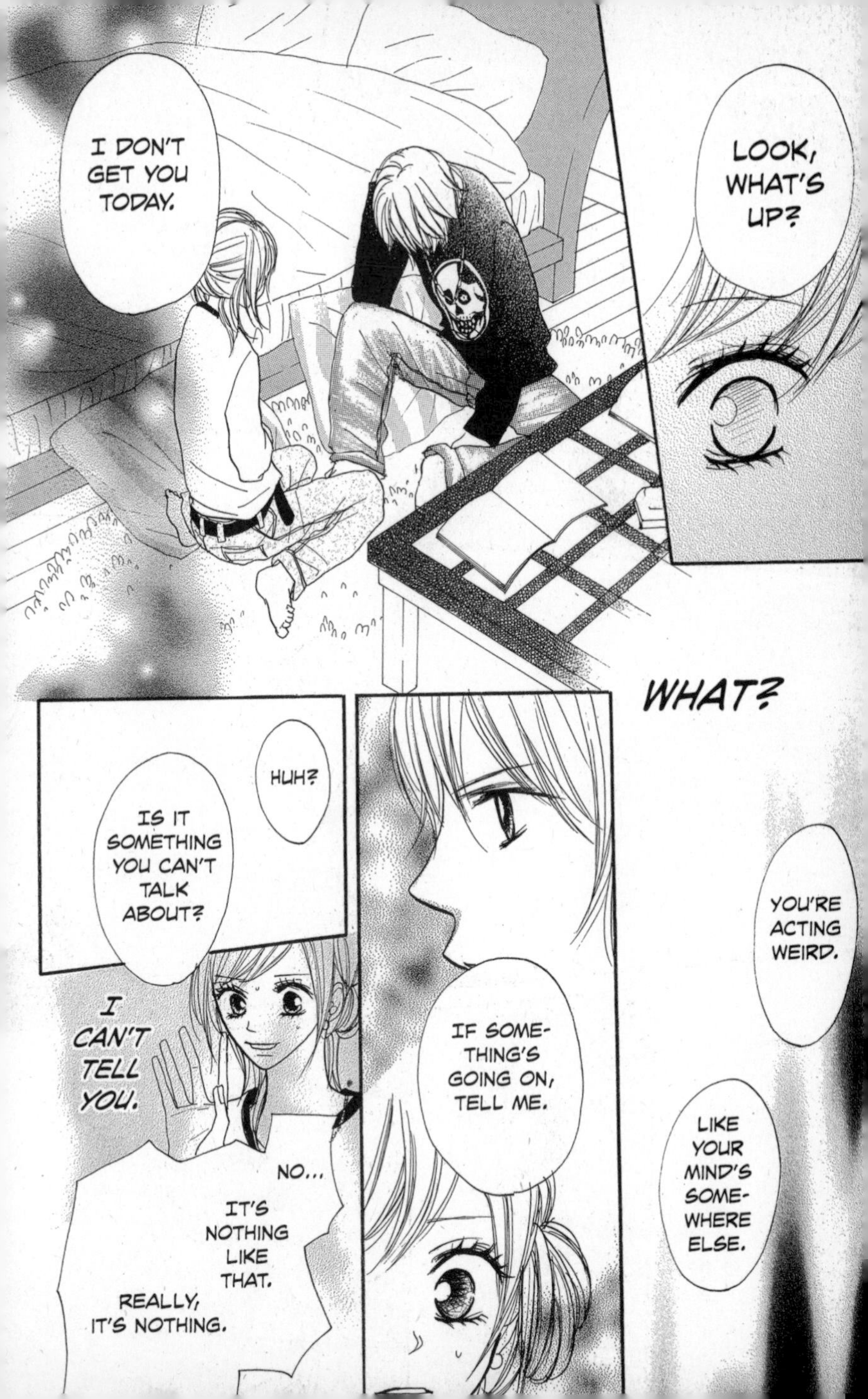
LOOK, WHAT'S UP?
I DON'T GET YOU TODAY.
WHAT?
YOU'RE ACTING WEIRD.
LIKE YOUR MIND'S SOME-WHERE ELSE.
IF SOME-THING'S GOING ON, TELL ME.
HUH?
IS IT SOMETHING YOU CAN'T TALK ABOUT?
I CAN'T TELL YOU.
NO...
IT'S NOTHING LIKE THAT.
REALLY, IT'S NOTHING.

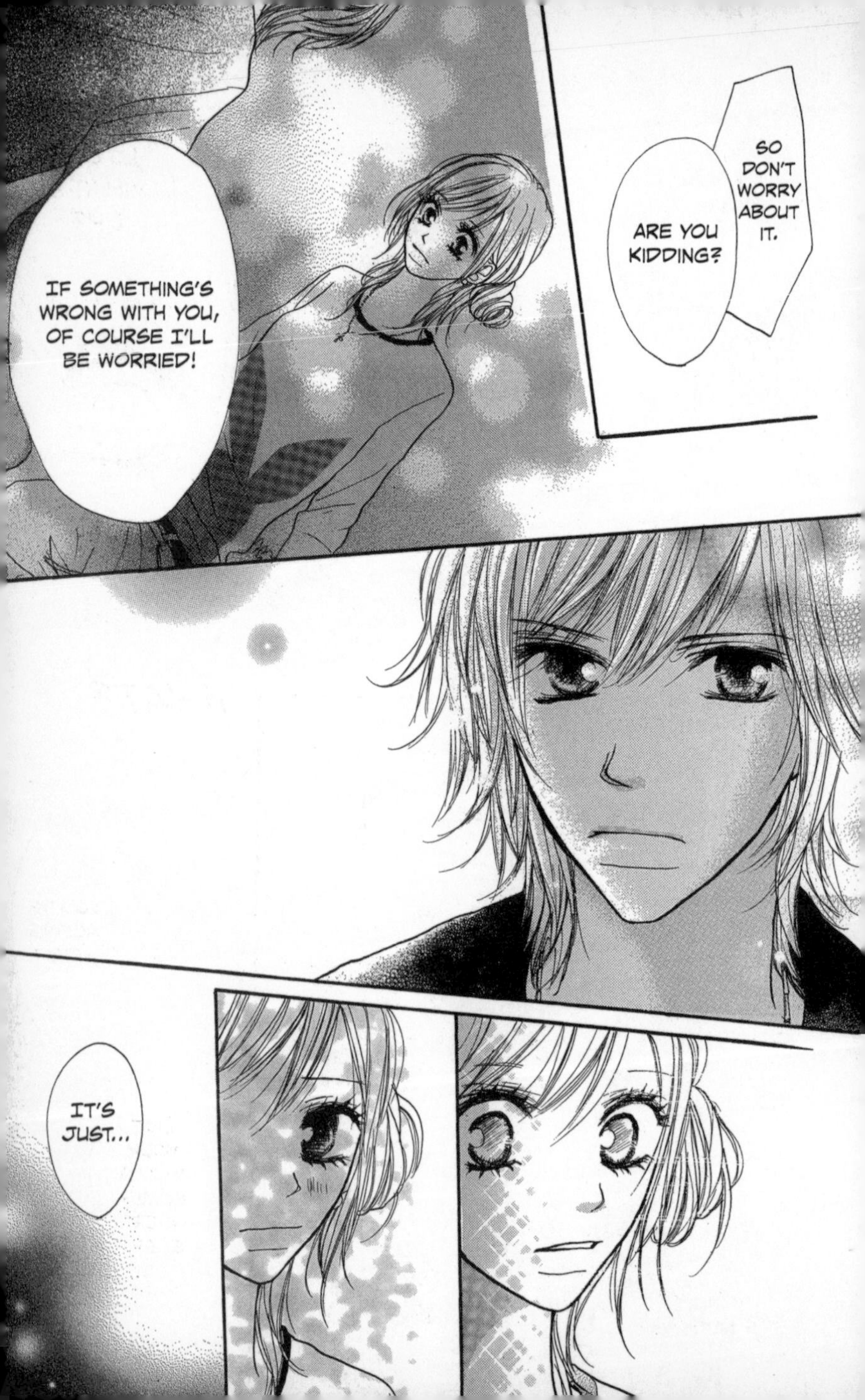
SO DON'T WORRY ABOUT IT.
ARE YOU KIDDING?
IF SOMETHING'S WRONG WITH YOU, OF COURSE I'LL BE WORRIED!
IT'S JUST...

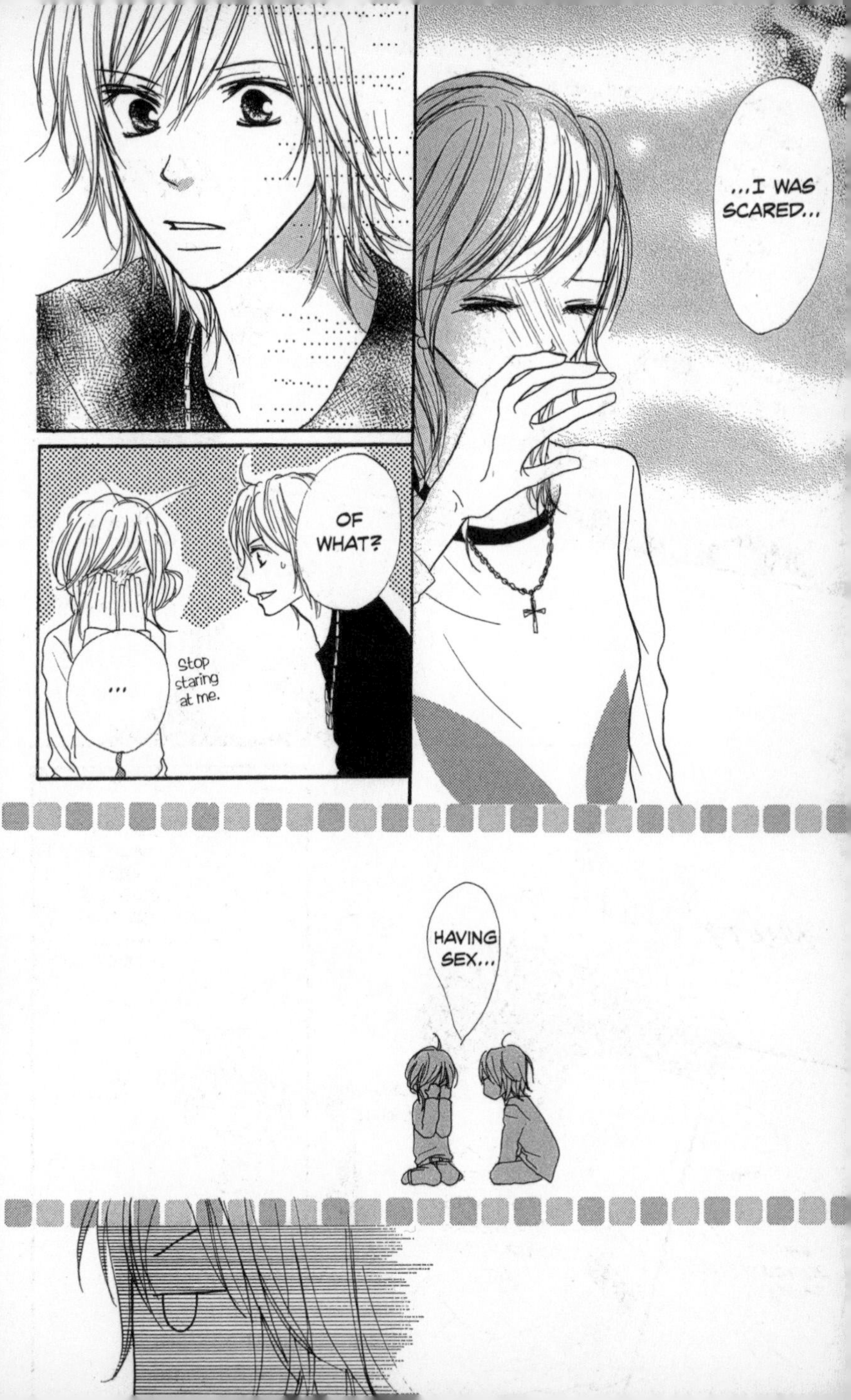
...I WAS SCARED...
OF WHAT?
...
Stop staring at me.
HAVING SEX...

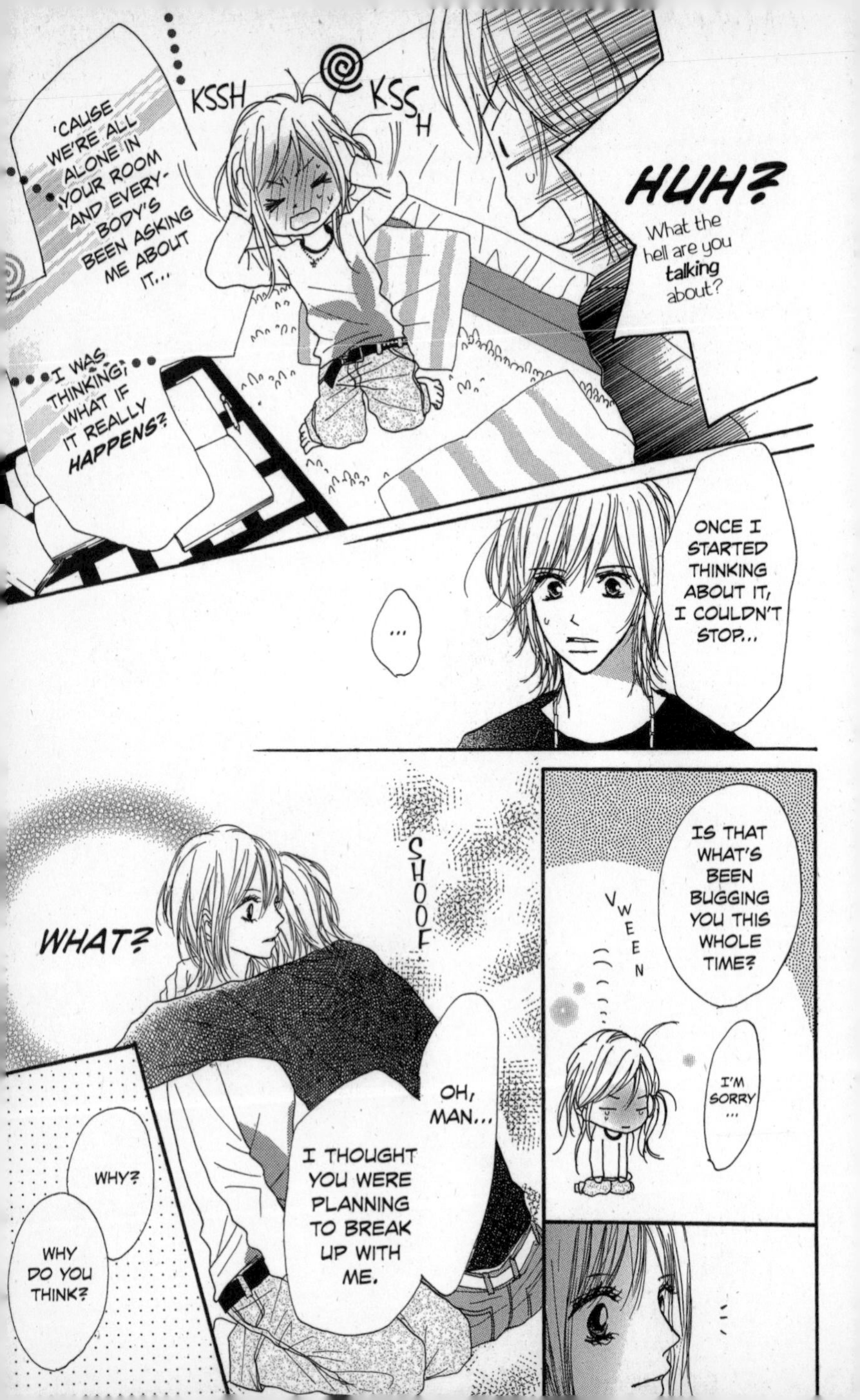
HUH?
What the hell are you **talking** about?
KSSH
KSSH
'CAUSE WE'RE ALL ALONE IN YOUR ROOM AND EVERY-BODY'S BEEN ASKING ME ABOUT IT...
I WAS THINKING; WHAT IF IT REALLY ***HAPPENS?***
ONCE I STARTED THINKING ABOUT IT, I COULDN'T STOP...
...
IS THAT WHAT'S BEEN BUGGING YOU THIS WHOLE TIME?
VWEEN
I'M SORRY...
SHOOF
OH, MAN...
I THOUGHT YOU WERE PLANNING TO BREAK UP WITH ME.
WHAT?
WHY?
WHY DO YOU THINK?

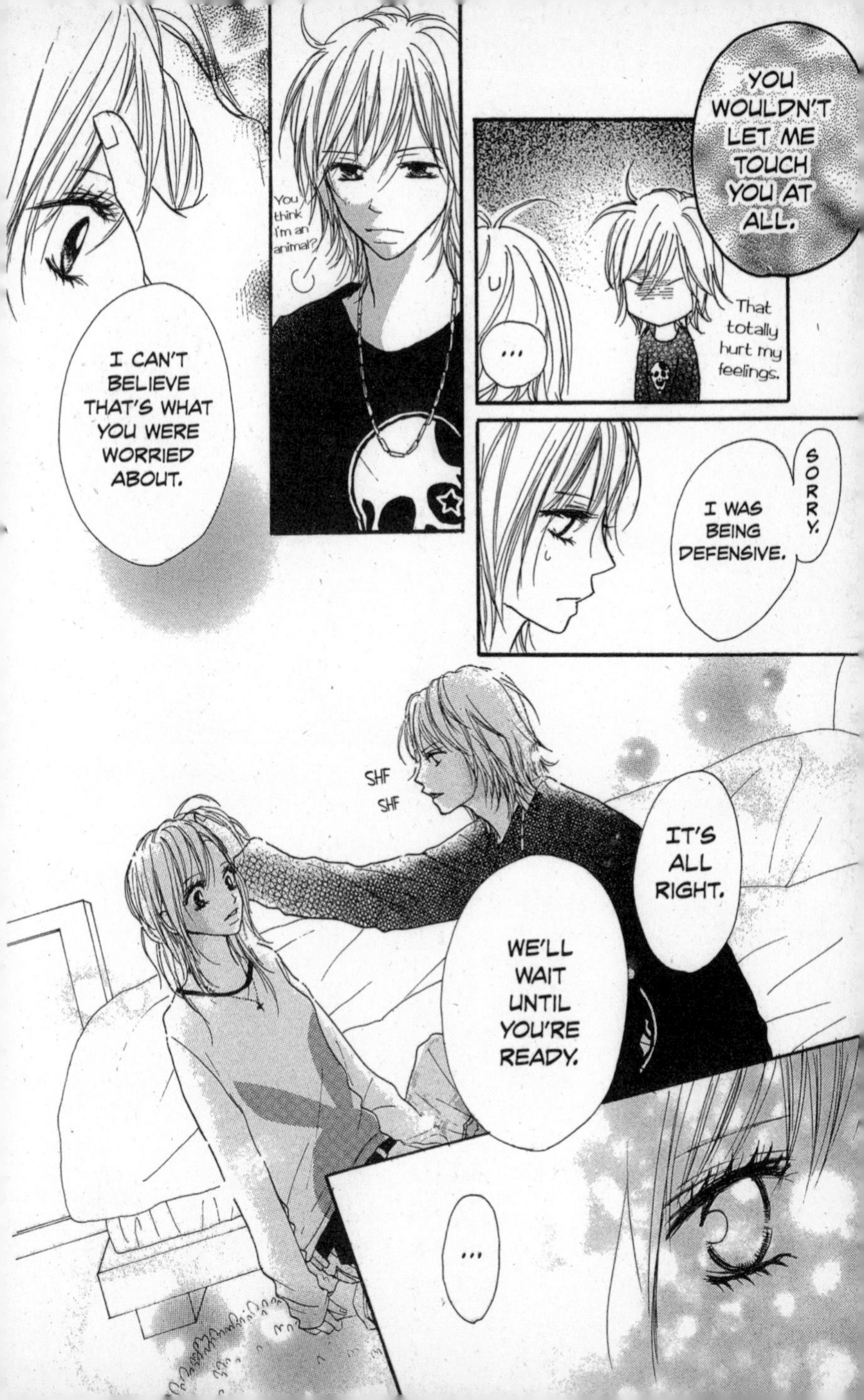

YOU WOULDN'T LET ME TOUCH YOU AT ALL.
...
That totally hurt my feelings.
SORRY.
I WAS BEING DEFENSIVE.
You think I'm an animal?
I CAN'T BELIEVE THAT'S WHAT YOU WERE WORRIED ABOUT.
IT'S ALL RIGHT.
SHF
SHF
WE'LL WAIT UNTIL YOU'RE READY.
...

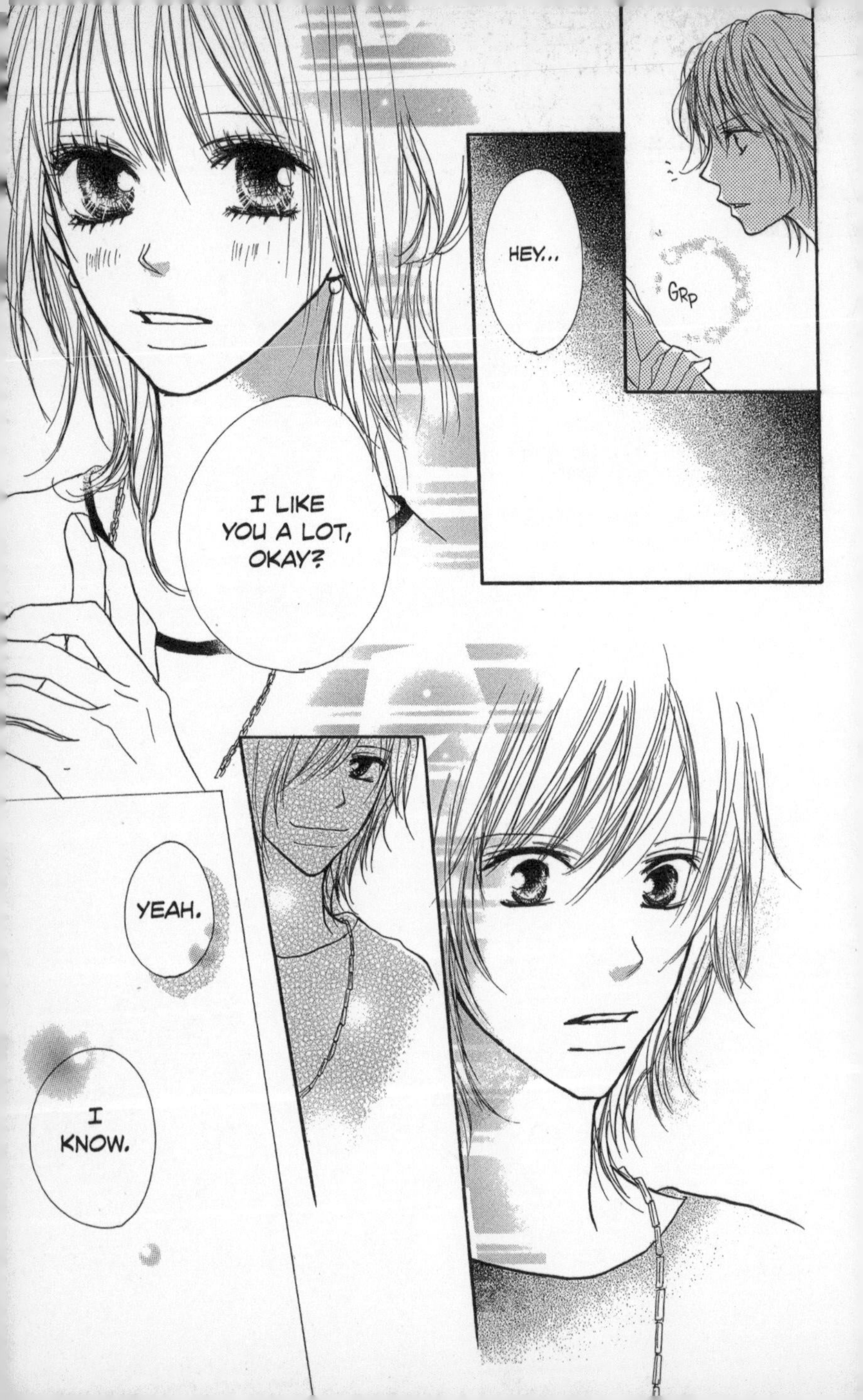
GRP
HEY...
I LIKE YOU A LOT, OKAY?
YEAH.
I KNOW.

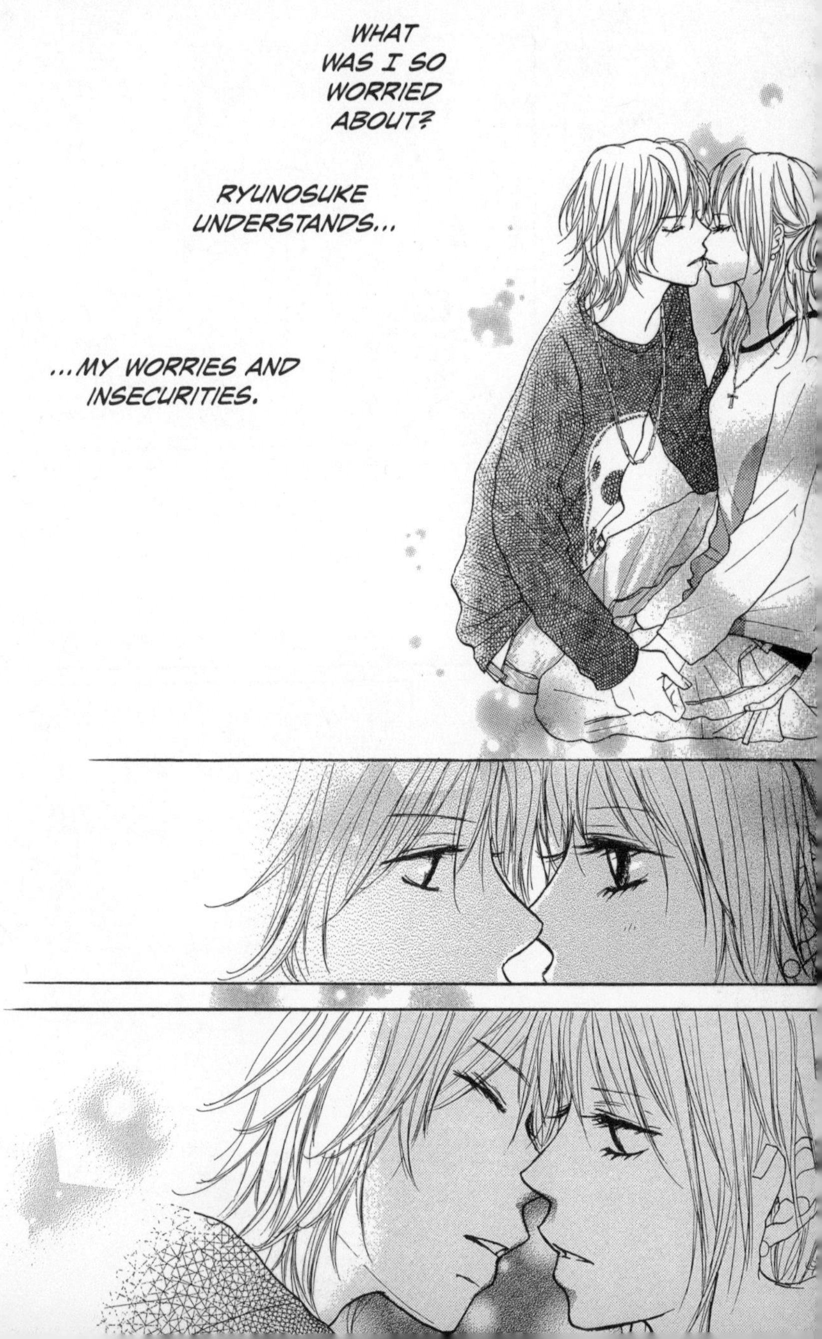
WHAT WAS I SO WORRIED ABOUT?
RYUNOSUKE UNDERSTANDS...
...MY WORRIES AND INSECURITIES.

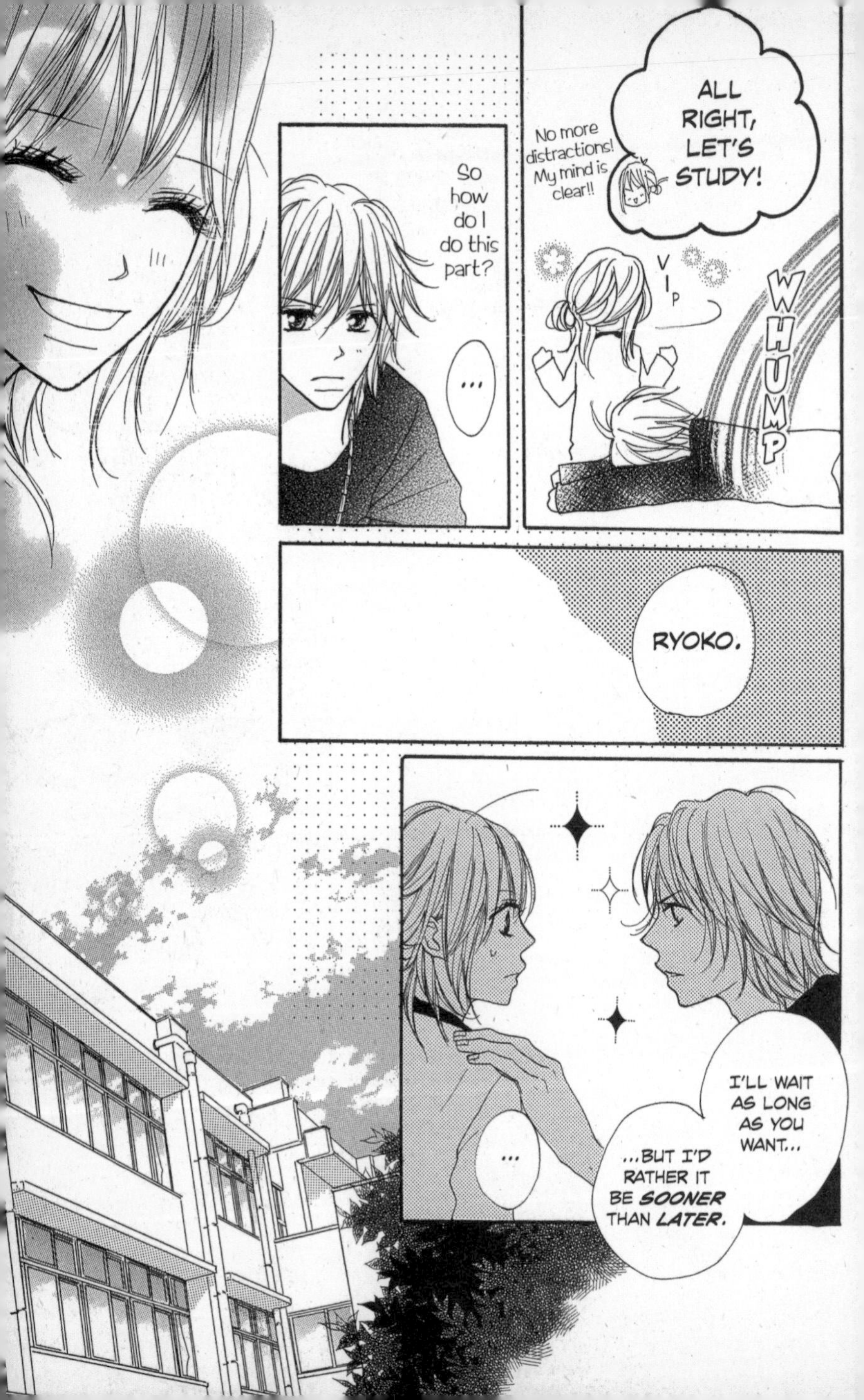
ALL RIGHT, LET'S STUDY!
No more distractions! My mind is clear!!
VIP
WHUMP
So how do I do this part?
...
RYOKO.
I'LL WAIT AS LONG AS YOU WANT...
...BUT I'D RATHER IT BE *SOONER* THAN *LATER.*
...

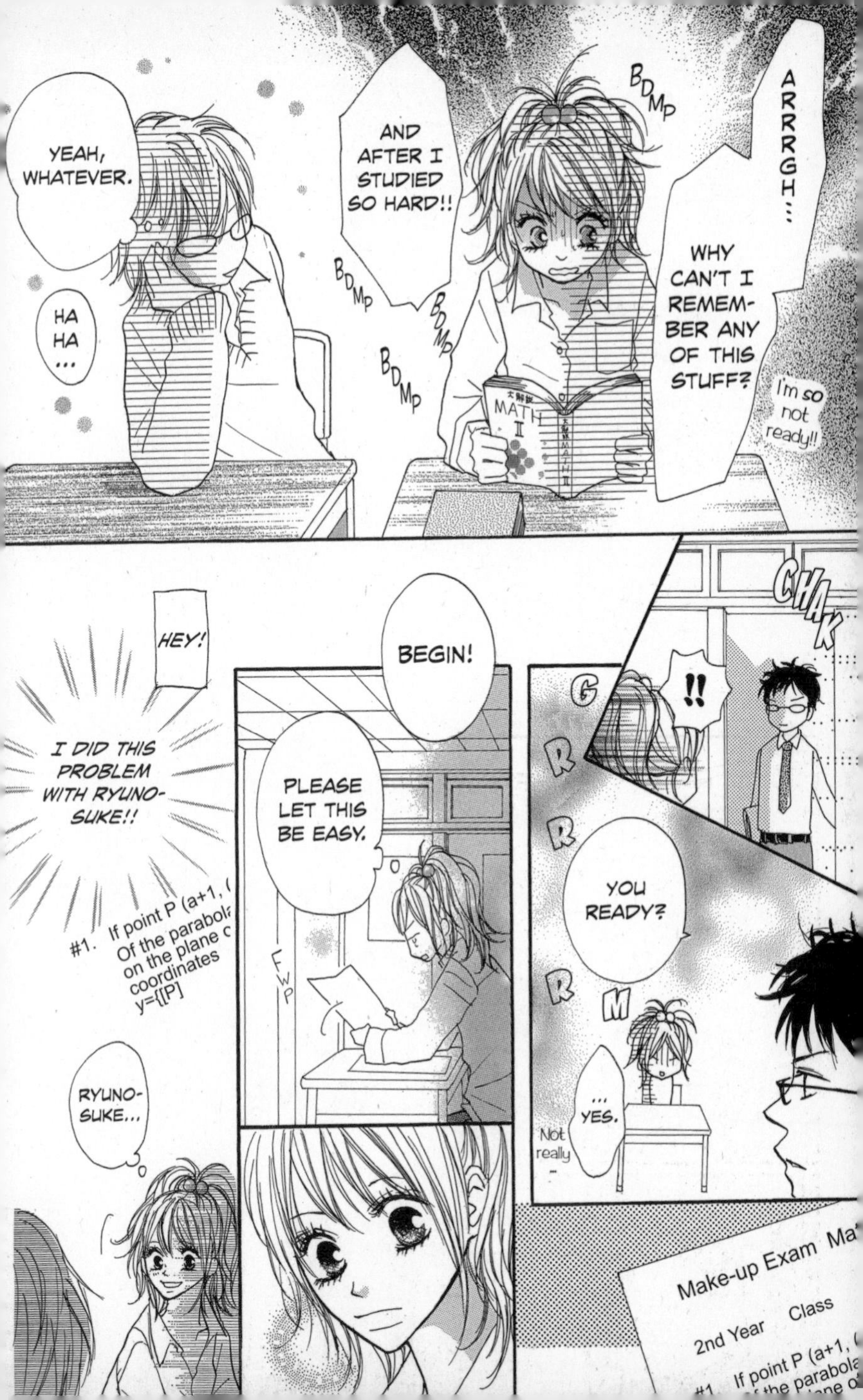
ARRRGH...
WHY CAN'T I REMEMBER ANY OF THIS STUFF?
I'm so not ready!!
BDMP
AND AFTER I STUDIED SO HARD!!
BDMP
BDMP
BDMP
MATH II
YEAH, WHATEVER.
HA HA ...
CHAK
!!
GRRRM
YOU READY?
... YES.
Not really -
BEGIN!
PLEASE LET THIS BE EASY.
FWP
HEY!
I DID THIS PROBLEM WITH RYUNOSUKE!!
#1. If point P (a+1, (
Of the parabola
on the plane c
coordinates
y={[P]
Make-up Exam Ma
2nd Year Class
#1 If point P (a+1, (
the parabola
RYUNOSUKE...

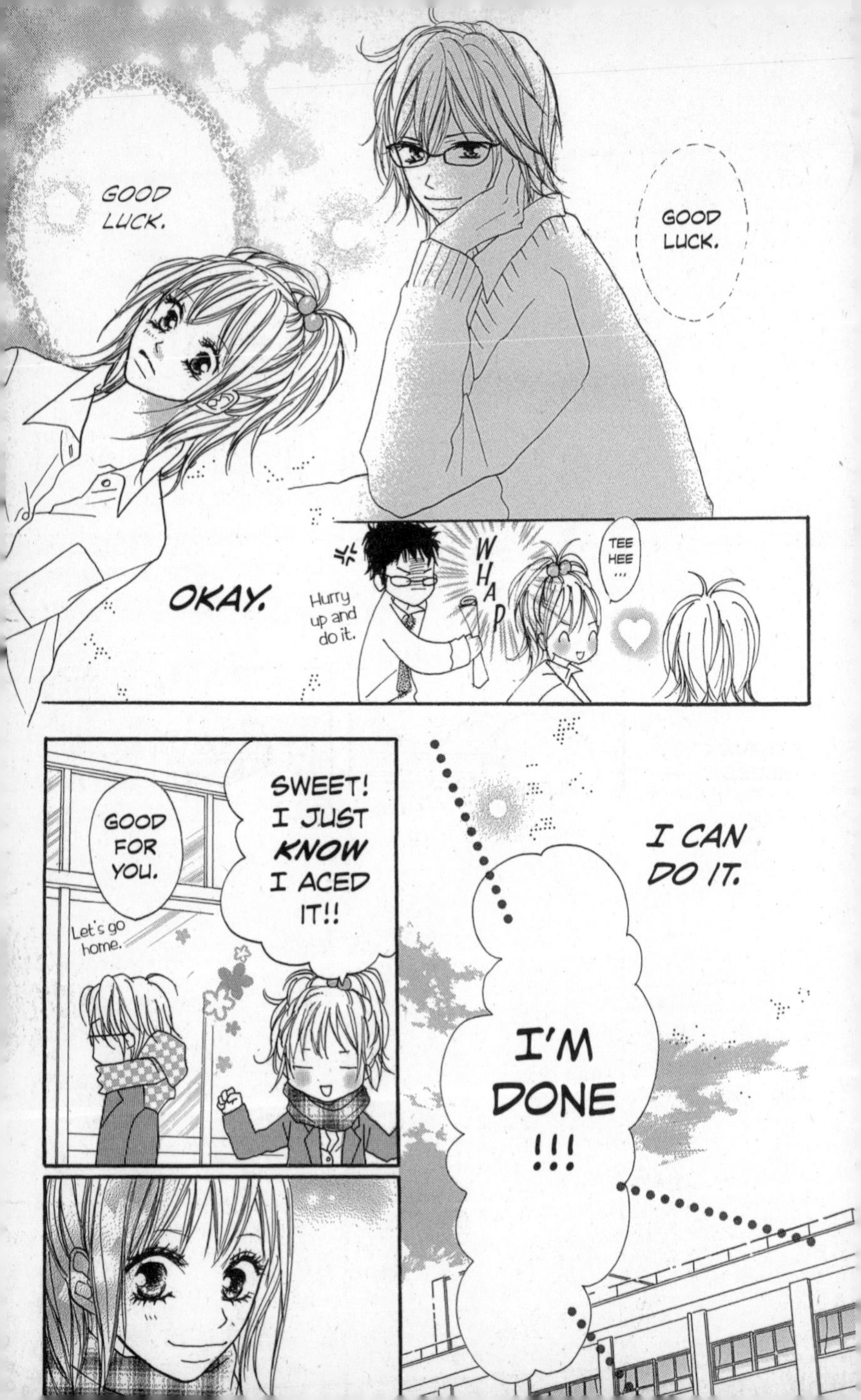
GOOD LUCK.
GOOD LUCK.
OKAY.
TEE HEE ...
WHAP
Hurry up and do it.
I CAN DO IT.
I'M DONE !!!
SWEET! I JUST KNOW I ACED IT!!
GOOD FOR YOU.
Let's go home.

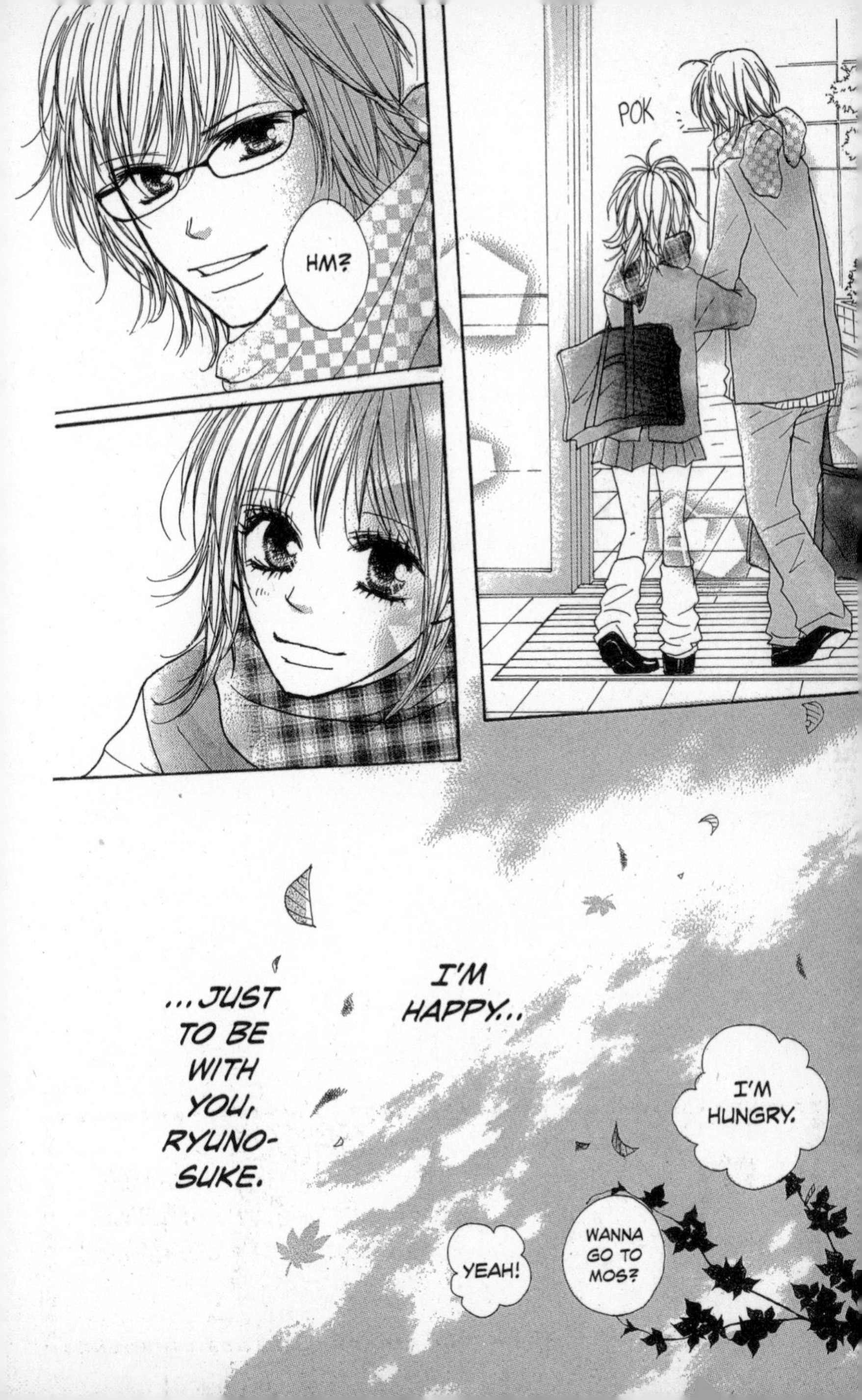
POK
HM?
I'M HAPPY...
...JUST TO BE WITH YOU, RYUNOSUKE.
I'M HUNGRY.
WANNA GO TO MOS?
YEAH!

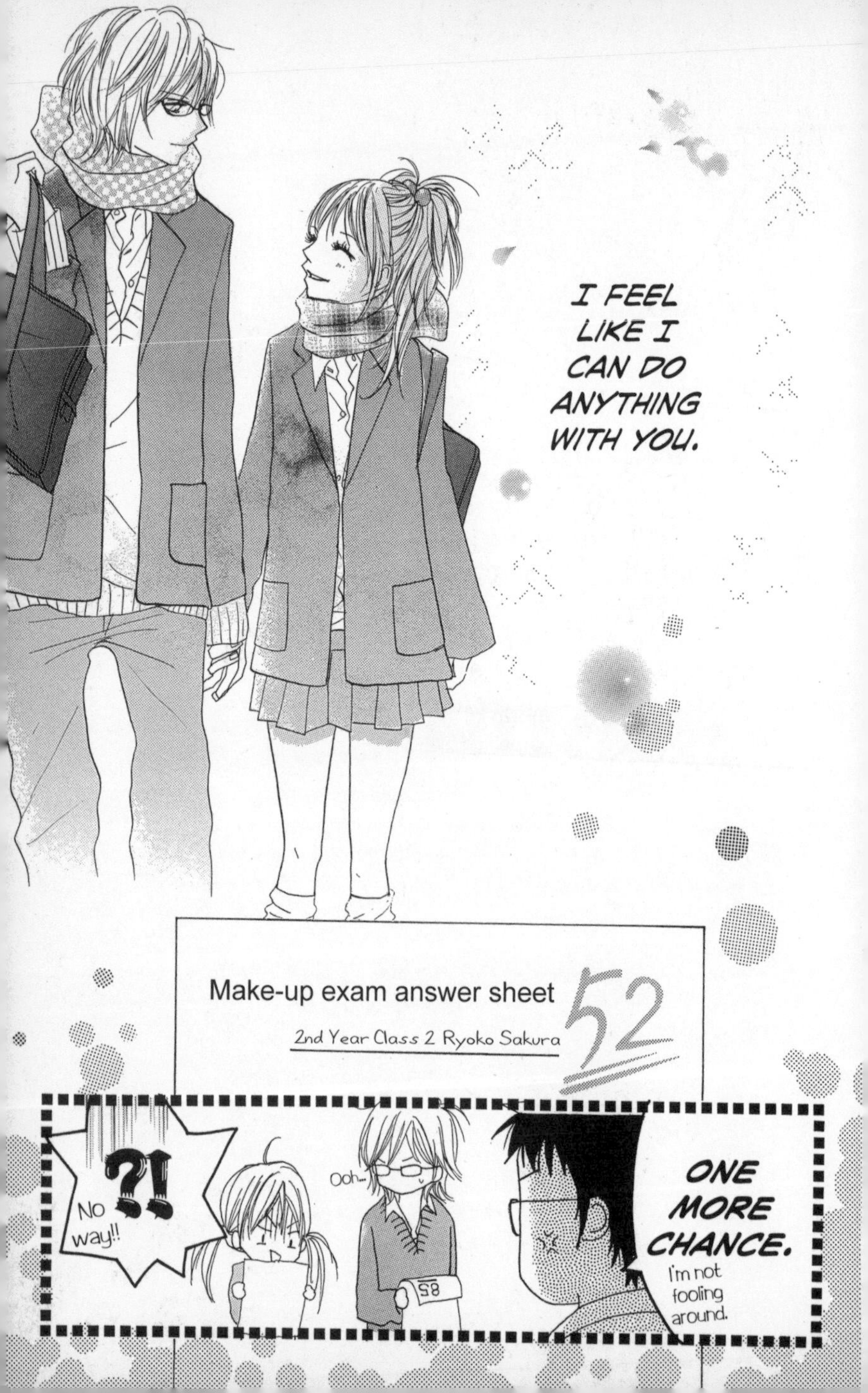
I FEEL LIKE I CAN DO ANYTHING WITH YOU.
Make-up exam answer sheet
2nd Year Class 2 Ryoko Sakura
52
ONE MORE CHANCE.
I'm not fooling around.
Ooh...
?!
No way!!

FAN MAIL CORNER——

Yes, it's the beloved (?) Fan Mail Corner!! I barely have time to reply to anyone who writes, so I hope you can enjoy the responses here. ♡

Well then, let's go———!

"When I tried to buy B.O.D.Y. at the bookstore today, my mom was like, 'You're still too young for that!! That's for high schoolers,' and got really mad at me. I thought, 'But it's hardly smutty at all.'"
Kagoshima H.Y.

Ma'am...Please listen...So far I've been writing B.O.D.Y. without any smutty bits...So there's no need to worry!! I'd like to say this loud and clear: there is no smut!! I actually think it could use a little!!

"My boyfriend and I rarely see each other because we're both in lots of after-school clubs. We couldn't even be together on Xmas, but he came to my house later and brought B.O.D.Y. with him. He knew I liked it so he went and found it for me. ♡"
Fukuoka K.M

How sweet...What a heartwarming story...B.O.D.Y. in the lives of youth!! Wow, that makes me so happy!! Thank you, boyfriend!! I wish you two the best!!

"I started reading B.O.D.Y. because when my mother and I were walking through the bookstore she said to me, 'This looks good!! Her boyfriend's a host. ♪'"
Saitama S.Y

Hey, Kagoshima H.Y.'s mother...as you can see, B.O.D.Y. can be enjoyed by the entire family. So please don't worry!!

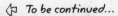 To be continued...

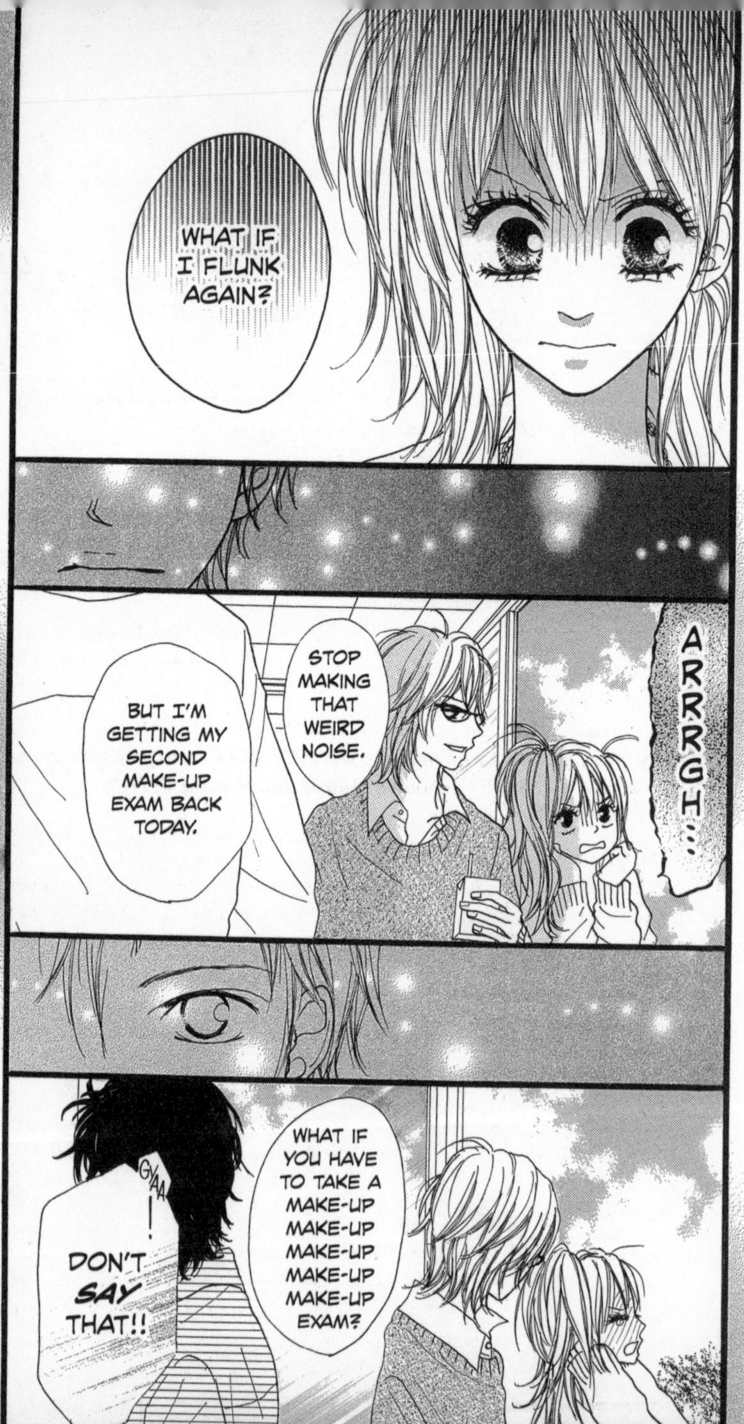
WHAT IF I FLUNK AGAIN?
ARRRGH...
STOP MAKING THAT WEIRD NOISE.
BUT I'M GETTING MY SECOND MAKE-UP EXAM BACK TODAY.
WHAT IF YOU HAVE TO TAKE A MAKE-UP MAKE-UP MAKE-UP MAKE-UP MAKE-UP EXAM?
GYAA!
DON'T SAY THAT!!

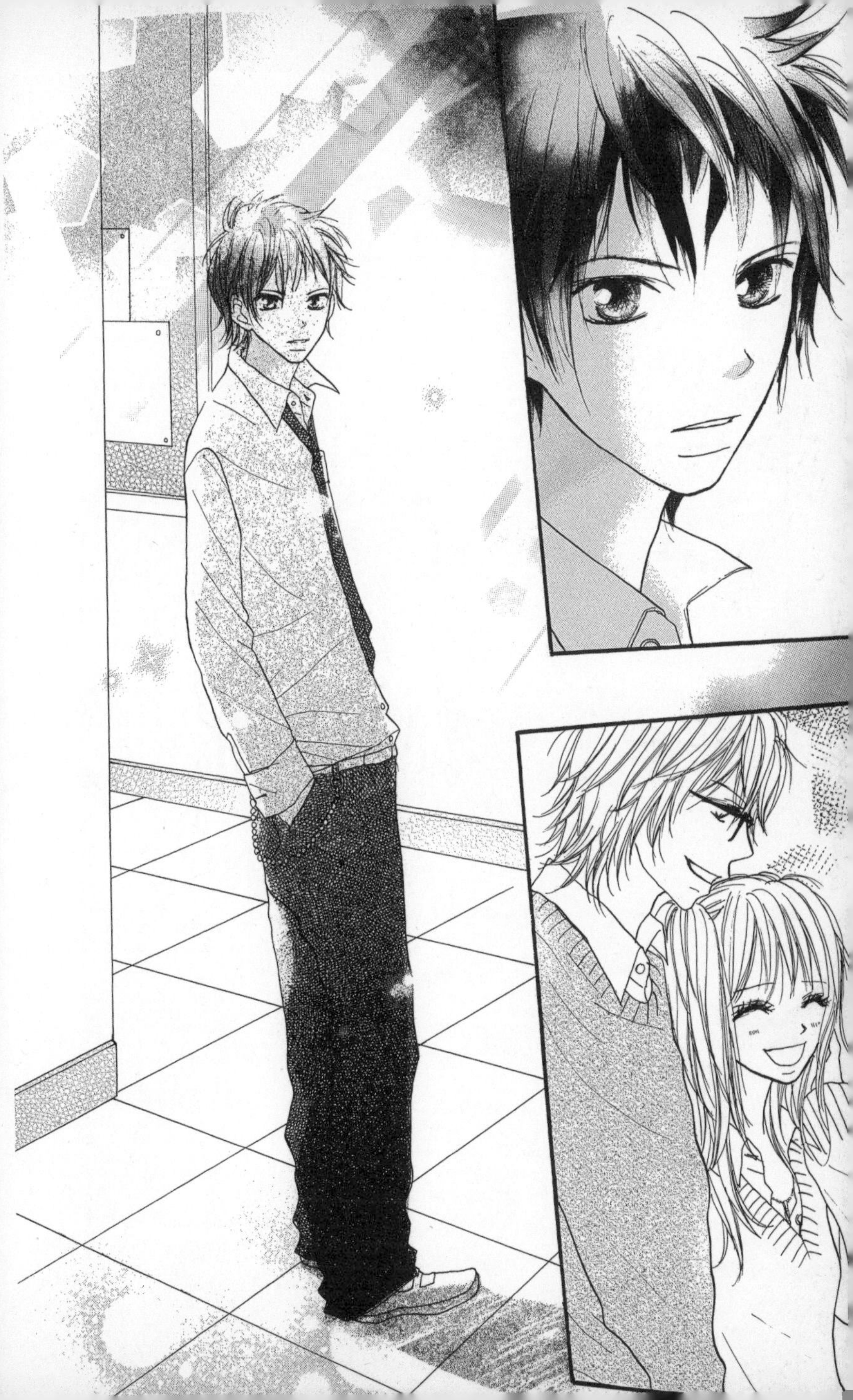

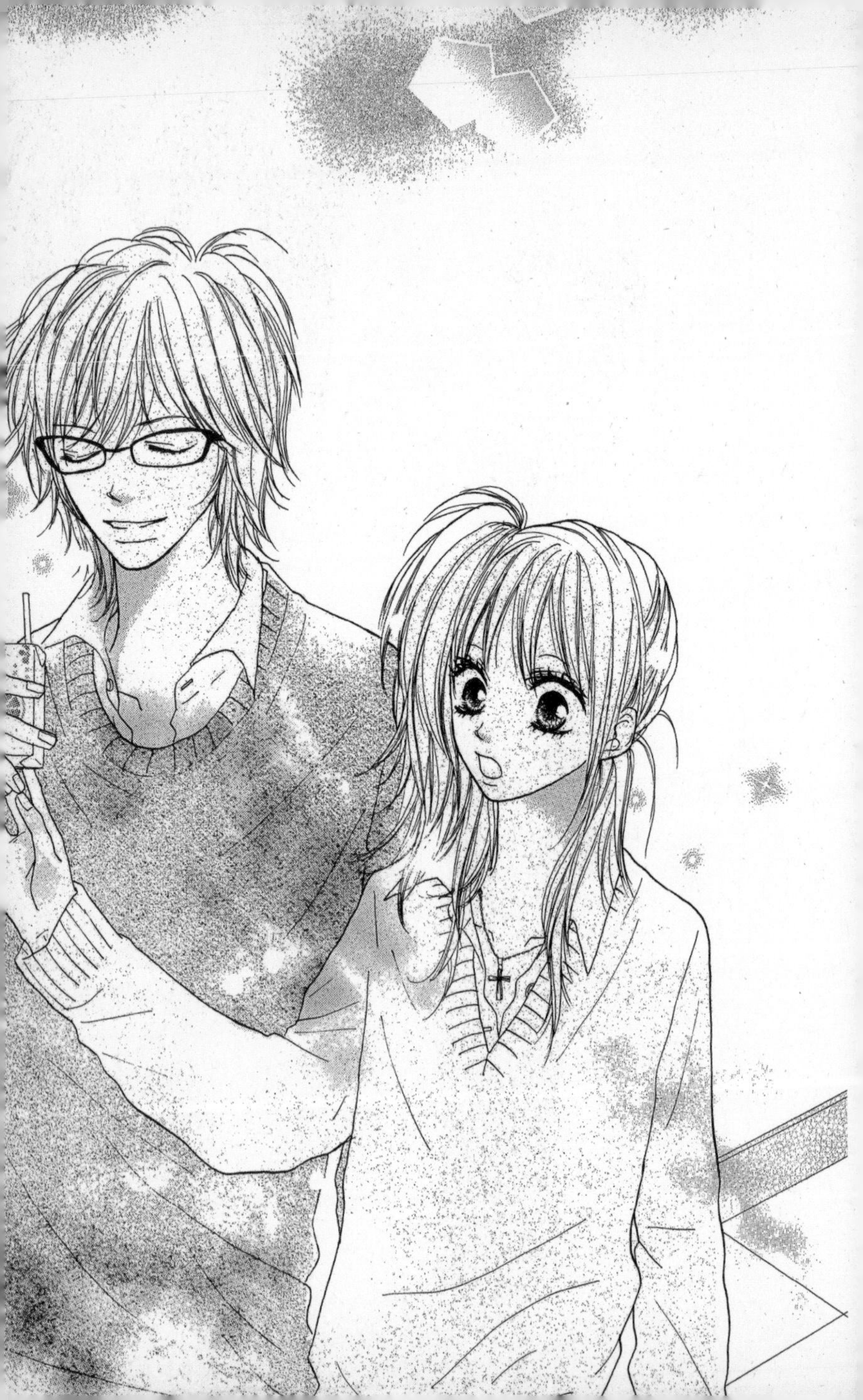

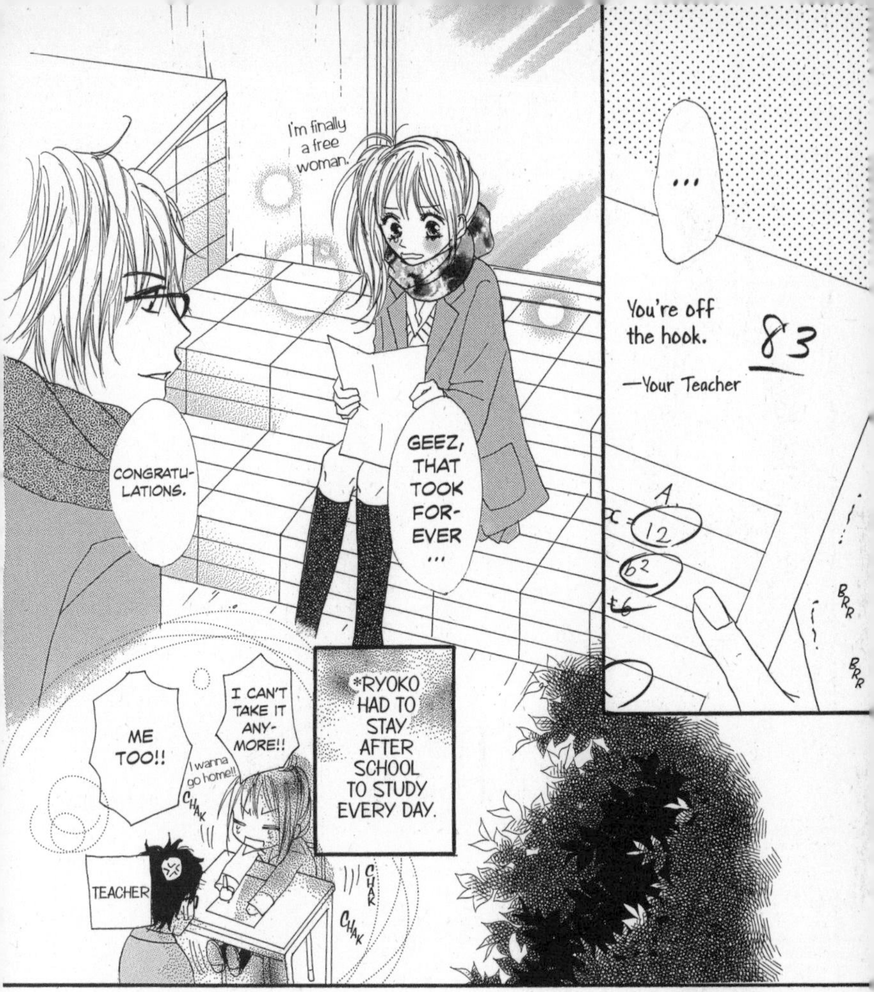
...
You're off the hook.
83
—Your Teacher
A.
x = 12
BRR
BRR
I'm finally a free woman.
GEEZ, THAT TOOK FOREVER...
CONGRATULATIONS.
*RYOKO HAD TO STAY AFTER SCHOOL TO STUDY EVERY DAY.
I CAN'T TAKE IT ANYMORE!!
ME TOO!!
I wanna go home!!
CHAK
TEACHER
CHAK
CHAK

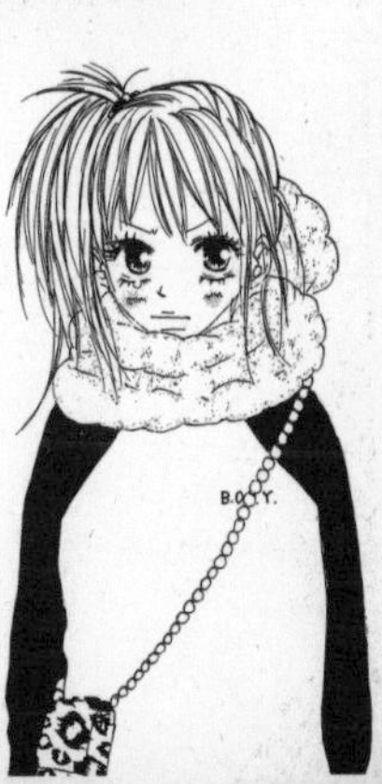
B.O.T.Y.

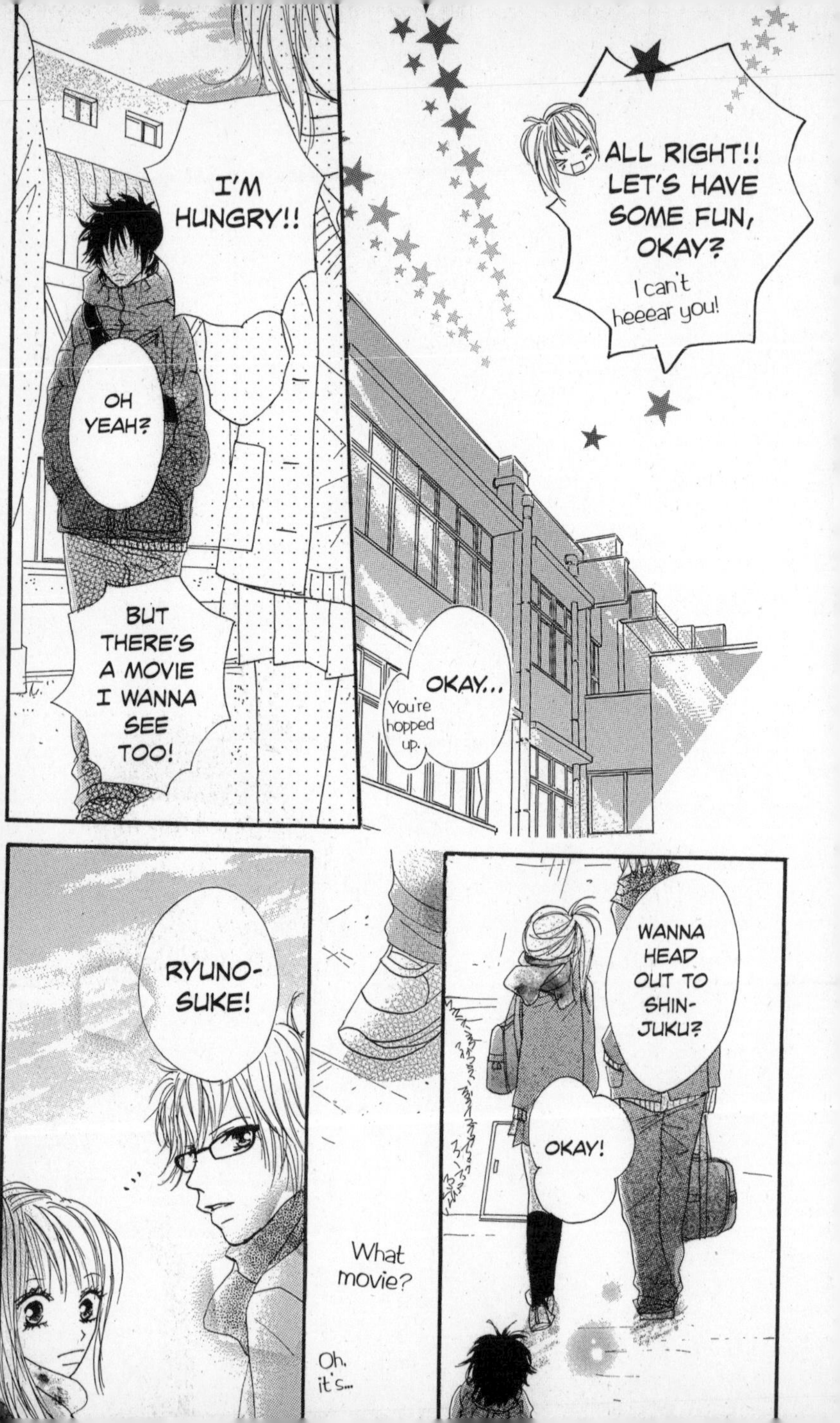
ALL RIGHT!! LET'S HAVE SOME FUN, OKAY?
I can't heeear you!
OKAY...
You're hopped up.
I'M HUNGRY!!
OH YEAH?
BUT THERE'S A MOVIE I WANNA SEE TOO!
WANNA HEAD OUT TO SHIN-JUKU?
OKAY!
What movie?
Oh, it's...
RYUNO-SUKE!

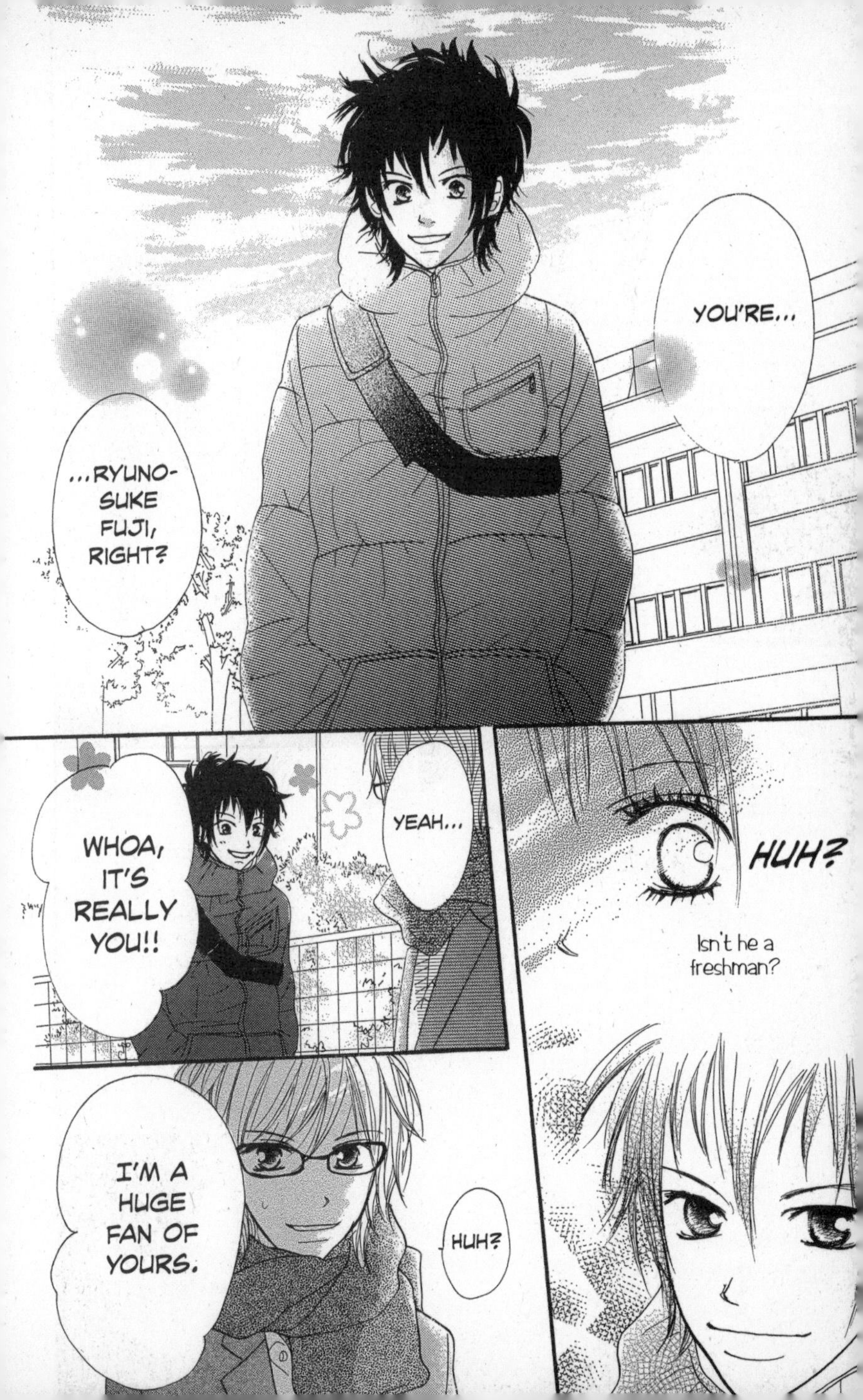
YOU'RE...
...RYUNO-SUKE FUJI, RIGHT?
HUH?
Isn't he a freshman?
YEAH...
WHOA, IT'S REALLY YOU!!
HUH?
I'M A HUGE FAN OF YOURS.

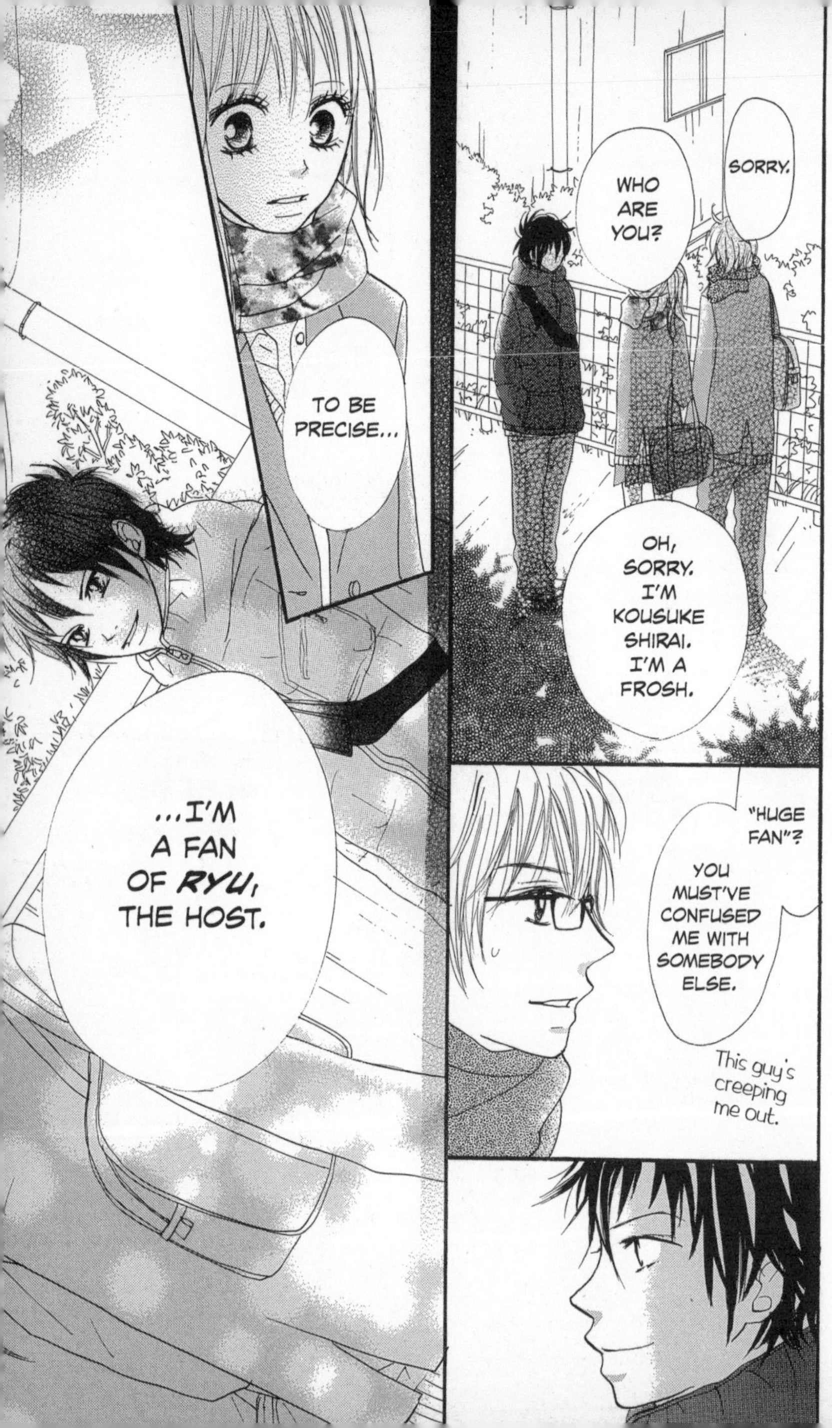
SORRY.
WHO ARE YOU?
OH, SORRY. I'M KOUSUKE SHIRAI. I'M A FROSH.
"HUGE FAN"? YOU MUST'VE CONFUSED ME WITH SOMEBODY ELSE.
This guy's creeping me out.
TO BE PRECISE...
...I'M A FAN OF RYU, THE HOST.

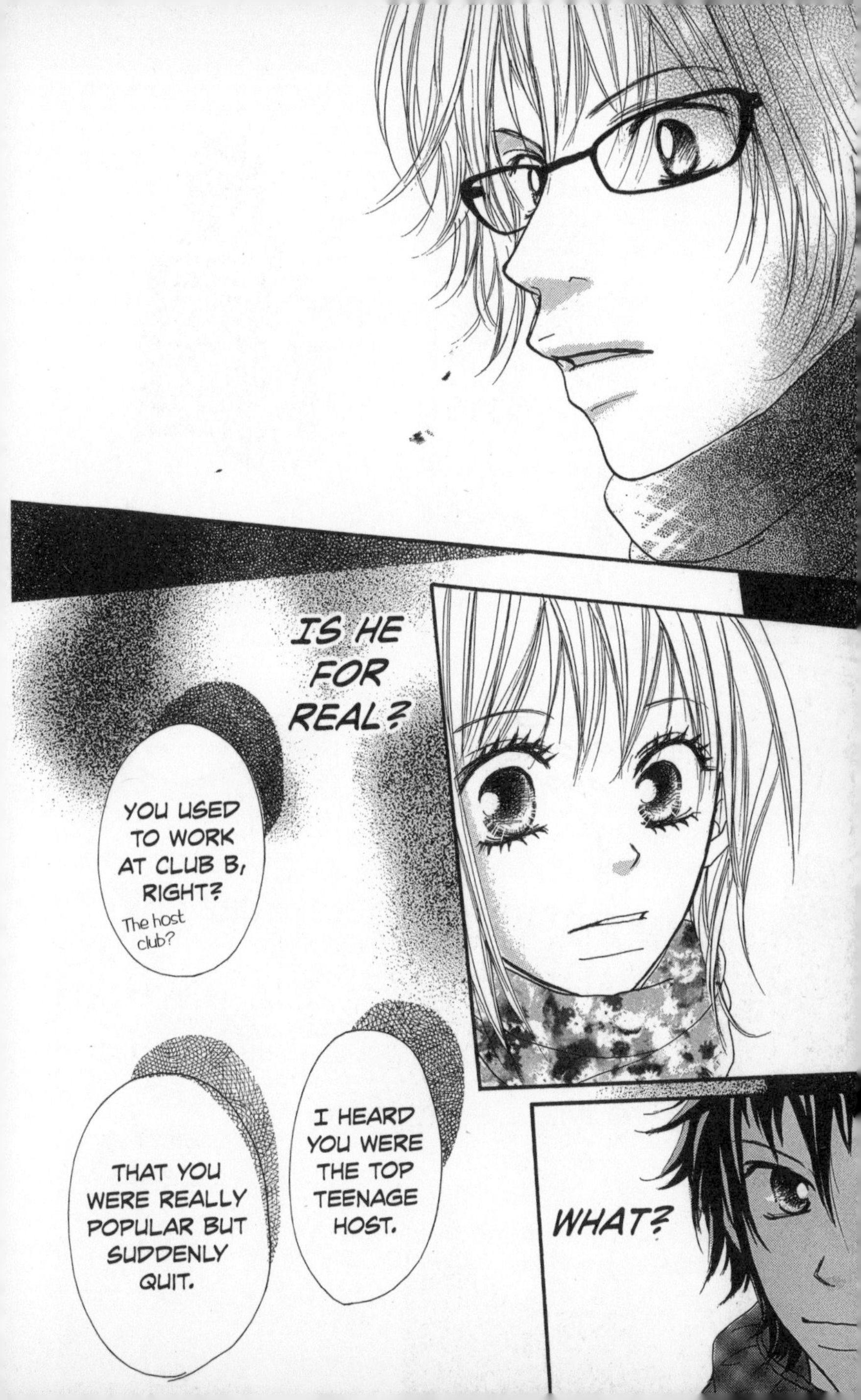
IS HE FOR REAL?
YOU USED TO WORK AT CLUB B, RIGHT?
The host club?
WHAT?
I HEARD YOU WERE THE TOP TEENAGE HOST.
THAT YOU WERE REALLY POPULAR BUT SUDDENLY QUIT.

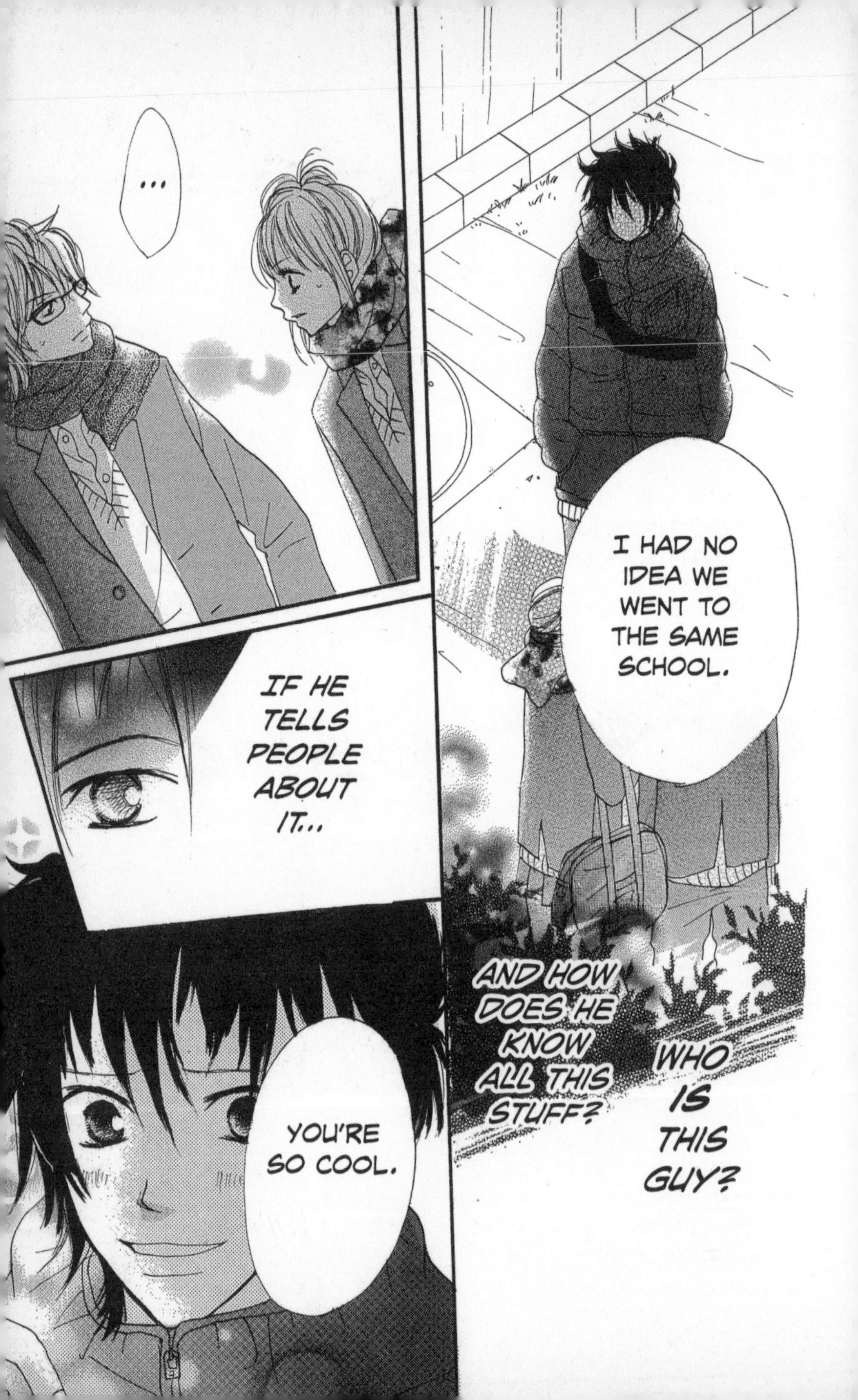
I HAD NO IDEA WE WENT TO THE SAME SCHOOL.
WHO IS THIS GUY?
AND HOW DOES HE KNOW ALL THIS STUFF?
...
IF HE TELLS PEOPLE ABOUT IT...
YOU'RE SO COOL.

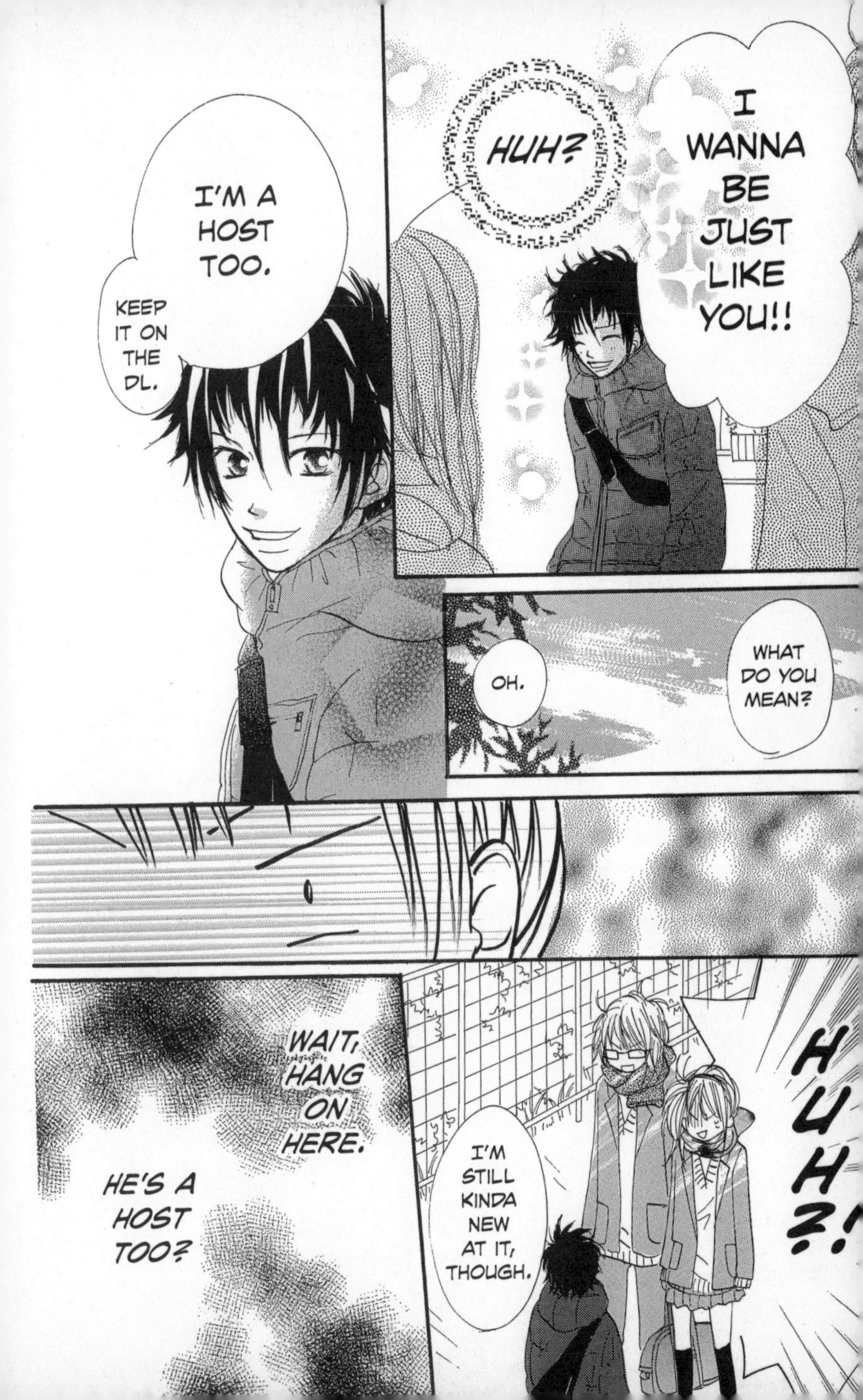
I WANNA BE JUST LIKE YOU!!
HUH?
WHAT DO YOU MEAN?
OH.
I'M A HOST TOO.
KEEP IT ON THE DL.
HUH?!
I'M STILL KINDA NEW AT IT, THOUGH.
WAIT, HANG ON HERE.
HE'S A HOST TOO?

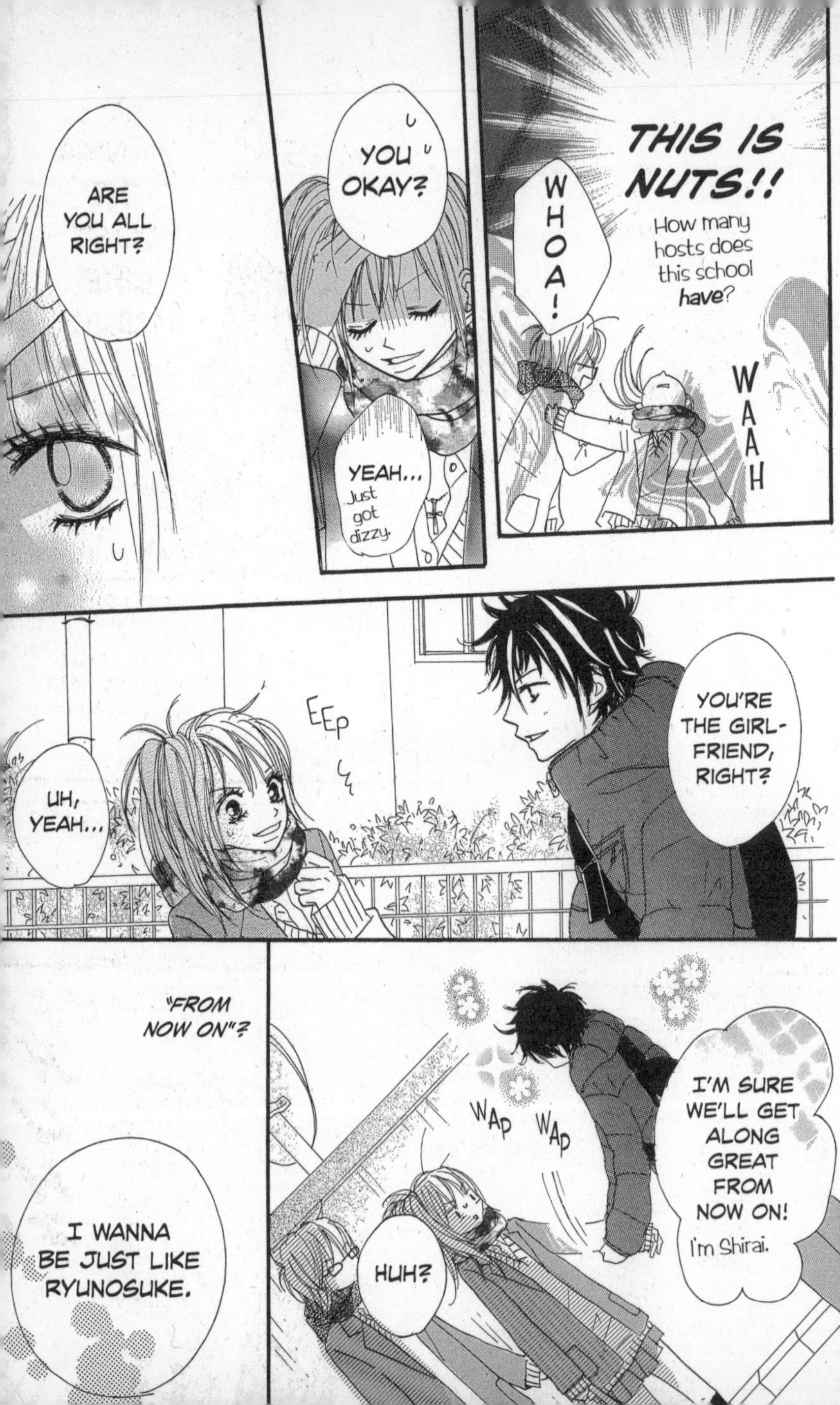
WHOA!
THIS IS NUTS!!
How many hosts does this school have?
WAAAH
YOU OKAY?
YEAH... Just got dizzy.
ARE YOU ALL RIGHT?
YOU'RE THE GIRL-FRIEND, RIGHT?
EEP
UH, YEAH...
I'M SURE WE'LL GET ALONG GREAT FROM NOW ON!
I'm Shirai.
WAP WAP
HUH?
"FROM NOW ON"?
I WANNA BE JUST LIKE RYUNOSUKE.

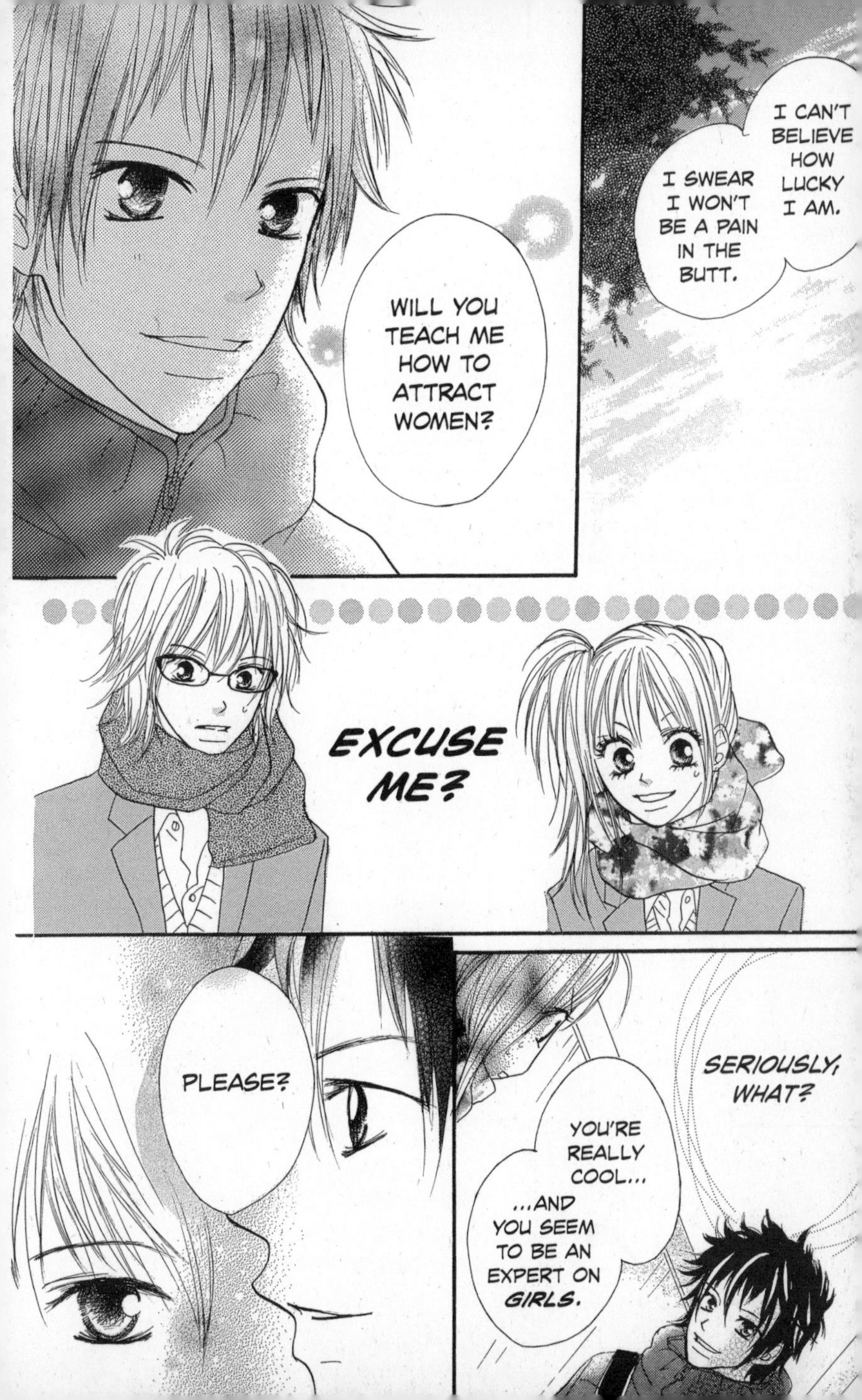
I CAN'T BELIEVE HOW LUCKY I AM.
I SWEAR I WON'T BE A PAIN IN THE BUTT.
WILL YOU TEACH ME HOW TO ATTRACT WOMEN?
EXCUSE ME?
SERIOUSLY, WHAT?
YOU'RE REALLY COOL... ...AND YOU SEEM TO BE AN EXPERT ON *GIRLS*.
PLEASE?

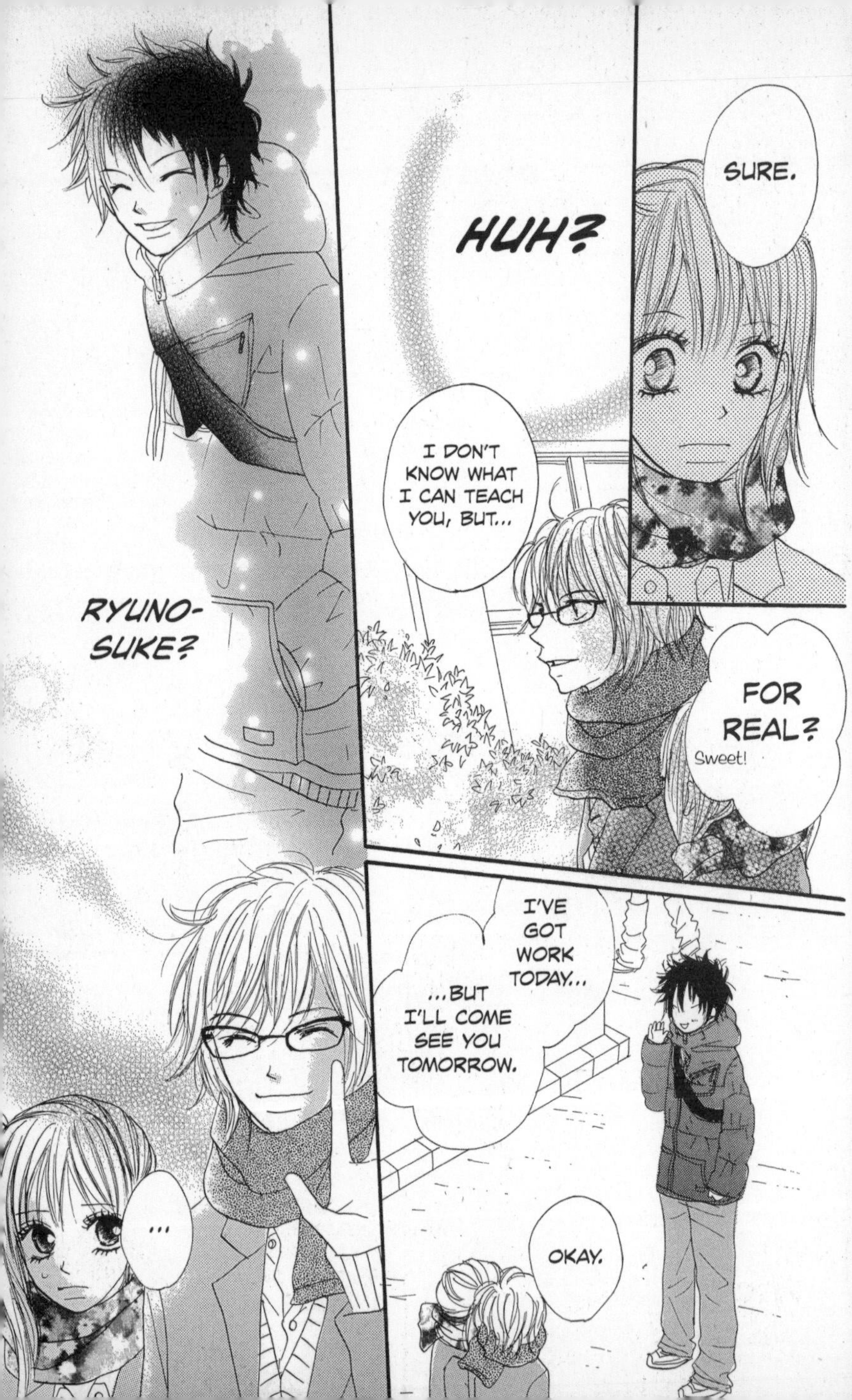
SURE.
HUH?
I DON'T KNOW WHAT I CAN TEACH YOU, BUT...
FOR REAL?
Sweet!
RYUNO-SUKE?
I'VE GOT WORK TODAY...
...BUT I'LL COME SEE YOU TOMORROW.
OKAY.
...

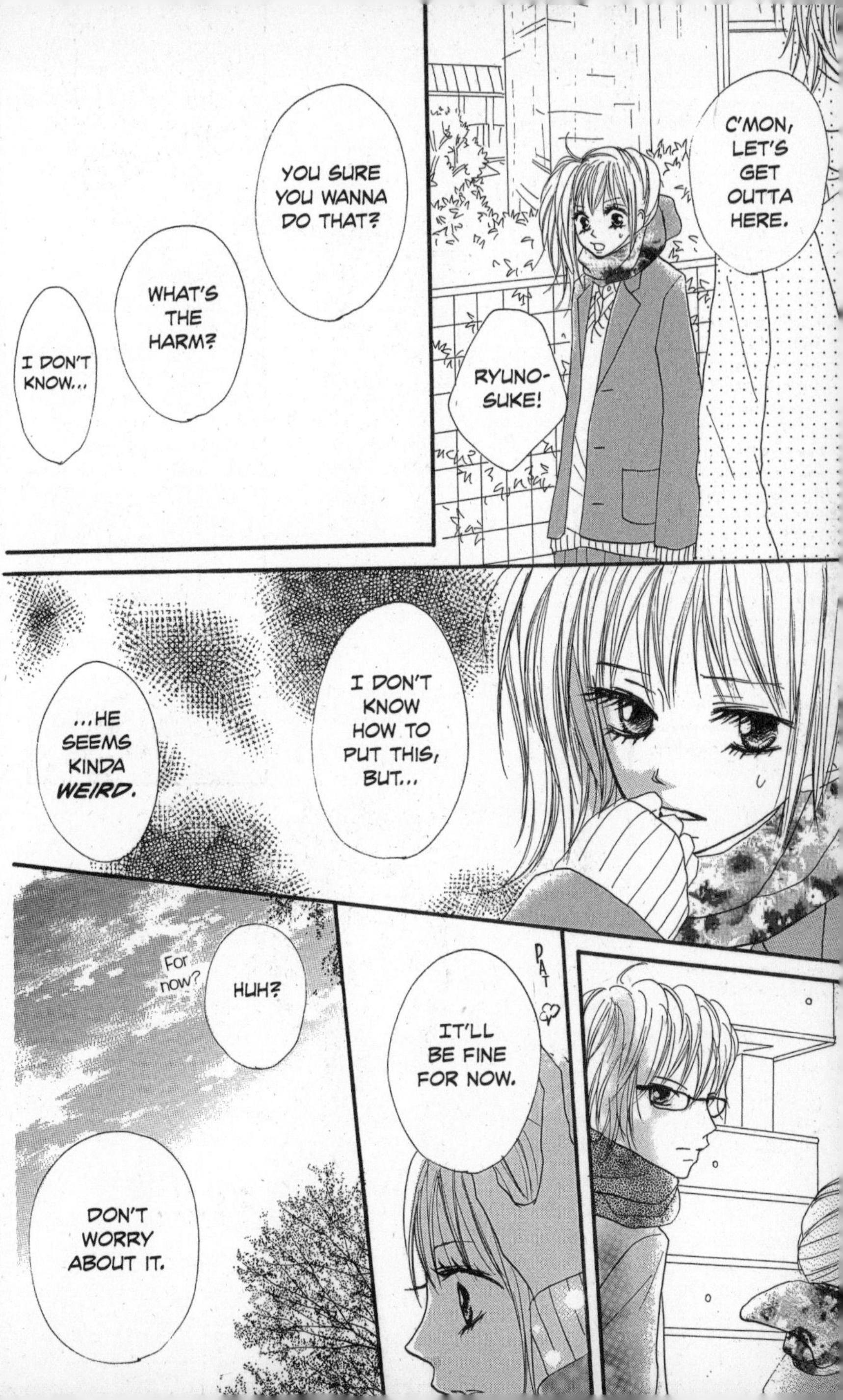
C'MON, LET'S GET OUTTA HERE.
RYUNO-SUKE!
YOU SURE YOU WANNA DO THAT?
WHAT'S THE HARM?
I DON'T KNOW...
I DON'T KNOW HOW TO PUT THIS, BUT...
...HE SEEMS KINDA WEIRD.
PAT
IT'LL BE FINE FOR NOW.
HUH?
For now?
DON'T WORRY ABOUT IT.

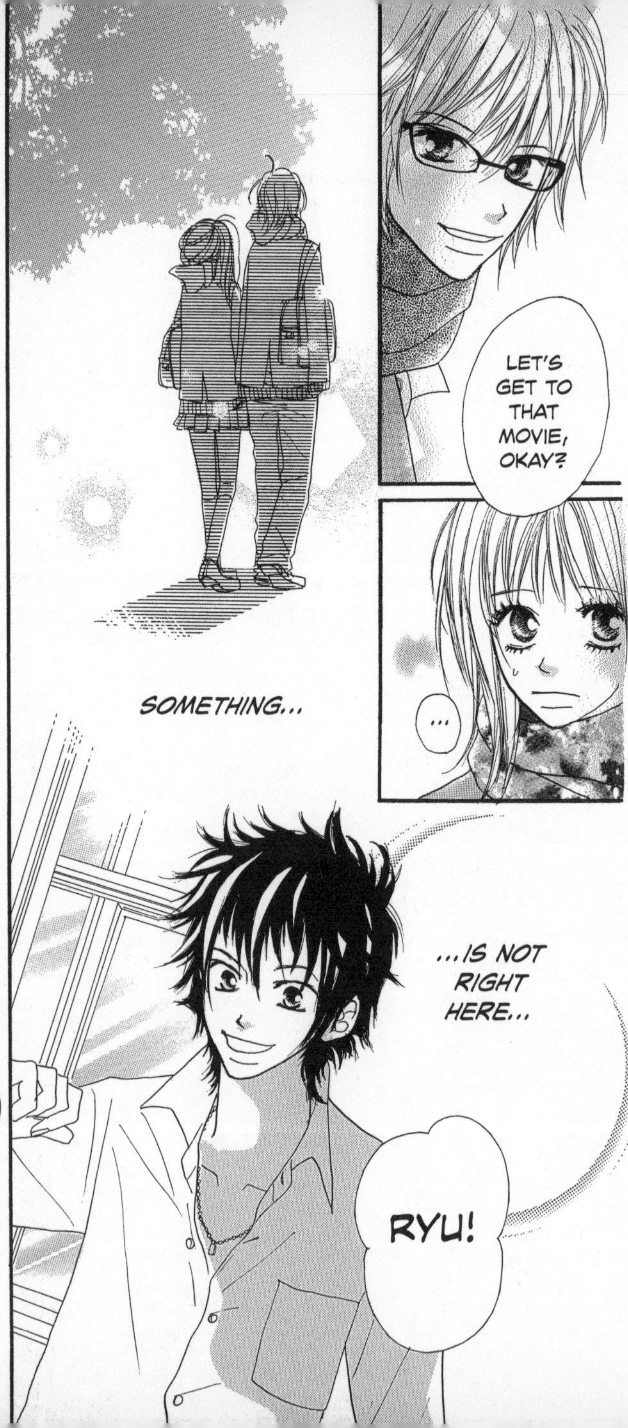
LET'S GET TO THAT MOVIE, OKAY?
...
SOMETHING...
...IS NOT RIGHT HERE...
RYU!

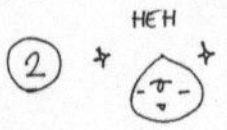
HEH

I just bought the balance ball, so I don't know how well it'll work, but I plan to keep using it.

I was texting Karuho Shiina the other day and she was like, "What're you doing right now?" I told her, "I'm smelling my toenails," and she started cracking up. She said, "I've never heard anyone report something like that! Ha ha ha!" She got a big kick out of it... I was so happy!! I'm glad I said it. It made me want to go on just being myself. But we all take a whiff, don't we?

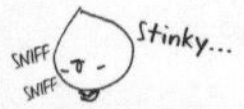
SNIFF
SNIFF
Stinky...

Karuho always says nice things about me. She makes me so happy. I need the encouragement, since I don't hear a lot of praise...and I gained weight...heh heh.

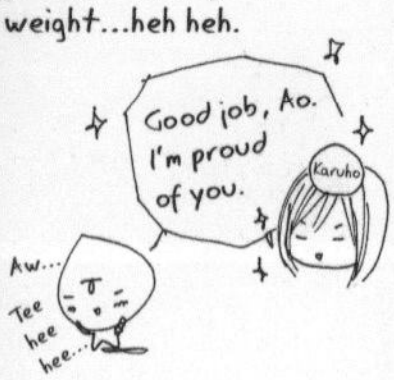
Good job, Ao. I'm proud of you.
Karuho
Aw... Tee hee hee...

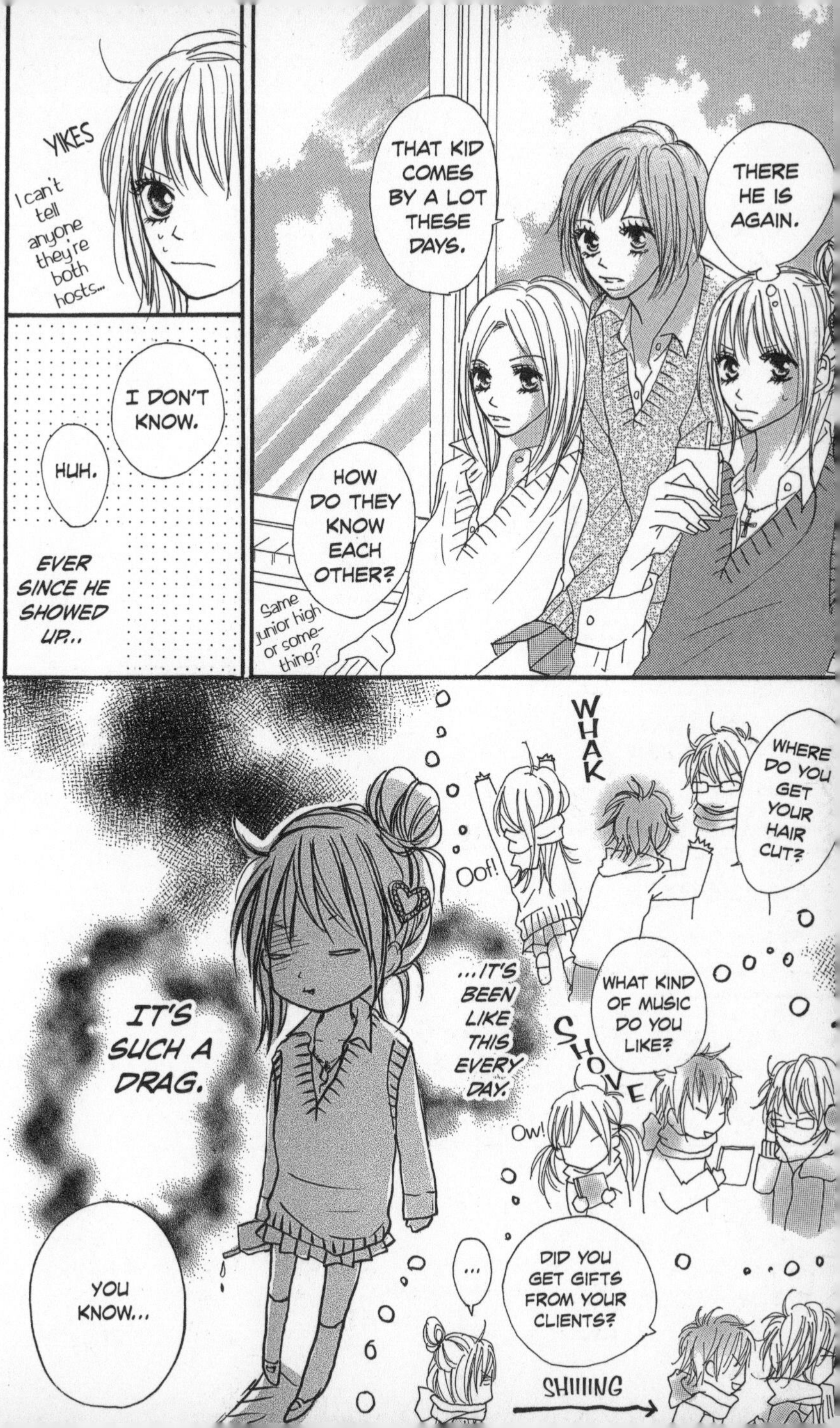
THERE HE IS AGAIN.
THAT KID COMES BY A LOT THESE DAYS.
HOW DO THEY KNOW EACH OTHER?
Same junior high or something?
YIKES
I can't tell anyone they're both hosts...
I DON'T KNOW.
HUH.
EVER SINCE HE SHOWED UP...
WHAK
WHERE DO YOU GET YOUR HAIR CUT?
Oof!
WHAT KIND OF MUSIC DO YOU LIKE?
SHOVE
Ow!
DID YOU GET GIFTS FROM YOUR CLIENTS?
SHIIIING
...
...IT'S BEEN LIKE THIS EVERY DAY.
IT'S SUCH A DRAG.
YOU KNOW...

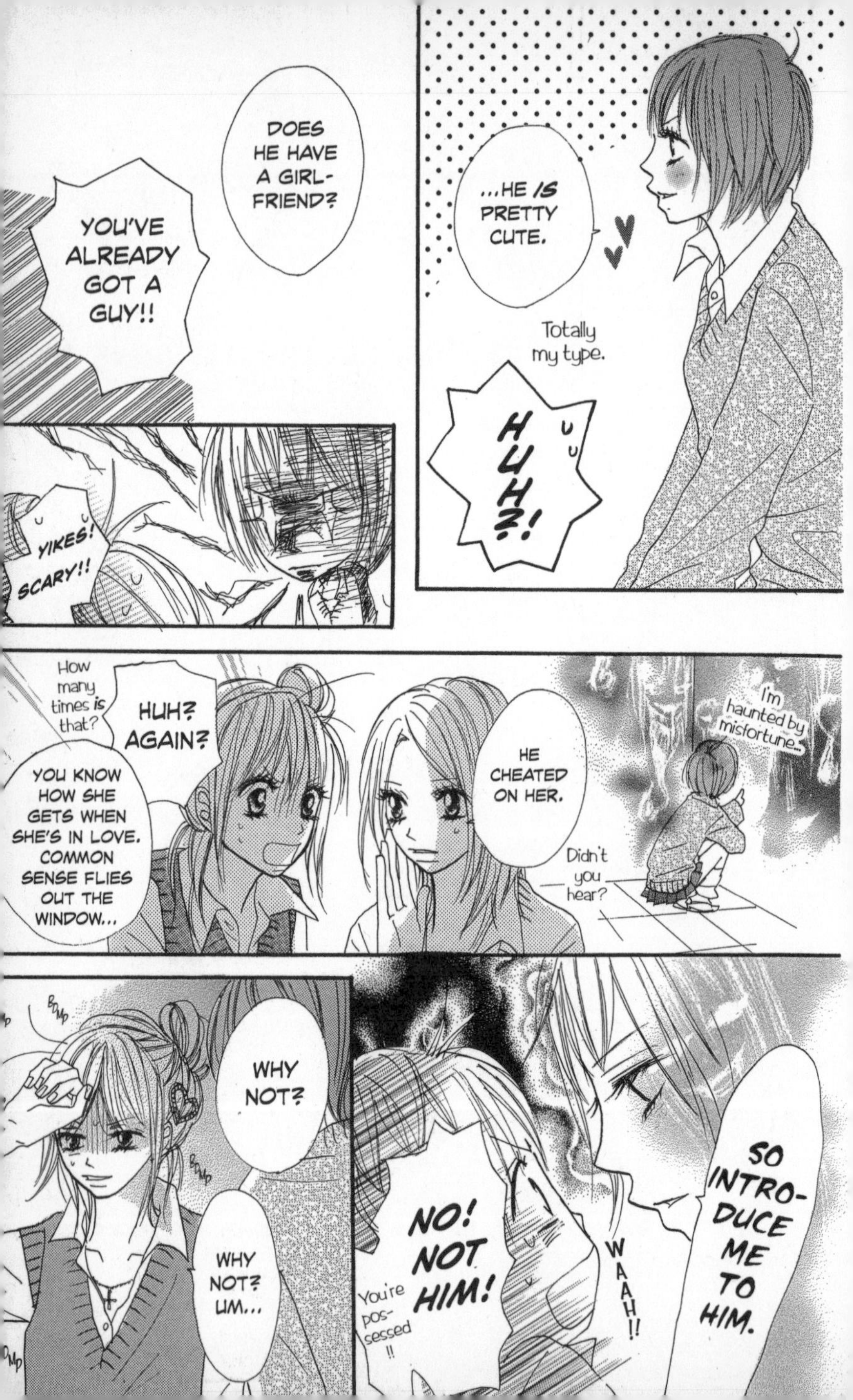

...HE IS PRETTY CUTE.
Totally my type.
HUH?!
DOES HE HAVE A GIRLFRIEND?
YOU'VE ALREADY GOT A GUY!!
YIKES! SCARY!!
I'm haunted by misfortune...
HE CHEATED ON HER.
Didn't you hear?
HUH? AGAIN?
How many times is that?
YOU KNOW HOW SHE GETS WHEN SHE'S IN LOVE. COMMON SENSE FLIES OUT THE WINDOW...
SO INTRODUCE ME TO HIM.
WAAH!!
NO! NOT HIM!
You're possessed!!
WHY NOT?
BDMP
BDMP
WHY NOT? UM...

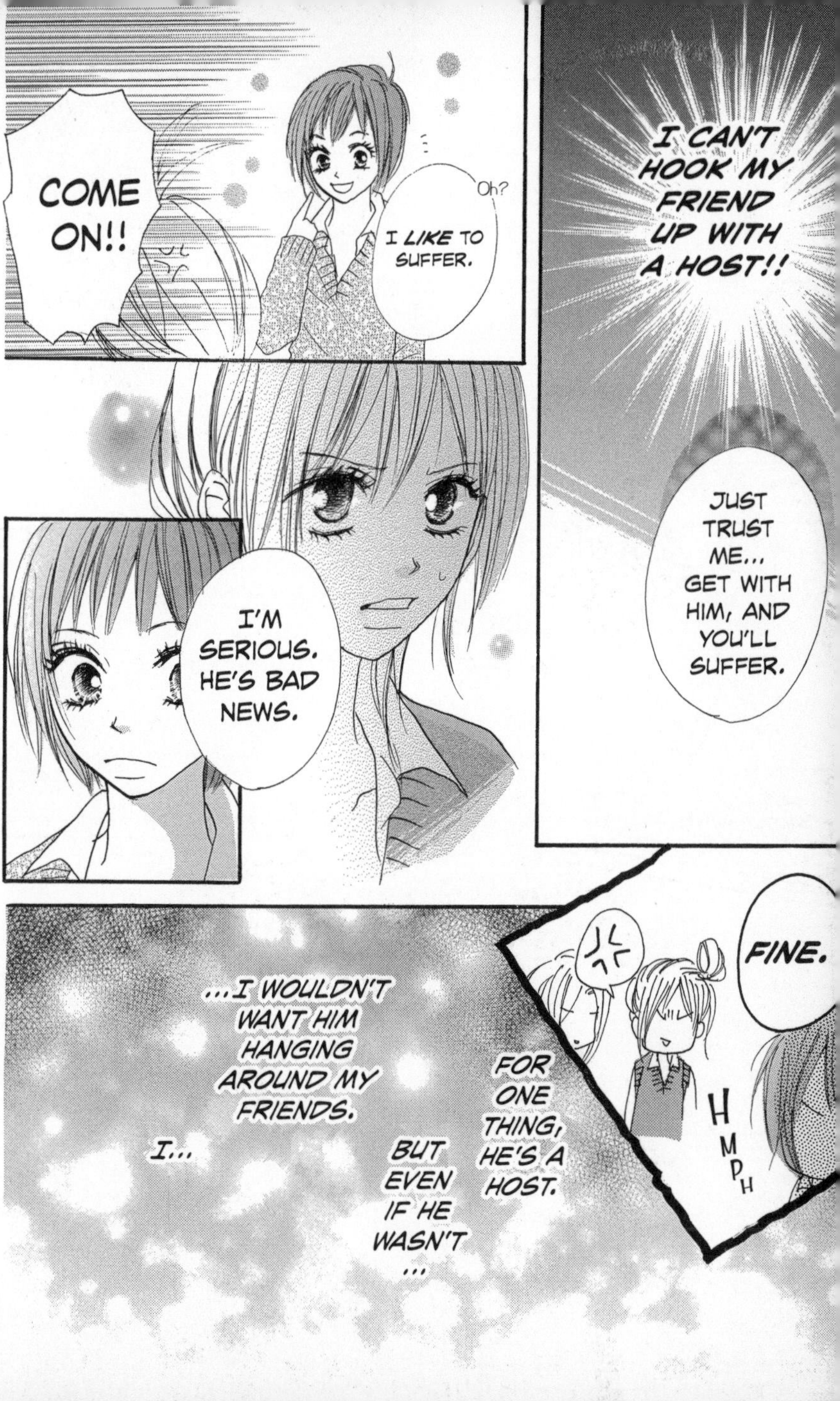
I CAN'T HOOK MY FRIEND UP WITH A HOST!!
JUST TRUST ME... GET WITH HIM, AND YOU'LL SUFFER.
Oh?
I LIKE TO SUFFER.
COME ON!!
I'M SERIOUS. HE'S BAD NEWS.
FINE.
HMPH
FOR ONE THING, HE'S A HOST.
BUT EVEN IF HE WASN'T...
...I WOULDN'T WANT HIM HANGING AROUND MY FRIENDS.
I...

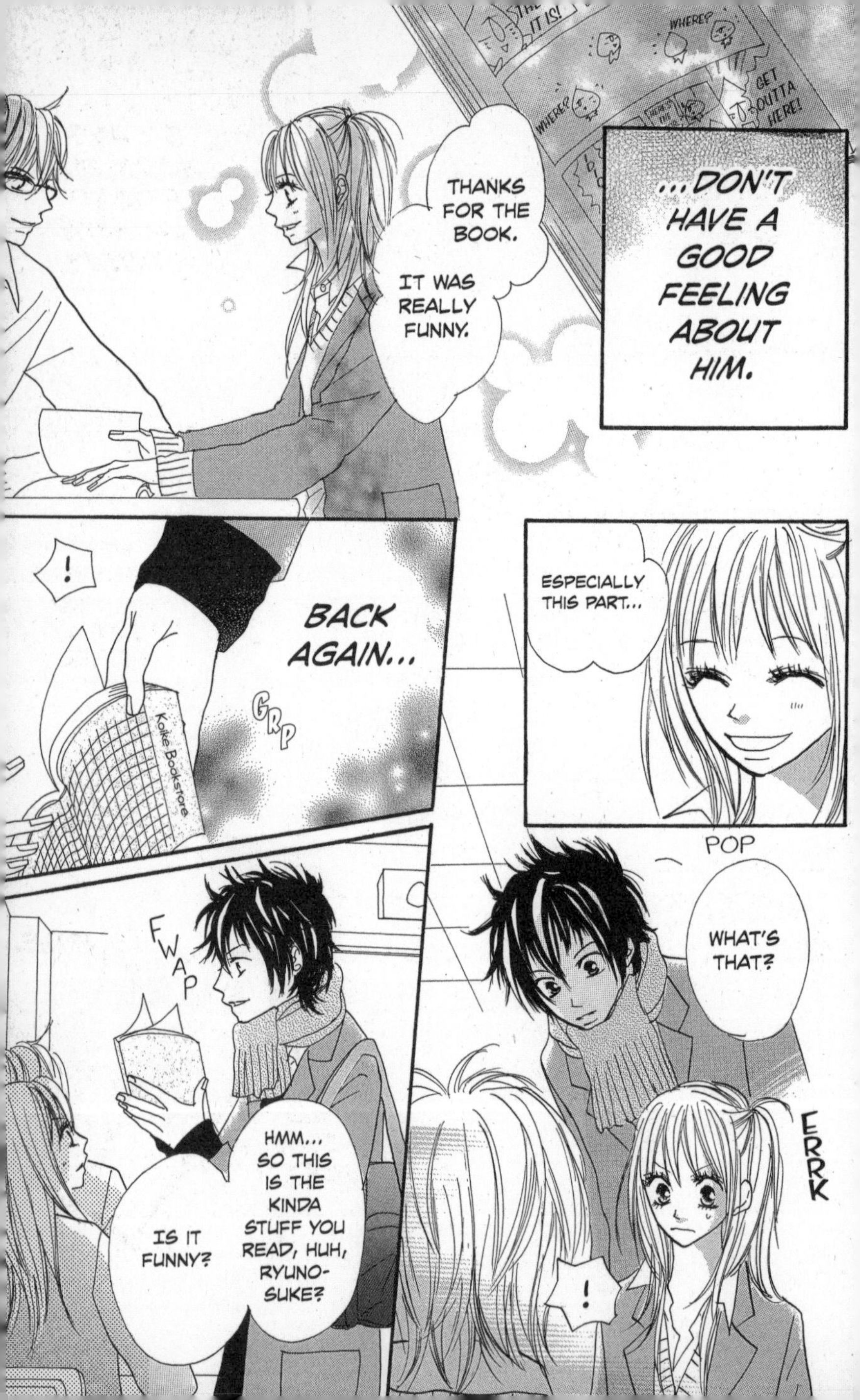

...DON'T HAVE A GOOD FEELING ABOUT HIM.
WHERE?
GET OUTTA HERE!
THANKS FOR THE BOOK.
IT WAS REALLY FUNNY.
ESPECIALLY THIS PART...
!
BACK AGAIN...
GRP
Koike Bookstore
POP
WHAT'S THAT?
ERRK
!
FWAP
HMM... SO THIS IS THE KINDA STUFF YOU READ, HUH, RYUNOSUKE?
IS IT FUNNY?

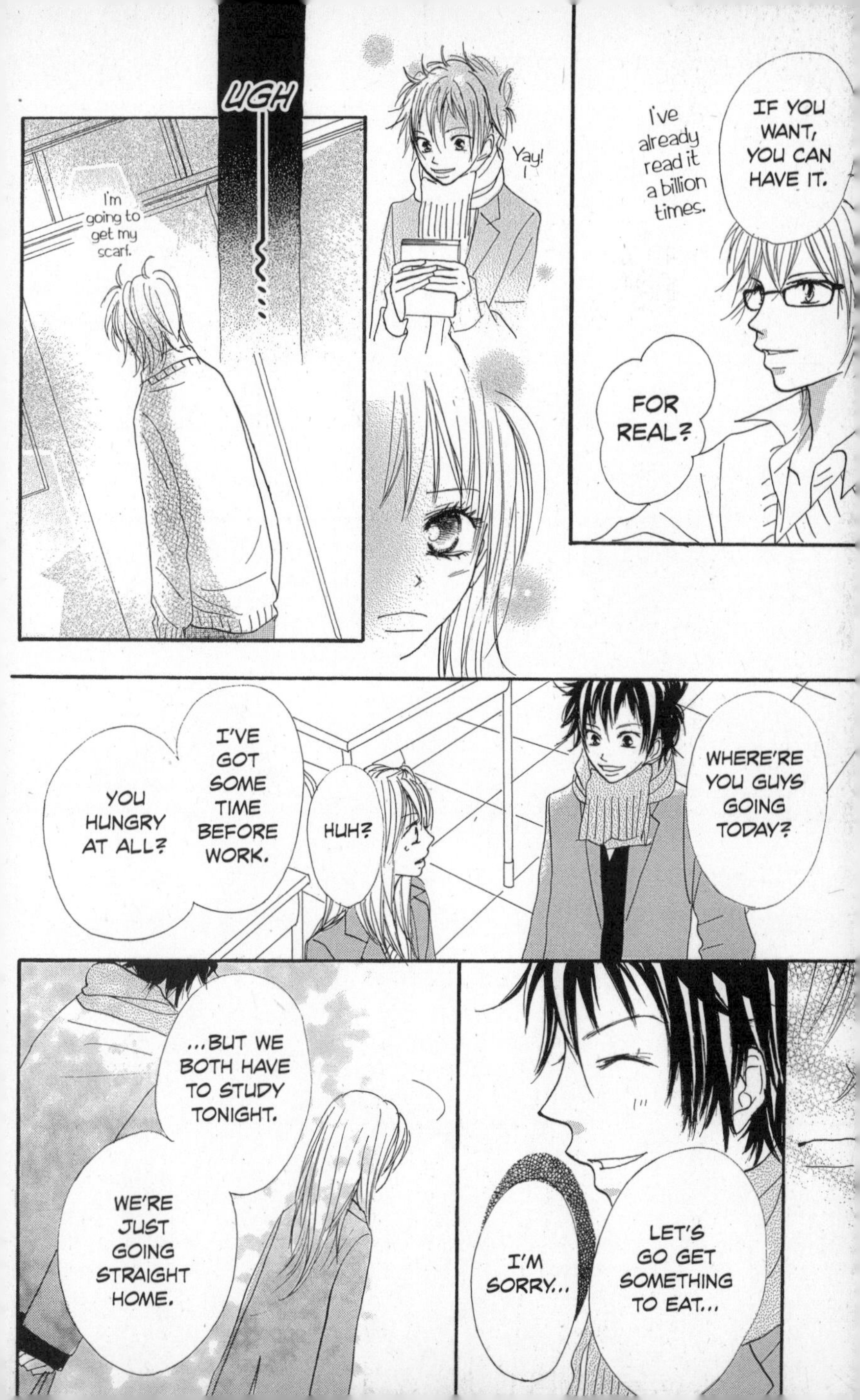
IF YOU WANT, YOU CAN HAVE IT.
I've already read it a billion times.
FOR REAL?
Yay!
UGH
I'm going to get my scarf.
WHERE'RE YOU GUYS GOING TODAY?
HUH?
I'VE GOT SOME TIME BEFORE WORK.
YOU HUNGRY AT ALL?
LET'S GO GET SOMETHING TO EAT...
I'M SORRY...
...BUT WE BOTH HAVE TO STUDY TONIGHT.
WE'RE JUST GOING STRAIGHT HOME.

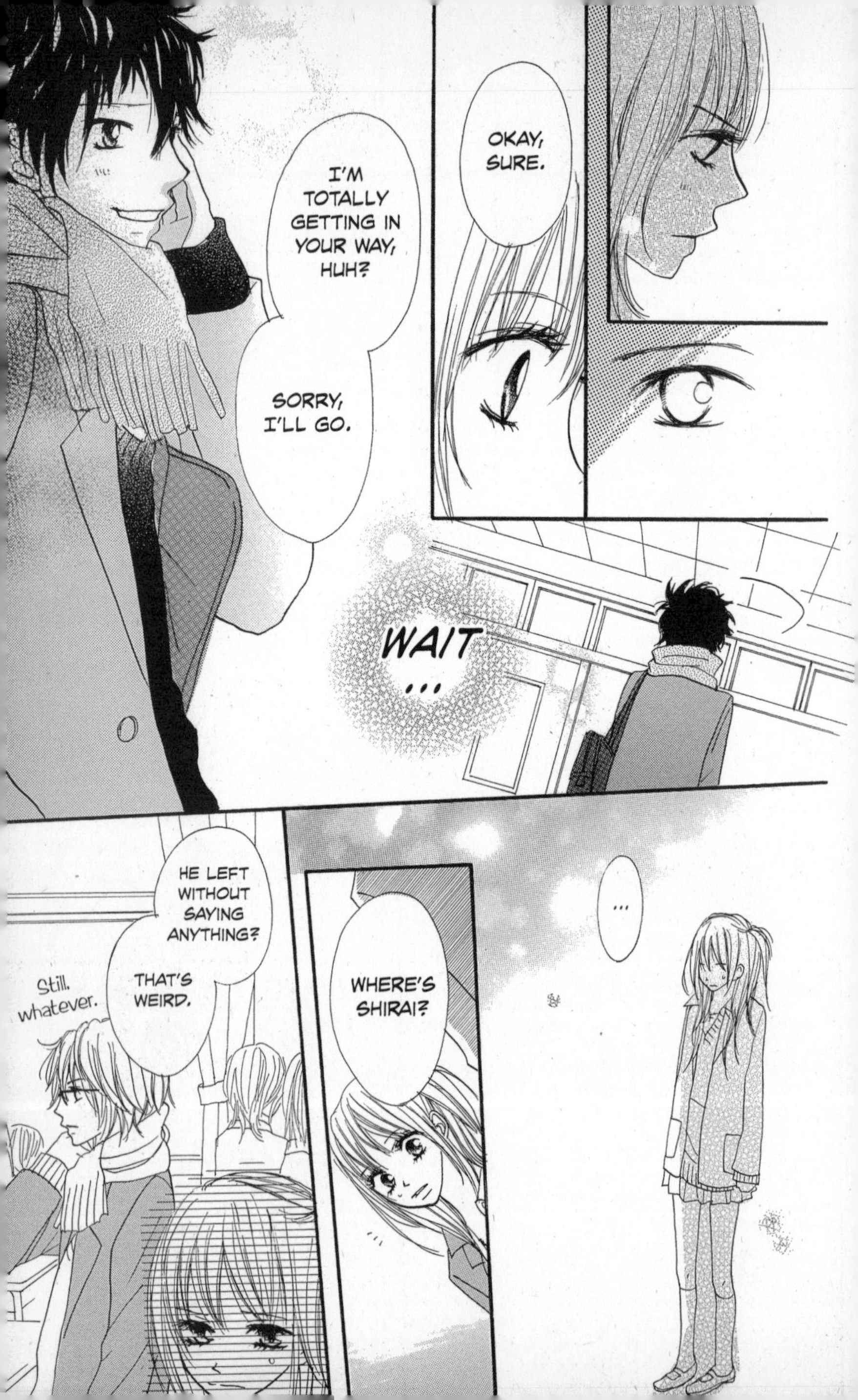

OKAY, SURE.
I'M TOTALLY GETTING IN YOUR WAY, HUH?
SORRY, I'LL GO.
WAIT ...
...
WHERE'S SHIRAI?
HE LEFT WITHOUT SAYING ANYTHING?
THAT'S WEIRD.
Still, whatever.

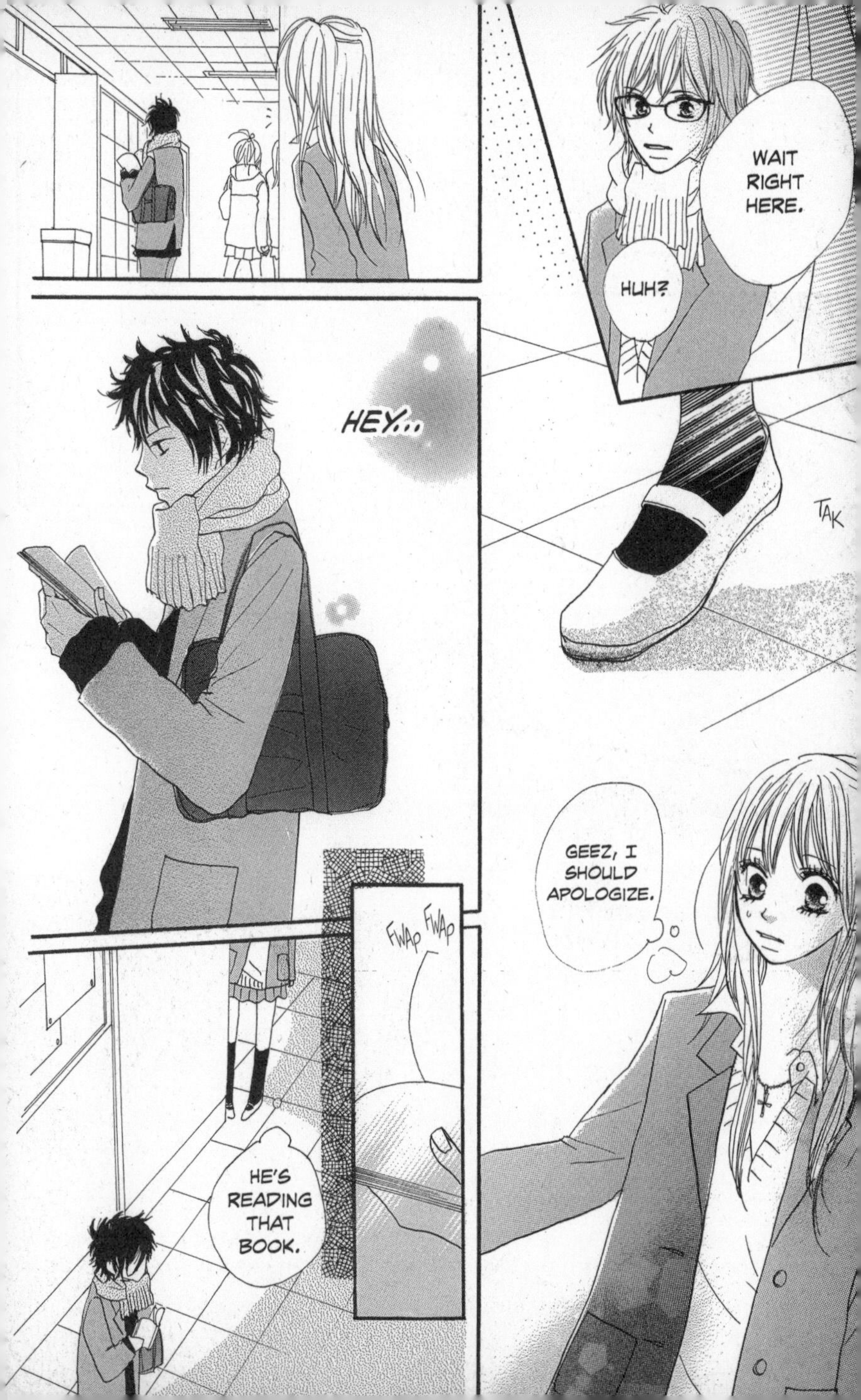
WAIT RIGHT HERE.
HUH?
TAK
GEEZ, I SHOULD APOLOGIZE.
HEY...
FWAP FWAP
HE'S READING THAT BOOK.

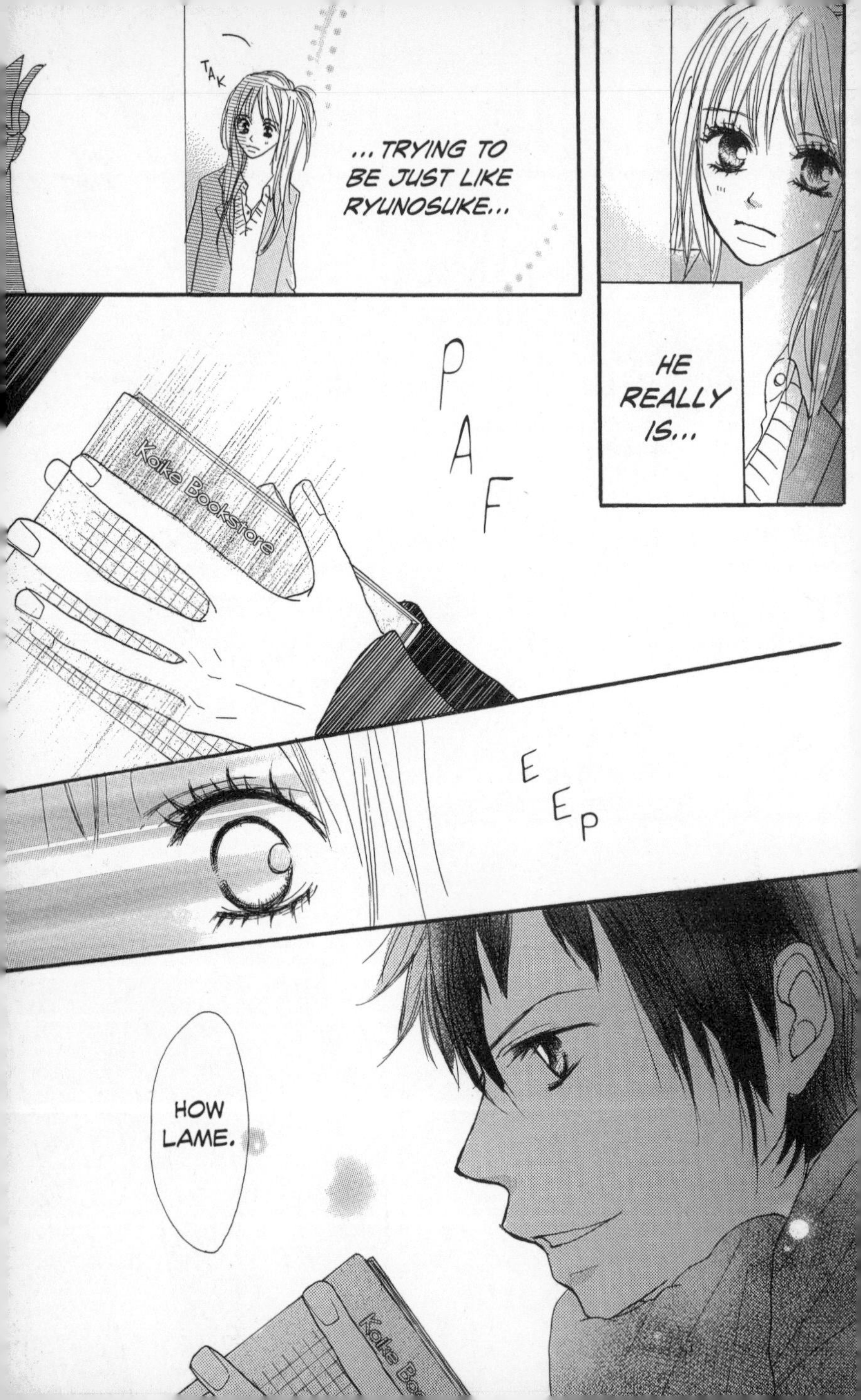
HE REALLY IS...
TAK
...TRYING TO BE JUST LIKE RYUNOSUKE...
PAF
Koike Bookstore
EEP
HOW LAME.

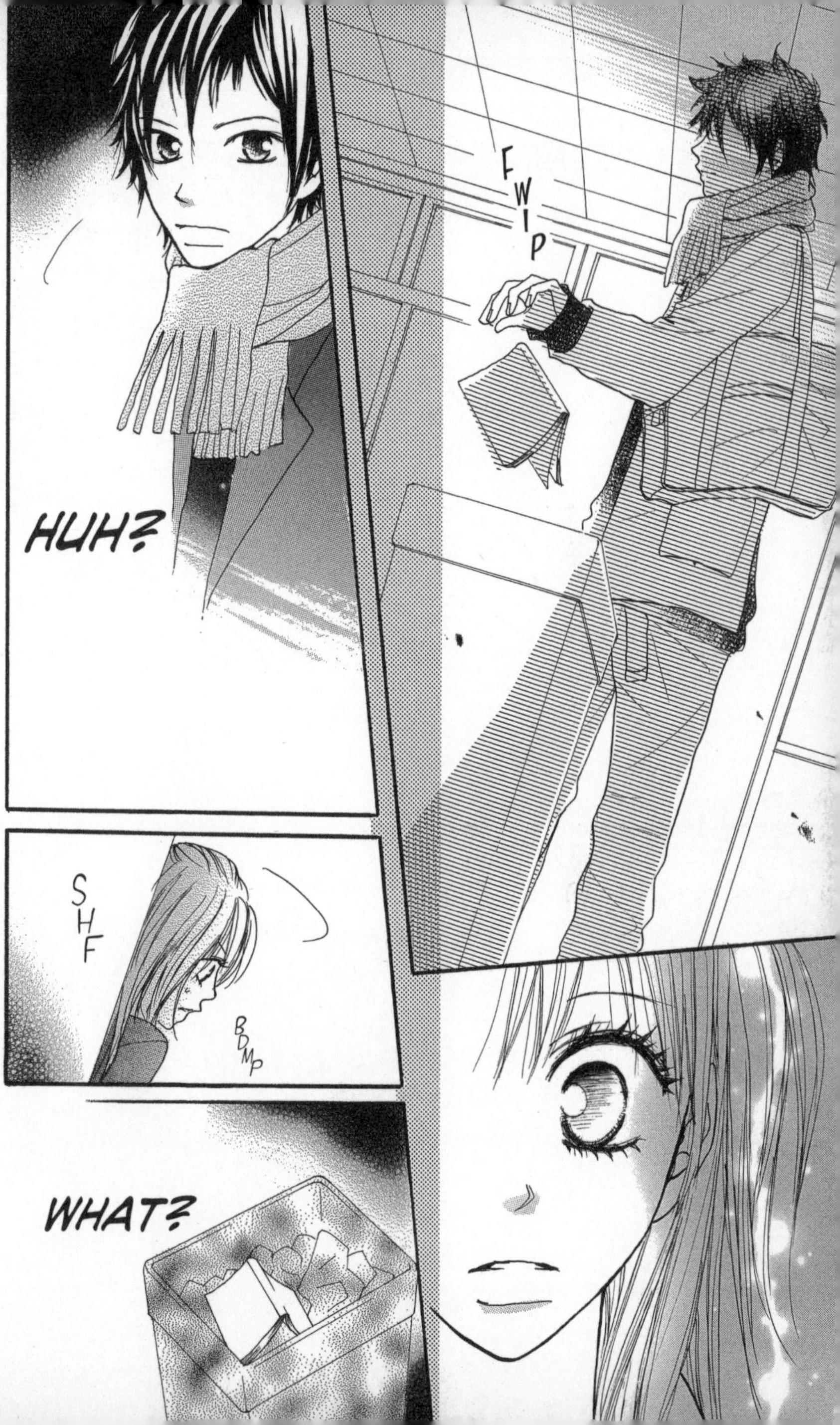
FWIP
HUH?
SHF
BDMP
WHAT?

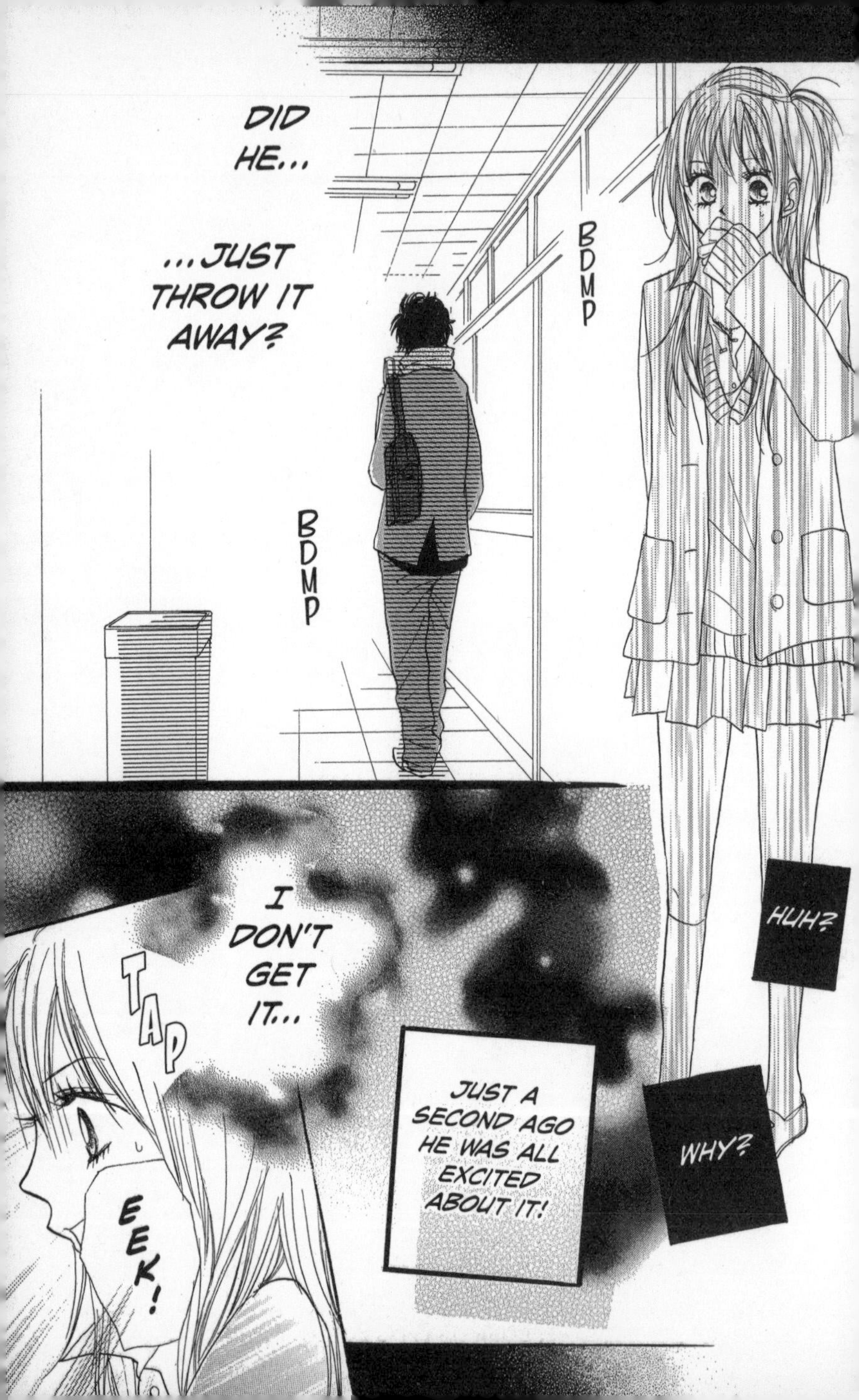
HUH?
WHY?
DID HE...
...JUST THROW IT AWAY?
BDMP
BDMP
JUST A SECOND AGO HE WAS ALL EXCITED ABOUT IT!
I DON'T GET IT...
TAP
EEK!

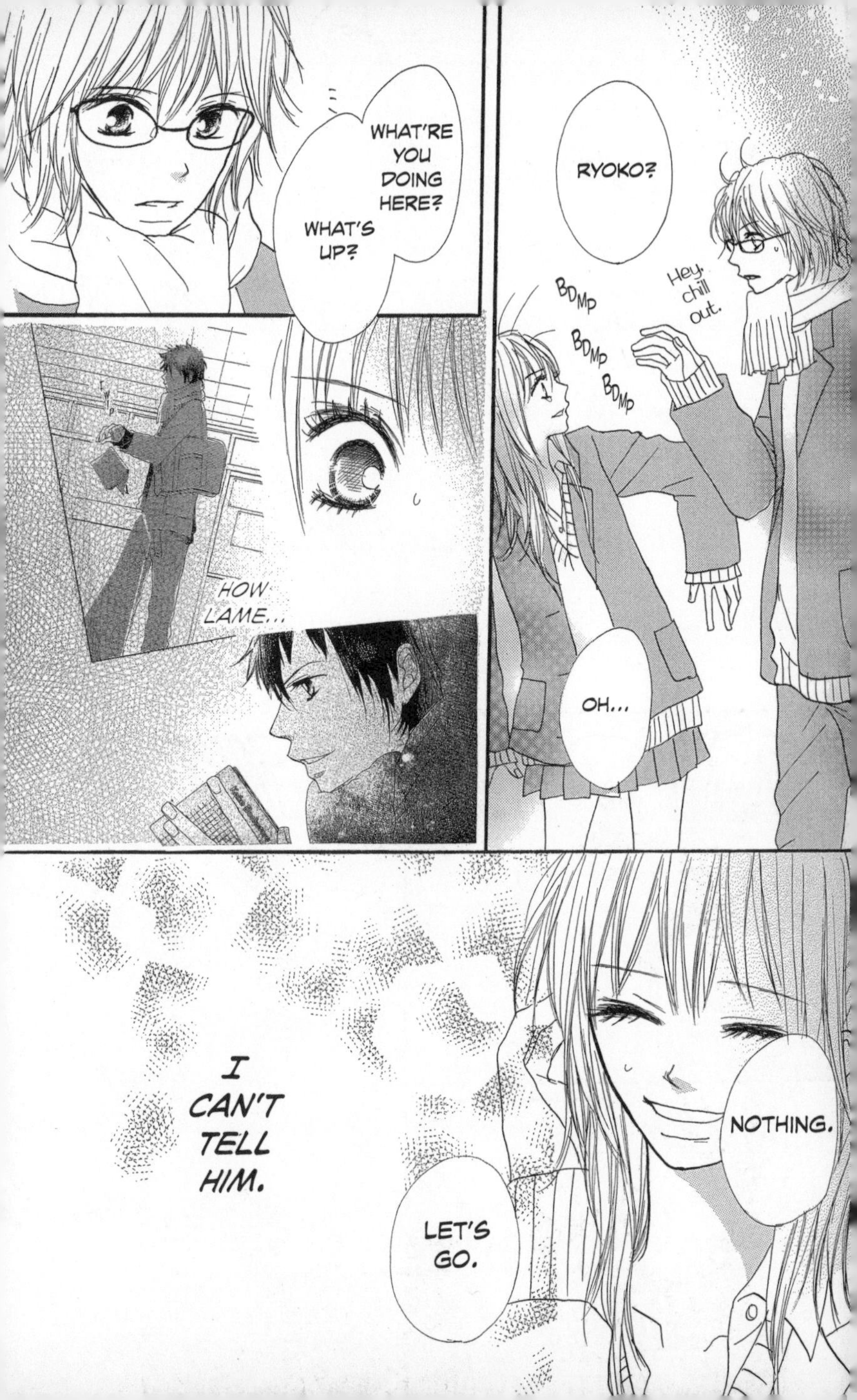
RYOKO?
BDMP
BDMP
BDMP
Hey, chill out.
OH...
WHAT'RE YOU DOING HERE?
WHAT'S UP?
HOW LAME...
NOTHING.
LET'S GO.
I CAN'T TELL HIM.

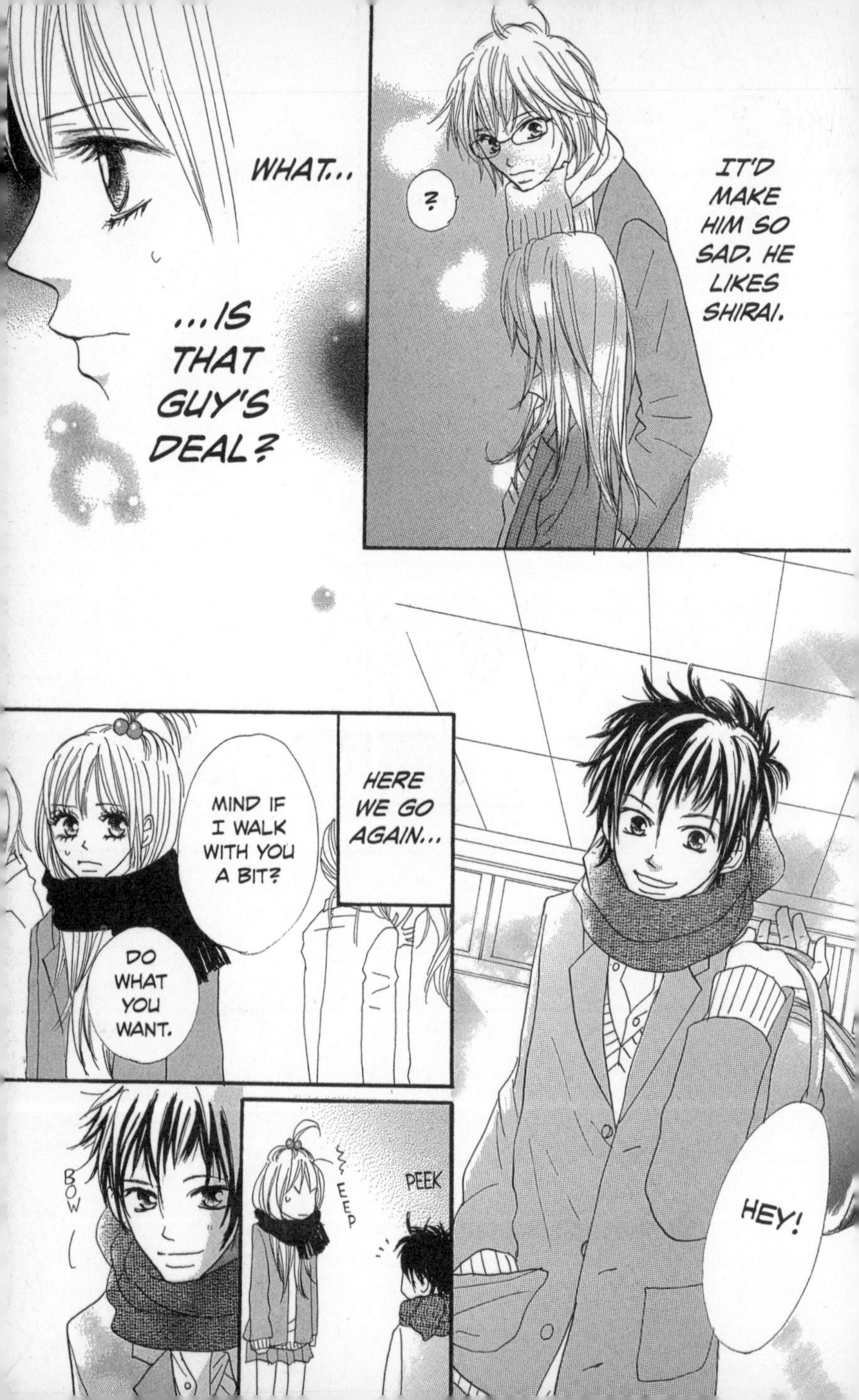
?
IT'D MAKE HIM SO SAD. HE LIKES SHIRAI.
WHAT...
...IS THAT GUY'S DEAL?
HEY!
HERE WE GO AGAIN...
MIND IF I WALK WITH YOU A BIT?
DO WHAT YOU WANT.
PEEK
EEP
BOW

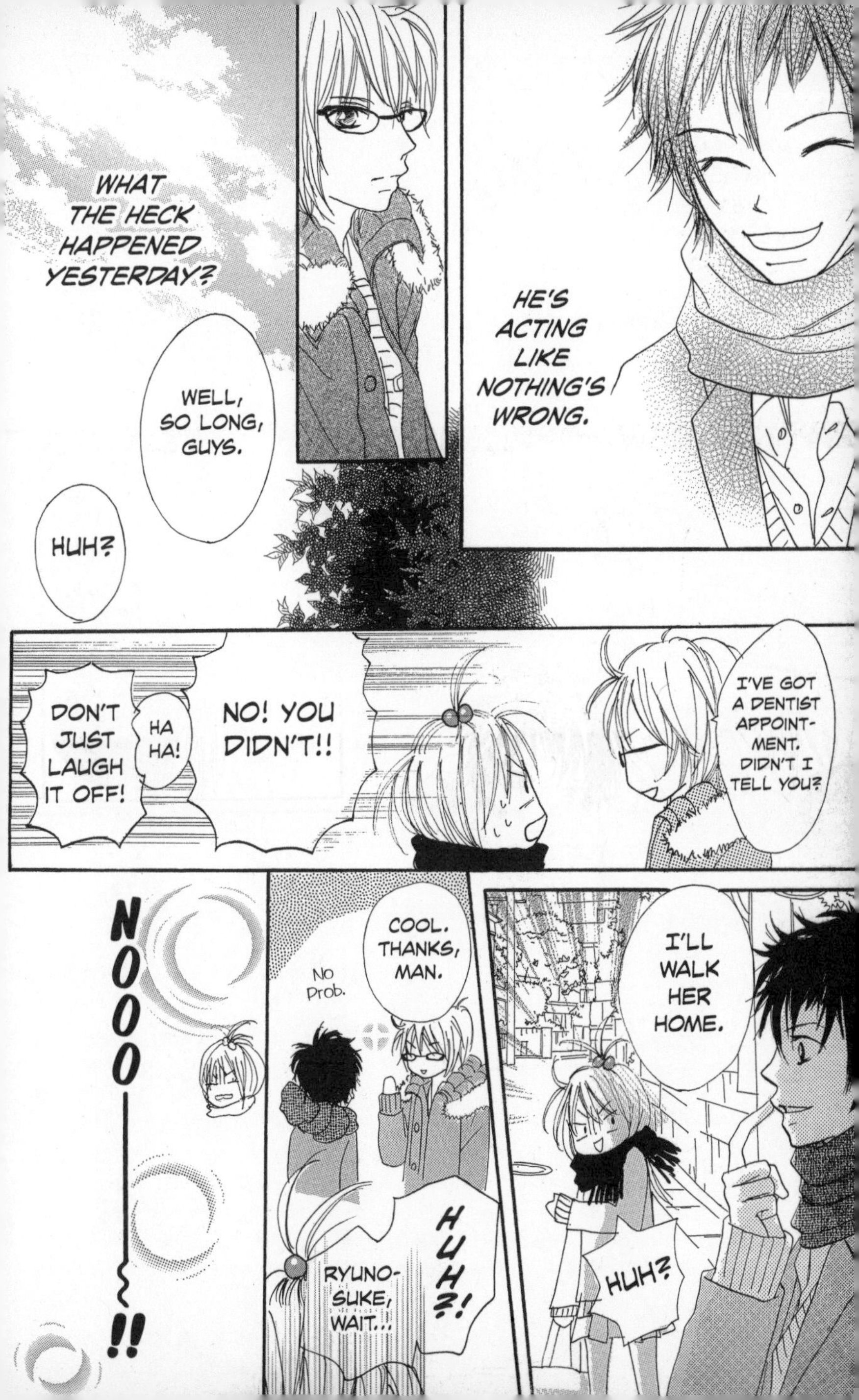
HE'S ACTING LIKE NOTHING'S WRONG.
WHAT THE HECK HAPPENED YESTERDAY?
WELL, SO LONG, GUYS.
HUH?
I'VE GOT A DENTIST APPOINT-MENT. DIDN'T I TELL YOU?
NO! YOU DIDN'T!!
HA HA!
DON'T JUST LAUGH IT OFF!
I'LL WALK HER HOME.
HUH?
COOL. THANKS, MAN.
No Prob.
HUH?!
RYUNO-SUKE, WAIT...!
NOOOO—~!!

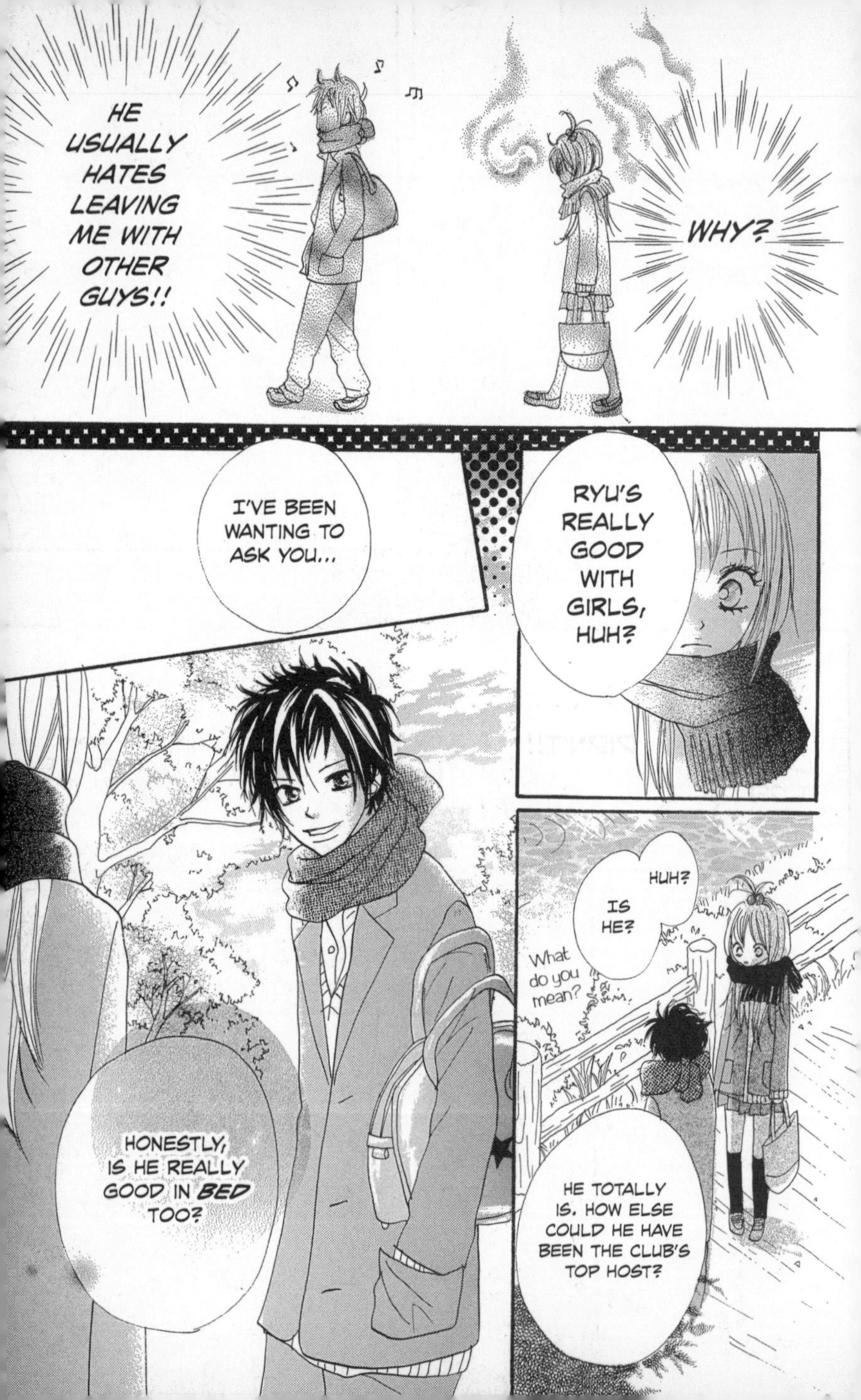
WHY?
HE USUALLY HATES LEAVING ME WITH OTHER GUYS!!
RYU'S REALLY GOOD WITH GIRLS, HUH?
HUH?
IS HE?
What do you mean?
HE TOTALLY IS. HOW ELSE COULD HE HAVE BEEN THE CLUB'S TOP HOST?
I'VE BEEN WANTING TO ASK YOU...
HONESTLY, IS HE REALLY GOOD IN BED TOO?

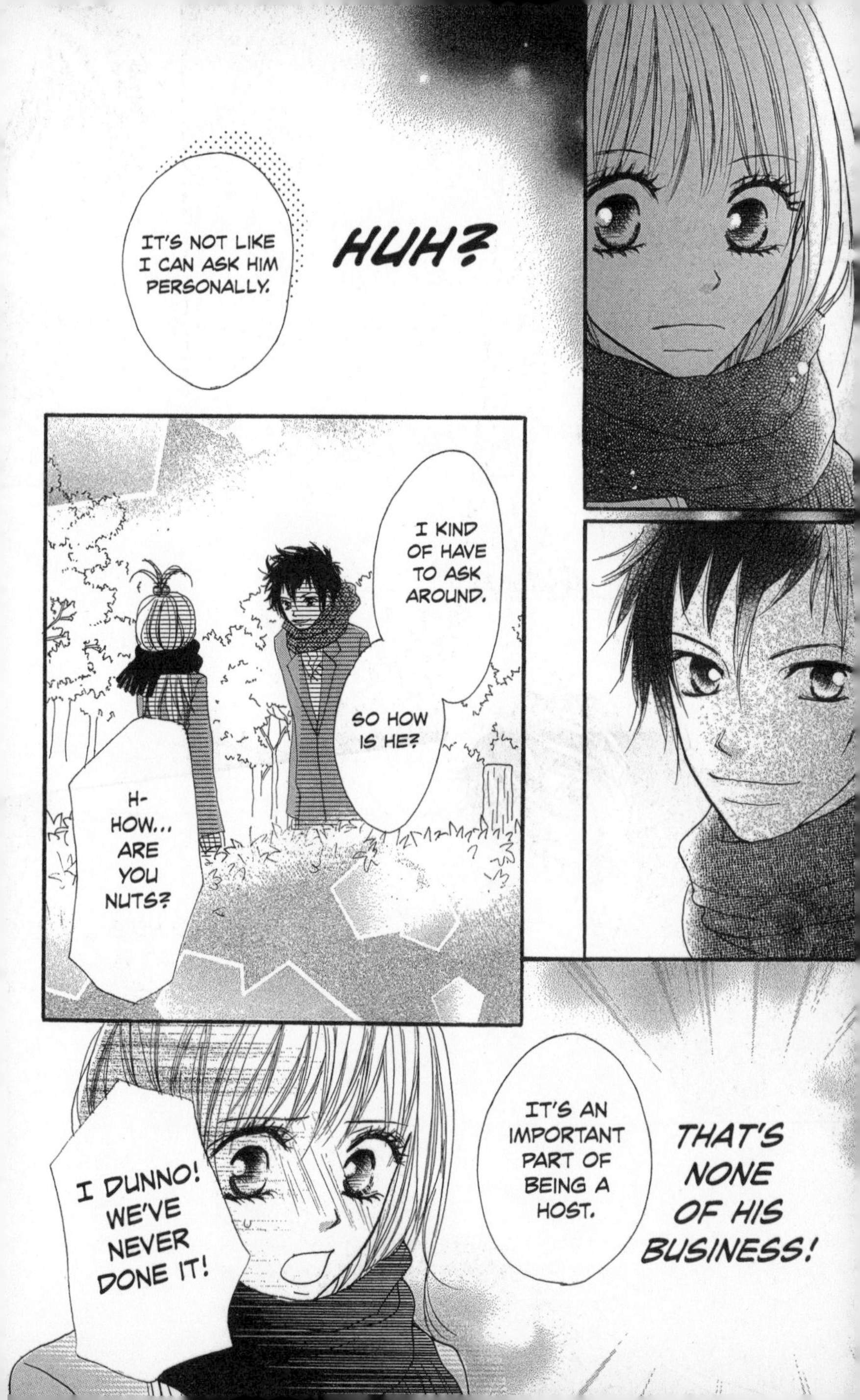

IT'S NOT LIKE I CAN ASK HIM PERSONALLY.
HUH?
I KIND OF HAVE TO ASK AROUND.
SO HOW IS HE?
H-HOW... ARE YOU NUTS?
IT'S AN IMPORTANT PART OF BEING A HOST.
THAT'S NONE OF HIS BUSINESS!
I DUNNO! WE'VE NEVER DONE IT!

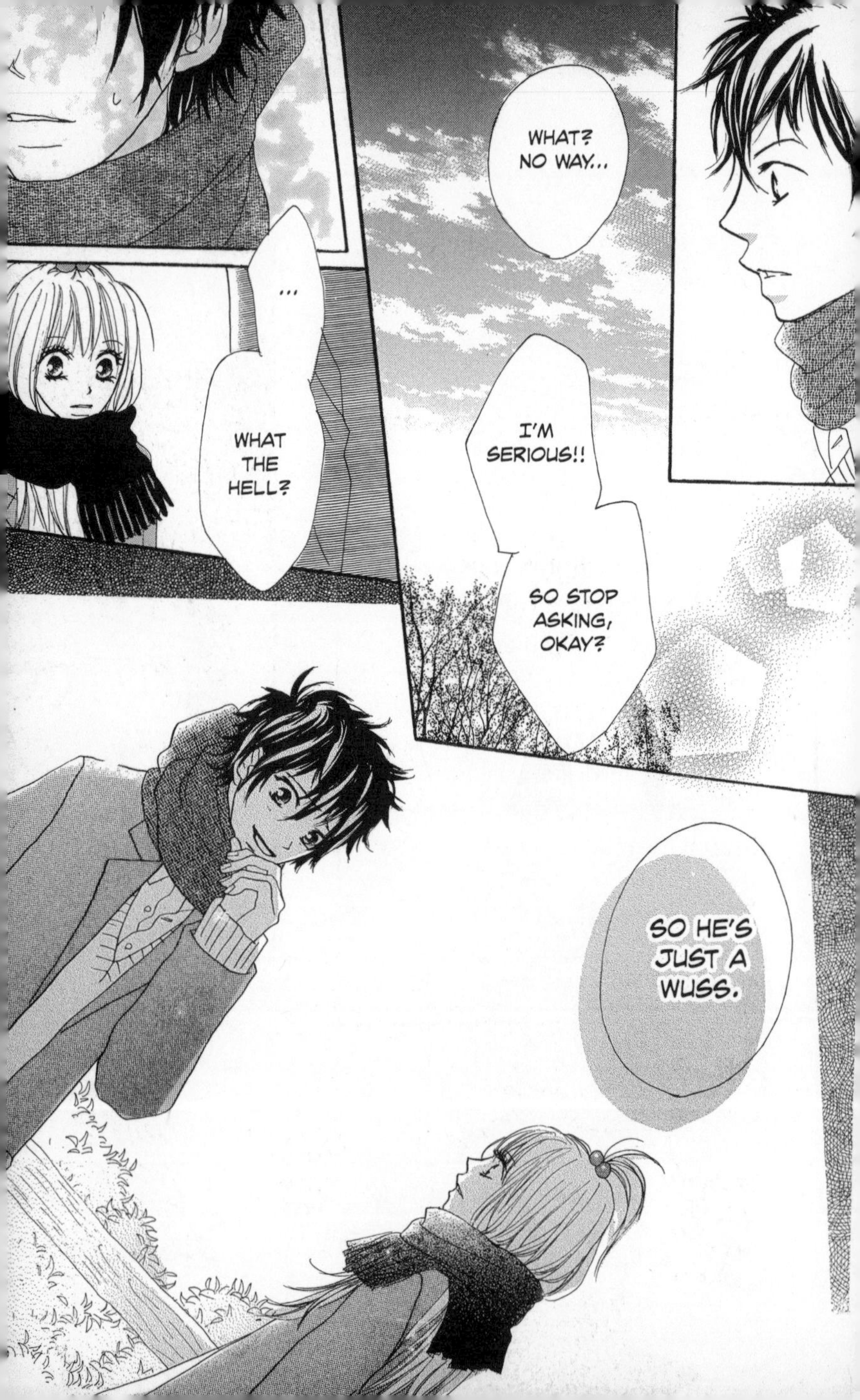
WHAT? NO WAY...
I'M SERIOUS!!
SO STOP ASKING, OKAY?
...
WHAT THE HELL?
SO HE'S JUST A WUSS.

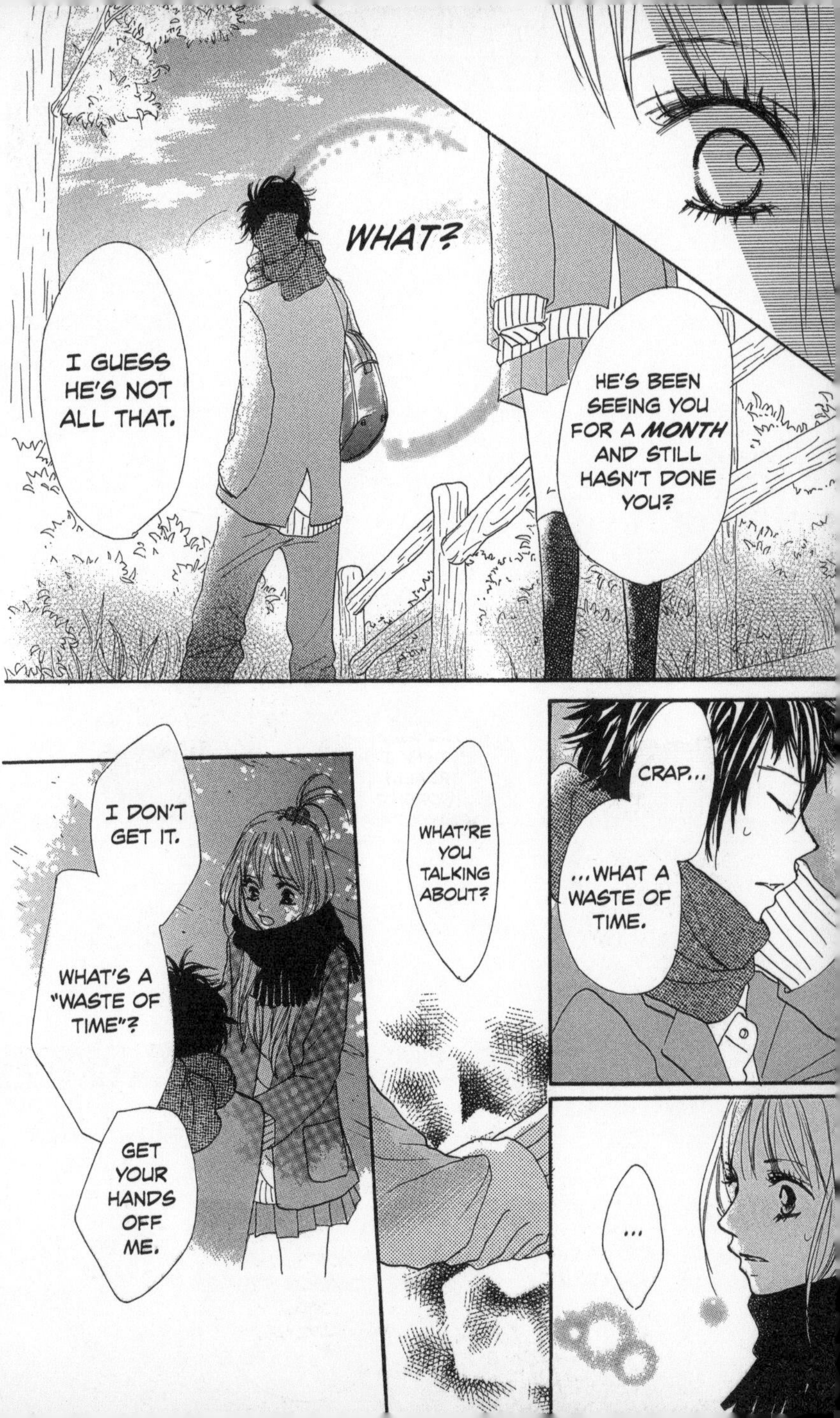
HE'S BEEN SEEING YOU FOR A *MONTH* AND STILL HASN'T DONE YOU?
I GUESS HE'S NOT ALL THAT.
WHAT?
CRAP...
...WHAT A WASTE OF TIME.
...
WHAT'RE YOU TALKING ABOUT?
I DON'T GET IT.
WHAT'S A "WASTE OF TIME"?
GET YOUR HANDS OFF ME.

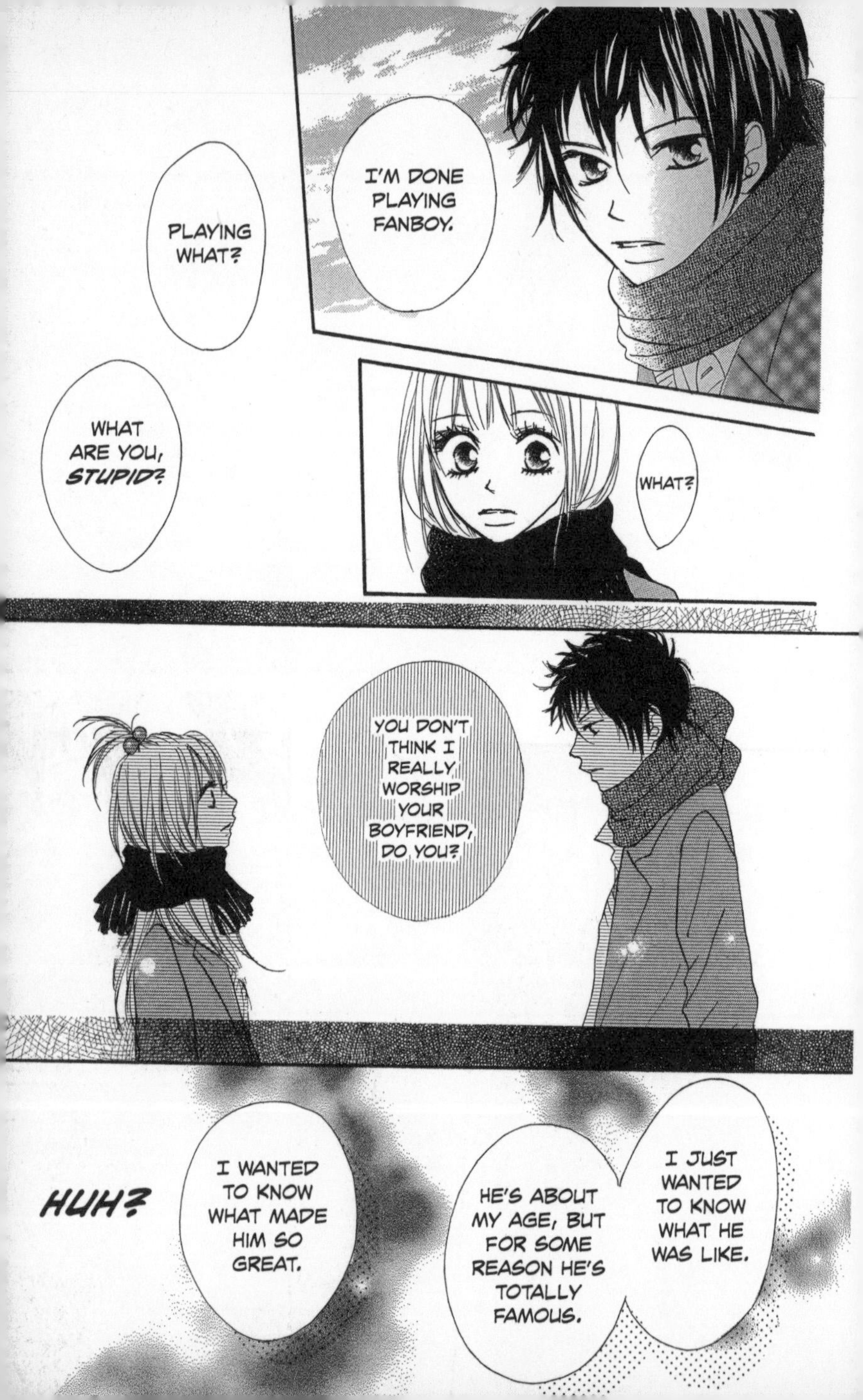
I'M DONE PLAYING FANBOY.
PLAYING WHAT?
WHAT?
WHAT ARE YOU, *STUPID?*
YOU DON'T THINK I REALLY WORSHIP YOUR BOYFRIEND, DO YOU?
I JUST WANTED TO KNOW WHAT HE WAS LIKE.
HE'S ABOUT MY AGE, BUT FOR SOME REASON HE'S TOTALLY FAMOUS.
I WANTED TO KNOW WHAT MADE HIM SO GREAT.
HUH?

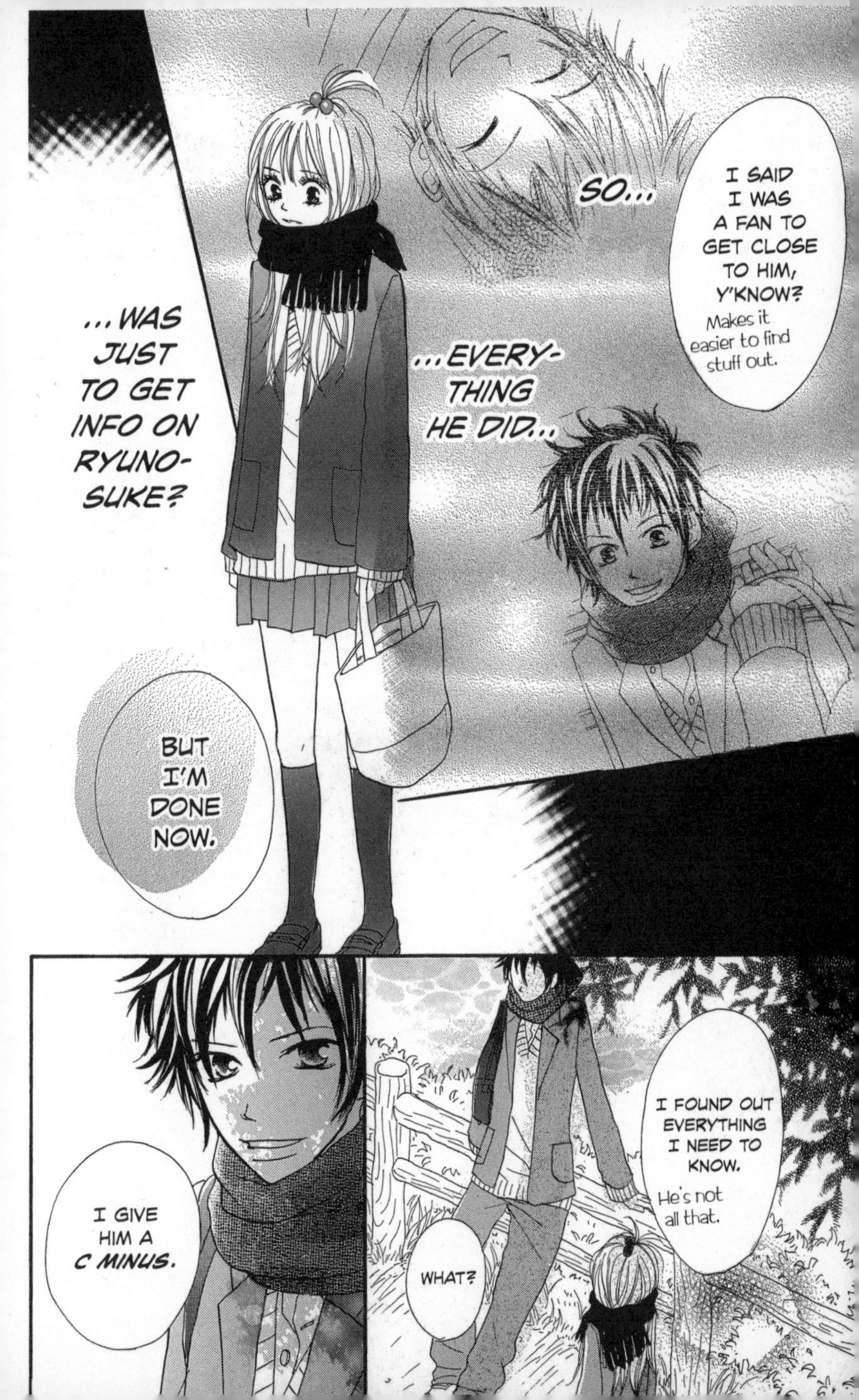
I SAID I WAS A FAN TO GET CLOSE TO HIM, Y'KNOW? Makes it easier to find stuff out.
SO...
...EVERY-THING HE DID...
...WAS JUST TO GET INFO ON RYUNO-SUKE?
BUT I'M DONE NOW.
I FOUND OUT EVERYTHING I NEED TO KNOW. He's not all that.
WHAT?
I GIVE HIM A C MINUS.

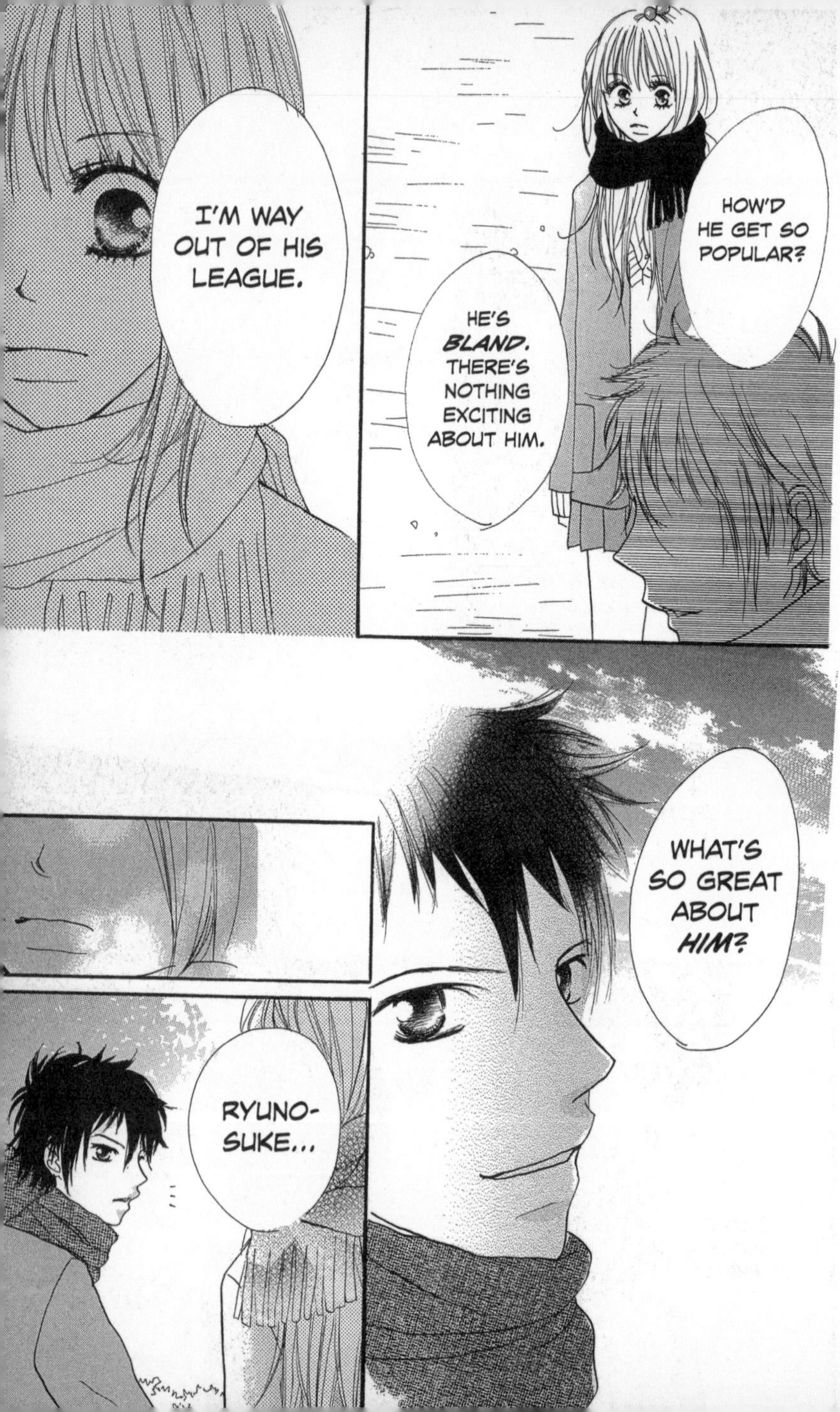
HOW'D HE GET SO POPULAR?
HE'S BLAND. THERE'S NOTHING EXCITING ABOUT HIM.
I'M WAY OUT OF HIS LEAGUE.
WHAT'S SO GREAT ABOUT HIM?
RYUNO-SUKE...

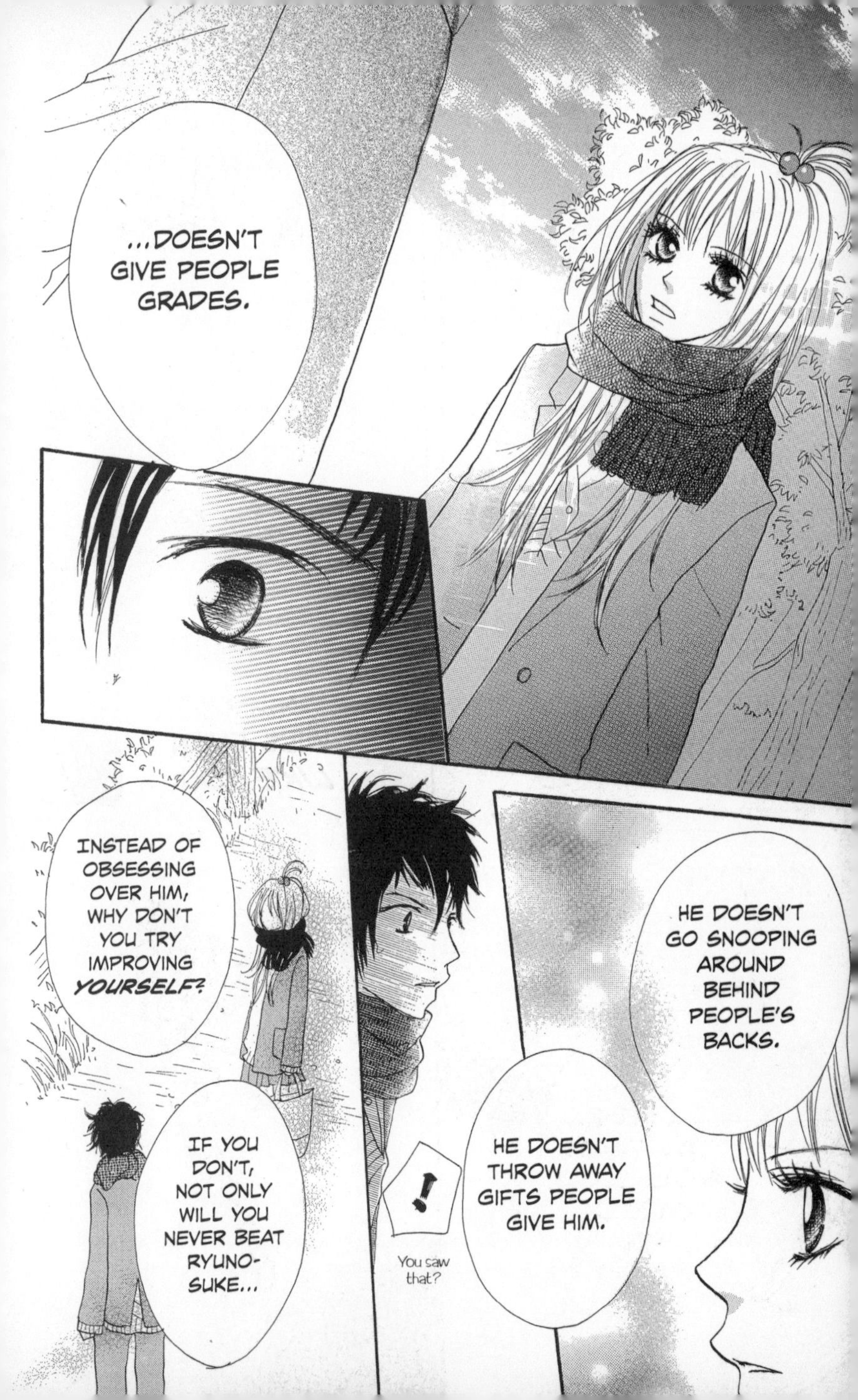
...DOESN'T GIVE PEOPLE GRADES.
HE DOESN'T GO SNOOPING AROUND BEHIND PEOPLE'S BACKS.
HE DOESN'T THROW AWAY GIFTS PEOPLE GIVE HIM.
!
You saw that?
INSTEAD OF OBSESSING OVER HIM, WHY DON'T YOU TRY IMPROVING YOURSELF?
IF YOU DON'T, NOT ONLY WILL YOU NEVER BEAT RYUNO-SUKE...

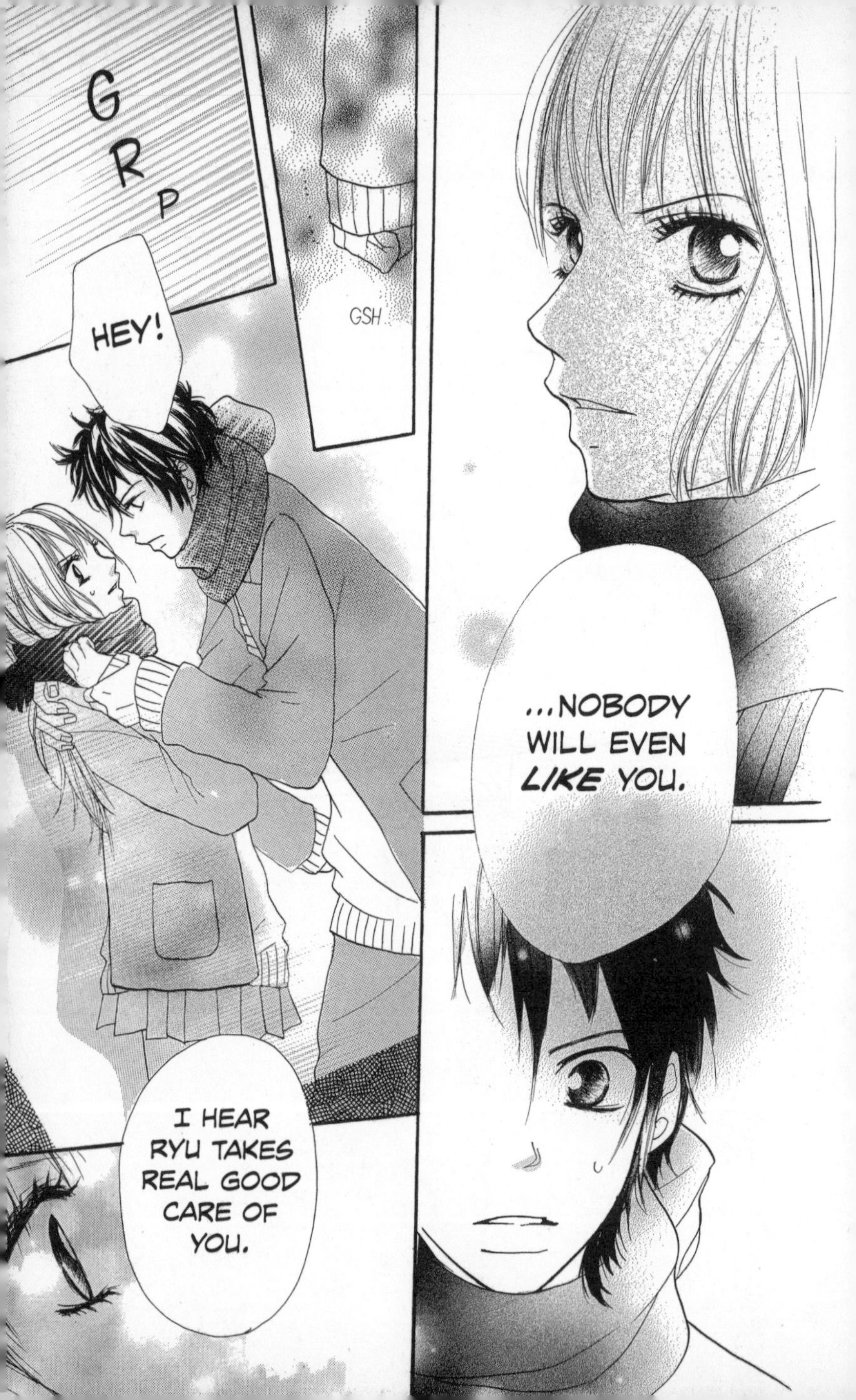

...NOBODY WILL EVEN *LIKE* YOU.
GSH
GRP
HEY!
I HEAR RYU TAKES REAL GOOD CARE OF YOU.

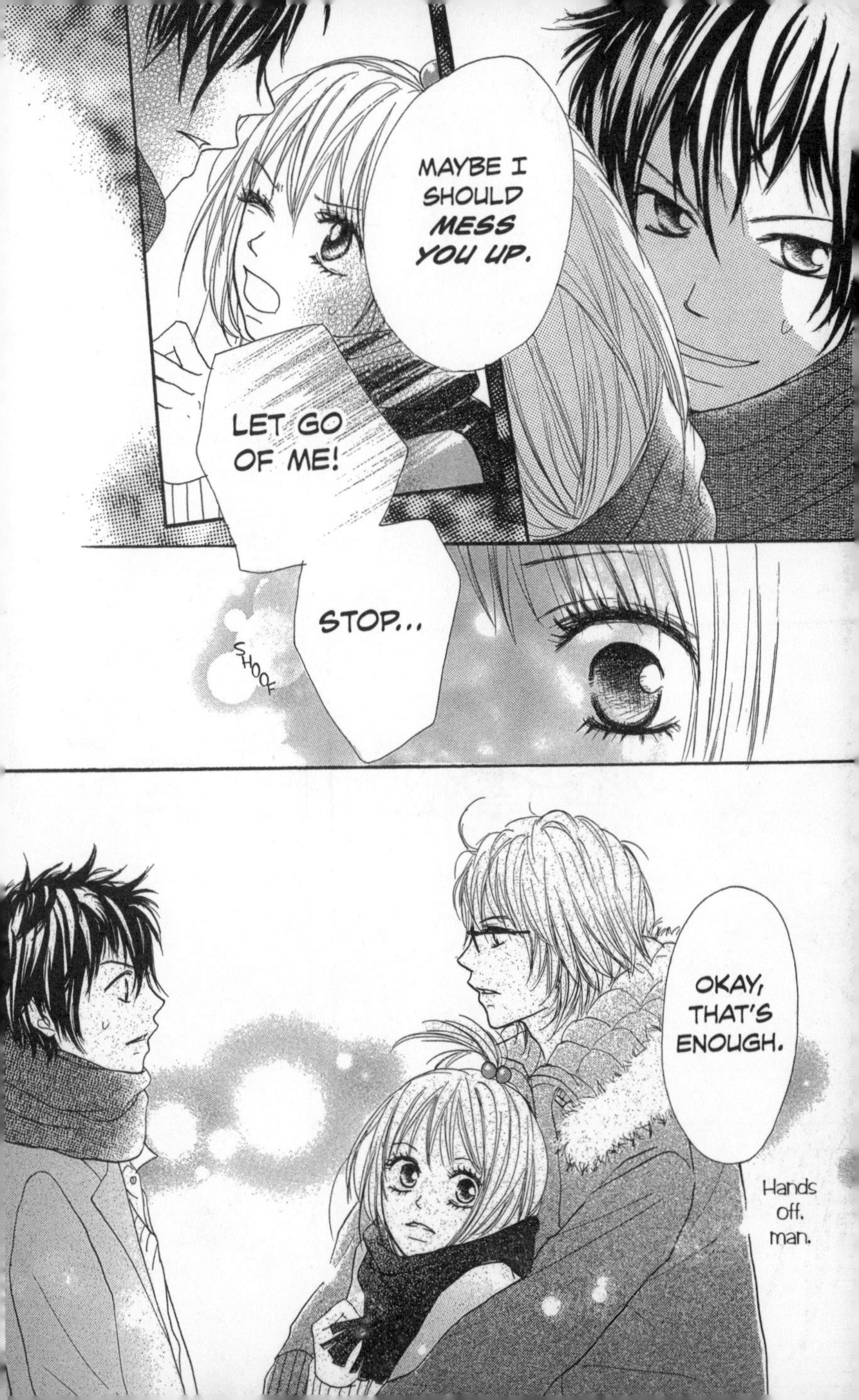
MAYBE I SHOULD MESS YOU UP.
LET GO OF ME!
STOP...
SHOOK
OKAY, THAT'S ENOUGH.
Hands off, man.

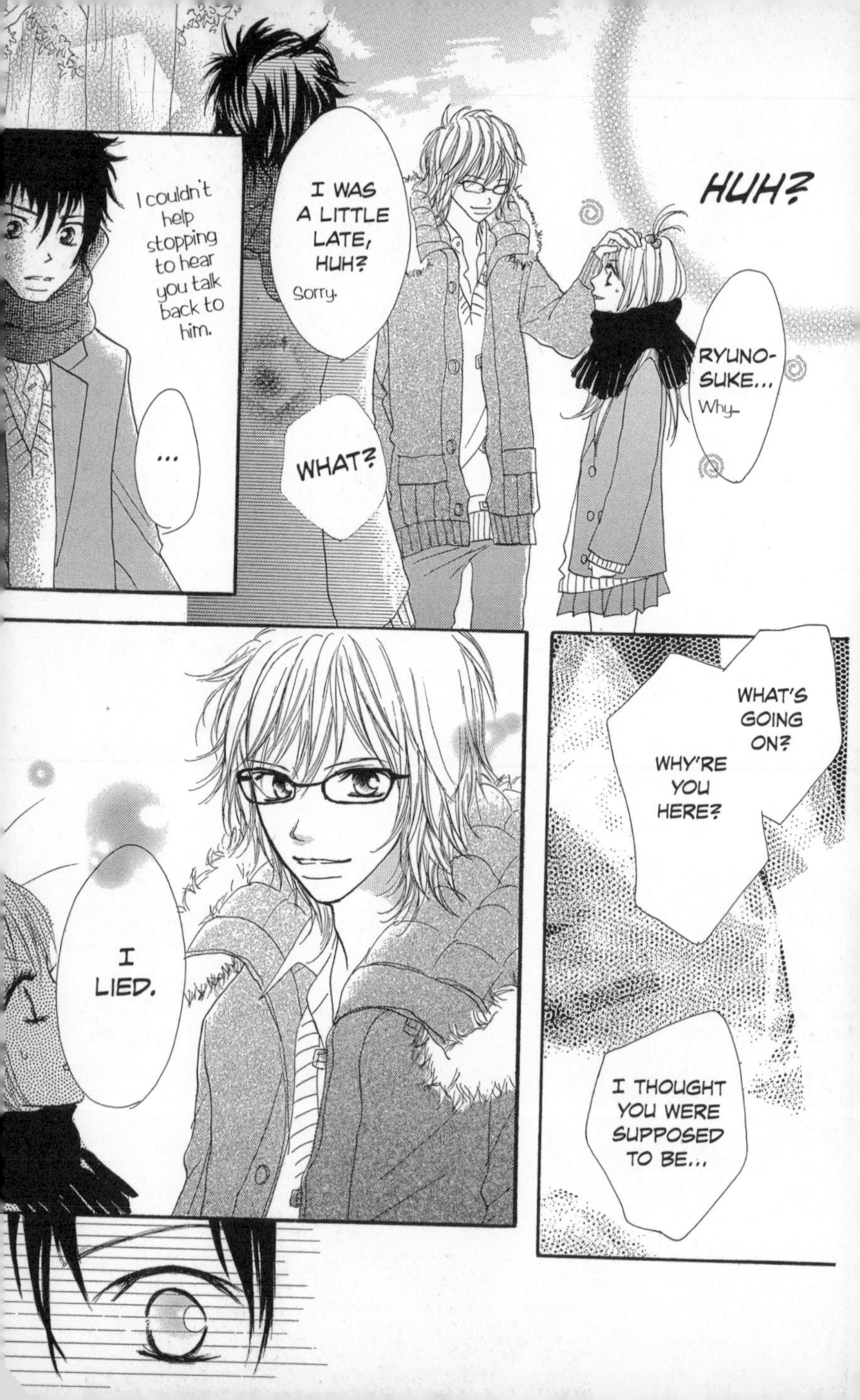
HUH?
RYUNO-SUKE... Why...
I WAS A LITTLE LATE, HUH? Sorry.
WHAT?
I couldn't help stopping to hear you talk back to him.
...
WHAT'S GOING ON? WHY'RE YOU HERE?
I THOUGHT YOU WERE SUPPOSED TO BE...
I LIED.

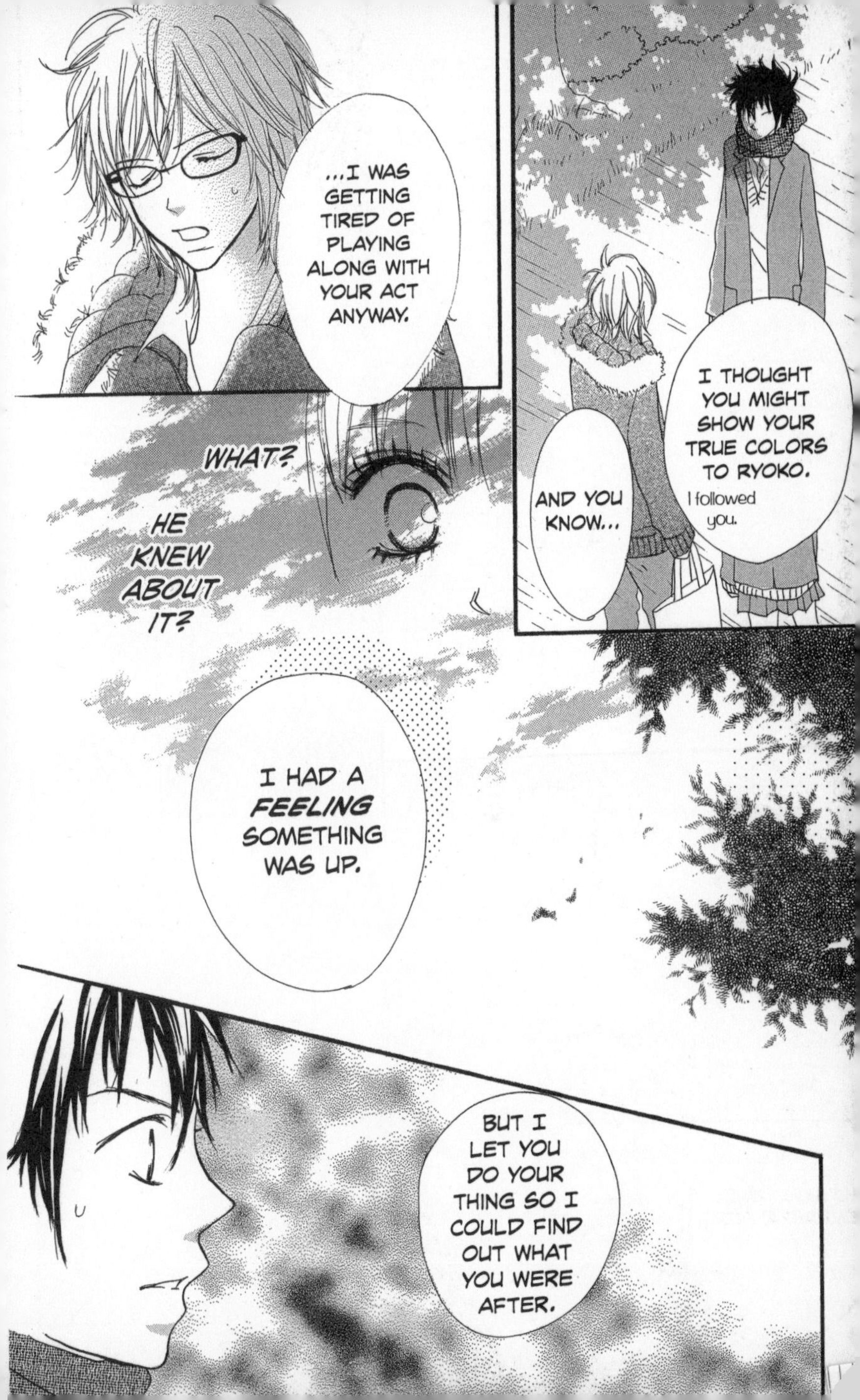

I THOUGHT YOU MIGHT SHOW YOUR TRUE COLORS TO RYOKO.
I followed you.
AND YOU KNOW...
...I WAS GETTING TIRED OF PLAYING ALONG WITH YOUR ACT ANYWAY.
WHAT?
HE KNEW ABOUT IT?
I HAD A *FEELING* SOMETHING WAS UP.
BUT I LET YOU DO YOUR THING SO I COULD FIND OUT WHAT YOU WERE AFTER.

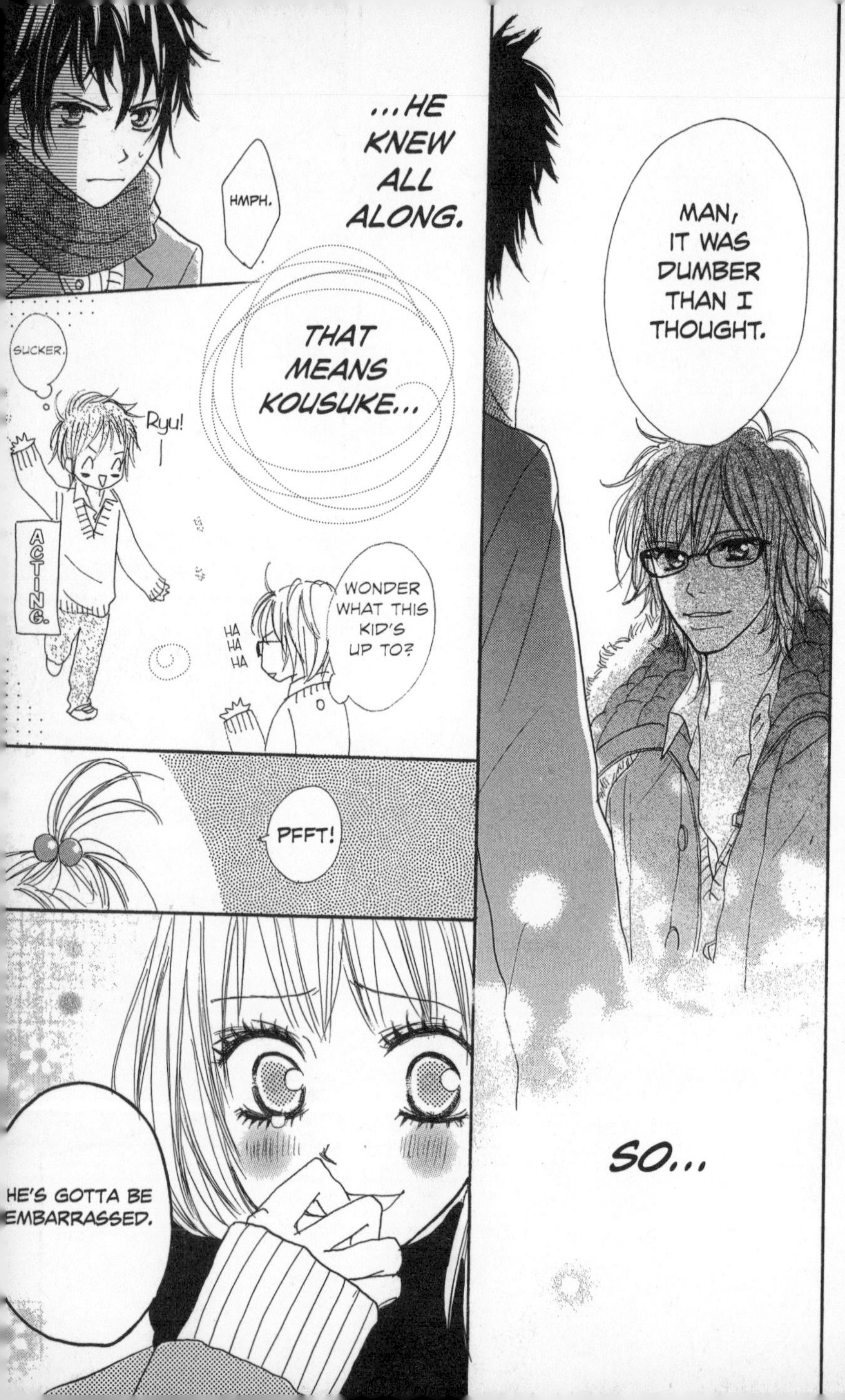
MAN, IT WAS DUMBER THAN I THOUGHT.
SO...
...HE KNEW ALL ALONG.
HMPH.
THAT MEANS KOUSUKE...
SUCKER.
Ryu!
WONDER WHAT THIS KID'S UP TO?
HA HA HA
ACTING.
PFFT!
HE'S GOTTA BE EMBARRASSED.

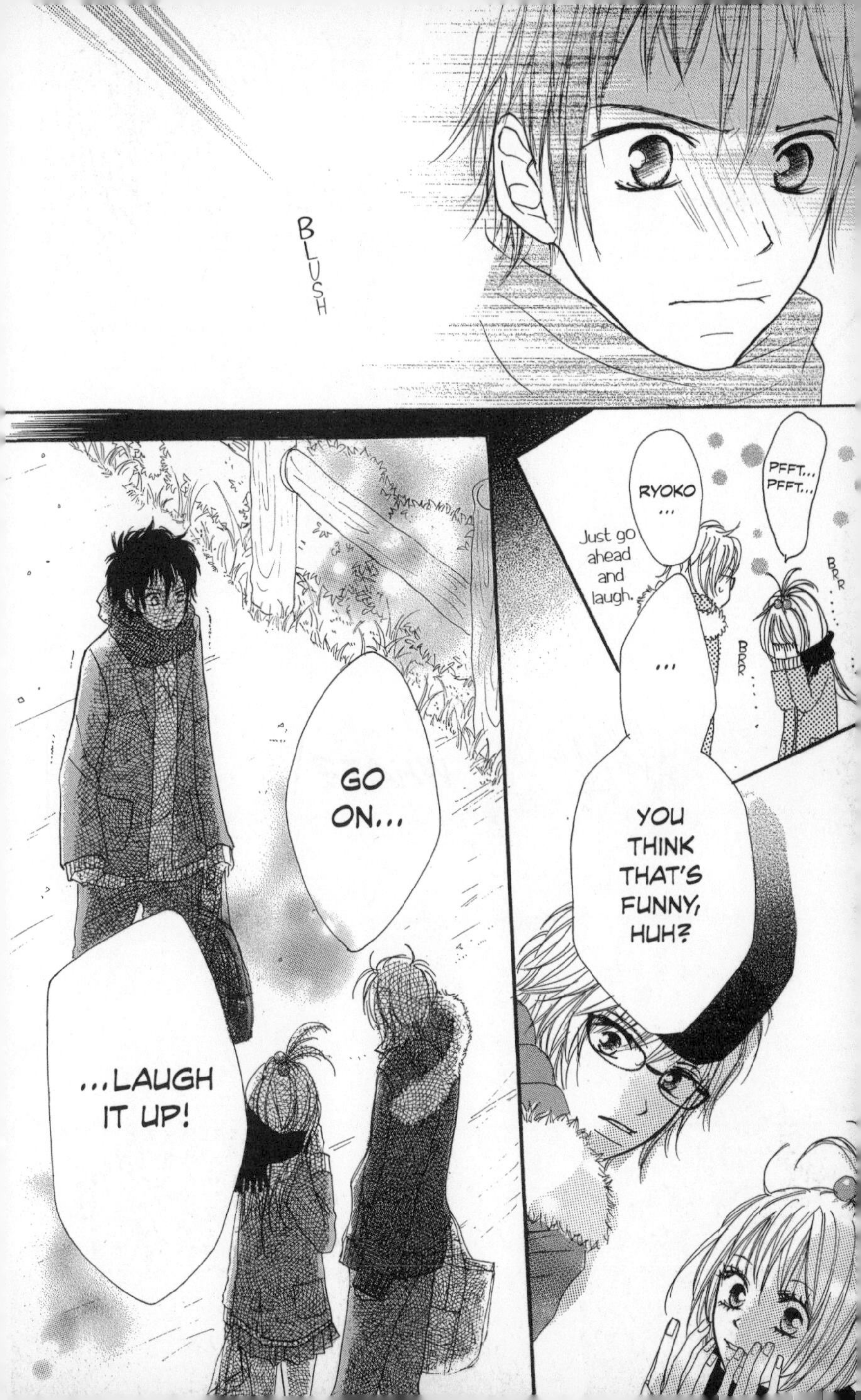
BLUSH
PFFT... PFFT...
RYOKO...
Just go ahead and laugh.
BRR...
BRR...
...
YOU THINK THAT'S FUNNY, HUH?
GO ON...
...LAUGH IT UP!

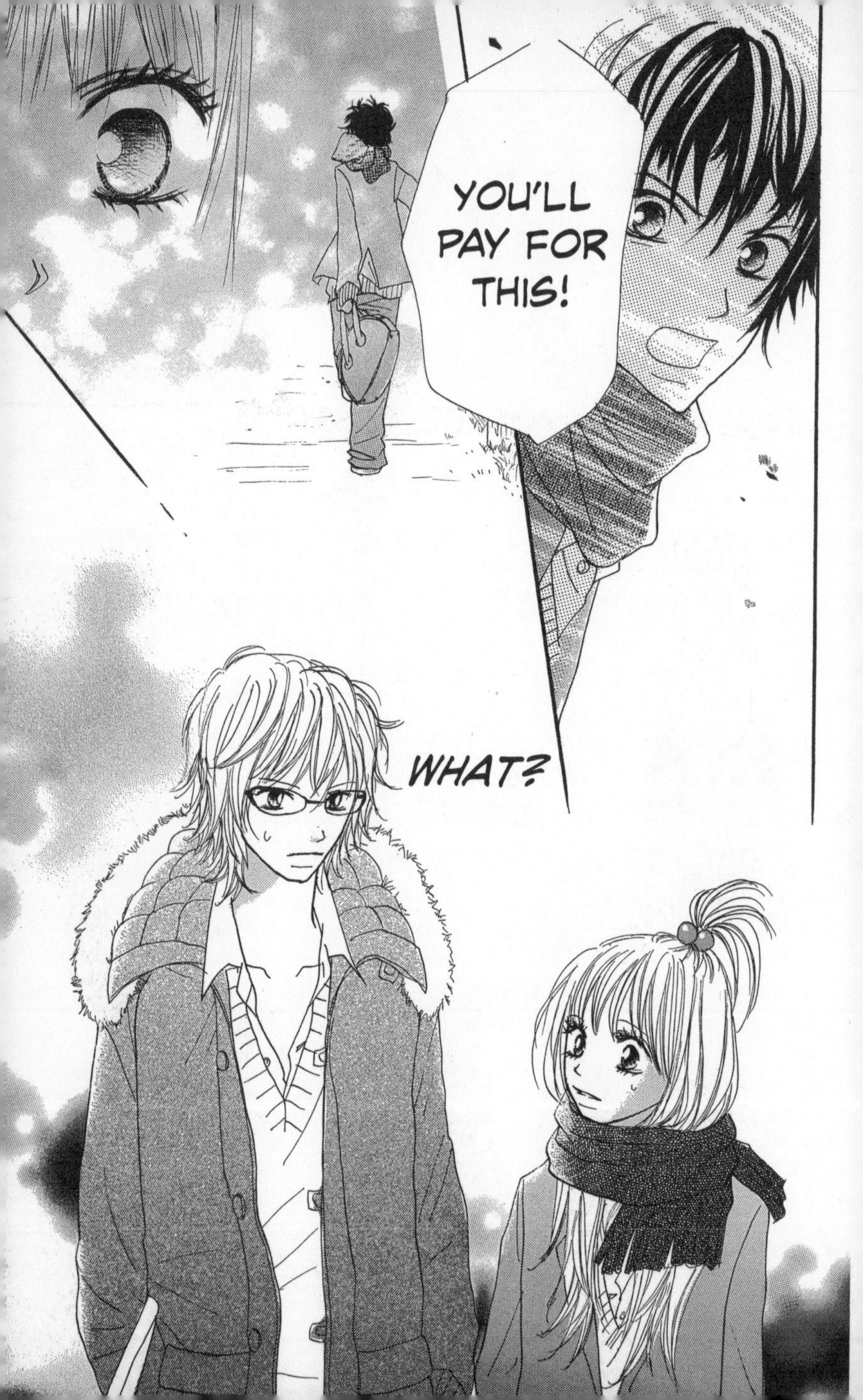
YOU'LL PAY FOR THIS!
WHAT?

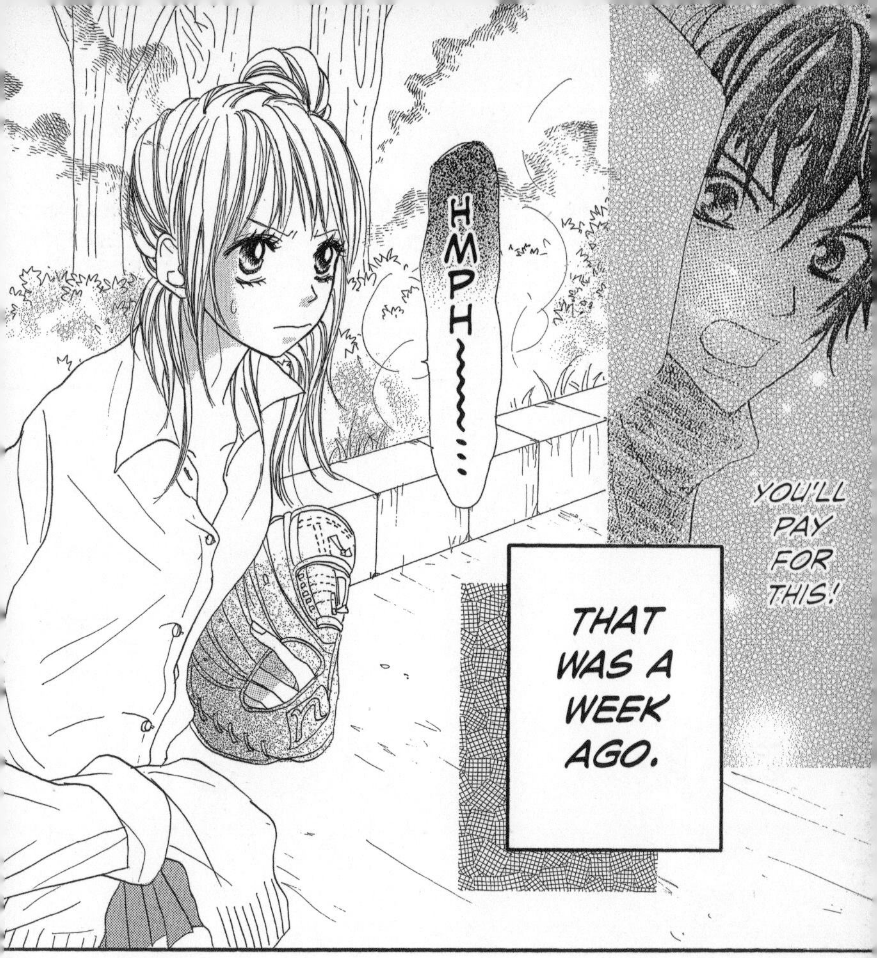
YOU'LL PAY FOR THIS!
THAT WAS A WEEK AGO.
HMPH~~~...

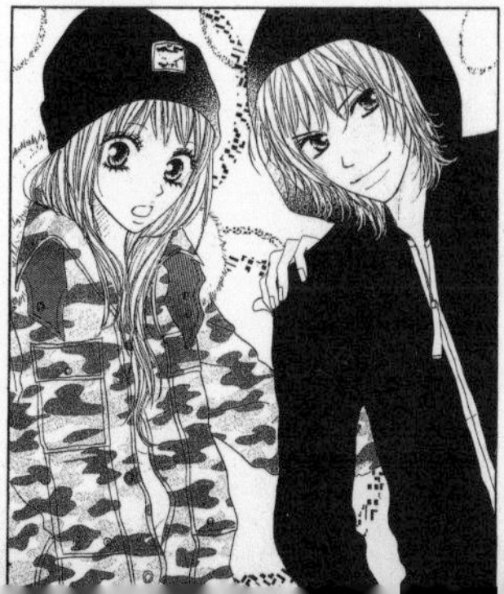

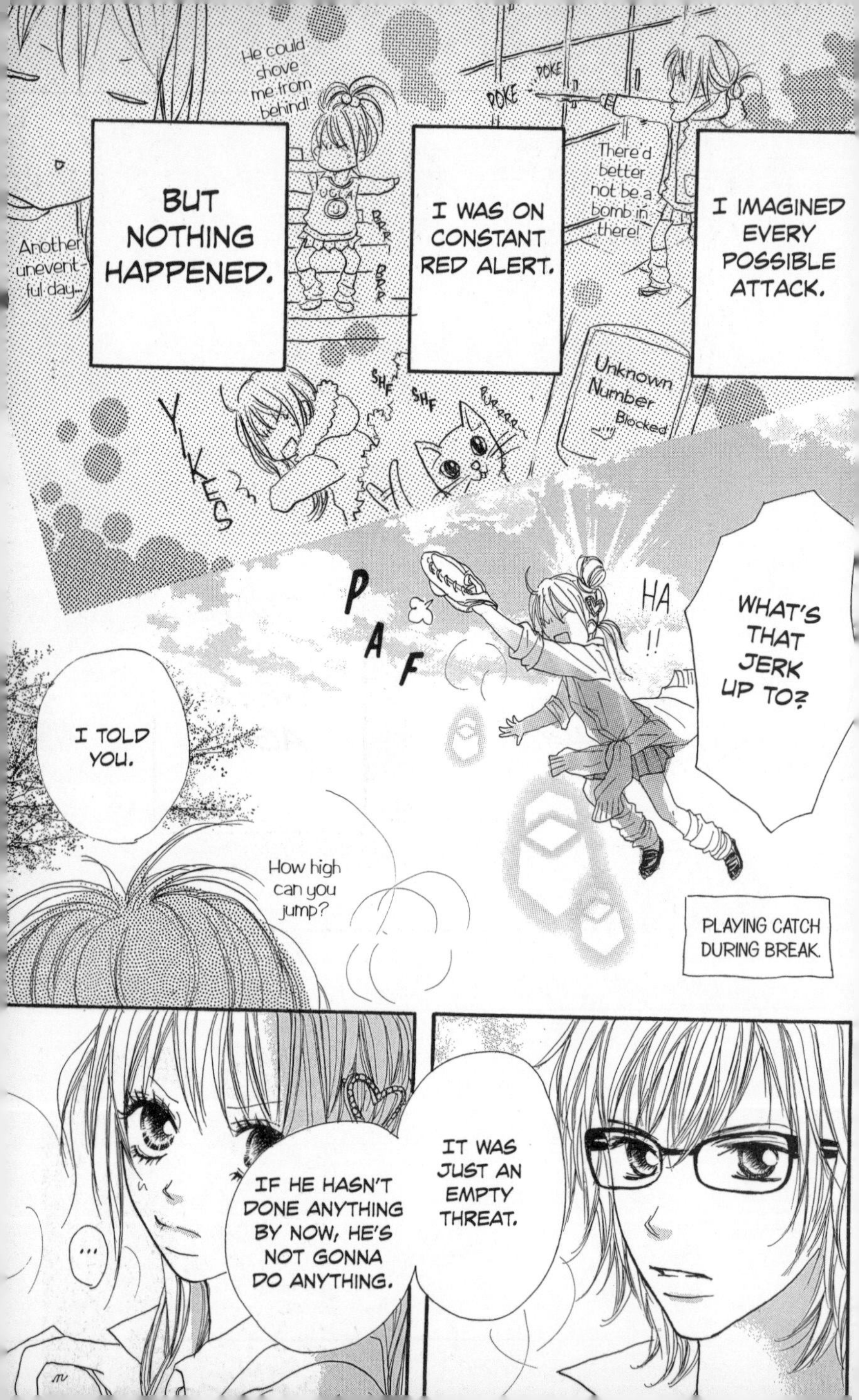
I IMAGINED EVERY POSSIBLE ATTACK.
There'd better not be a bomb in there!
POKE
POKE
Unknown Number
Blocked
I WAS ON CONSTANT RED ALERT.
He could shove me from behind!
BRRR
BRRR
PURRRR
SHF
SHF
YIKES
BUT NOTHING HAPPENED.
Another uneventful day...
PLAYING CATCH DURING BREAK.
WHAT'S THAT JERK UP TO?
HA!!
PAF
How high can you jump?
I TOLD YOU.
IT WAS JUST AN EMPTY THREAT.
IF HE HASN'T DONE ANYTHING BY NOW, HE'S NOT GONNA DO ANYTHING.
...

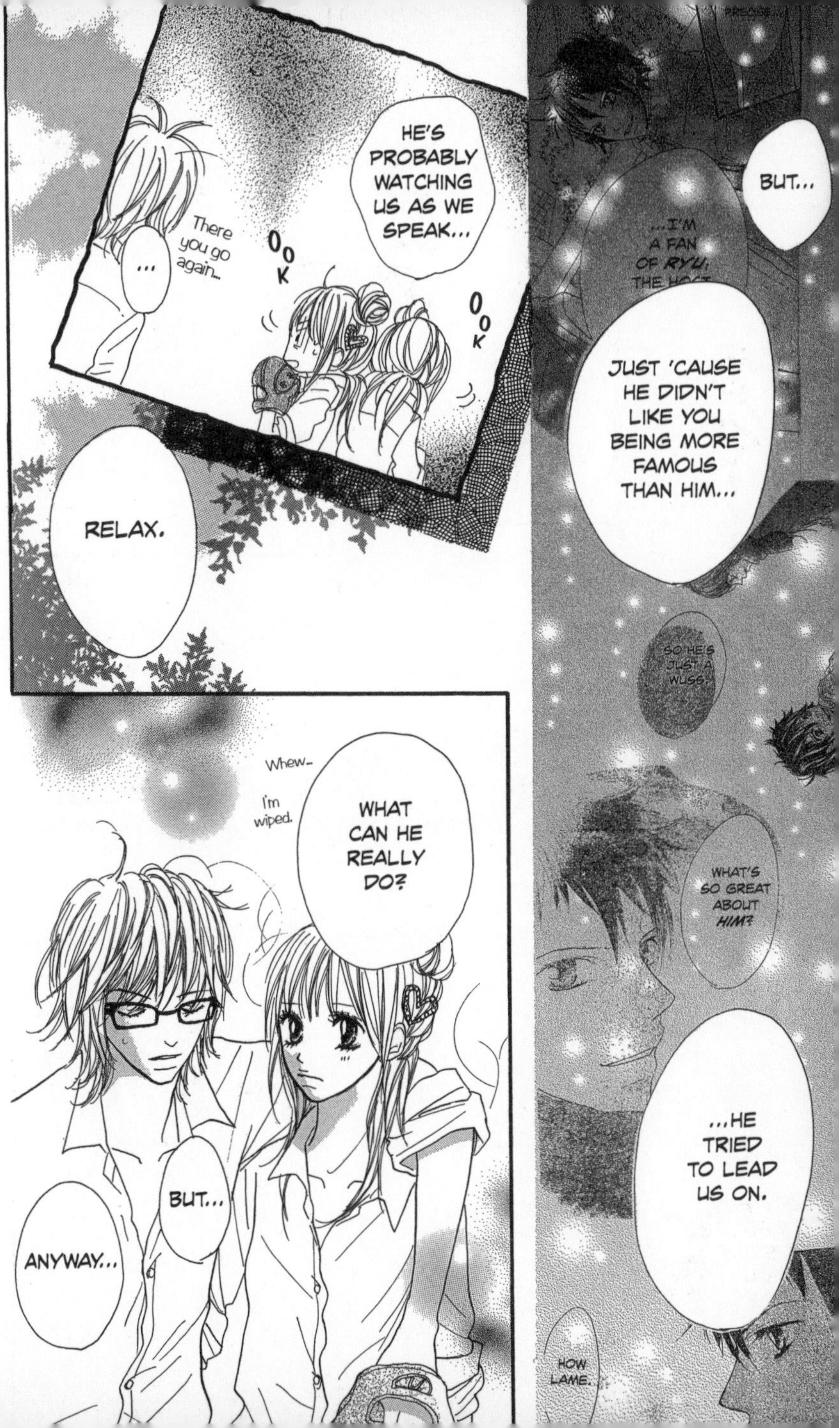
BUT...
...I'M A FAN OF RYU,
JUST 'CAUSE HE DIDN'T LIKE YOU BEING MORE FAMOUS THAN HIM...
SO HE'S JUST A WUSS.
WHAT'S SO GREAT ABOUT HIM?
...HE TRIED TO LEAD US ON.
HOW LAME.
HE'S PROBABLY WATCHING US AS WE SPEAK...
OOK
OOK
There you go again...
...
RELAX.
WHAT CAN HE REALLY DO?
Whew...
I'm wiped.
BUT...
ANYWAY...

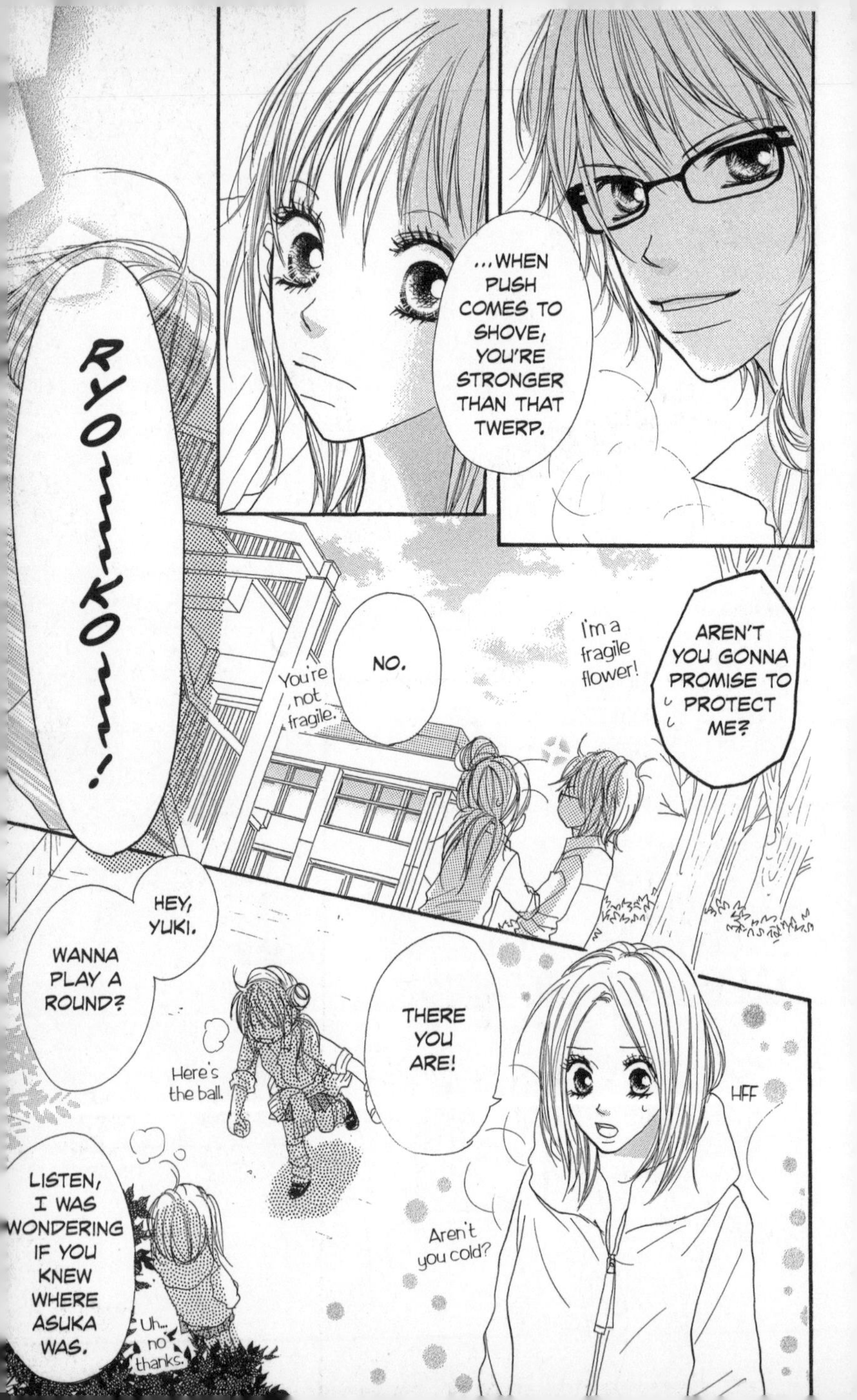

...WHEN PUSH COMES TO SHOVE, YOU'RE STRONGER THAN THAT TWERP.
AREN'T YOU GONNA PROMISE TO PROTECT ME?
I'm a fragile flower!
NO.
You're not fragile.
RYOKO-!
THERE YOU ARE!
HFF
Aren't you cold?
HEY, YUKI.
WANNA PLAY A ROUND?
Here's the ball.
LISTEN, I WAS WONDERING IF YOU KNEW WHERE ASUKA WAS.
Uh... no thanks.

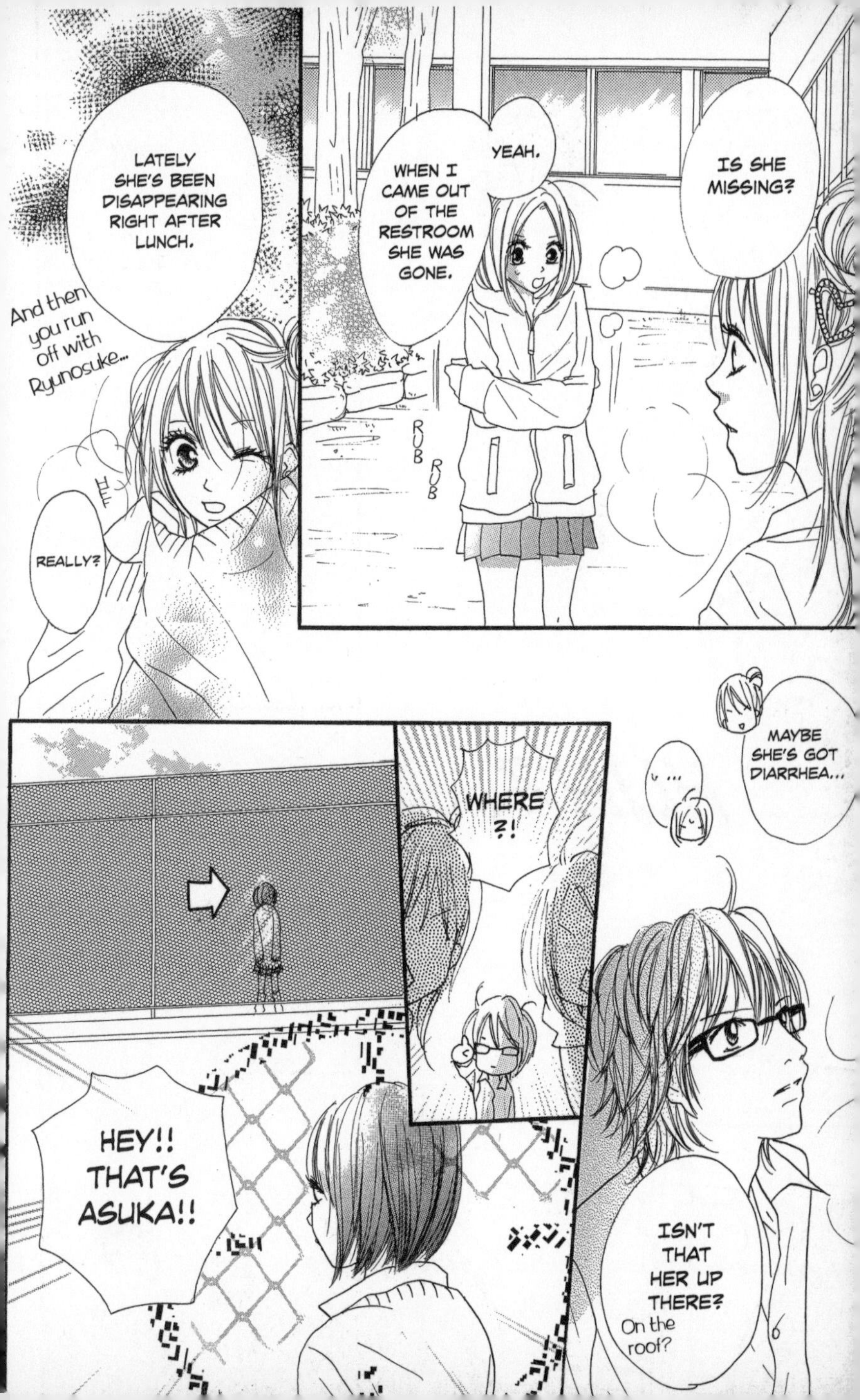
IS SHE MISSING?
YEAH.
WHEN I CAME OUT OF THE RESTROOM SHE WAS GONE.
RUB RUB
LATELY SHE'S BEEN DISAPPEARING RIGHT AFTER LUNCH.
And then you run off with Ryunosuke...
REALLY?
MAYBE SHE'S GOT DIARRHEA...
...
ISN'T THAT HER UP THERE?
On the roof?
WHERE?!
HEY!! THAT'S ASUKA!!

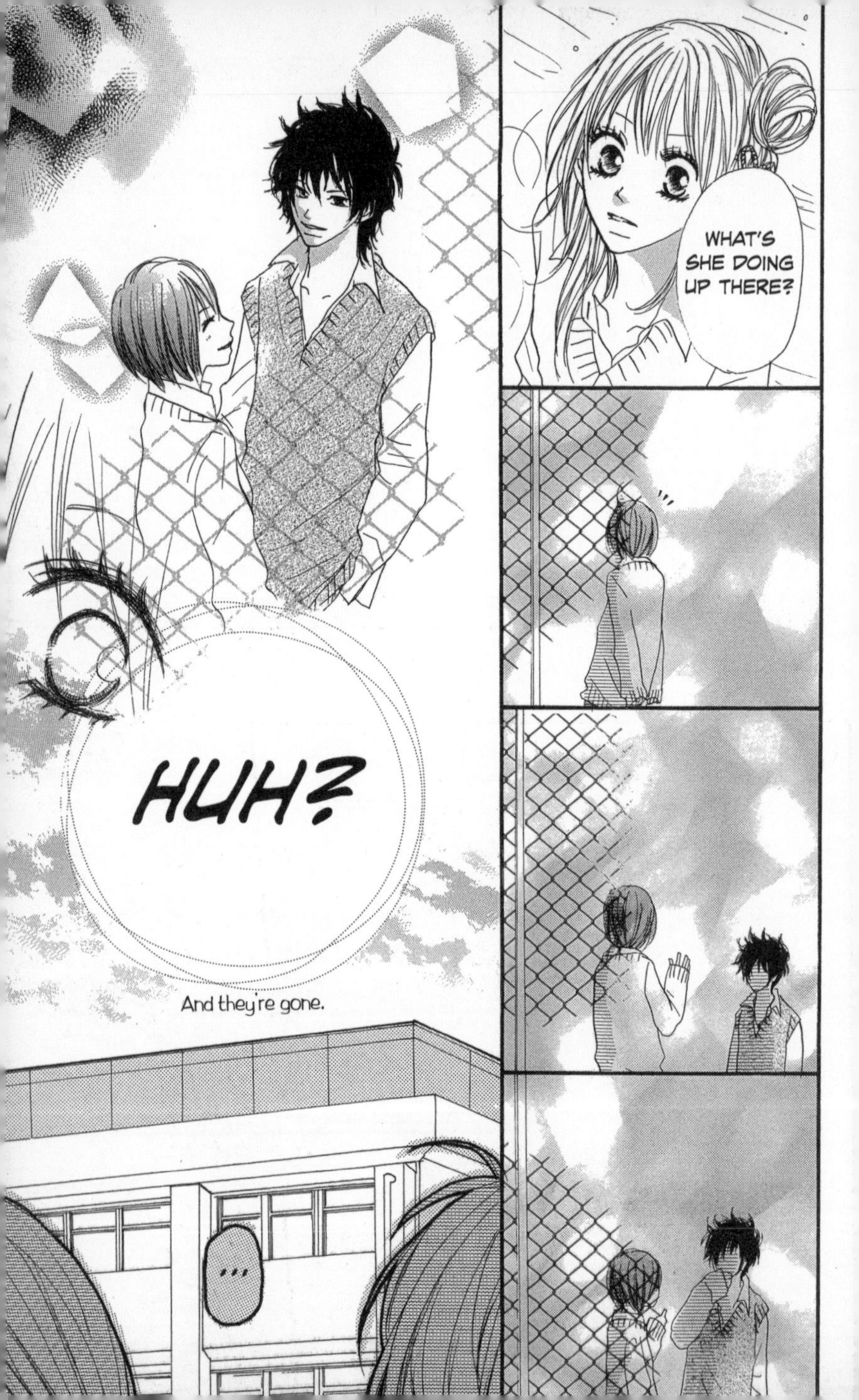
WHAT'S SHE DOING UP THERE?
HUH?
And they're gone.
...

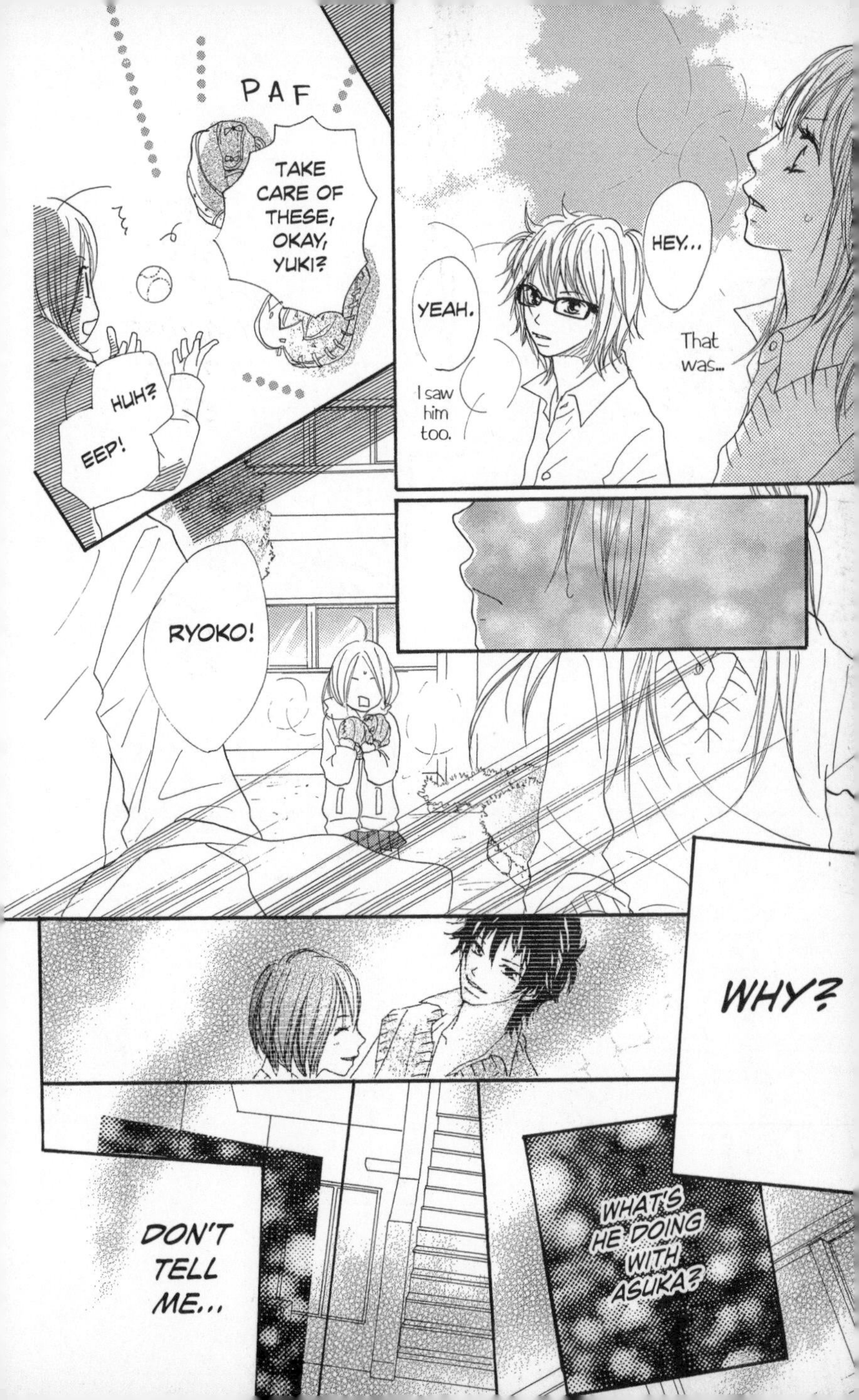
HEY...
That was...
YEAH.
I saw him too.
PAF
TAKE CARE OF THESE, OKAY, YUKI?
HUH?
EEP!
RYOKO!
WHY?
WHAT'S HE DOING WITH ASUKA?
DON'T TELL ME...

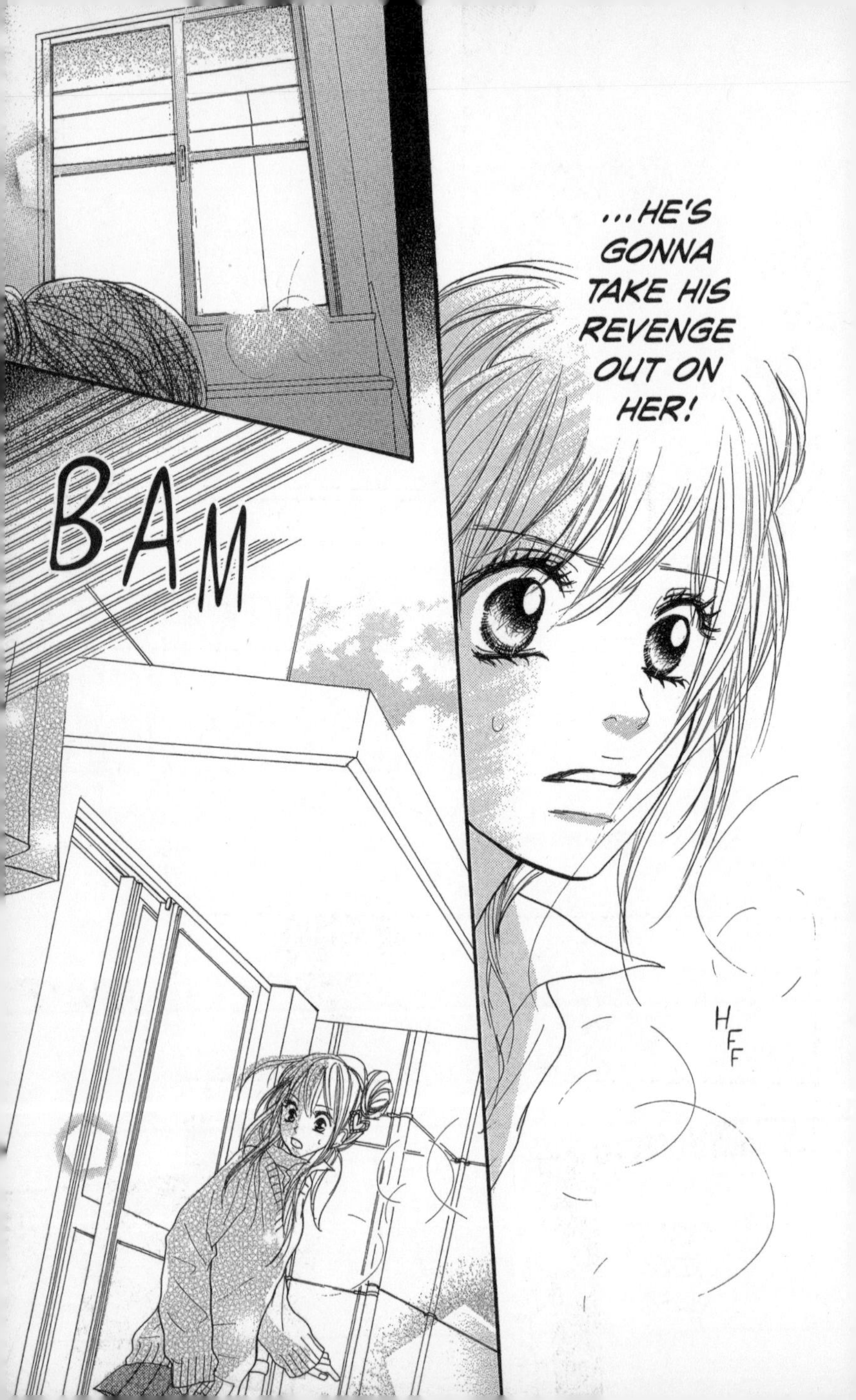
...HE'S GONNA TAKE HIS REVENGE OUT ON HER!
BAM
HFF

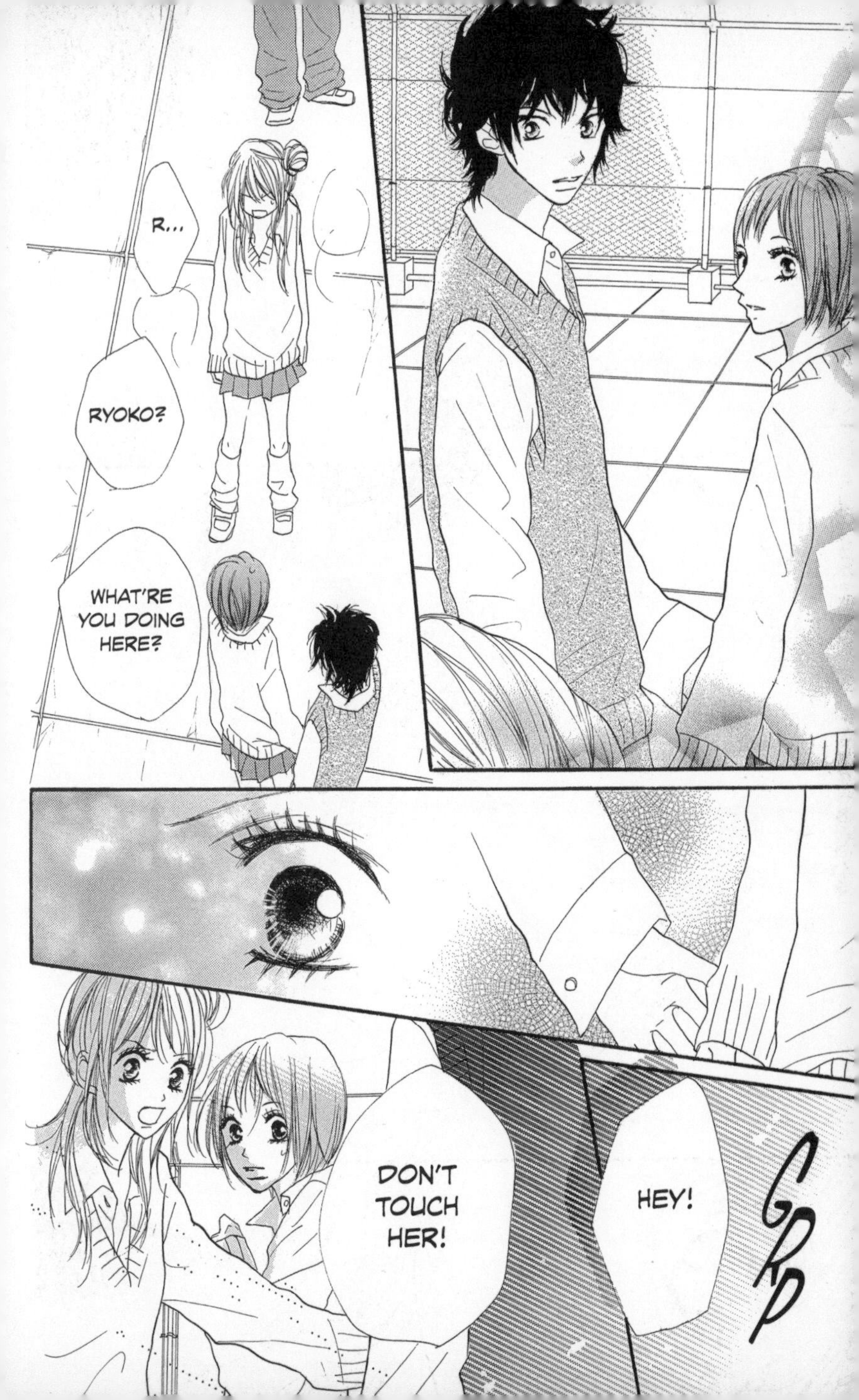
R...
RYOKO?
WHAT'RE YOU DOING HERE?
GRP
HEY!
DON'T TOUCH HER!

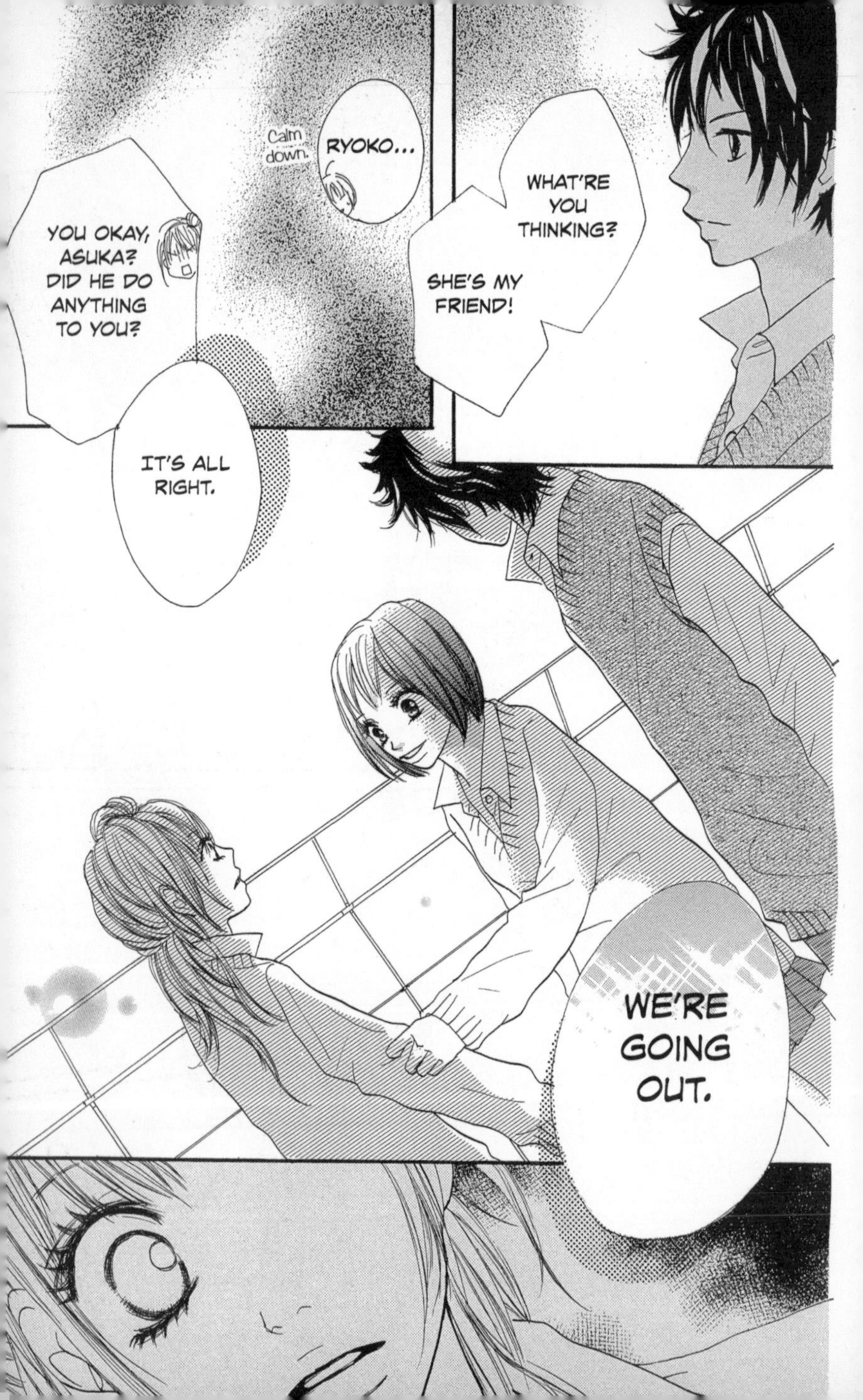
WHAT'RE YOU THINKING?
SHE'S MY FRIEND!
RYOKO...
Calm down.
YOU OKAY, ASUKA? DID HE DO ANYTHING TO YOU?
IT'S ALL RIGHT.
WE'RE GOING OUT.

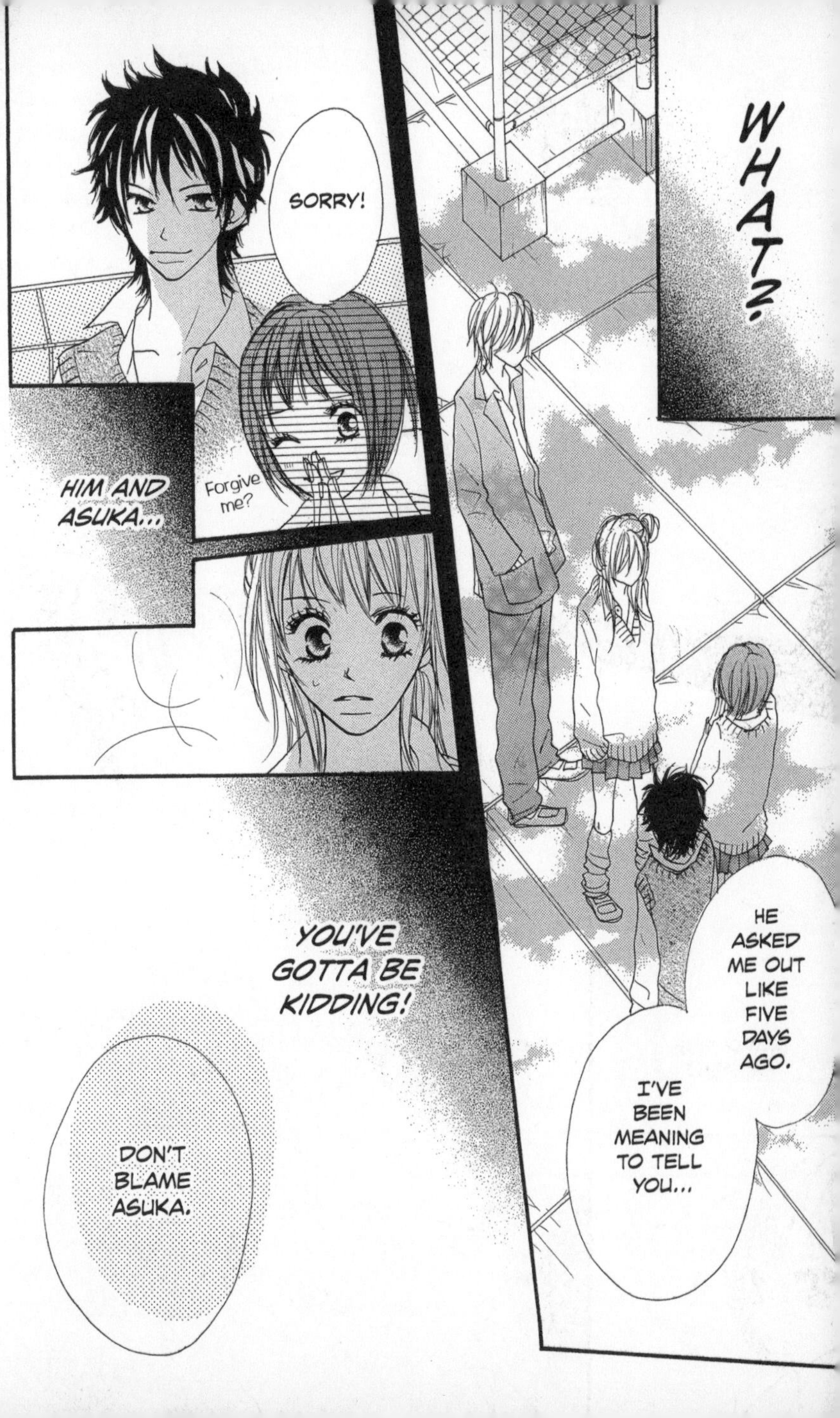
WHAT?
HE ASKED ME OUT LIKE FIVE DAYS AGO.
I'VE BEEN MEANING TO TELL YOU...
SORRY!
Forgive me?
HIM AND ASUKA...
YOU'VE GOTTA BE KIDDING!
DON'T BLAME ASUKA.

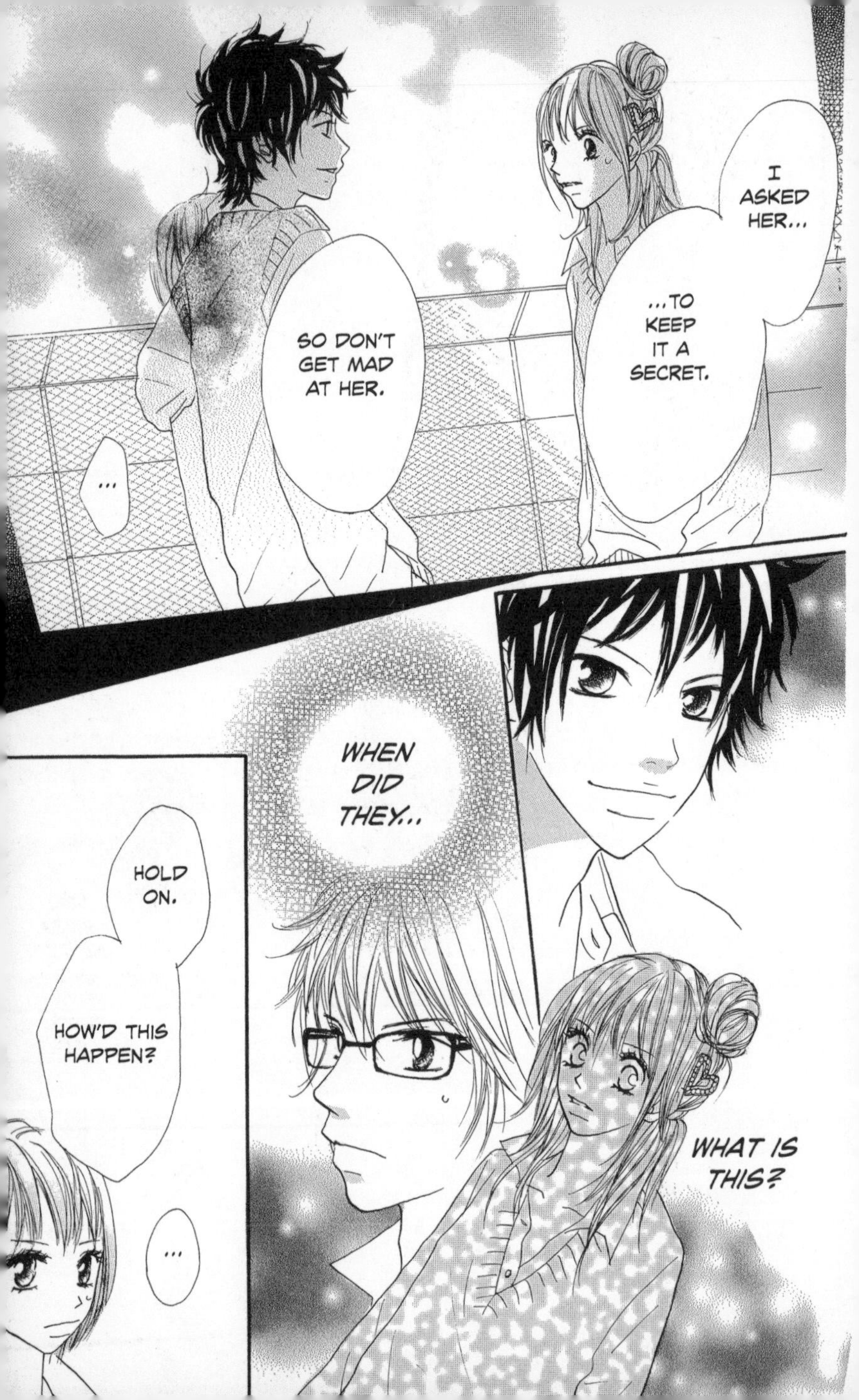
I ASKED HER...
...TO KEEP IT A SECRET.
SO DON'T GET MAD AT HER.
...
WHEN DID THEY...
WHAT IS THIS?
HOLD ON.
HOW'D THIS HAPPEN?
...

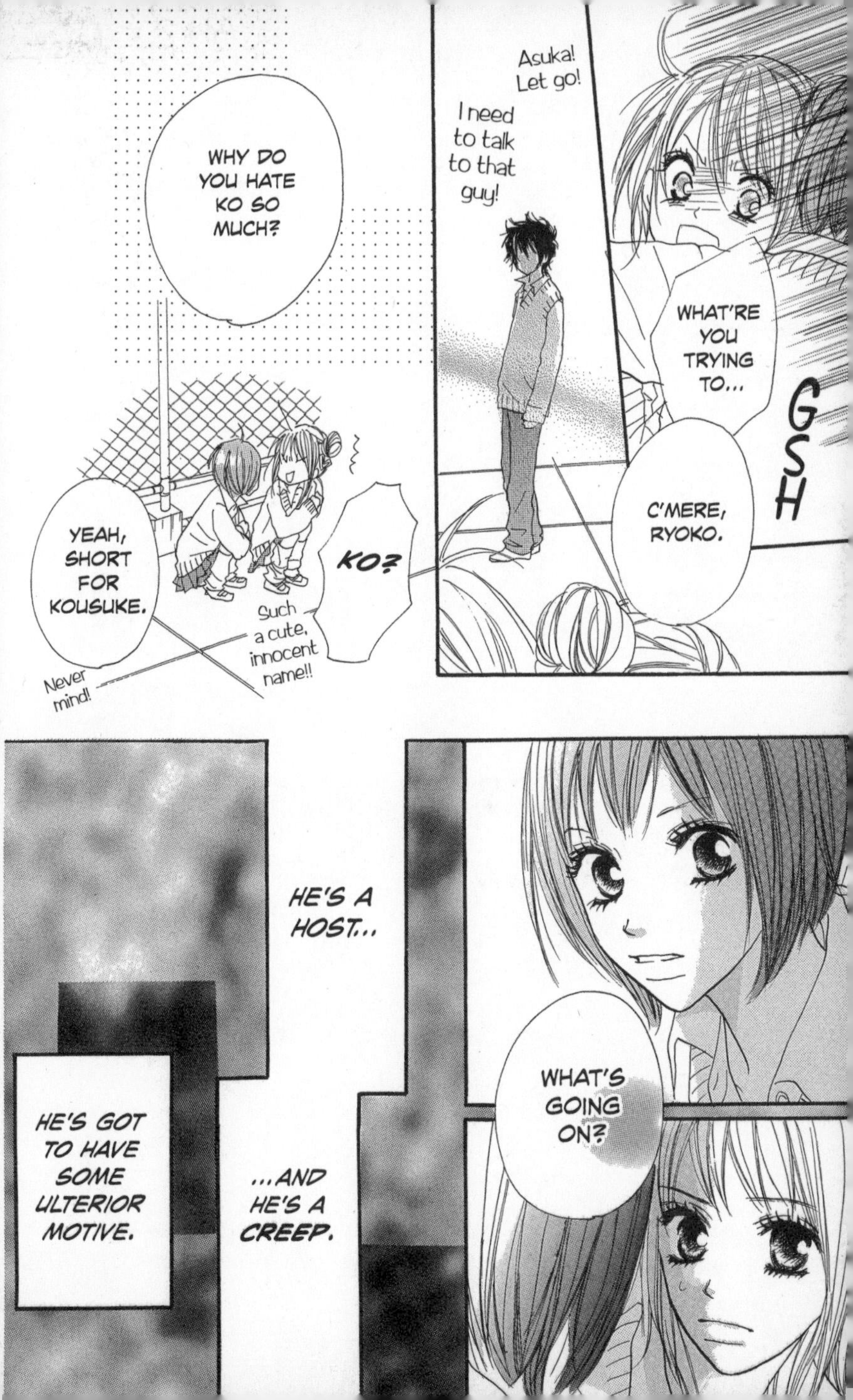
Asuka! Let go!
I need to talk to that guy!
WHAT'RE YOU TRYING TO...
GSH
C'MERE, RYOKO.
WHY DO YOU HATE KO SO MUCH?
KO?
YEAH, SHORT FOR KOUSUKE.
Such a cute, innocent name!!
Never mind!
WHAT'S GOING ON?
HE'S A HOST...
...AND HE'S A CREEP.
HE'S GOT TO HAVE SOME ULTERIOR MOTIVE.

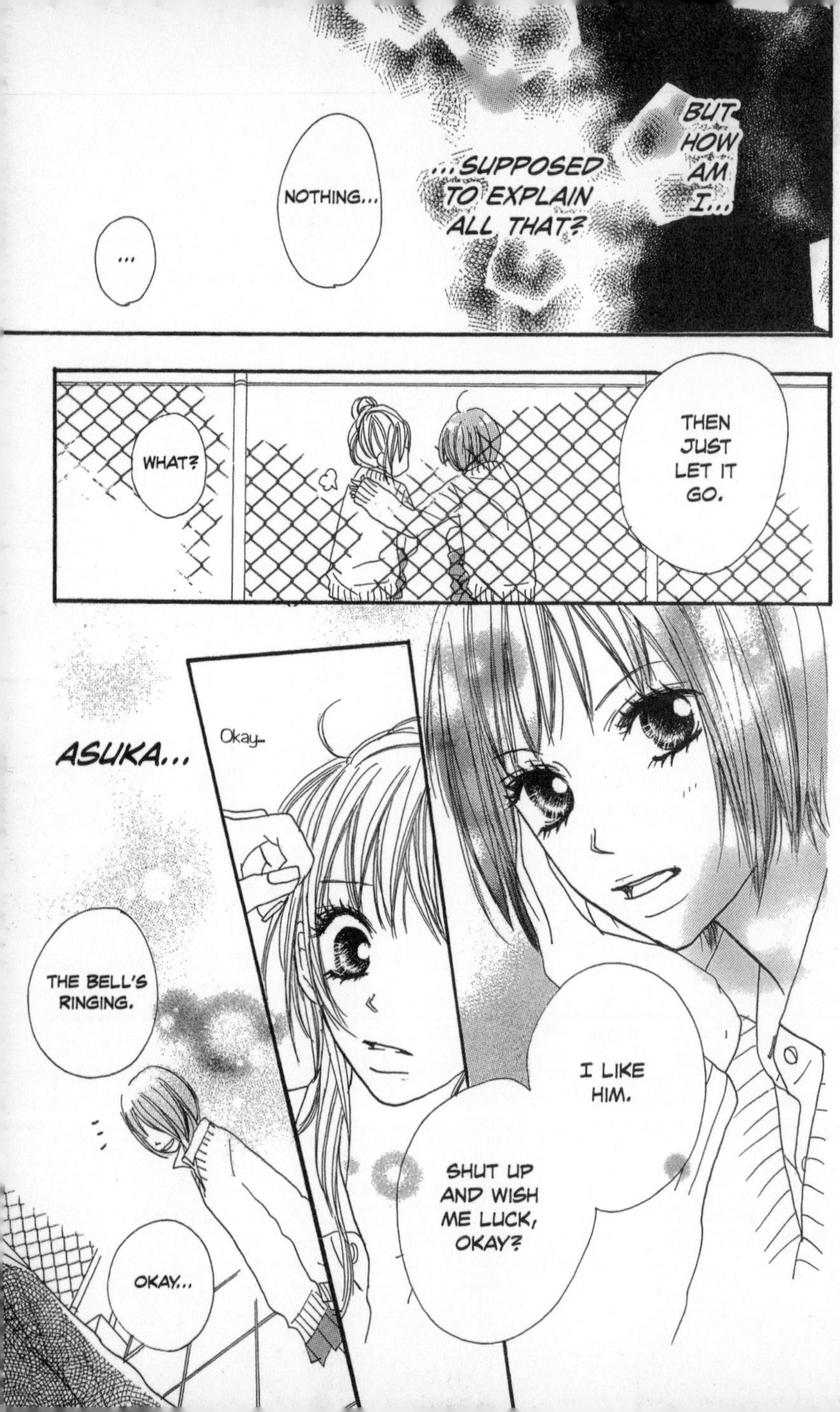
BUT HOW AM I...
...SUPPOSED TO EXPLAIN ALL THAT?
NOTHING...
...
THEN JUST LET IT GO.
WHAT?
I LIKE HIM.
SHUT UP AND WISH ME LUCK, OKAY?
Okay...
ASUKA...
THE BELL'S RINGING.
OKAY...

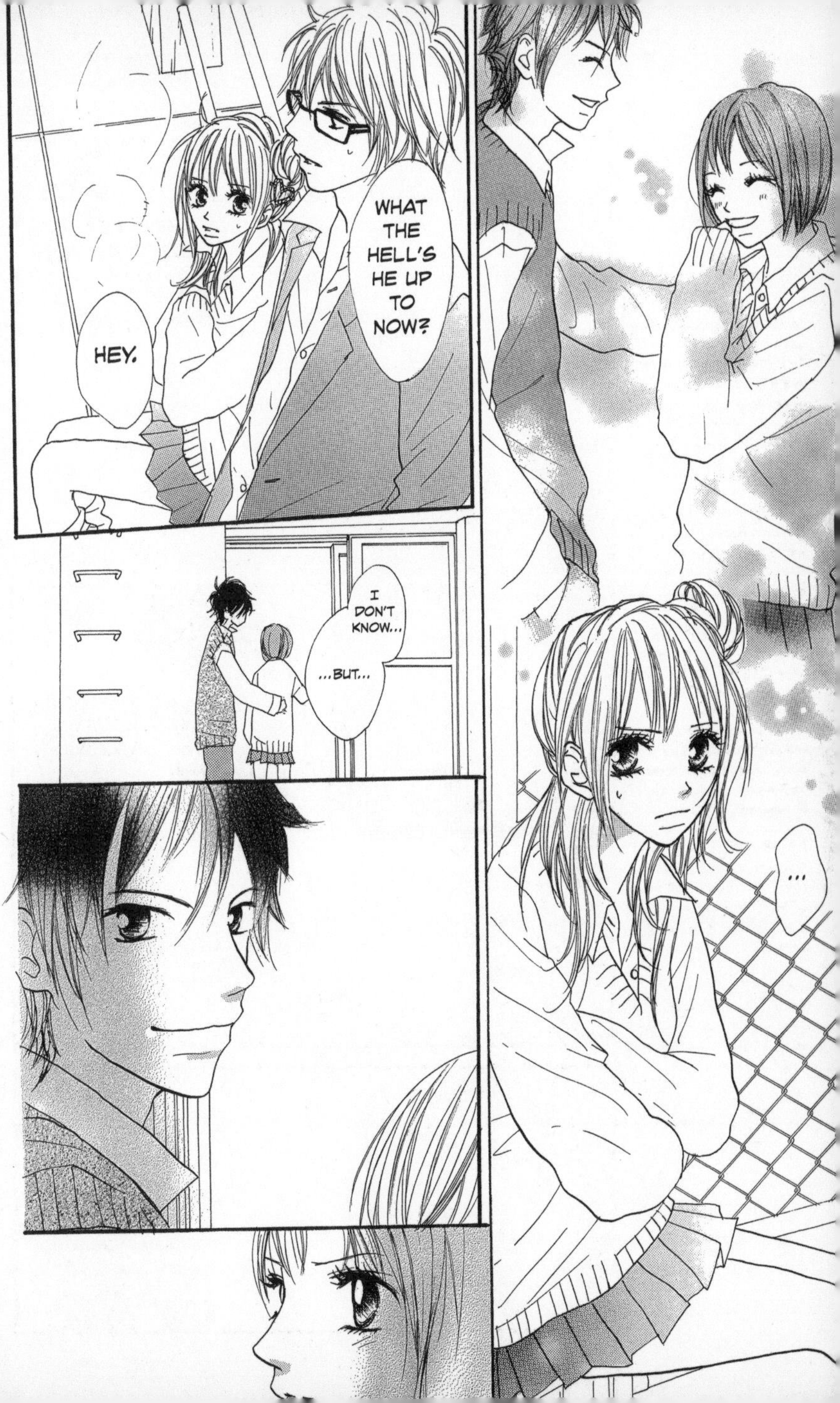
...
WHAT THE HELL'S HE UP TO NOW?
HEY.
I DON'T KNOW...
...BUT...

(3)

Lately I've gotten hooked on this period drama on TV. I'm watching it as I write this. I'm really into stuff I never used to be interested in, like period dramas and Shoten. I guess I'm turning into an old lady...

And if there's a special on ancient civilizations or world heritage sites I always watch it. Like crop circles...I wrote about this in one of the earlier volumes, but I just love stuff like that. Um...what else? Oh yeah. Sky Fish! What are they? They're so weird, aren't they? Why can't they be caught? What the hell are they? They're not birds...they couldn't really be from space, could they? It bugs me...

And that human-shaped thing that was sighted in the skies over Mexico!! What is that? It scares me!! If I ever see that thing in person...

Kyaa!! I'll faint!!
But I still wanna know what it is!! I hope they do another special on that stuff.

I'm sleepy...

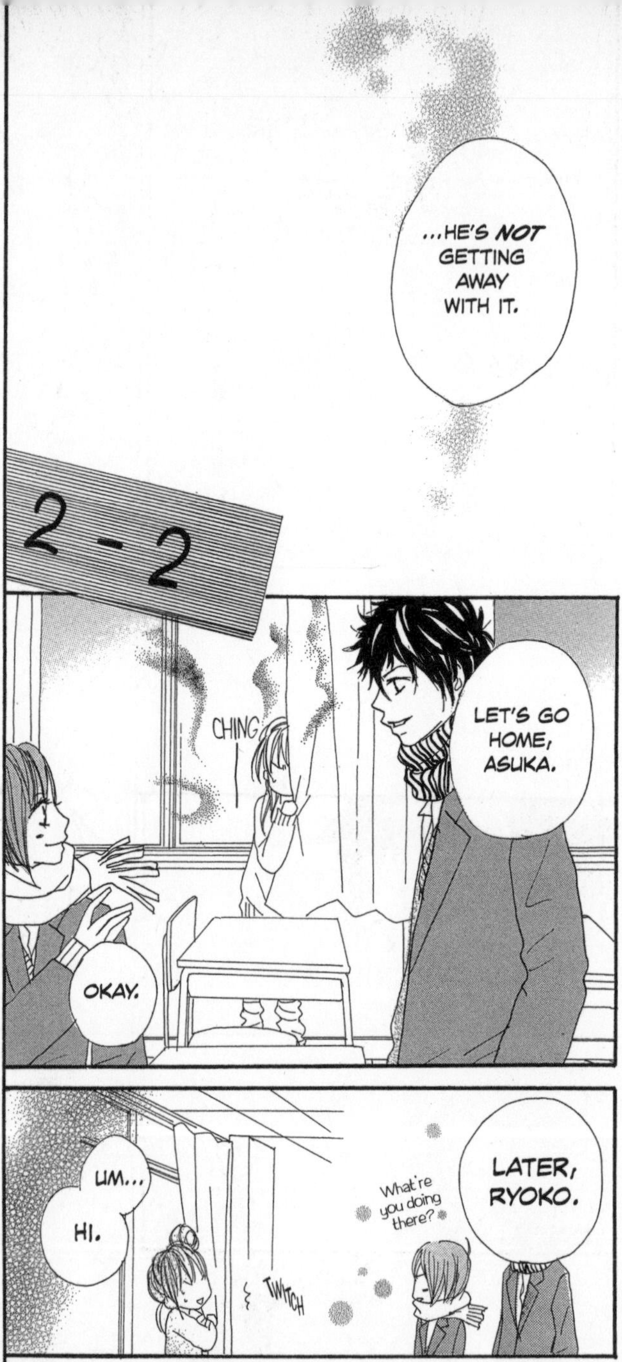
...HE'S NOT GETTING AWAY WITH IT.
2-2
LET'S GO HOME, ASUKA.
CHING
OKAY.
LATER, RYOKO.
What're you doing there?
UM...
HI.
TWITCH

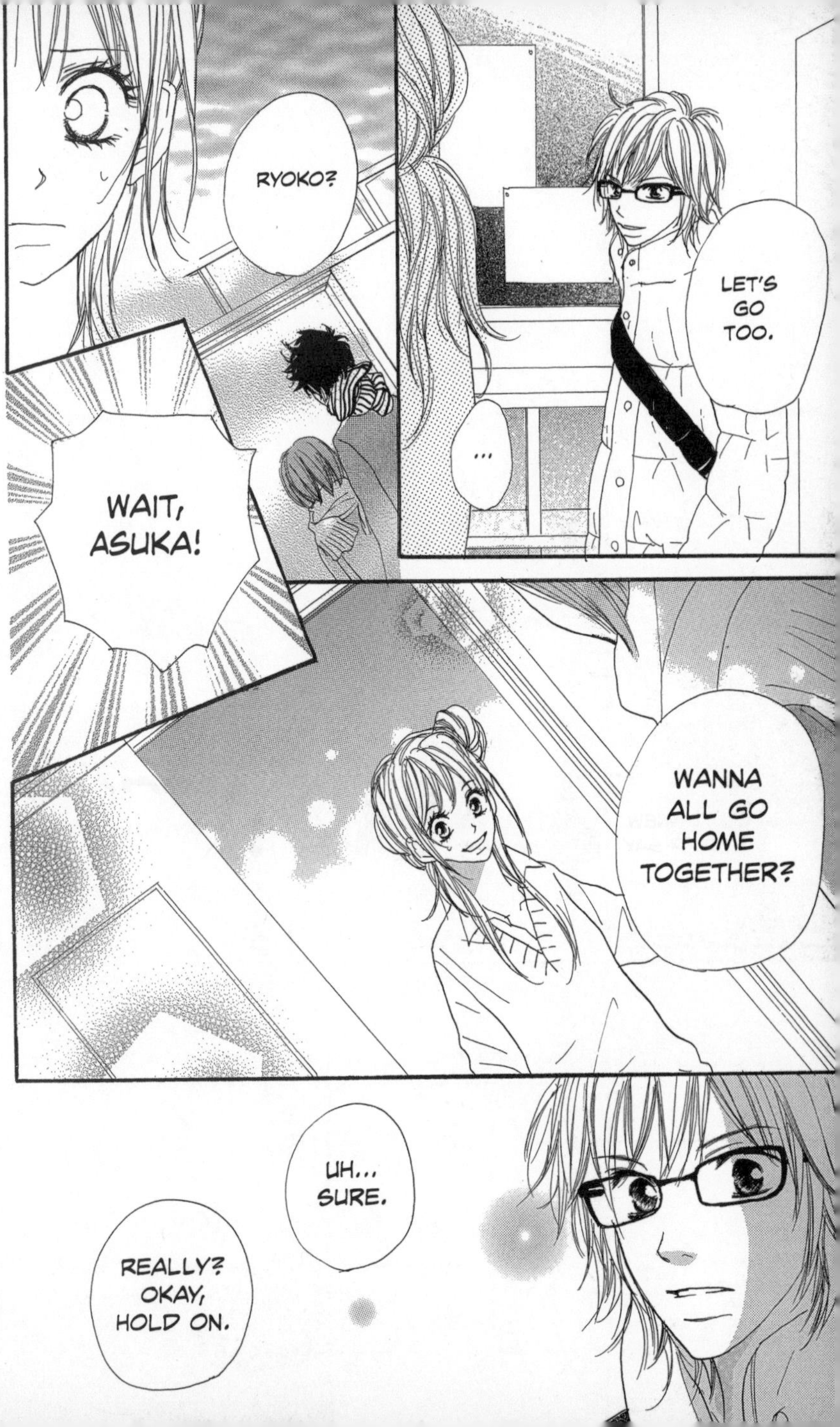
LET'S GO TOO.
...
RYOKO?
WAIT, ASUKA!
WANNA ALL GO HOME TOGETHER?
UH... SURE.
REALLY? OKAY, HOLD ON.

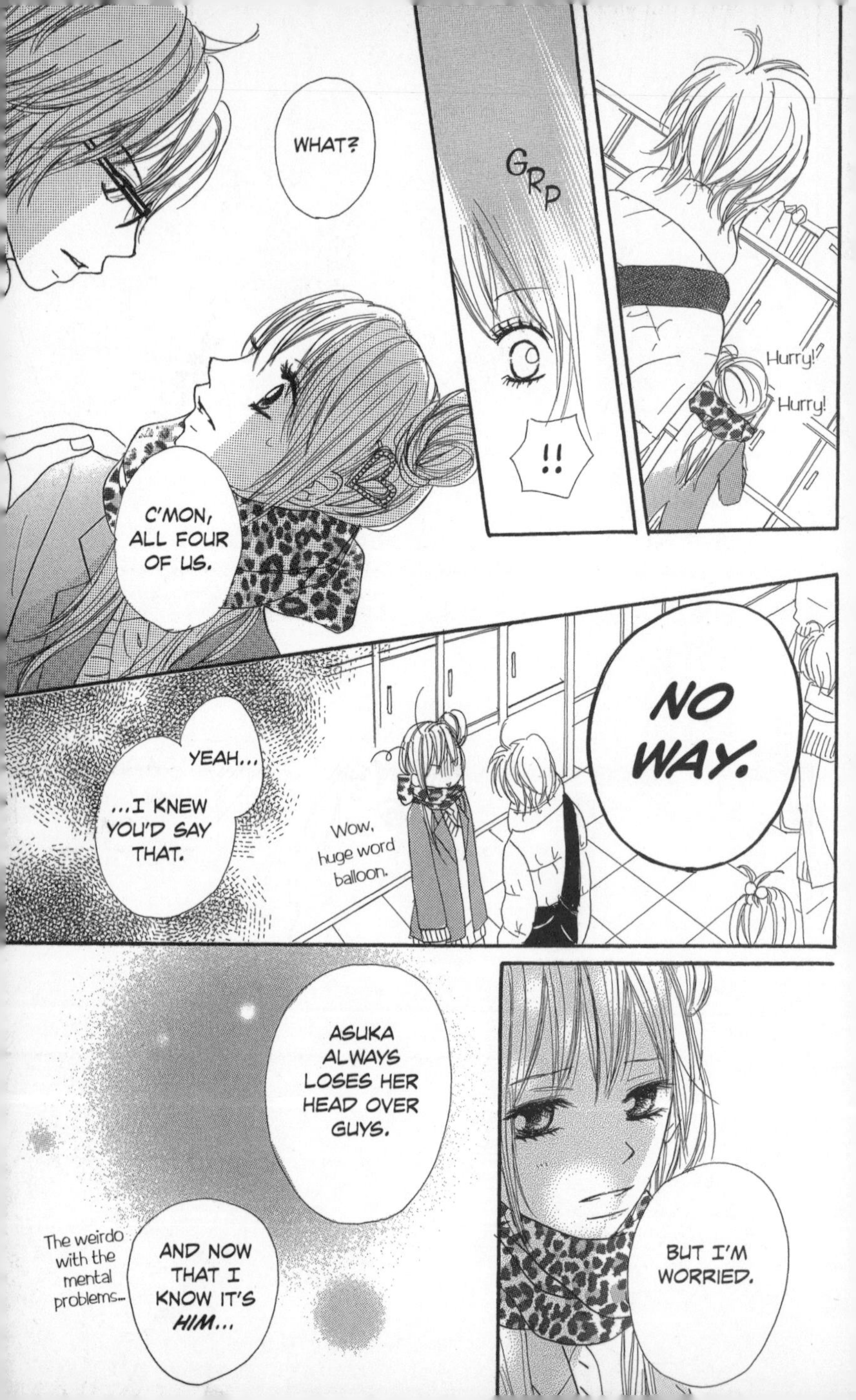
Hurry!
Hurry!
GRP
!!
WHAT?
C'MON, ALL FOUR OF US.
NO WAY.
YEAH...
...I KNEW YOU'D SAY THAT.
Wow, huge word balloon.
BUT I'M WORRIED.
ASUKA ALWAYS LOSES HER HEAD OVER GUYS.
AND NOW THAT I KNOW IT'S *HIM*...
The weirdo with the mental problems...

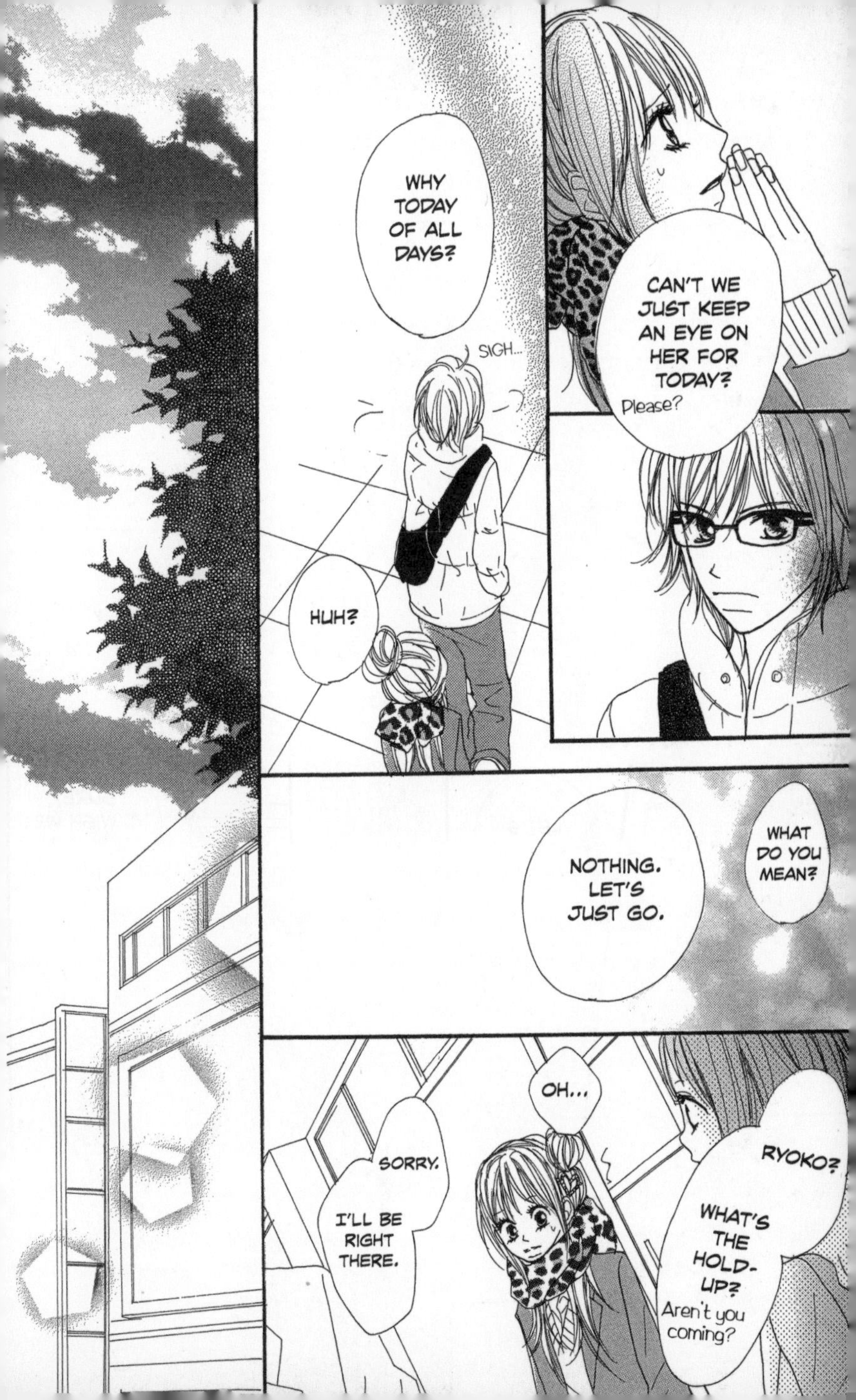

CAN'T WE JUST KEEP AN EYE ON HER FOR TODAY?
Please?
WHY TODAY OF ALL DAYS?
SIGH...
HUH?
WHAT DO YOU MEAN?
NOTHING. LET'S JUST GO.
RYOKO?
WHAT'S THE HOLD-UP?
Aren't you coming?
OH...
SORRY.
I'LL BE RIGHT THERE.

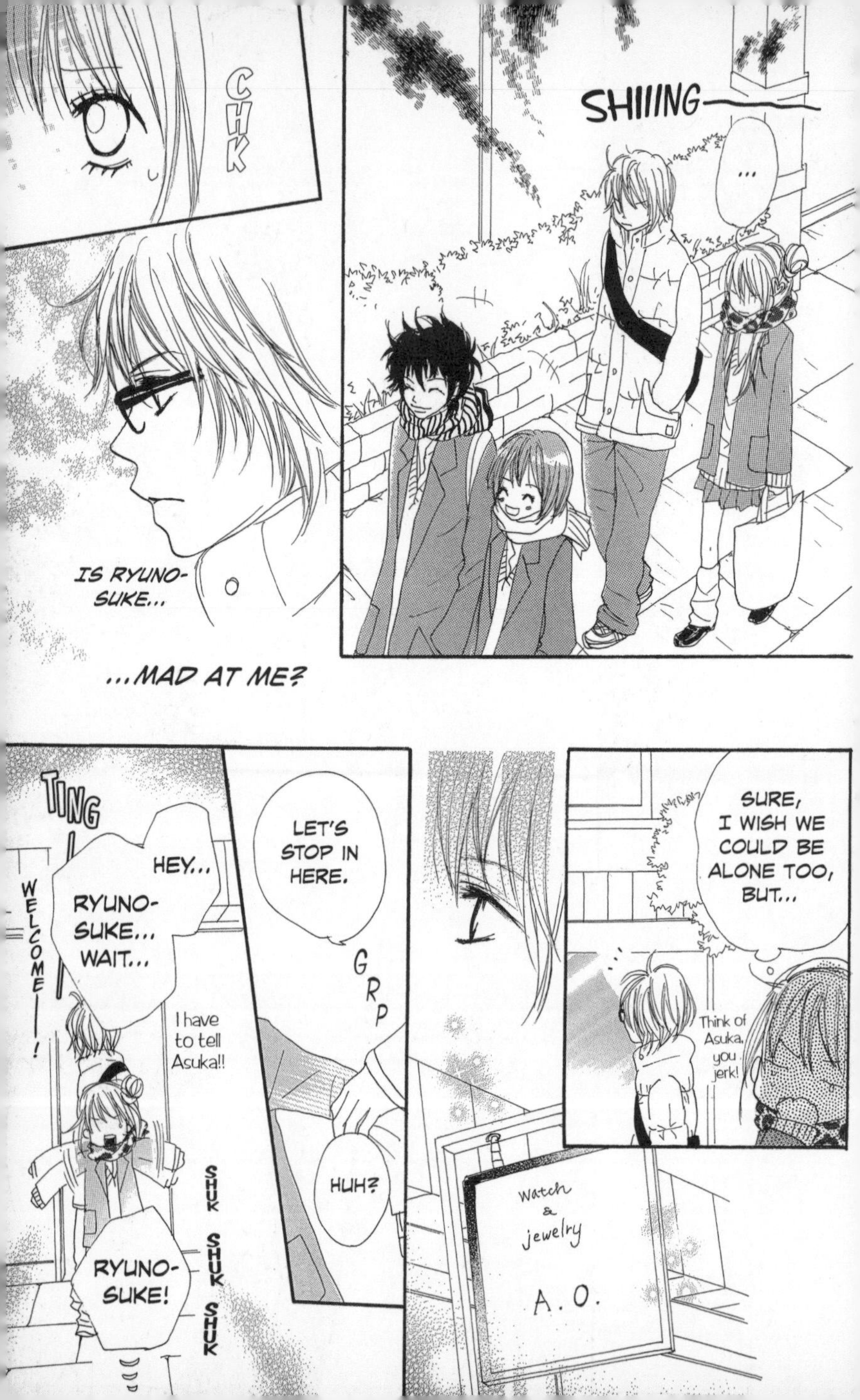
SHIIING
...
CHK
IS RYUNO-SUKE...
...MAD AT ME?
SURE, I WISH WE COULD BE ALONE TOO, BUT...
Think of Asuka, you jerk!
Watch & jewelry
A.O.
LET'S STOP IN HERE.
GRP
HUH?
TING
WELCOME—!
HEY... RYUNO-SUKE... WAIT...
I have to tell Asuka!!
SHUK SHUK SHUK
RYUNO-SUKE!

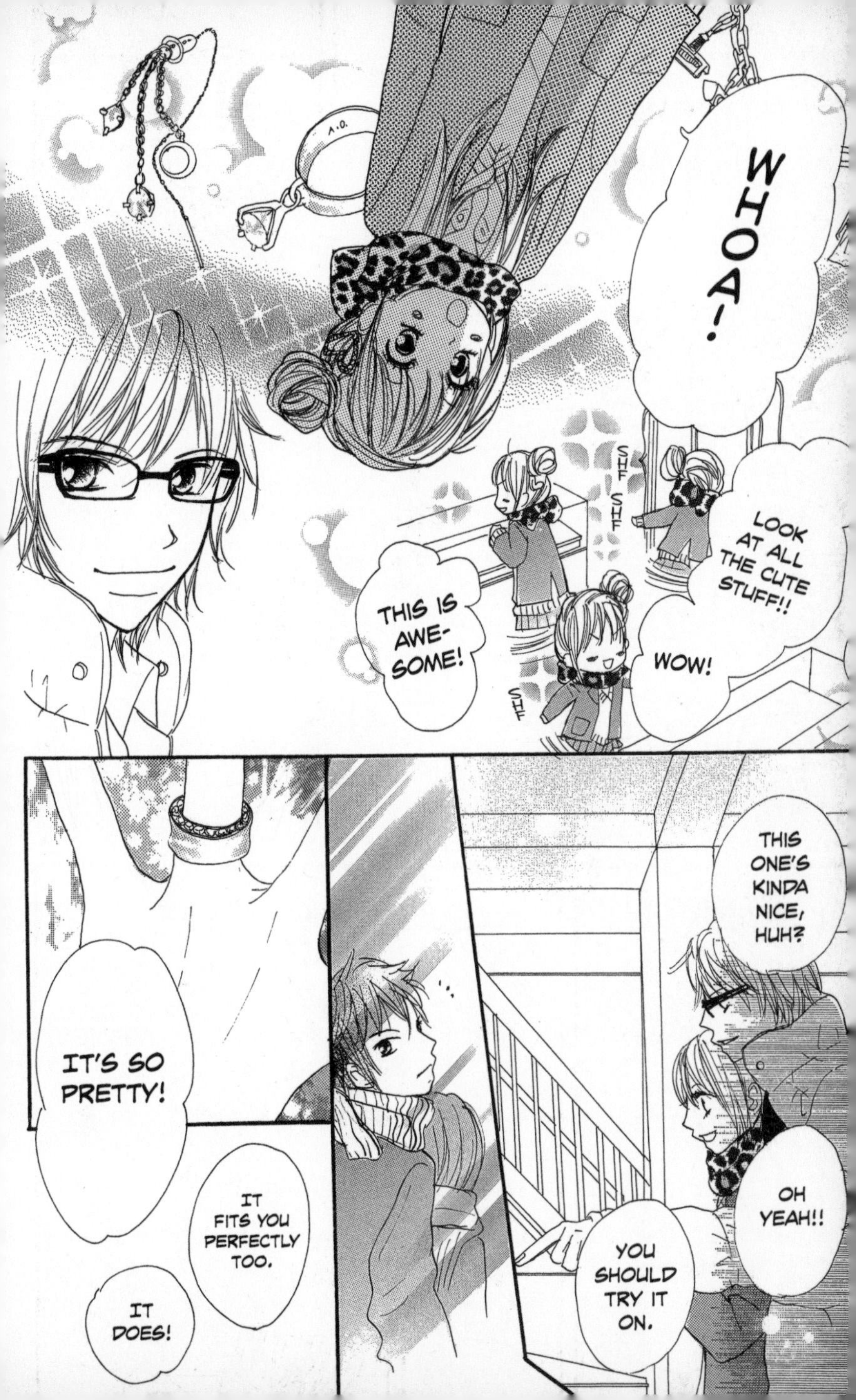
WHOA!
LOOK AT ALL THE CUTE STUFF!!
SHF SHF
WOW!
THIS IS AWE-SOME!
SHF
THIS ONE'S KINDA NICE, HUH?
OH YEAH!!
YOU SHOULD TRY IT ON.
IT'S SO PRETTY!
IT FITS YOU PERFECTLY TOO.
IT DOES!

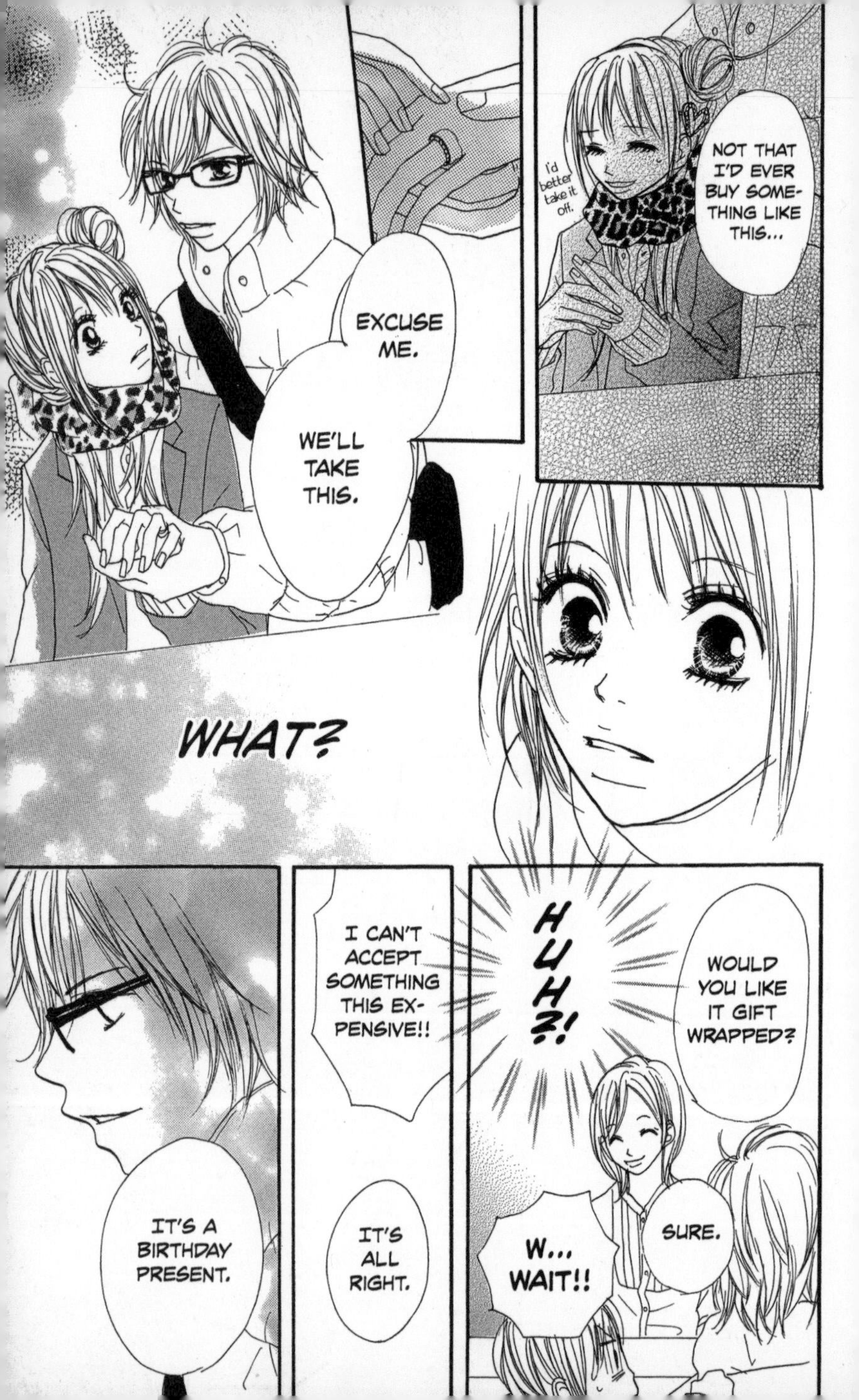
NOT THAT I'D EVER BUY SOME-THING LIKE THIS...
I'd better take it off.
EXCUSE ME.
WE'LL TAKE THIS.
WHAT?
WOULD YOU LIKE IT GIFT WRAPPED?
HUH?!
SURE.
W... WAIT!!
I CAN'T ACCEPT SOMETHING THIS EX-PENSIVE!!
IT'S ALL RIGHT.
IT'S A BIRTHDAY PRESENT.

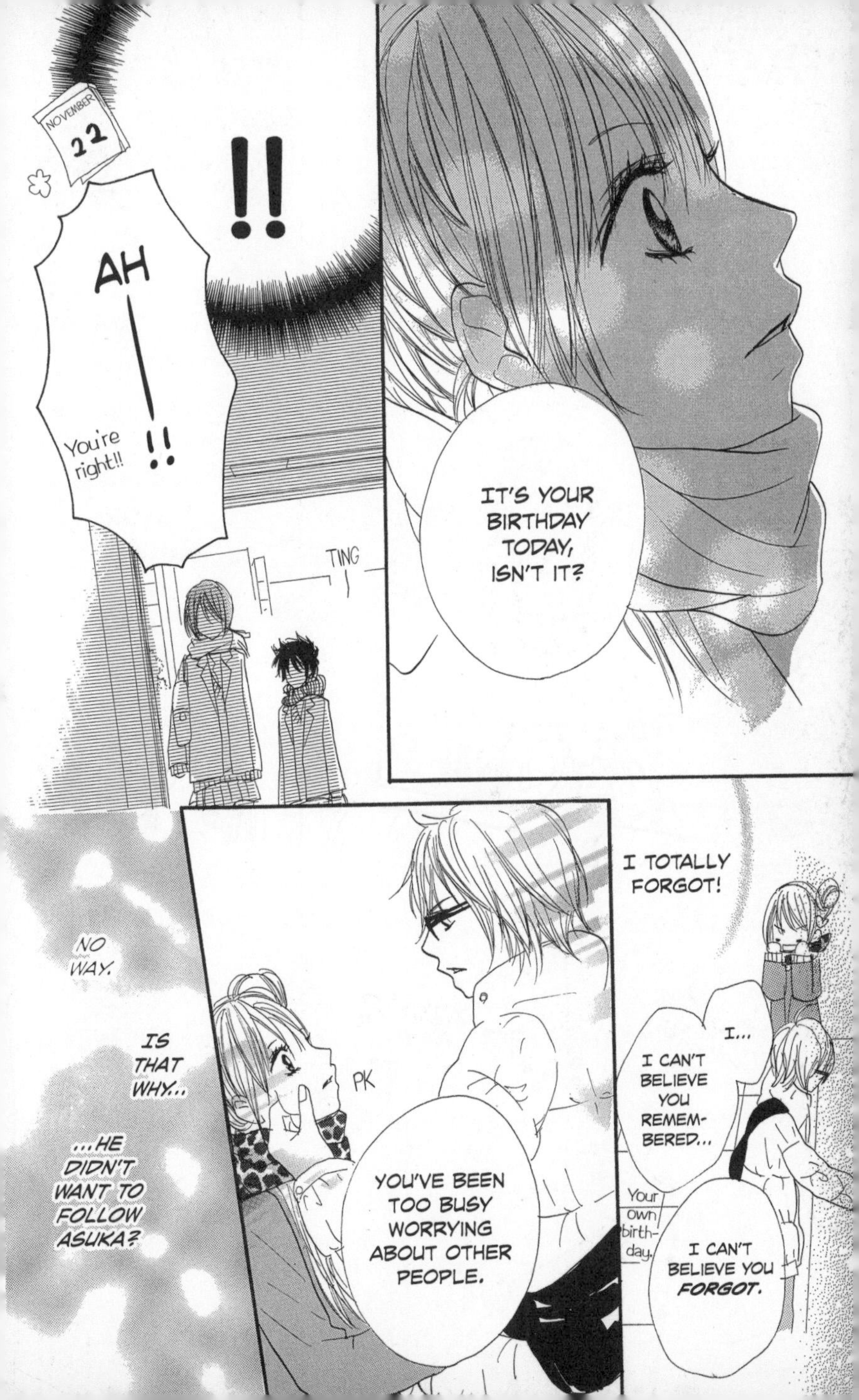
IT'S YOUR BIRTHDAY TODAY, ISN'T IT?
!!
NOVEMBER 22
AH—!!
You're right!!
TING
I TOTALLY FORGOT!
I...
I CAN'T BELIEVE YOU REMEMBERED...
I CAN'T BELIEVE YOU FORGOT.
Your own birthday.
PK
YOU'VE BEEN TOO BUSY WORRYING ABOUT OTHER PEOPLE.
NO WAY.
IS THAT WHY...
...HE DIDN'T WANT TO FOLLOW ASUKA?

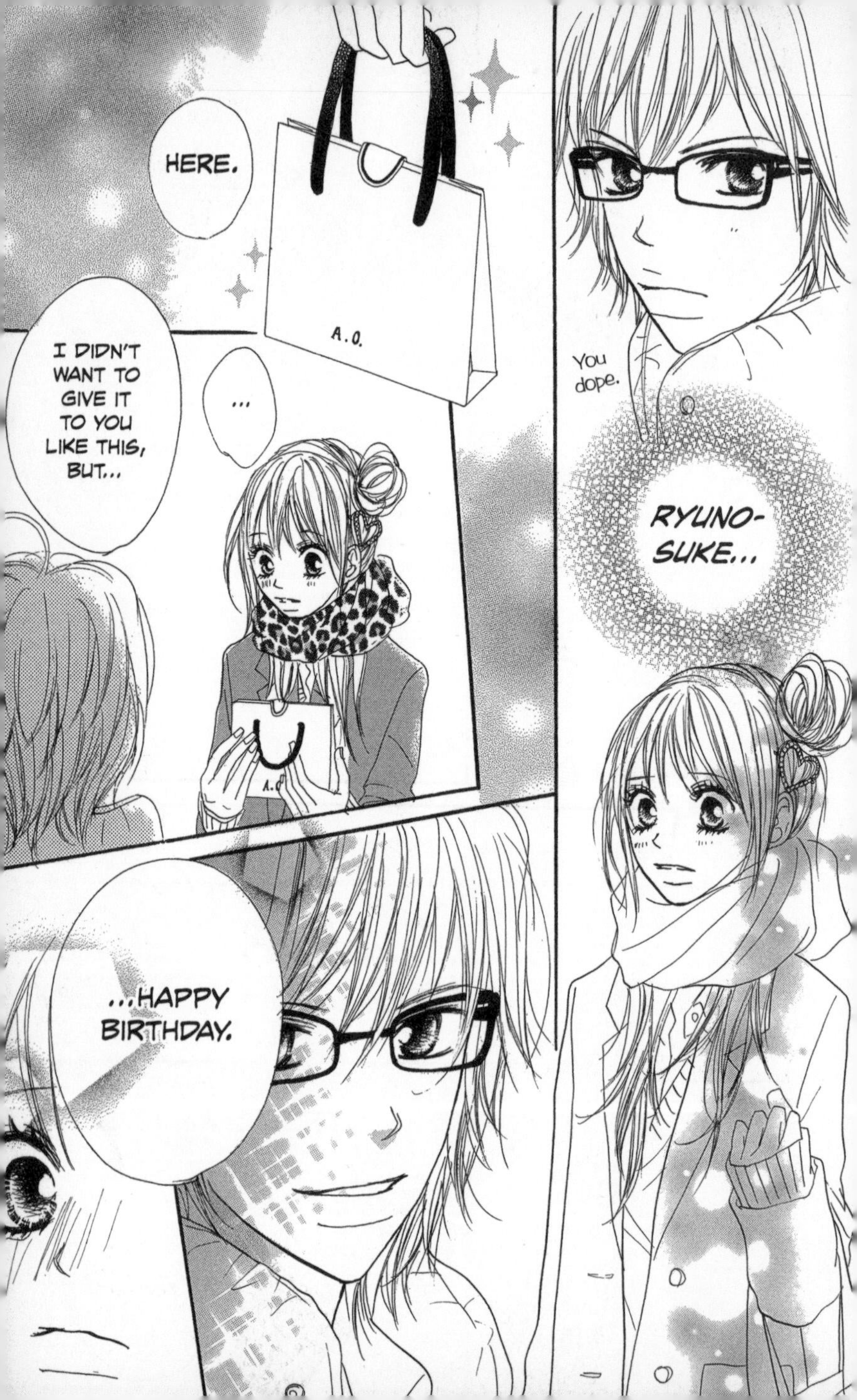
You dope.
RYUNO-SUKE...
HERE.
A.O.
I DIDN'T WANT TO GIVE IT TO YOU LIKE THIS, BUT...
...
...HAPPY BIRTHDAY.

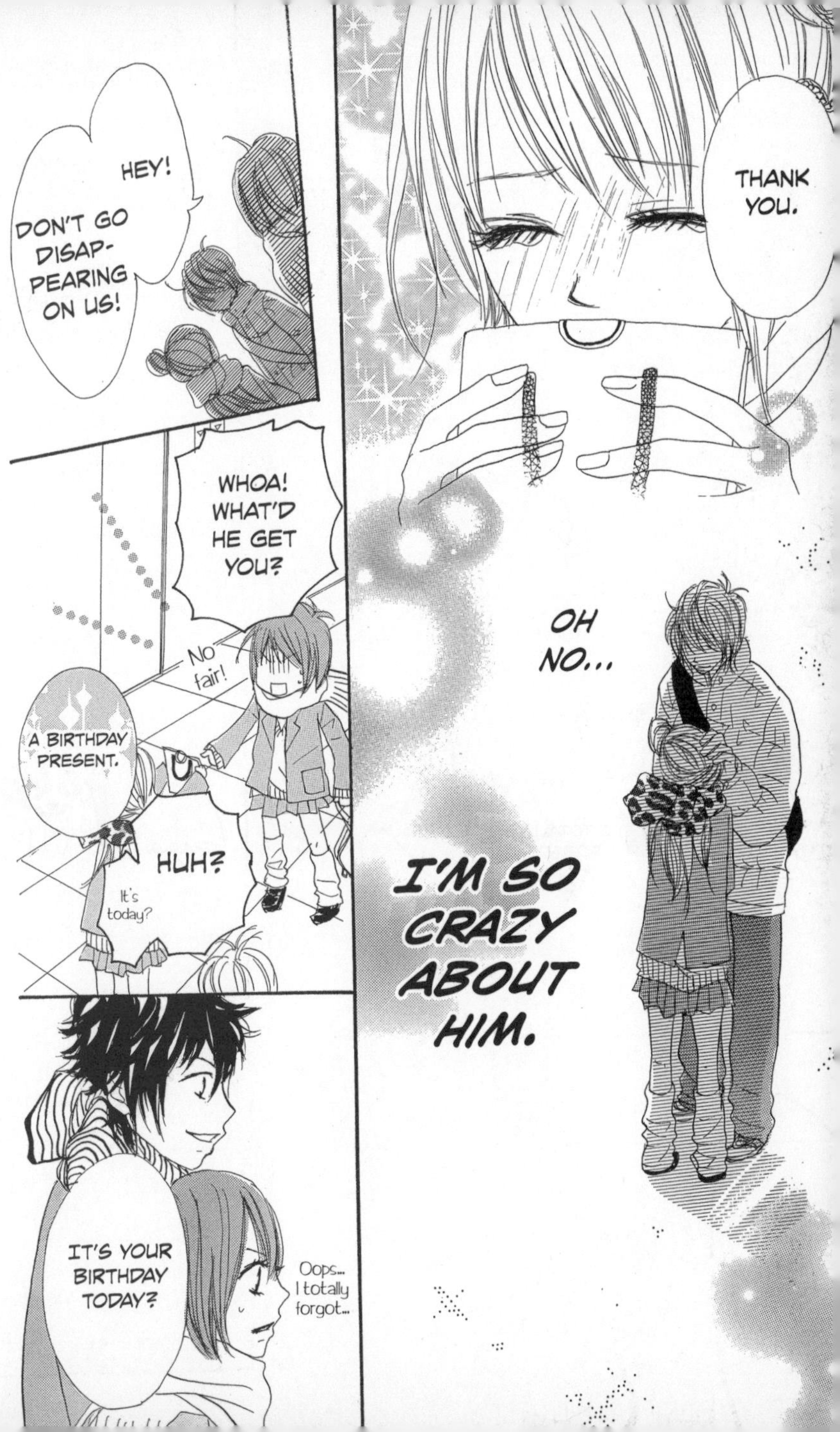
THANK YOU.
OH NO...
I'M SO CRAZY ABOUT HIM.
HEY! DON'T GO DISAP-PEARING ON US!
WHOA! WHAT'D HE GET YOU?
No fair!
A BIRTHDAY PRESENT.
HUH?
It's today?
IT'S YOUR BIRTHDAY TODAY?
Oops... I totally forgot...

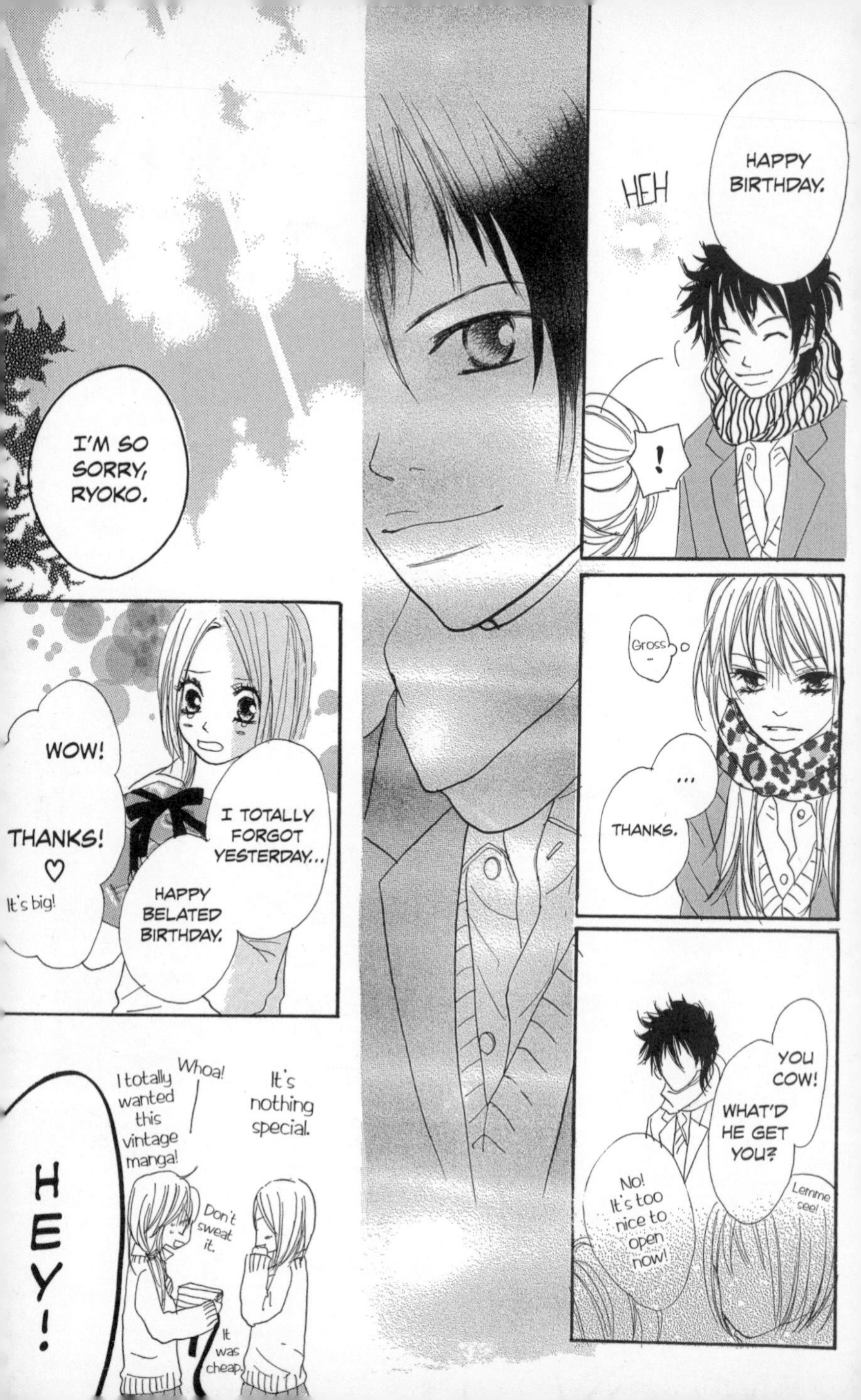
HAPPY BIRTHDAY.
HEH
!
Gross...
...
THANKS.
YOU COW!
WHAT'D HE GET YOU?
Lemme see!
No! It's too nice to open now!
I'M SO SORRY, RYOKO.
I TOTALLY FORGOT YESTERDAY...
HAPPY BELATED BIRTHDAY.
WOW!
THANKS! ♡
It's big!
It's nothing special.
It was cheap.
Whoa!
I totally wanted this vintage manga!
Don't sweat it.
HEY!

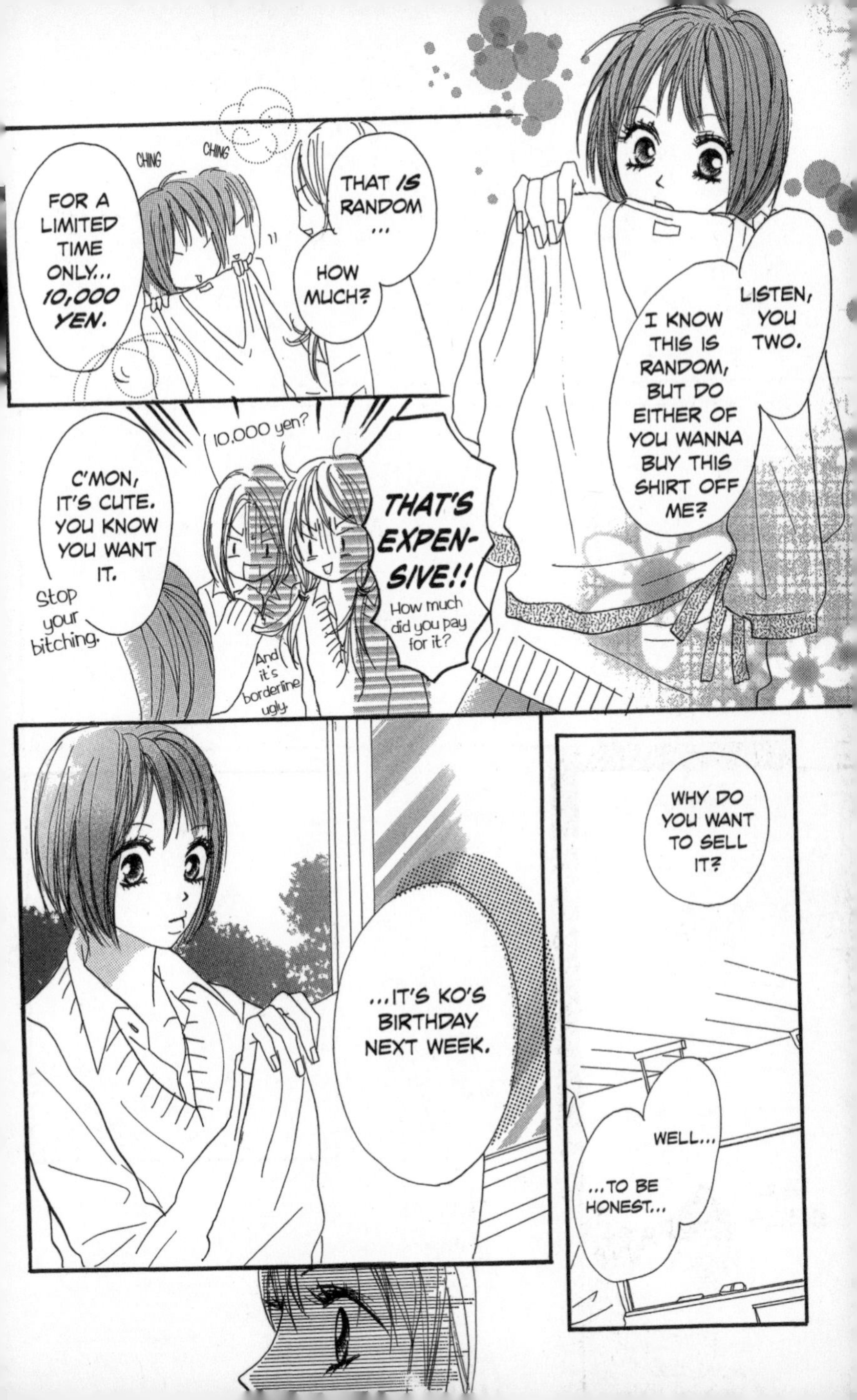
LISTEN, YOU TWO.
I KNOW THIS IS RANDOM, BUT DO EITHER OF YOU WANNA BUY THIS SHIRT OFF ME?
THAT *IS* RANDOM...
HOW MUCH?
CHING
CHING
FOR A LIMITED TIME ONLY... **10,000 YEN.**
10,000 yen?
THAT'S EXPEN-SIVE!!
How much did you pay for it?
And it's borderline ugly.
C'MON, IT'S CUTE. YOU KNOW YOU WANT IT.
Stop your bitching.
WHY DO YOU WANT TO SELL IT?
WELL...
...TO BE HONEST...
...IT'S KO'S BIRTHDAY NEXT WEEK.

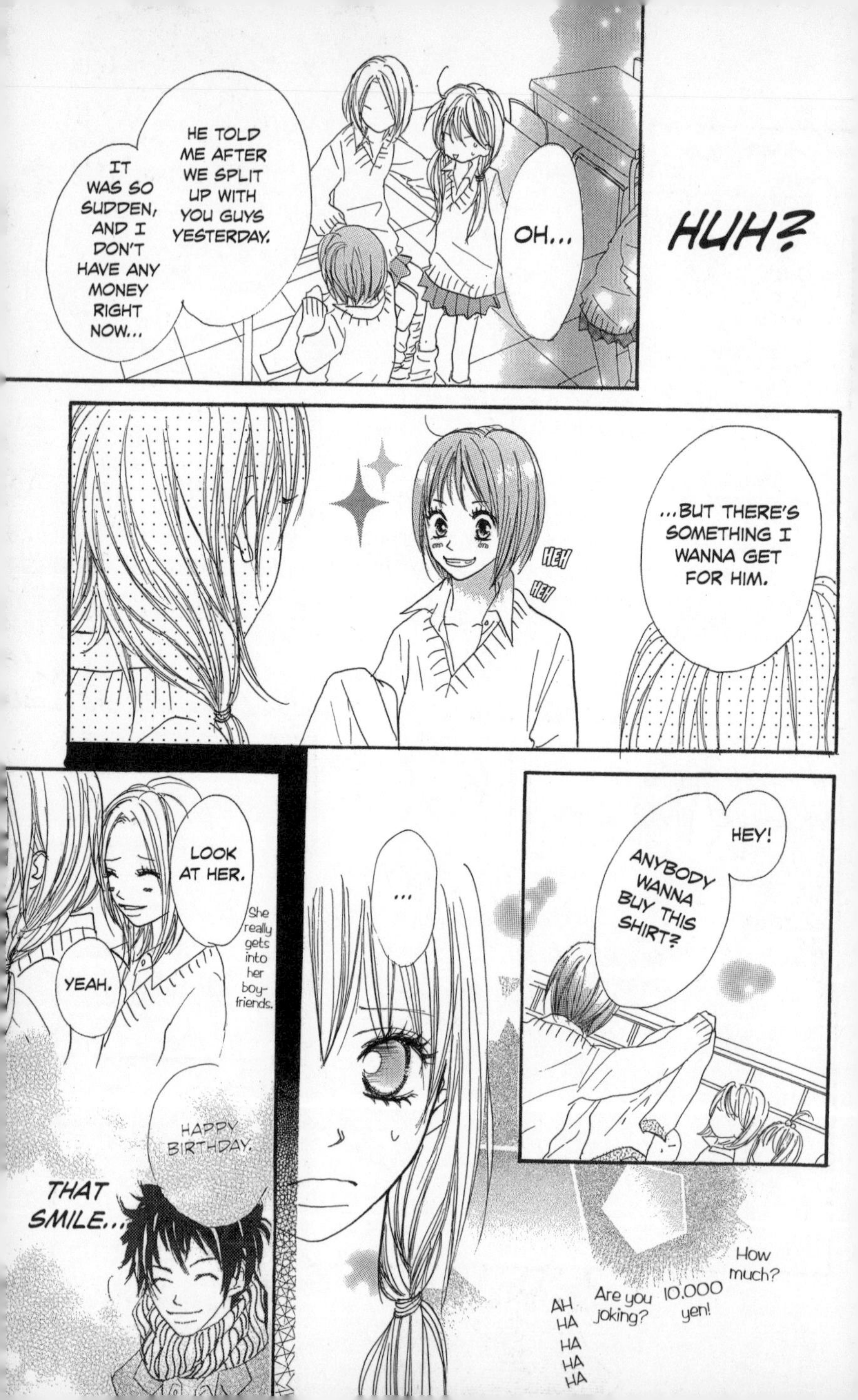
HUH?
OH...
HE TOLD ME AFTER WE SPLIT UP WITH YOU GUYS YESTERDAY.
IT WAS SO SUDDEN, AND I DON'T HAVE ANY MONEY RIGHT NOW...
...BUT THERE'S SOMETHING I WANNA GET FOR HIM.
HEH HEH
HEY!
ANYBODY WANNA BUY THIS SHIRT?
How much?
10,000 yen!
Are you joking?
AH HA HA HA HA
...
LOOK AT HER.
She really gets into her boyfriends.
YEAH.
HAPPY BIRTHDAY.
THAT SMILE...

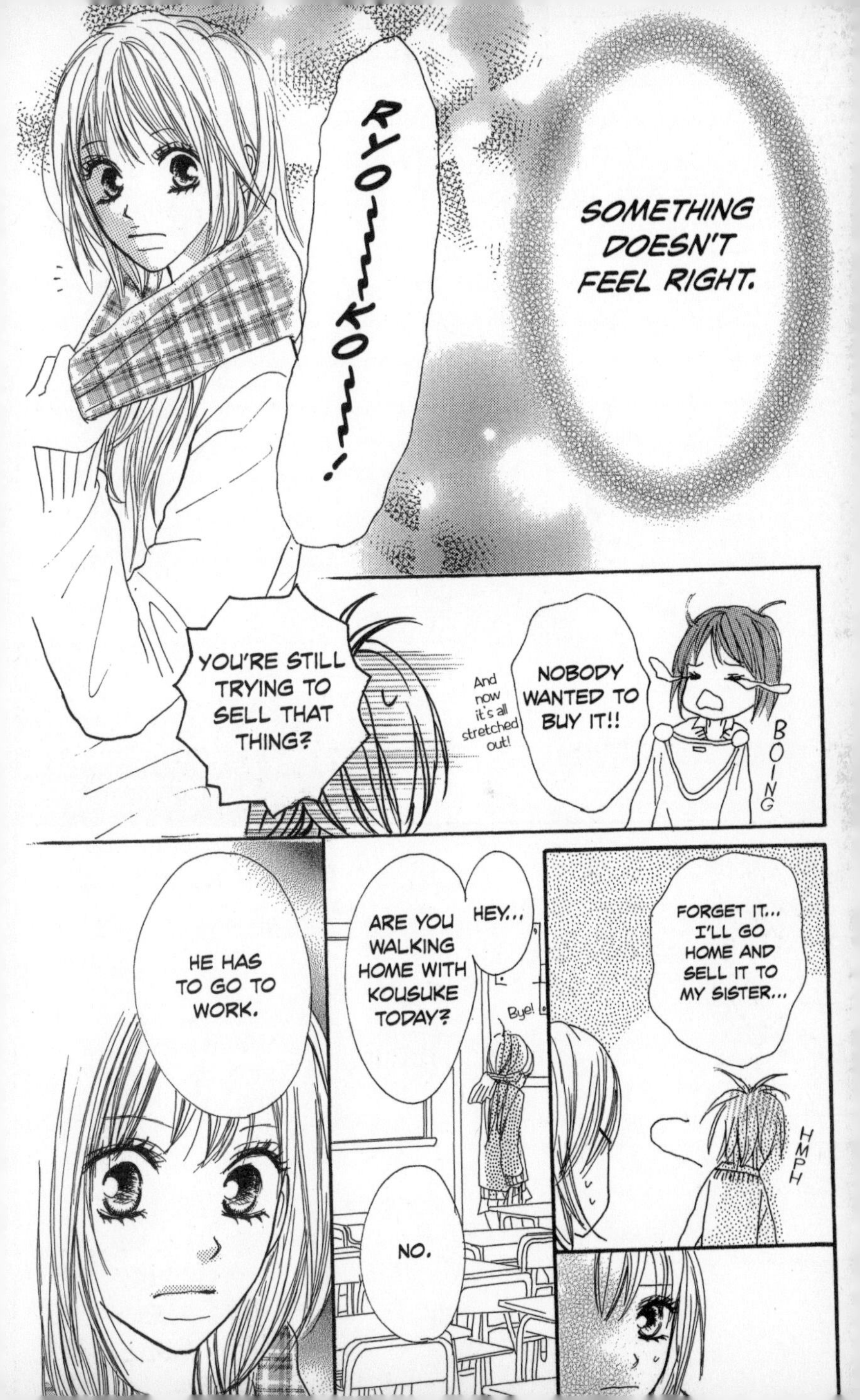
SOMETHING DOESN'T FEEL RIGHT.
RYO~KO~!
NOBODY WANTED TO BUY IT!!
And now it's all stretched out!
BOING
YOU'RE STILL TRYING TO SELL THAT THING?
FORGET IT... I'LL GO HOME AND SELL IT TO MY SISTER...
HMPH
HEY...
ARE YOU WALKING HOME WITH KOUSUKE TODAY?
Bye!
NO.
HE HAS TO GO TO WORK.

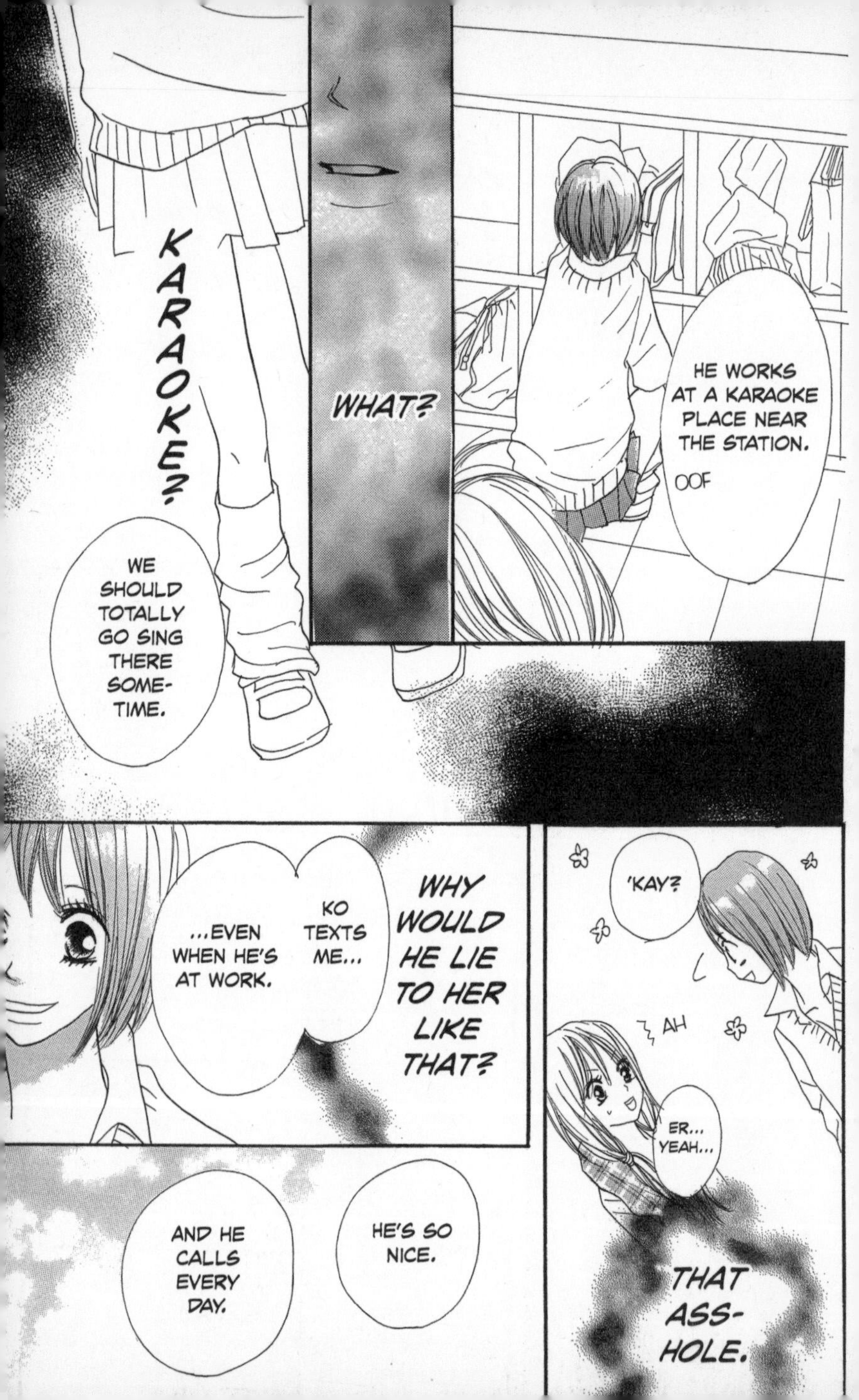
HE WORKS AT A KARAOKE PLACE NEAR THE STATION.
OOF
WHAT?
KARAOKE?
WE SHOULD TOTALLY GO SING THERE SOME-TIME.
'KAY?
AH
ER... YEAH...
THAT ASS-HOLE.
WHY WOULD HE LIE TO HER LIKE THAT?
KO TEXTS ME...
...EVEN WHEN HE'S AT WORK.
HE'S SO NICE.
AND HE CALLS EVERY DAY.

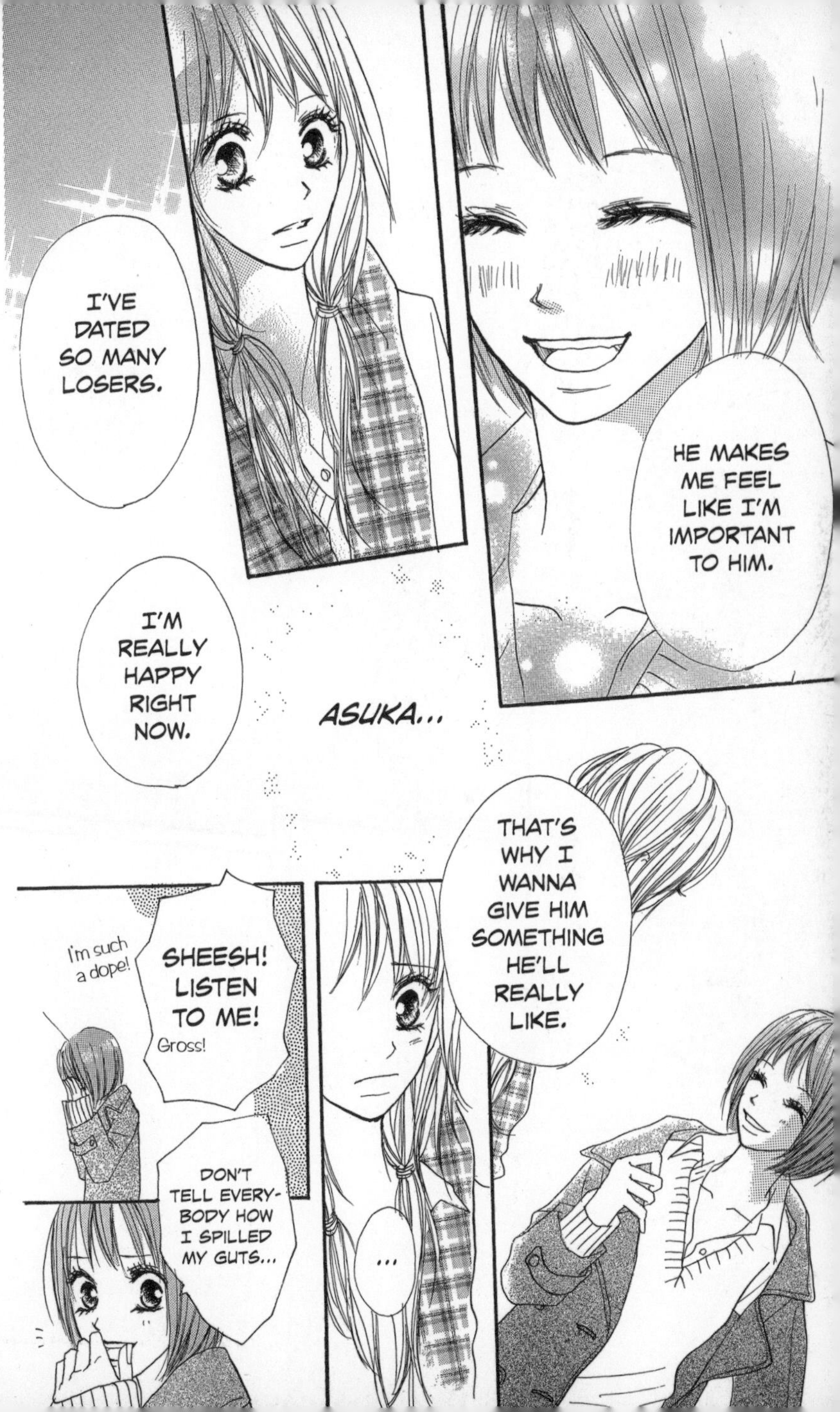
I'VE DATED SO MANY LOSERS.
HE MAKES ME FEEL LIKE I'M IMPORTANT TO HIM.
I'M REALLY HAPPY RIGHT NOW.
ASUKA...
THAT'S WHY I WANNA GIVE HIM SOMETHING HE'LL REALLY LIKE.
...
SHEESH! LISTEN TO ME!
Gross!
I'm such a dope!
DON'T TELL EVERY-BODY HOW I SPILLED MY GUTS...

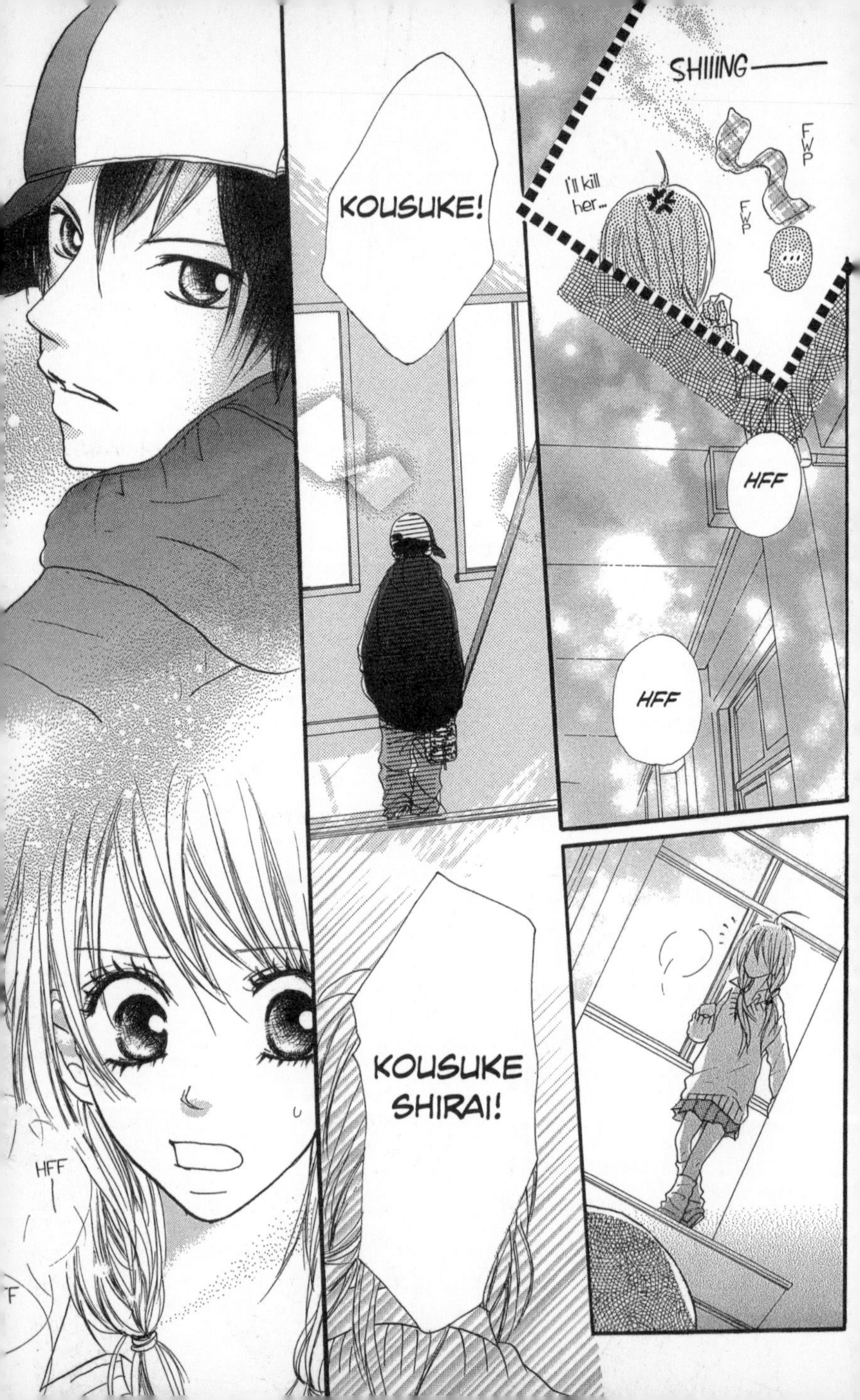
SHIIING
FWP
FWP
I'll kill her...
...
HFF
HFF
KOUSUKE!
KOUSUKE SHIRAI!
HFF
F

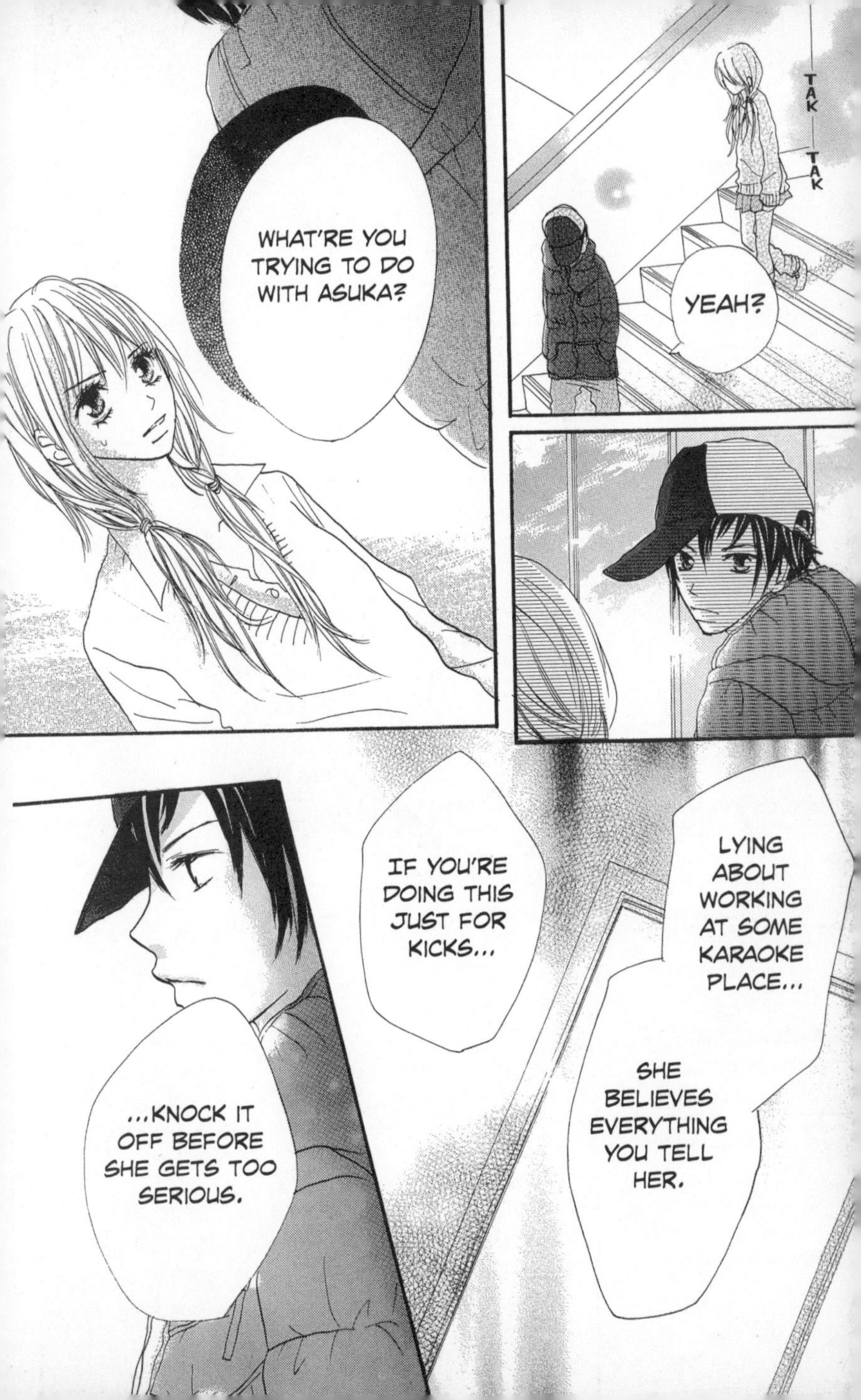
TAK TAK
YEAH?
WHAT'RE YOU TRYING TO DO WITH ASUKA?
LYING ABOUT WORKING AT SOME KARAOKE PLACE...
SHE BELIEVES EVERYTHING YOU TELL HER.
IF YOU'RE DOING THIS JUST FOR KICKS...
...KNOCK IT OFF BEFORE SHE GETS TOO SERIOUS.

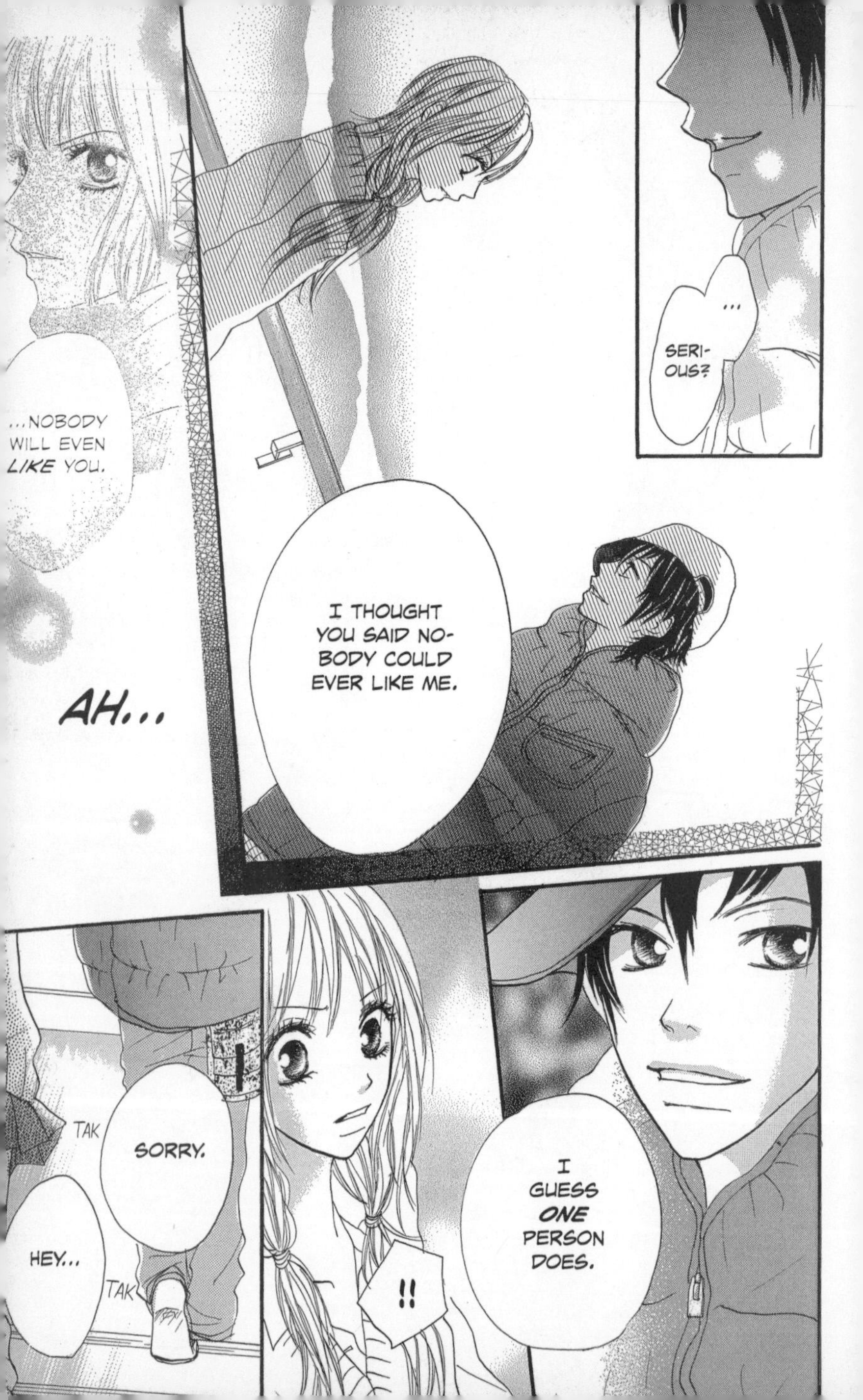
...
SERI-OUS?
I THOUGHT YOU SAID NO-BODY COULD EVER LIKE ME.
...NOBODY WILL EVEN LIKE YOU.
AH...
I GUESS ONE PERSON DOES.
!!
TAK
SORRY.
HEY...
TAK

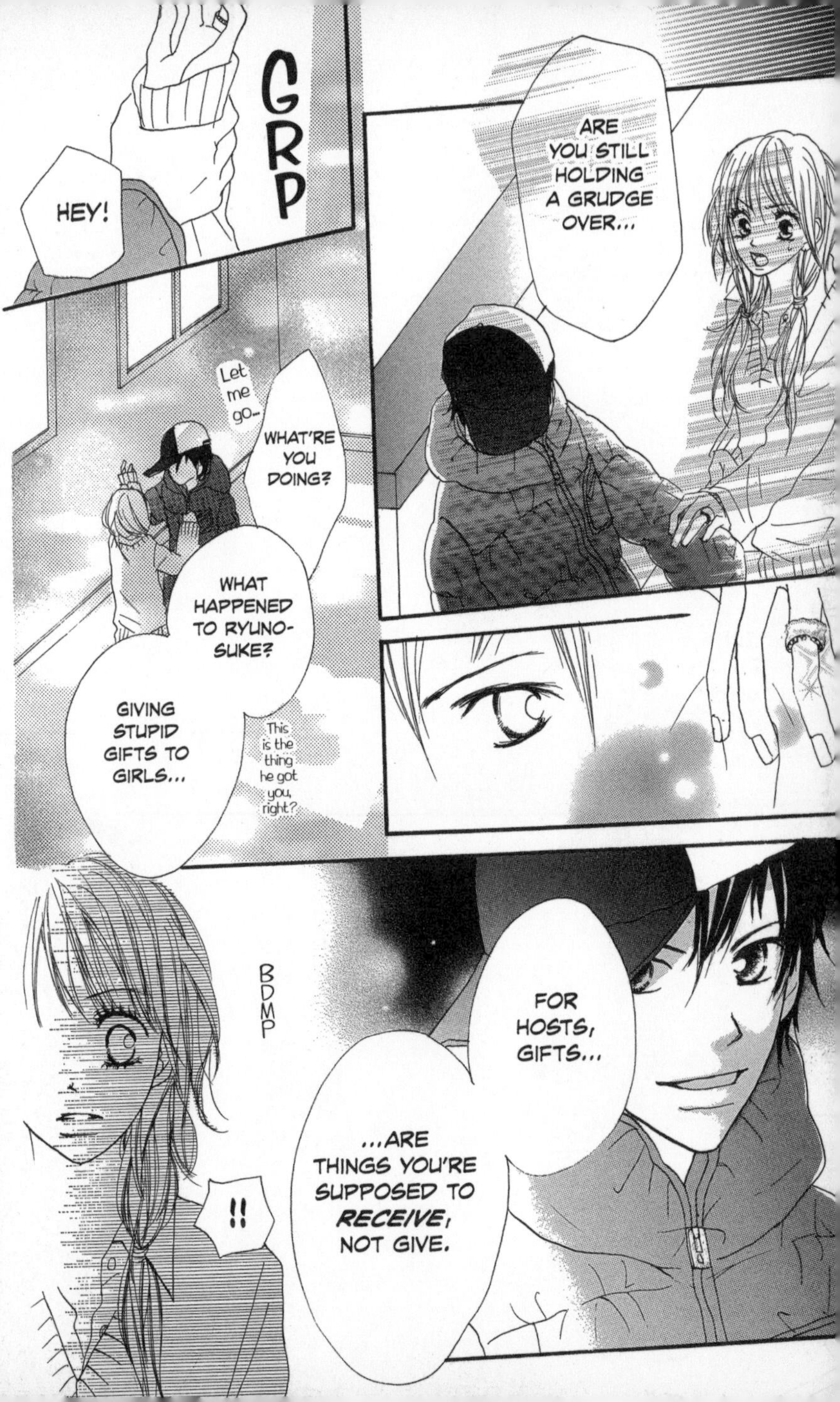
ARE YOU STILL HOLDING A GRUDGE OVER...
GRP
HEY!
WHAT'RE YOU DOING?
Let me go...
WHAT HAPPENED TO RYUNO-SUKE?
This is the thing he got you, right?
GIVING STUPID GIFTS TO GIRLS...
FOR HOSTS, GIFTS...
...ARE THINGS YOU'RE SUPPOSED TO *RECEIVE*, NOT GIVE.
BDMP
!!

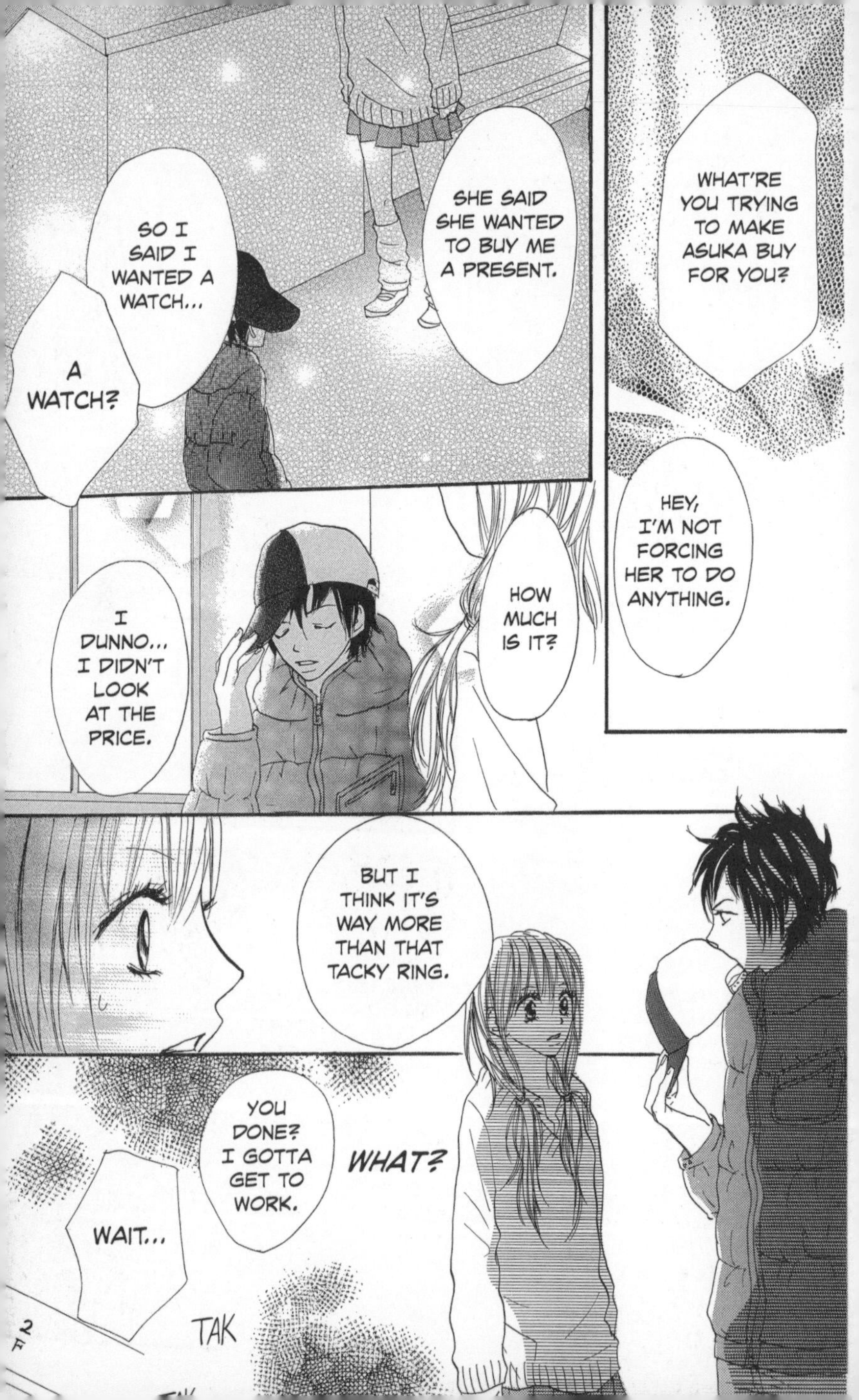
WHAT'RE YOU TRYING TO MAKE ASUKA BUY FOR YOU?
HEY, I'M NOT FORCING HER TO DO ANYTHING.
SHE SAID SHE WANTED TO BUY ME A PRESENT.
SO I SAID I WANTED A WATCH...
A WATCH?
HOW MUCH IS IT?
I DUNNO... I DIDN'T LOOK AT THE PRICE.
BUT I THINK IT'S WAY MORE THAN THAT TACKY RING.
WHAT?
YOU DONE? I GOTTA GET TO WORK.
WAIT...
TAK

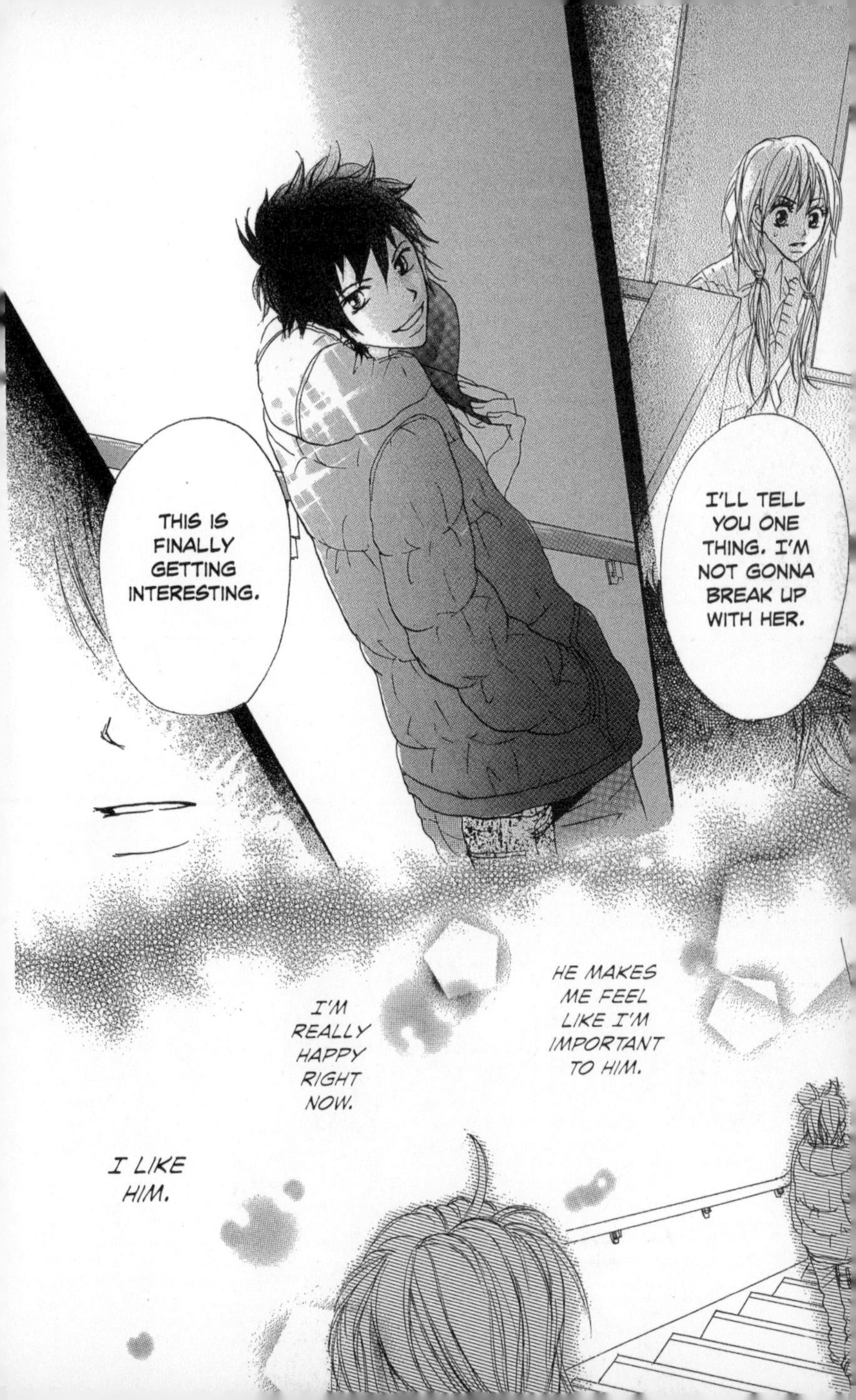
I'LL TELL YOU ONE THING. I'M NOT GONNA BREAK UP WITH HER.
THIS IS FINALLY GETTING INTERESTING.
HE MAKES ME FEEL LIKE I'M IMPORTANT TO HIM.
I'M REALLY HAPPY RIGHT NOW.
I LIKE HIM.

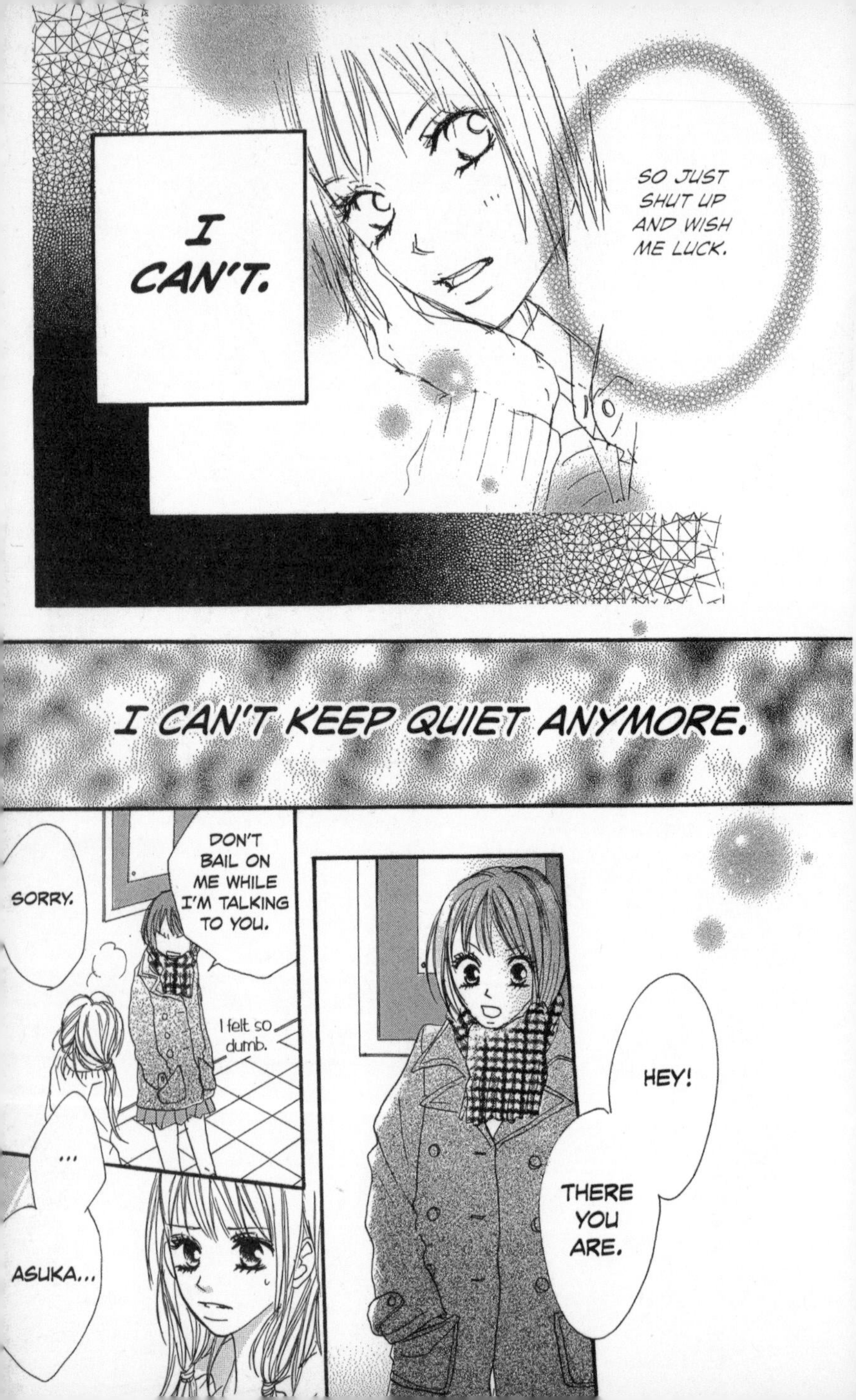
SO JUST SHUT UP AND WISH ME LUCK.
I CAN'T.
I CAN'T KEEP QUIET ANYMORE.
HEY!
THERE YOU ARE.
DON'T BAIL ON ME WHILE I'M TALKING TO YOU.
I felt so dumb.
SORRY.
...
ASUKA...

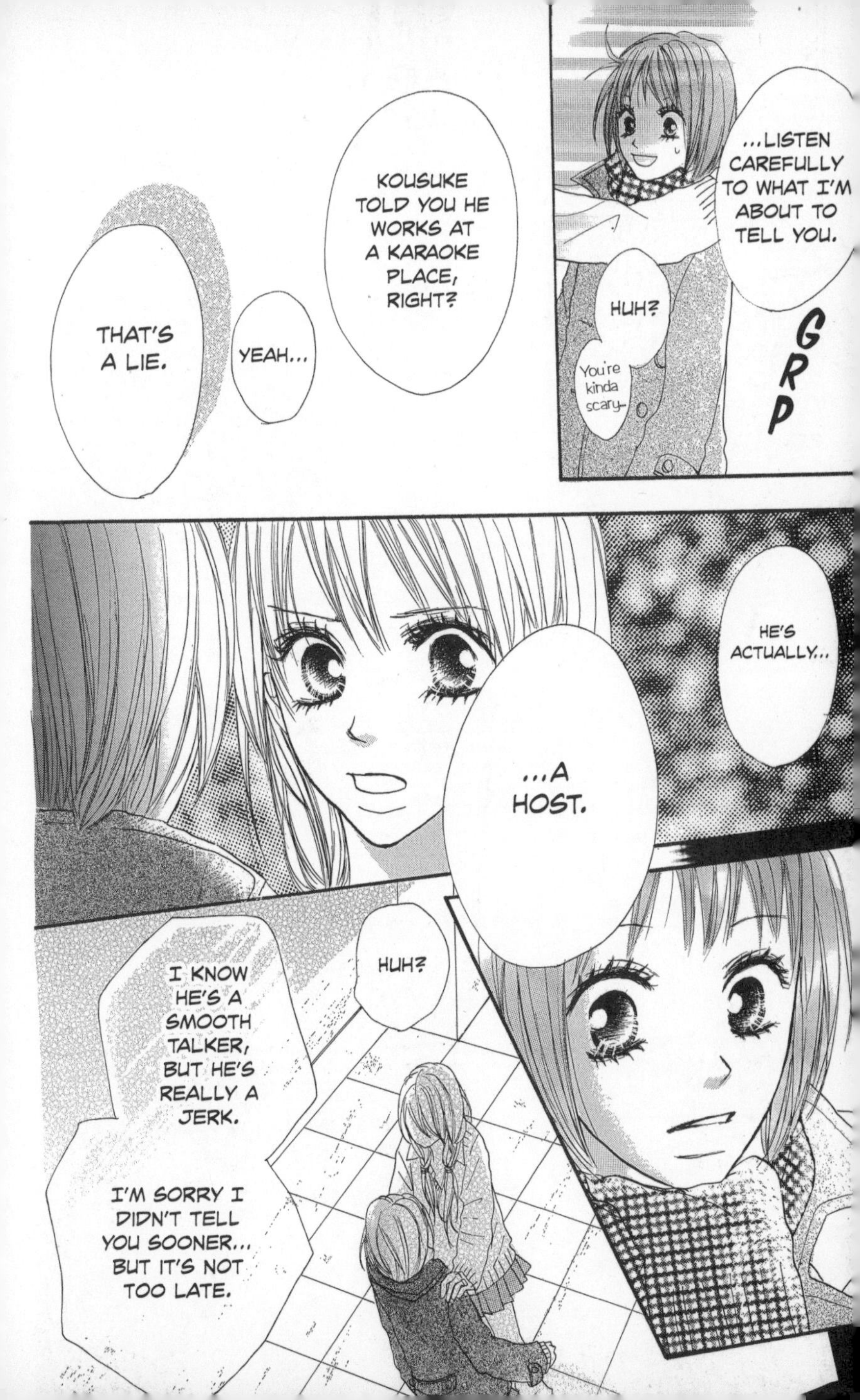
...LISTEN CAREFULLY TO WHAT I'M ABOUT TO TELL YOU.
GRP
HUH?
You're kinda scary...
KOUSUKE TOLD YOU HE WORKS AT A KARAOKE PLACE, RIGHT?
YEAH...
THAT'S A LIE.
HE'S ACTUALLY...
...A HOST.
HUH?
I KNOW HE'S A SMOOTH TALKER, BUT HE'S REALLY A JERK.
I'M SORRY I DIDN'T TELL YOU SOONER... BUT IT'S NOT TOO LATE.

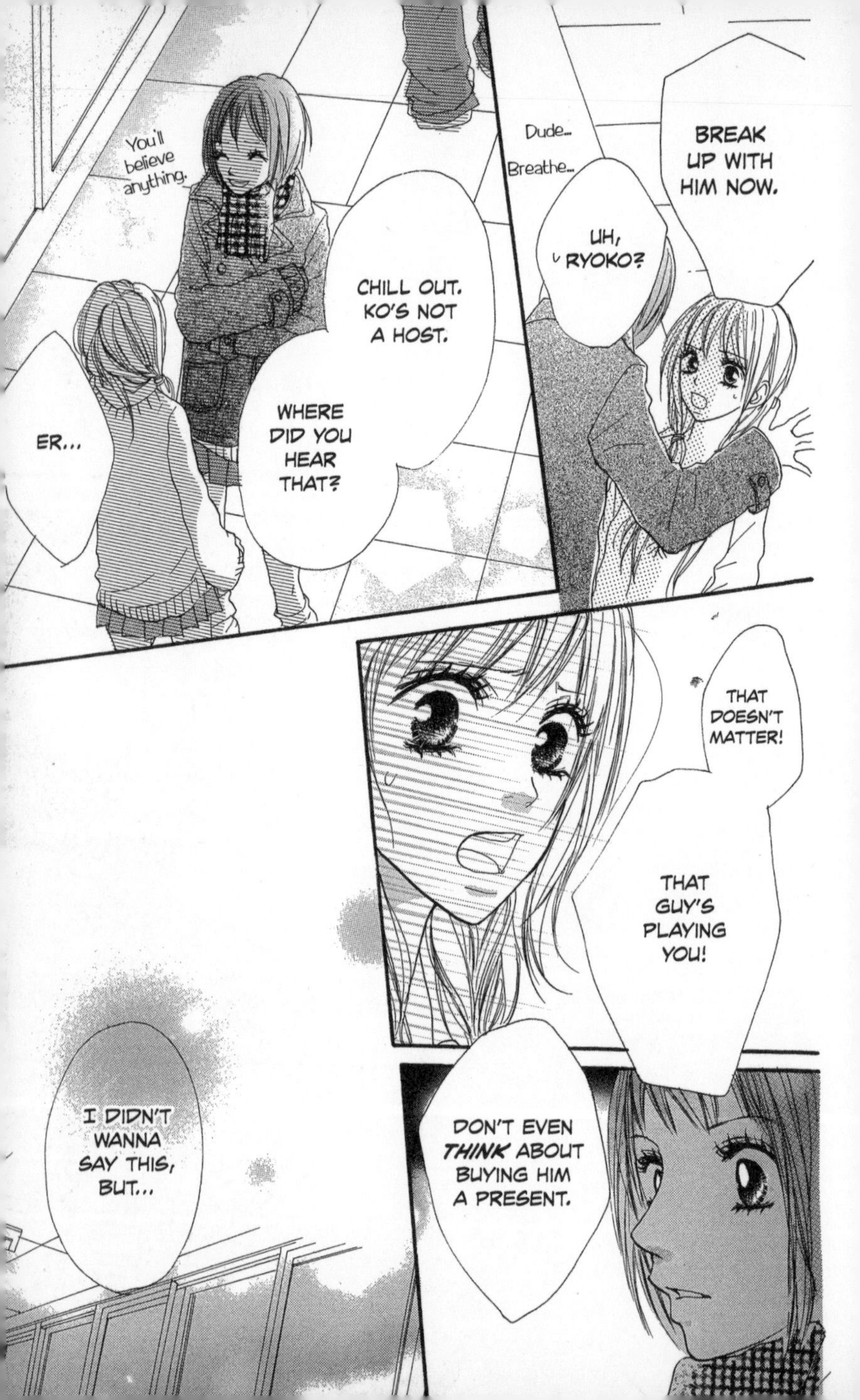
BREAK UP WITH HIM NOW.
Dude... Breathe...
UH, RYOKO?
CHILL OUT. KO'S NOT A HOST.
WHERE DID YOU HEAR THAT?
You'll believe anything.
ER...
THAT DOESN'T MATTER!
THAT GUY'S PLAYING YOU!
DON'T EVEN *THINK* ABOUT BUYING HIM A PRESENT.
I DIDN'T WANNA SAY THIS, BUT...

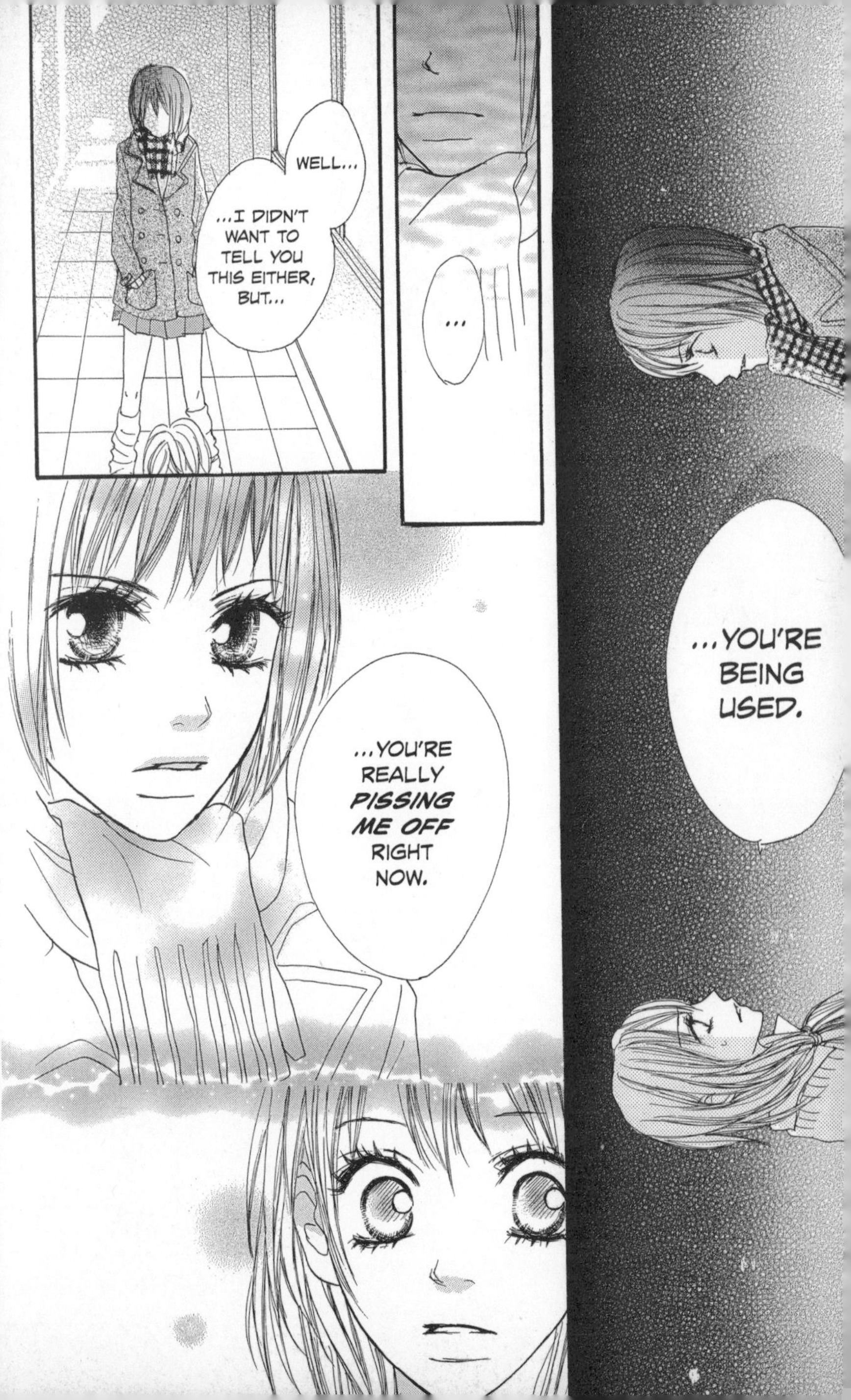
WELL...
...I DIDN'T WANT TO TELL YOU THIS EITHER, BUT...
...YOU'RE BEING USED.
...
...YOU'RE REALLY PISSING ME OFF RIGHT NOW.

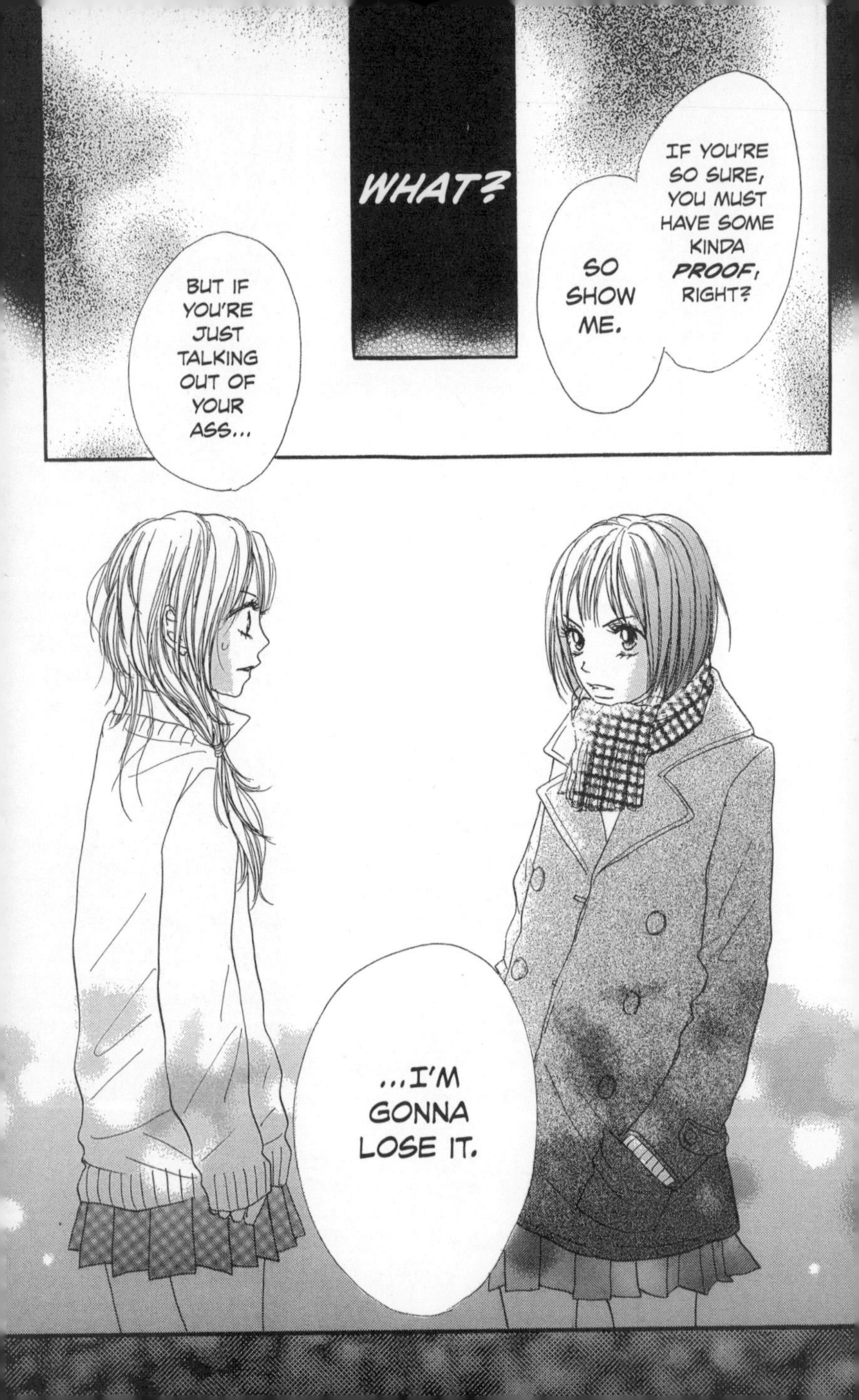
IF YOU'RE SO SURE, YOU MUST HAVE SOME KINDA PROOF, RIGHT?
SO SHOW ME.
WHAT?
BUT IF YOU'RE JUST TALKING OUT OF YOUR ASS...
...I'M GONNA LOSE IT.

Fan Mail Corner Continued ○ ○ ○

"At my school there's a saying that if you write the name of the guy you like on a new eraser and use it up, he'll fall for you. I have 'Ryuno-suke from B.O.D.Y.' ♥ on mine." ♥♥

U.K., Tokushima

‥‥‥ Cute...so cute!! U.K. says her dream is to have Ryunosuke say her name. I'll make that dream come true!! If that's all you want, it's yours!! Though the name on the eraser may be different by now...

○***natsu is so cute...

I drew her to look like the Print Club Photo she sent...

So pointless...

GASP....

Was it okay to reveal her name? It's fine, right? Waaa! I don't want to cause her any trouble, so I'll censor part of it!! ←Dummy.

"They should make a bookstore that sells only books by Ao Mimori!! That'd be the best!!"

O.A., Nagano

"That'd be the best..." That's funny. But they'd never make a profit!! Would they attract any customers? They'd only have ten books on sale...and a massive inventory of unsold copies. I could personally run the store, and at the end of the month I'd draw my comics at the counter....Hey...That sounds kinda fun.

"I'm a 17-year-old male senior in high school. I wasn't sure if it was okay for a teenage guy to write to you, but here's a letter anyway."

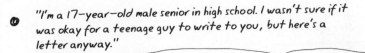

It's okay!! It's okay to write me letters!! He also wrote, "You seem pretty busy so I'll end it here." It's okay to write more!! I rarely get letters from boys, so I was surprised and happy. Send me another one!

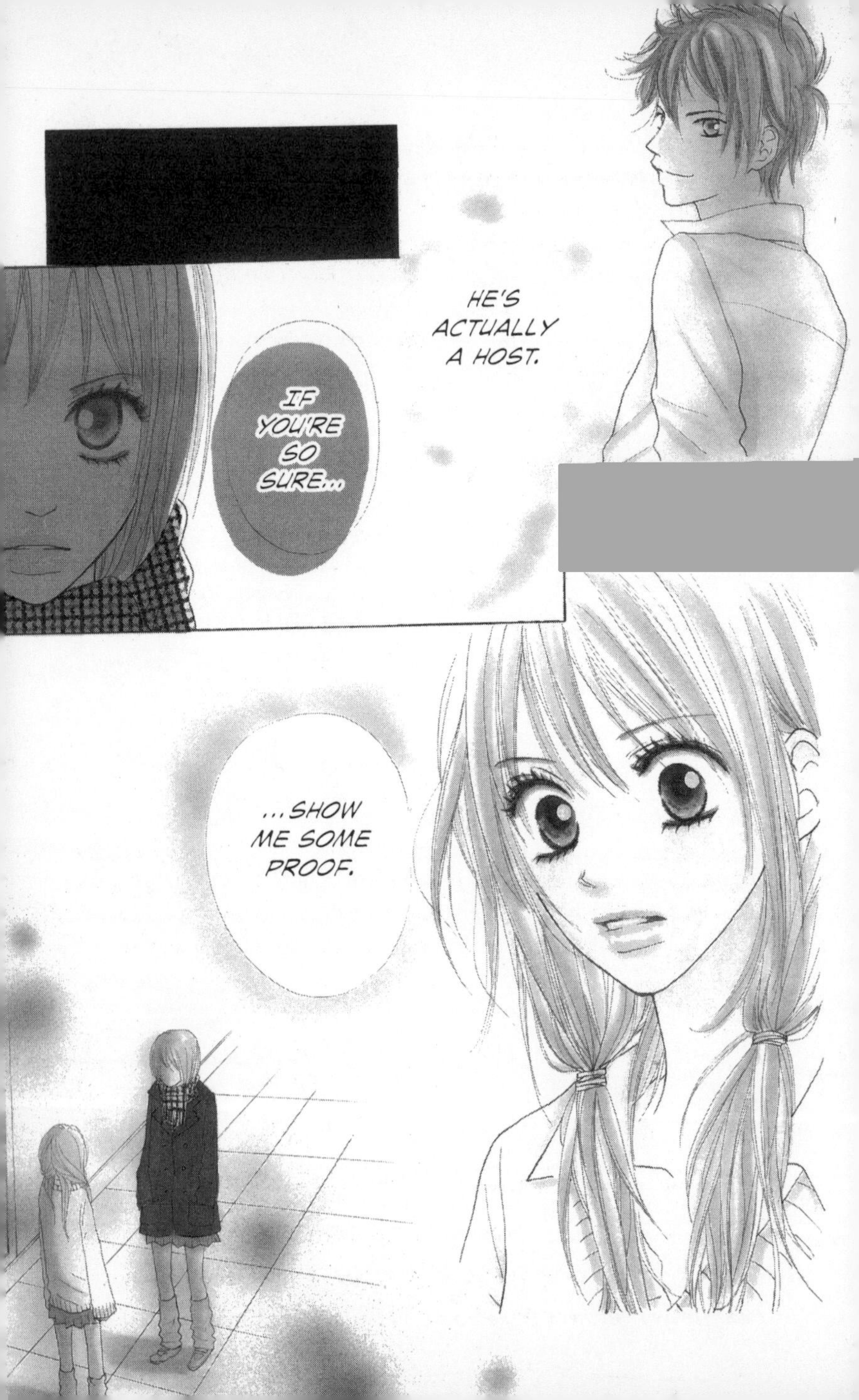
[redacted]
HE'S ACTUALLY A HOST.
IF YOU'RE SO SURE...
...SHOW ME SOME PROOF.

Something I Realized Recently

All the letters I get smell good.

Why? Is everybody putting perfume on their letters? You're all so mature. I think I started wearing perfume in college...I started wearing makeup pretty late too. I haven't worn makeup since I've become a manga artist...

Most people say they found out about B.O.D.Y. from their friends.

To all the members of The Ao Mimori Popularization Committee...Thanks for your hard work!! From hand to hand...delivered with love. Let's join in friendship...

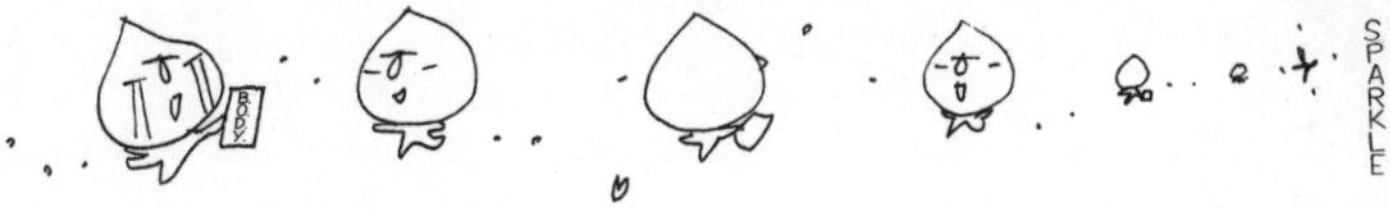
B.O.D.Y.
SPARKLE

I know I say this all the time, but I really appreciate your letters.

I always respond out loud to myself while I read them. I wish I could reply to everyone. I'll try to one of these days, so hang in there...but don't hold your breath... Hee Hee

Address

VIZ Media, LLC
P.O. BOX 77010
San Francisco, CA 94107

Ao Mimori

I'll be waiting!

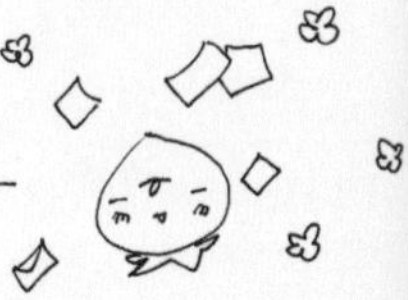

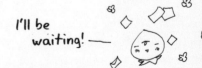

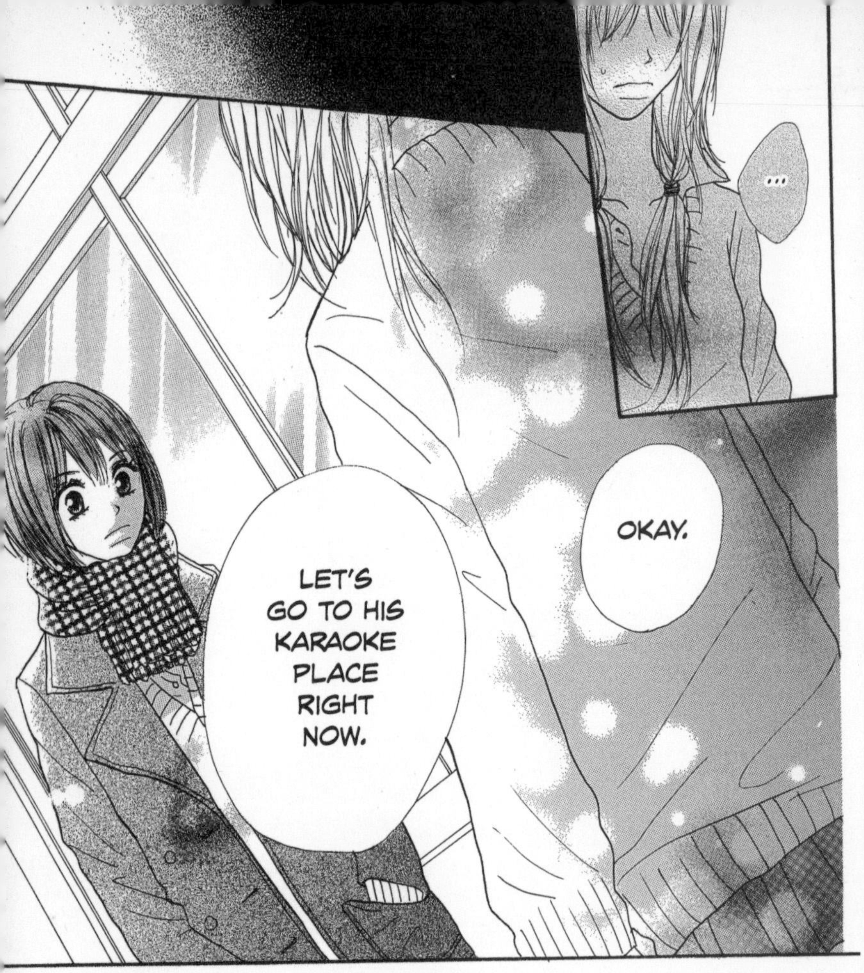
...
OKAY.
LET'S GO TO HIS KARAOKE PLACE RIGHT NOW.

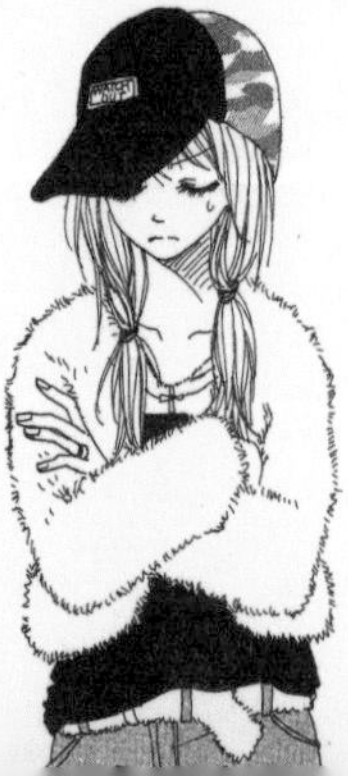

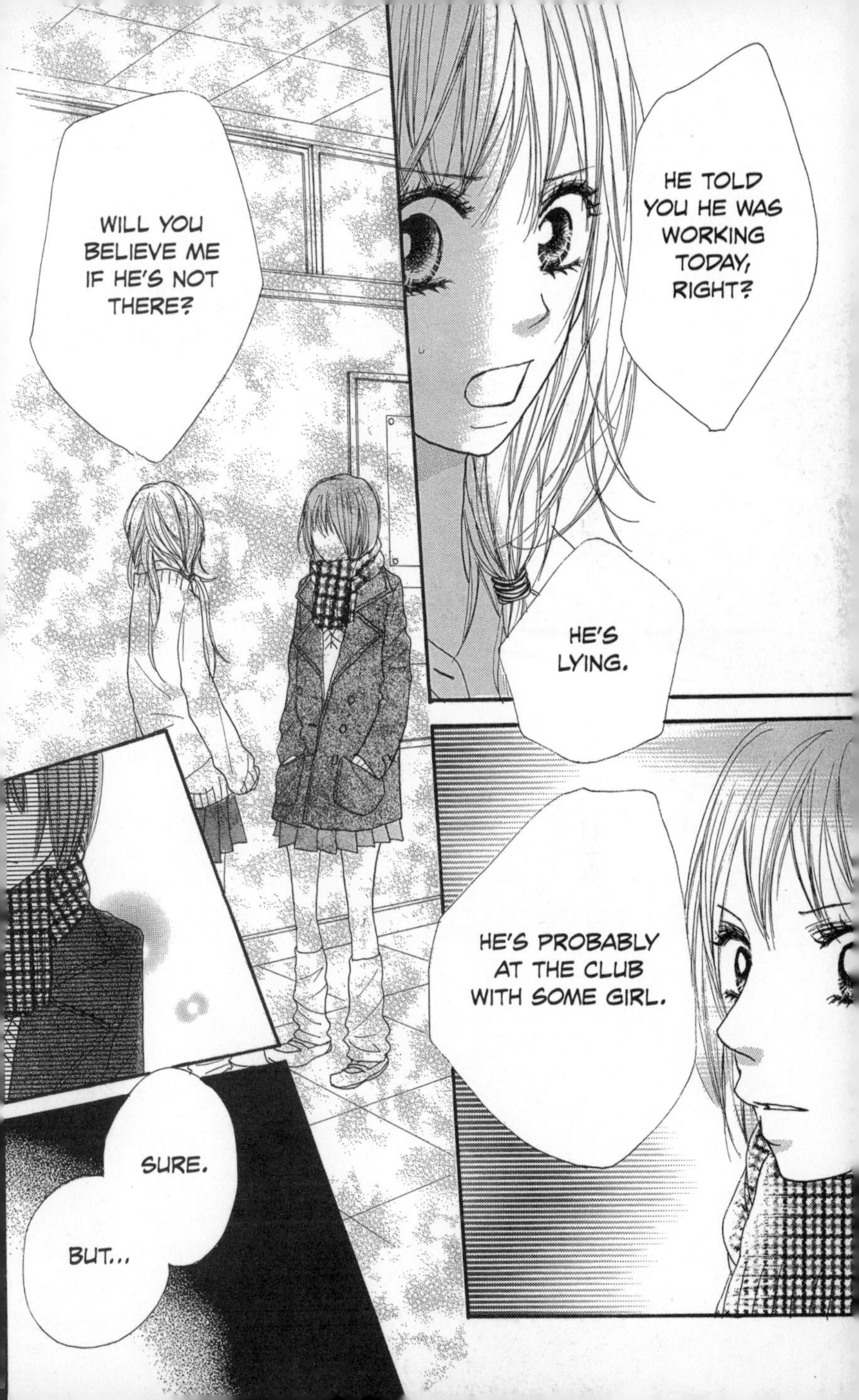
HE TOLD YOU HE WAS WORKING TODAY, RIGHT?
HE'S LYING.
HE'S PROBABLY AT THE CLUB WITH SOME GIRL.
WILL YOU BELIEVE ME IF HE'S NOT THERE?
SURE.
BUT...

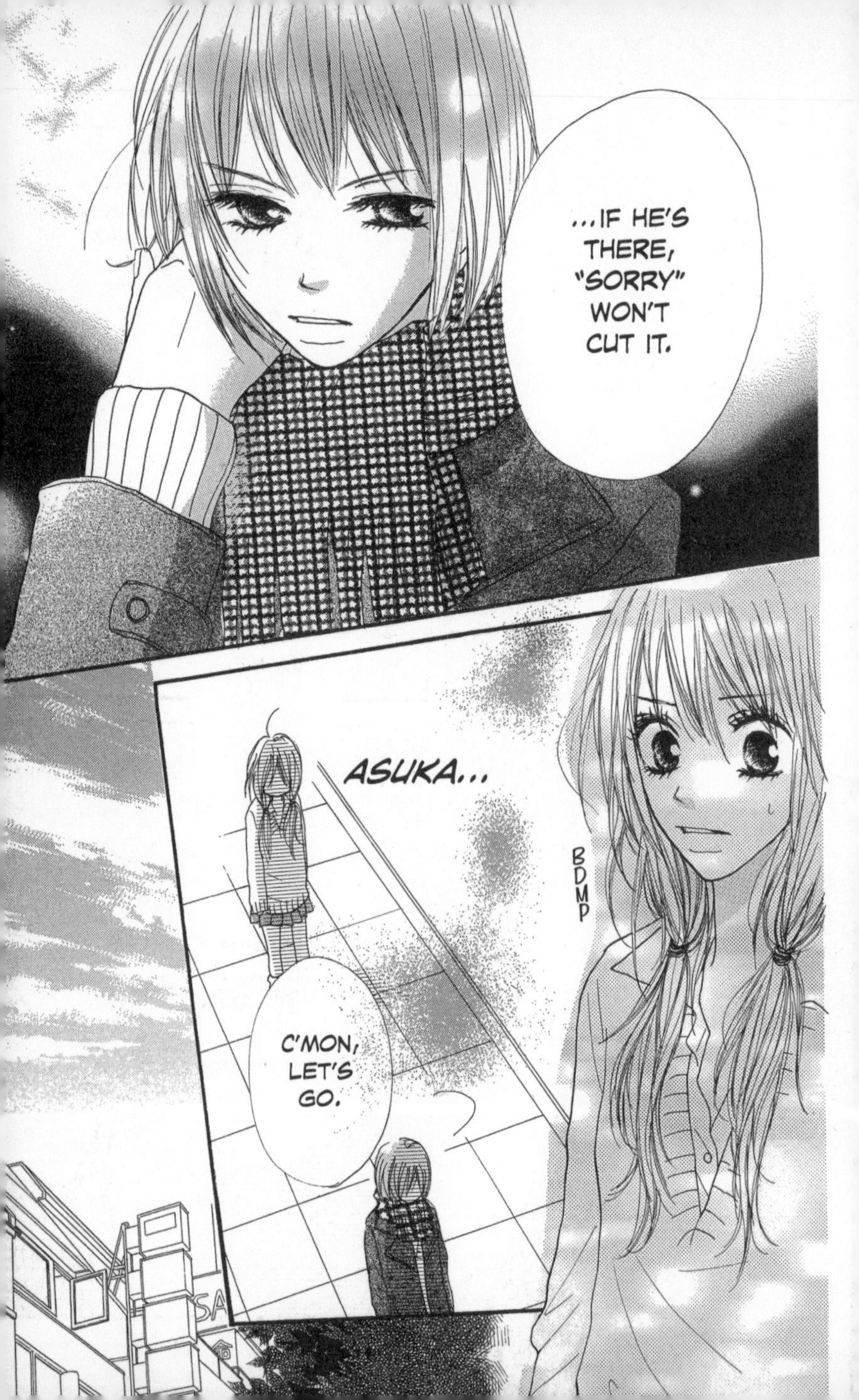
...IF HE'S THERE, "SORRY" WON'T CUT IT.
BDMP
ASUKA...
C'MON, LET'S GO.

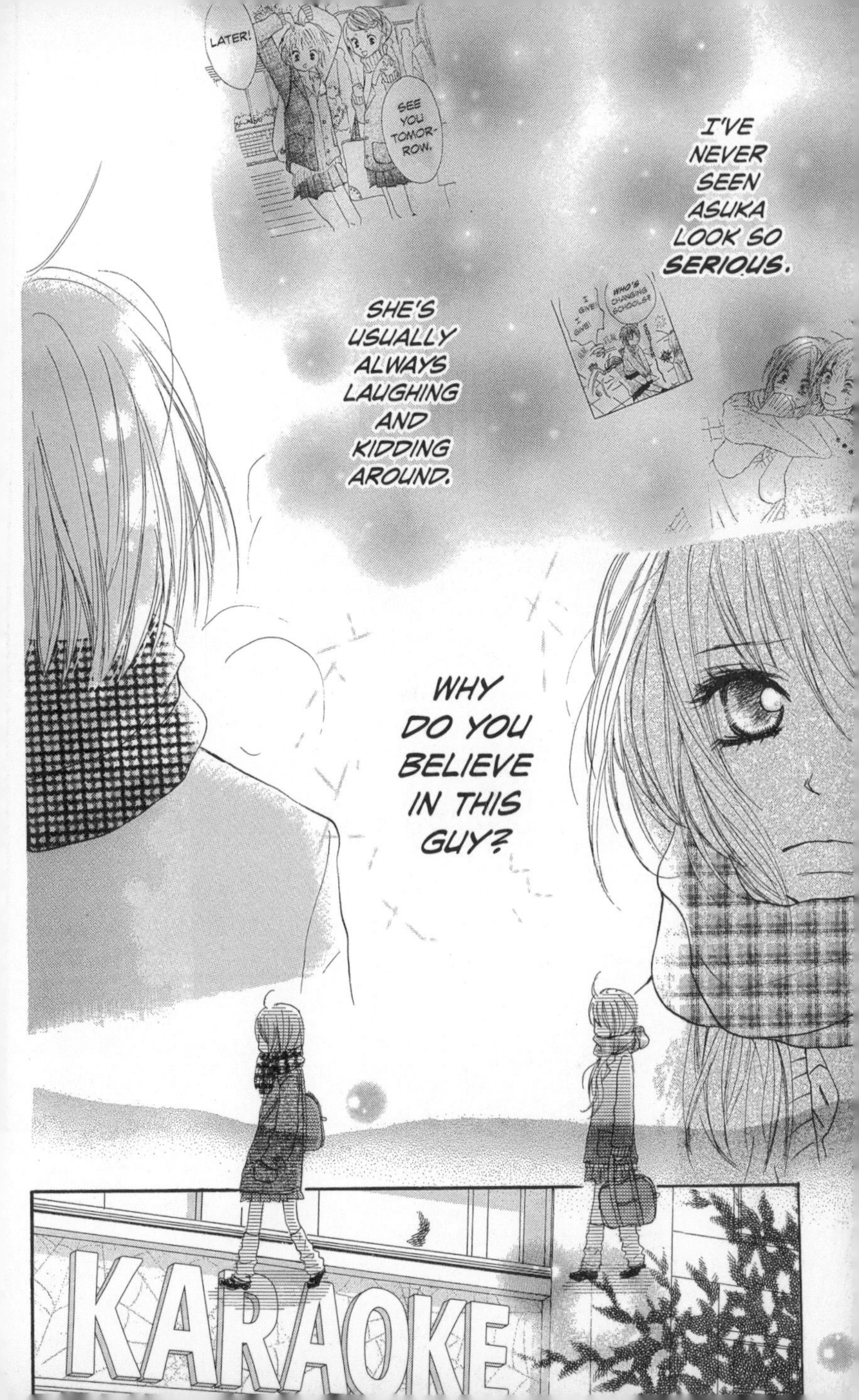
I'VE NEVER SEEN ASUKA LOOK SO SERIOUS.
LATER!
SEE YOU TOMORROW.
WHO'S CHANGING SCHOOLS?
I GIVE! I GIVE!
SHE'S USUALLY ALWAYS LAUGHING AND KIDDING AROUND.
WHY DO YOU BELIEVE IN THIS GUY?
KARAOKE

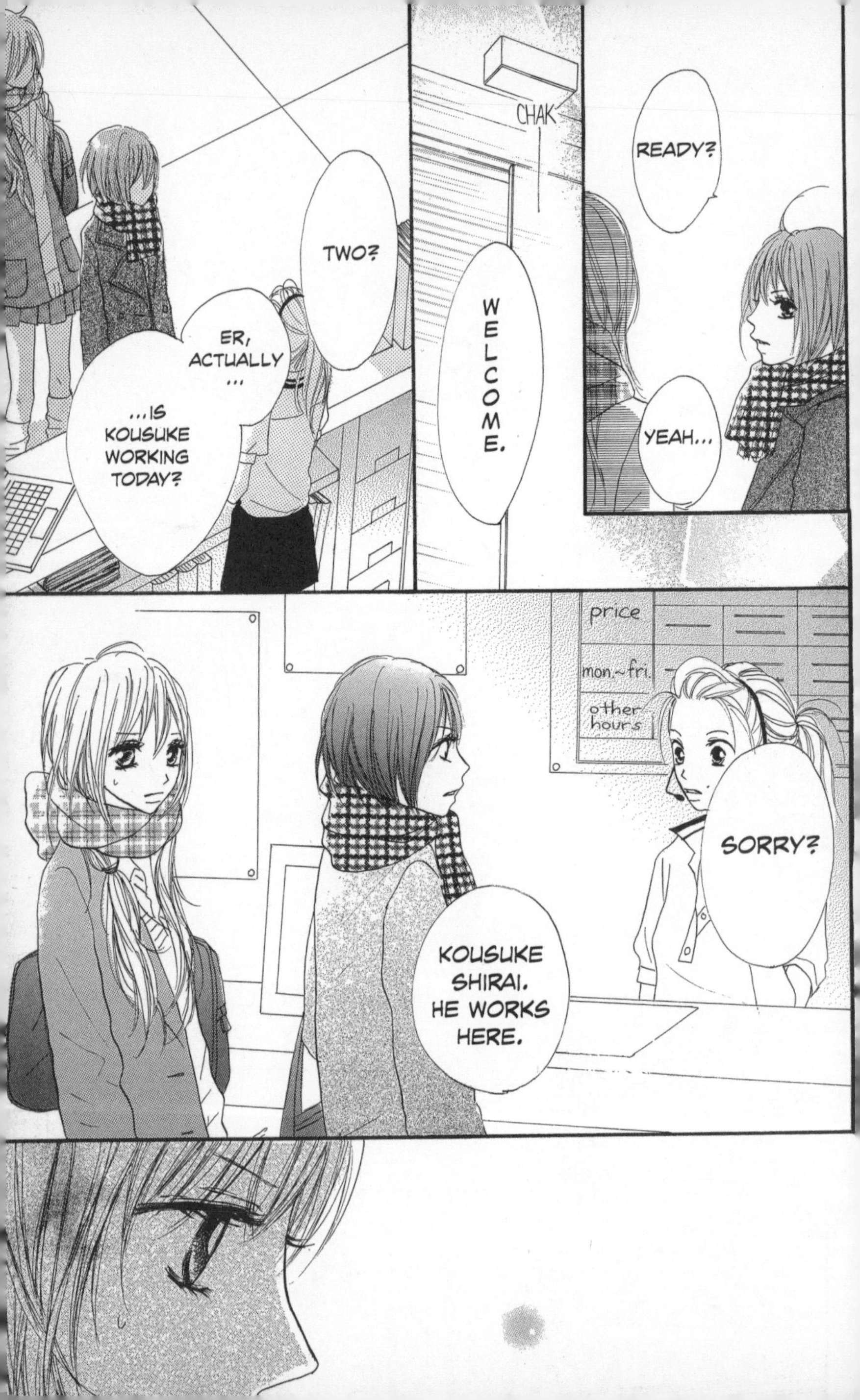
READY?
YEAH...
CHAK
WELCOME.
TWO?
ER, ACTUALLY...
...IS KOUSUKE WORKING TODAY?
price
mon.~fri.
other hours
SORRY?
KOUSUKE SHIRAI. HE WORKS HERE.

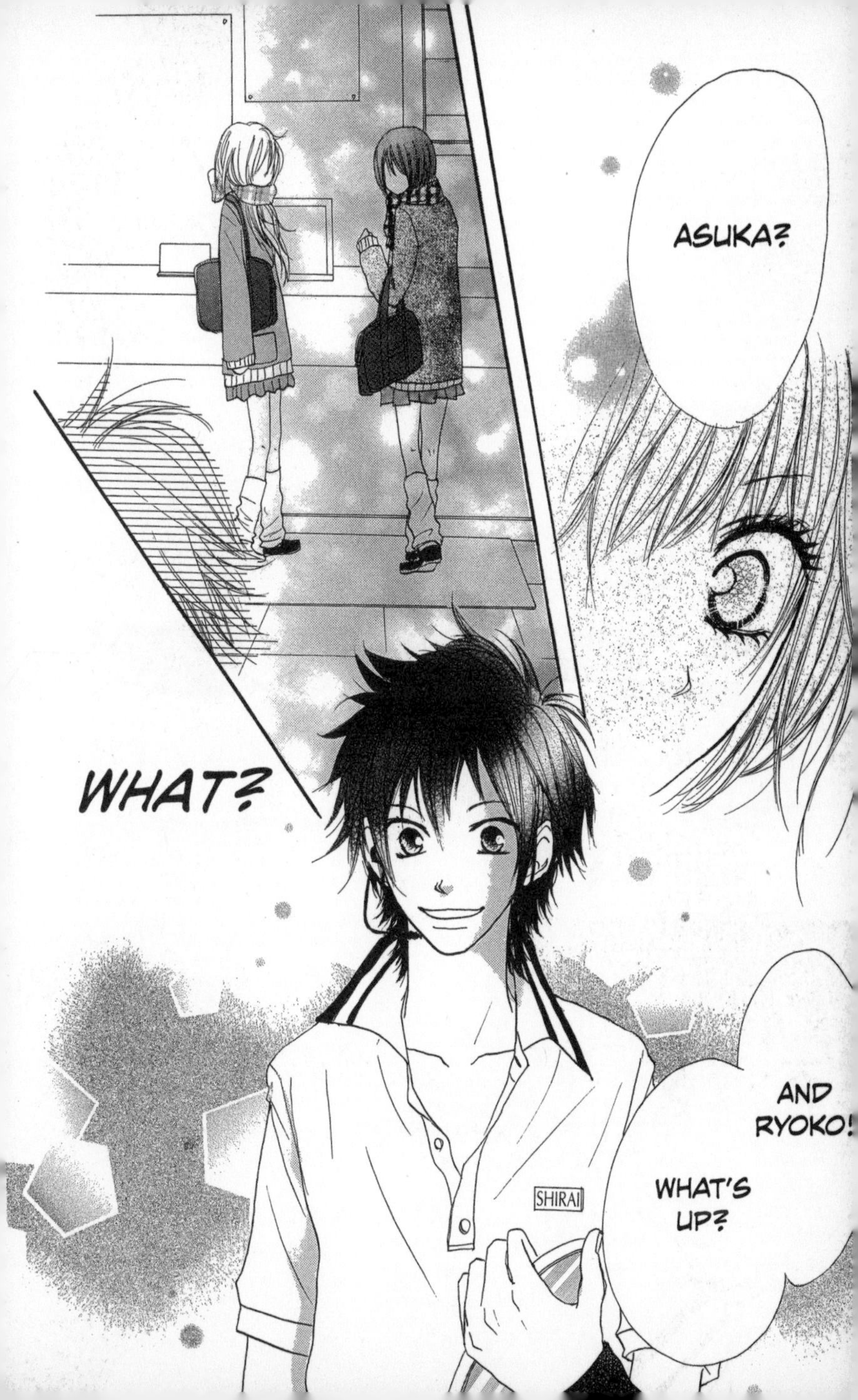
ASUKA?
WHAT?
SHIRAI
AND RYOKO!
WHAT'S UP?

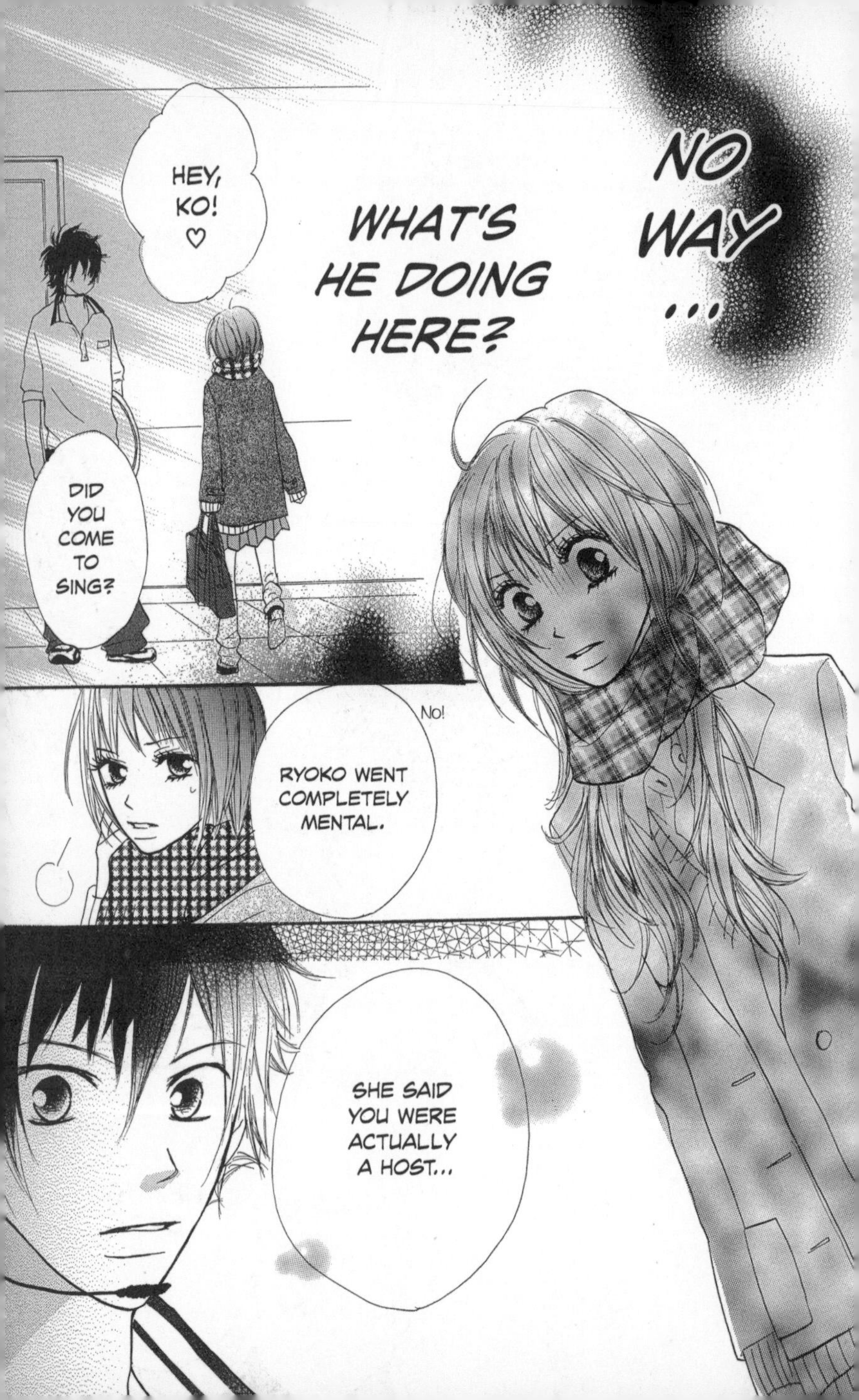
NO WAY...
WHAT'S HE DOING HERE?
HEY, KO! ♡
DID YOU COME TO SING?
No!
RYOKO WENT COMPLETELY MENTAL.
SHE SAID YOU WERE ACTUALLY A HOST...

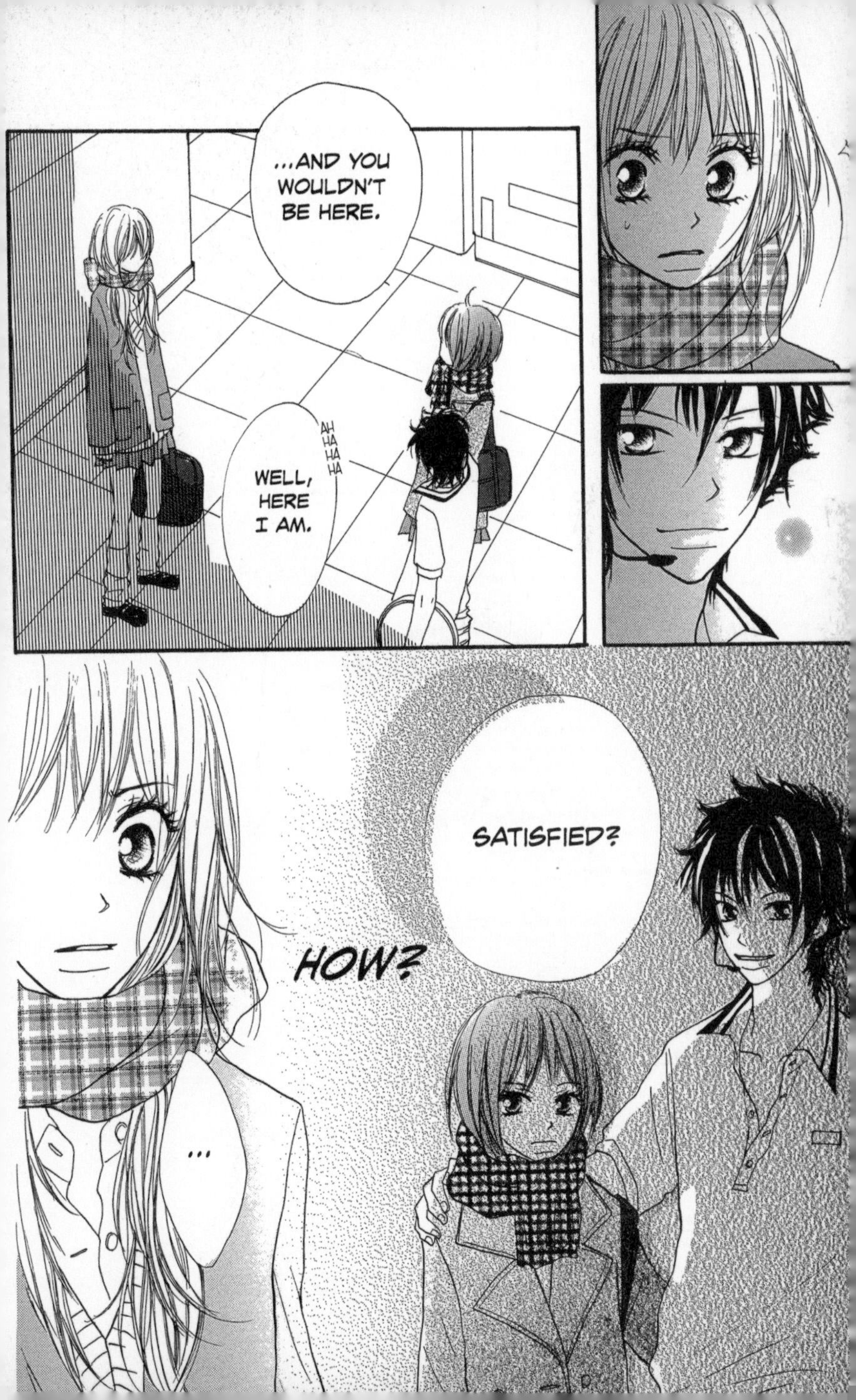
...AND YOU WOULDN'T BE HERE.
AH HA HA HA
WELL, HERE I AM.
SATISFIED?
HOW?
...

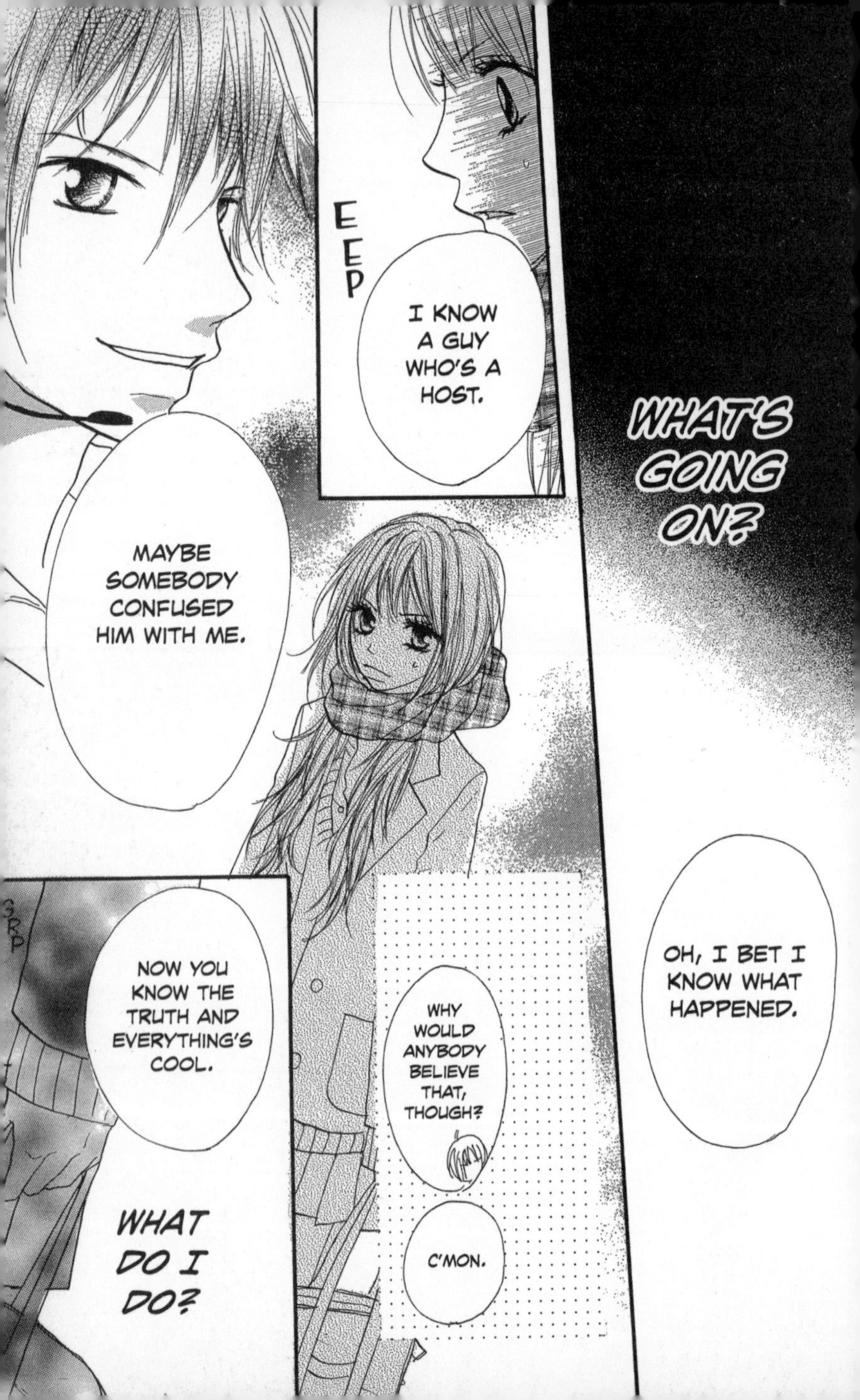
WHAT'S GOING ON?
OH, I BET I KNOW WHAT HAPPENED.
EEP
I KNOW A GUY WHO'S A HOST.
MAYBE SOMEBODY CONFUSED HIM WITH ME.
WHY WOULD ANYBODY BELIEVE THAT, THOUGH?
C'MON.
NOW YOU KNOW THE TRUTH AND EVERYTHING'S COOL.
GRP
WHAT DO I DO?

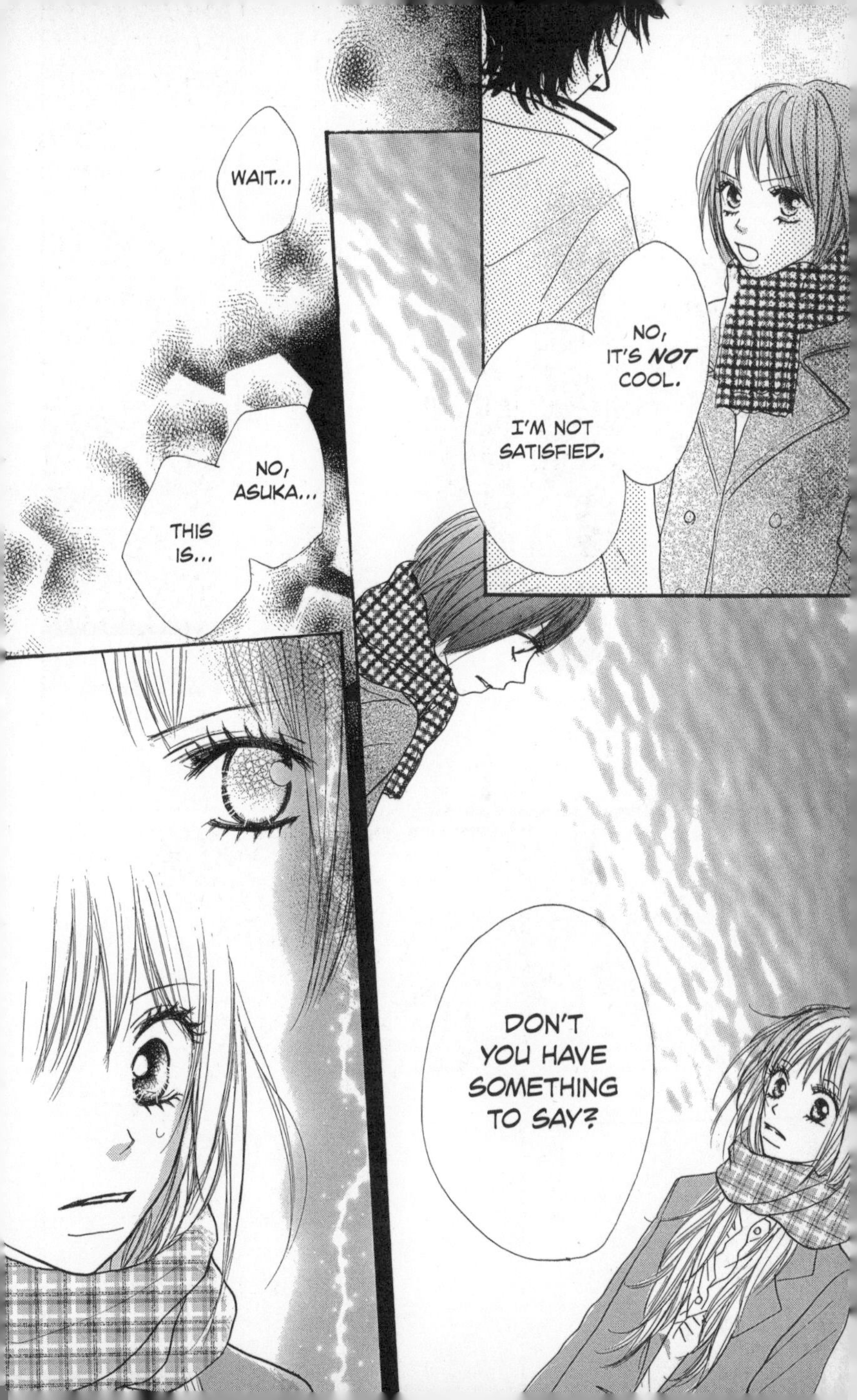
NO, IT'S NOT COOL.
I'M NOT SATISFIED.
WAIT...
NO, ASUKA...
THIS IS...
DON'T YOU HAVE SOMETHING TO SAY?

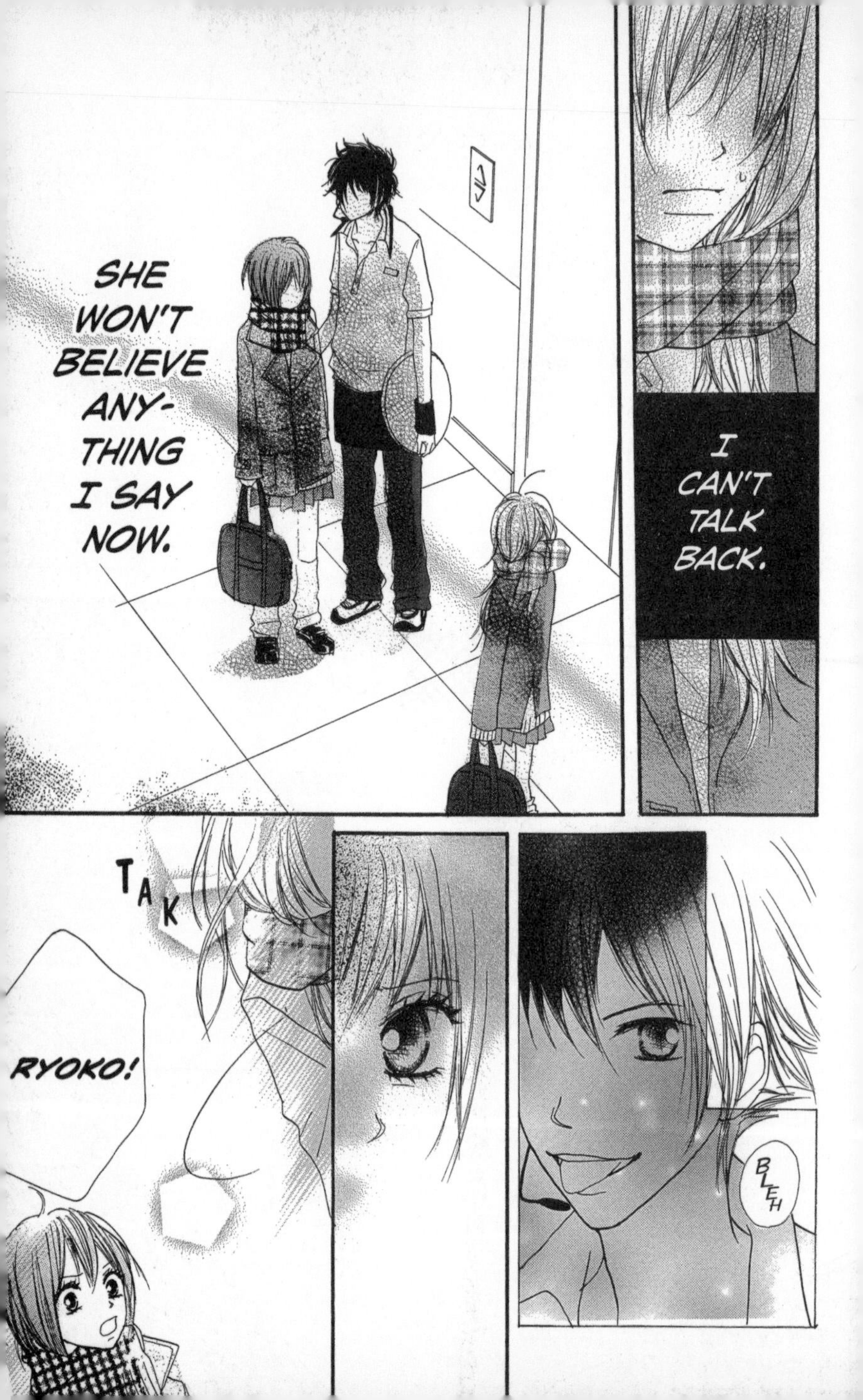
I CAN'T TALK BACK.
SHE WON'T BELIEVE ANYTHING I SAY NOW.
BLEH
TAK
RYOKO!

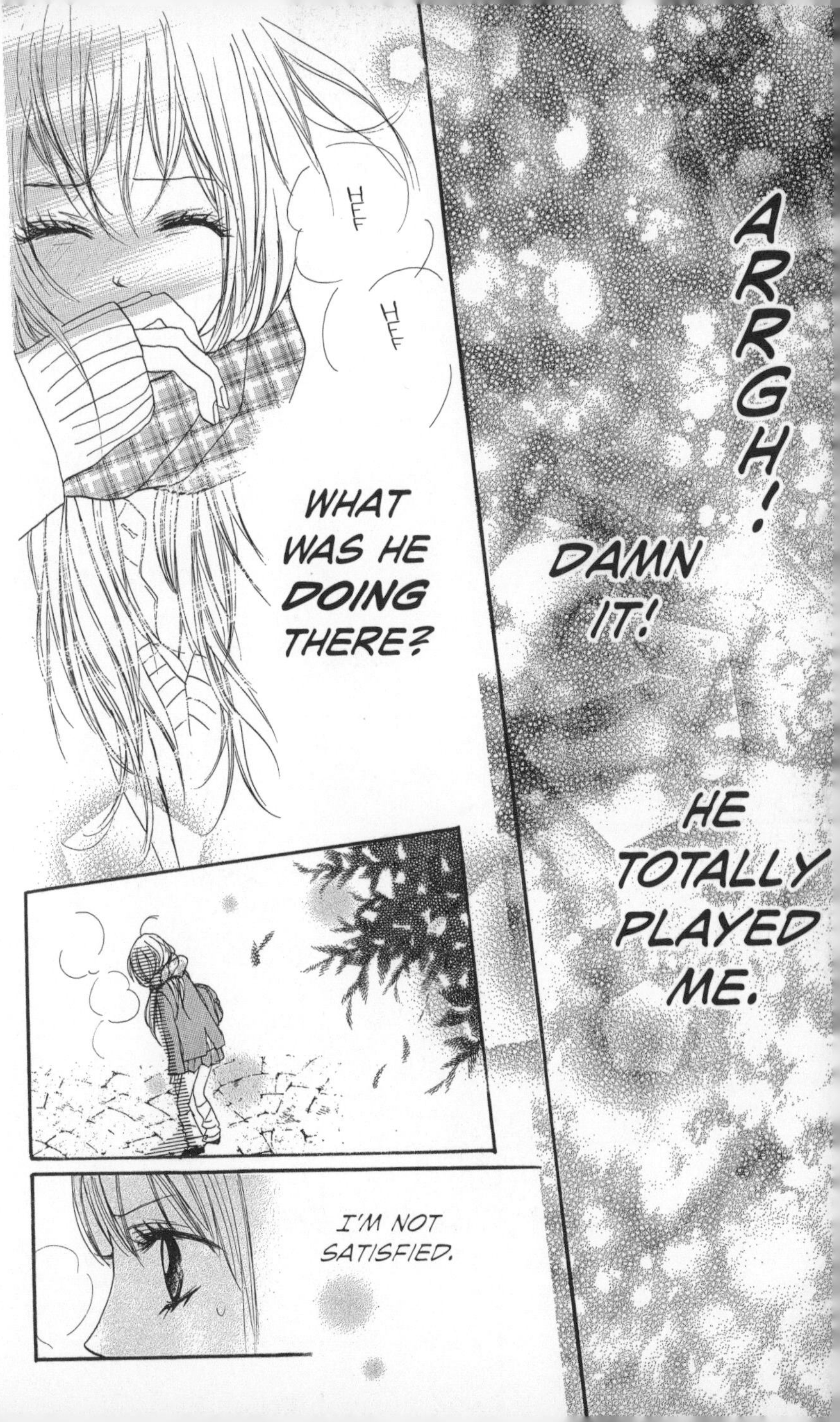
ARRGH!
DAMN IT!
HE TOTALLY PLAYED ME.
HEF
HEF
WHAT WAS HE DOING THERE?
I'M NOT SATISFIED.

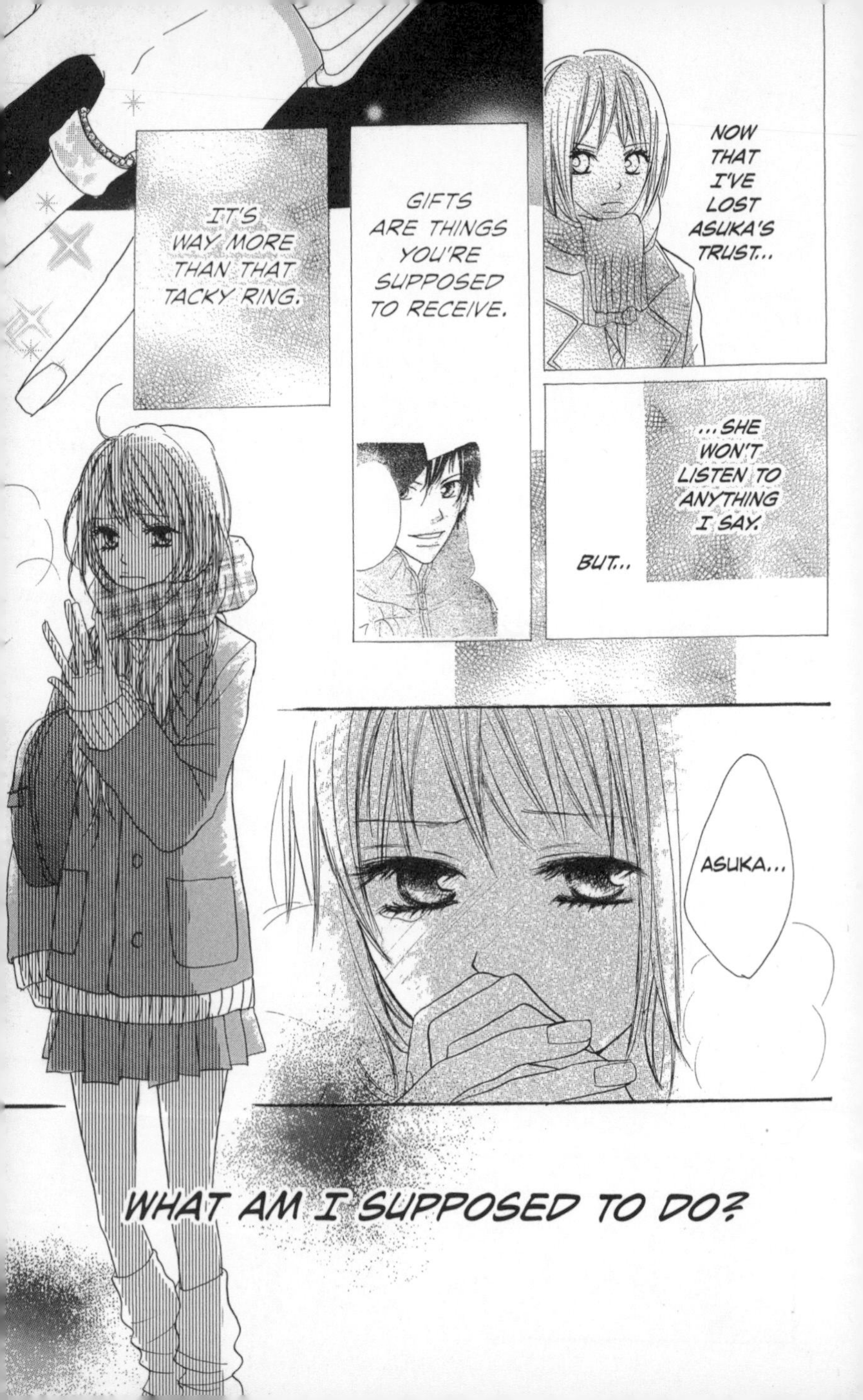
NOW THAT I'VE LOST ASUKA'S TRUST...
...SHE WON'T LISTEN TO ANYTHING I SAY.
BUT...
GIFTS ARE THINGS YOU'RE SUPPOSED TO RECEIVE.
IT'S WAY MORE THAN THAT TACKY RING.
ASUKA...
WHAT AM I SUPPOSED TO DO?

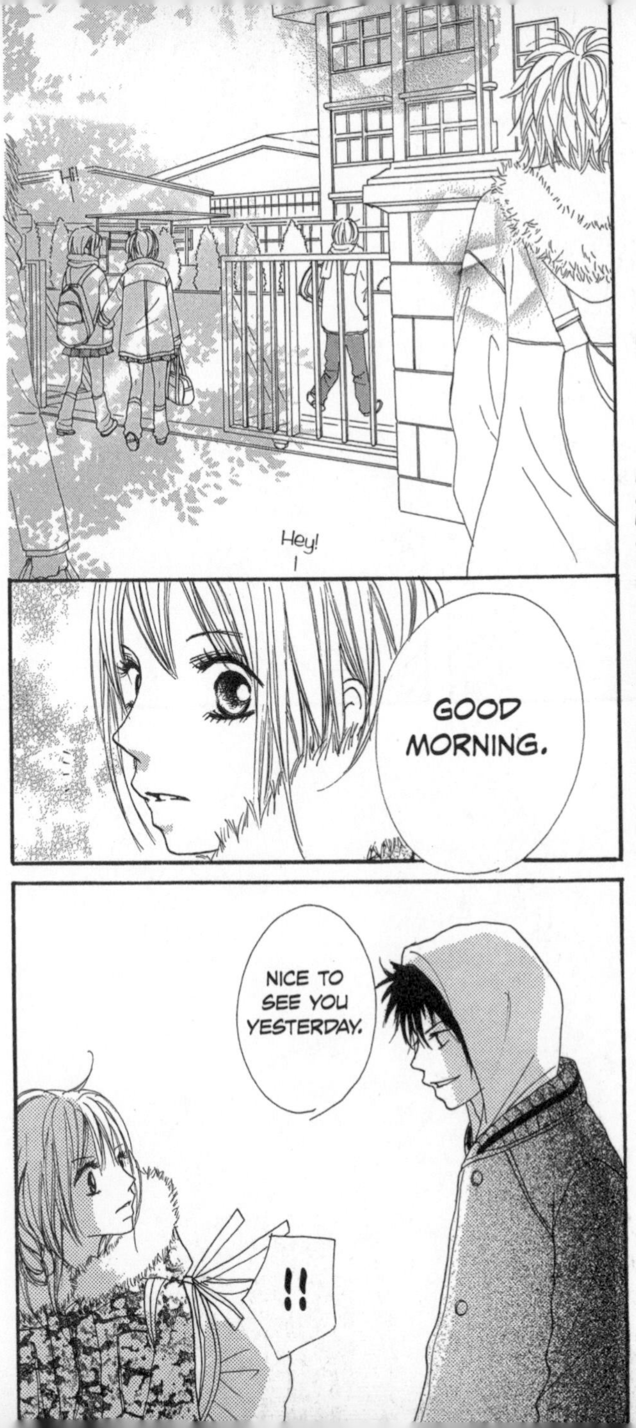
Hey!
GOOD MORNING.
NICE TO SEE YOU YESTERDAY.
!!

④ Four!

—I'd like to go see the Nazca Lines someday. I think it'd move me to tears. Even the parade at Disneyland makes me cry.

Meanwhile, we're already nearing the end. Kousuke makes his first appearance in this volume. Those of you who don't like him, please be patient...

My favorite albums right now are 100s's OZ and Spitz's *Souvenir*. I love them both about the same. I liked Asian Kung-Fu Generation for a while, but these days I basically only listen to those two albums. The other thing I'm into is putting serum in my hair...stuff like that. Man, I'm sleepy.

Well, see you next time.

Ten-hut!

Bow!

Whew...

The End

青

Ao

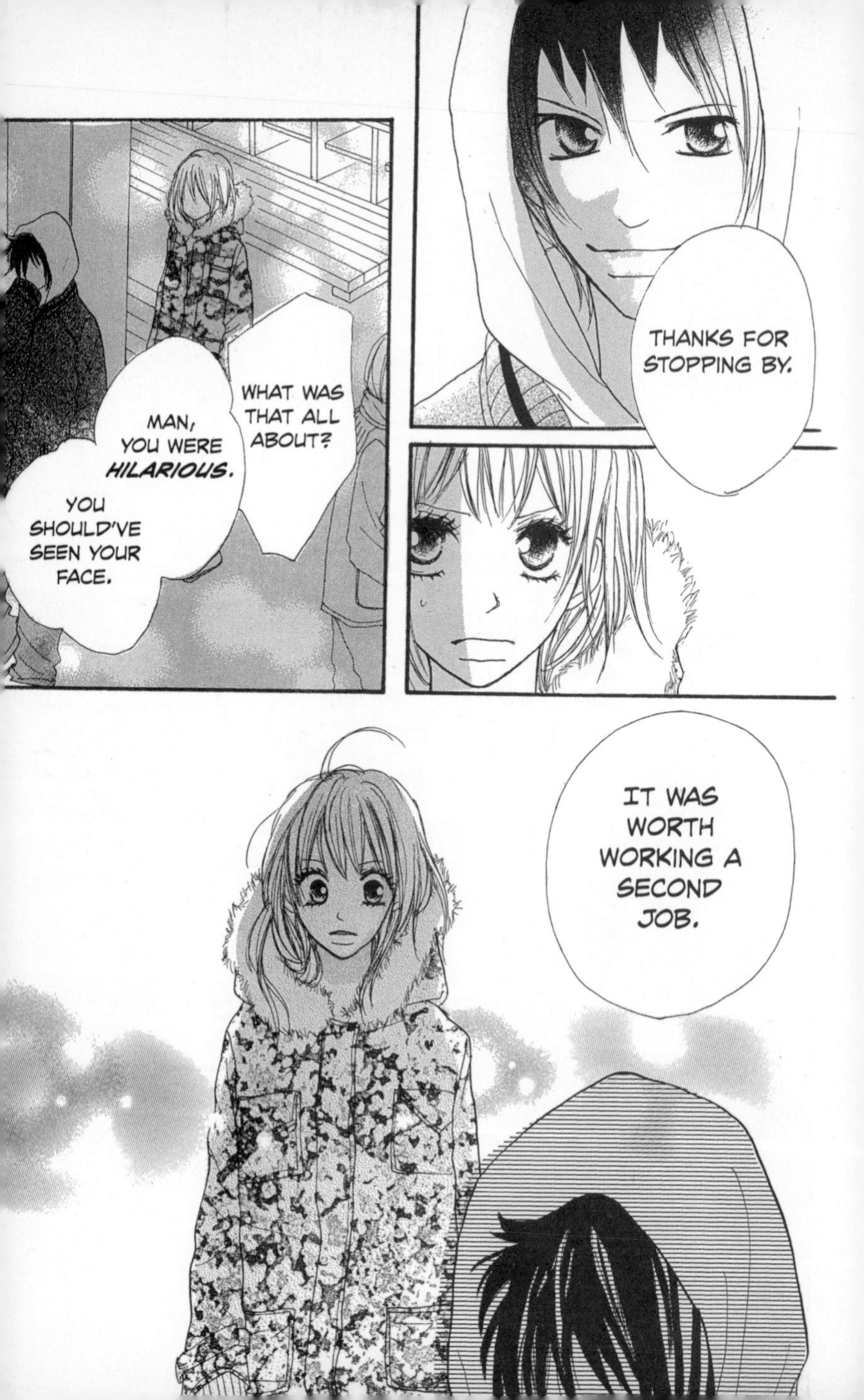
THANKS FOR STOPPING BY.
WHAT WAS THAT ALL ABOUT?
MAN, YOU WERE ***HILARIOUS***. YOU SHOULD'VE SEEN YOUR FACE.
IT WAS WORTH WORKING A SECOND JOB.

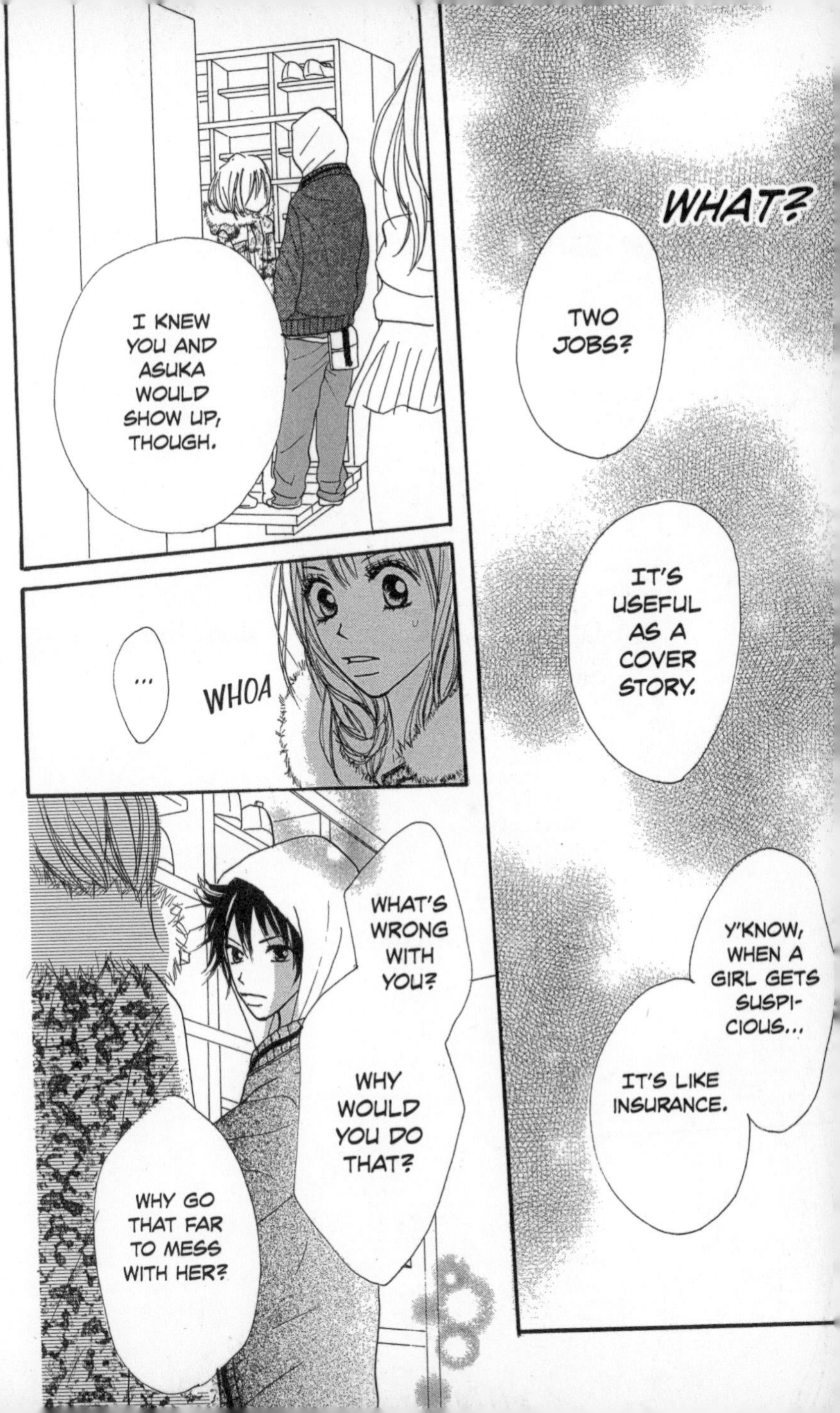
WHAT?
TWO JOBS?
IT'S USEFUL AS A COVER STORY.
Y'KNOW, WHEN A GIRL GETS SUSPI-CIOUS...
IT'S LIKE INSURANCE.
I KNEW YOU AND ASUKA WOULD SHOW UP, THOUGH.
...
WHOA
WHAT'S WRONG WITH YOU?
WHY WOULD YOU DO THAT?
WHY GO THAT FAR TO MESS WITH HER?

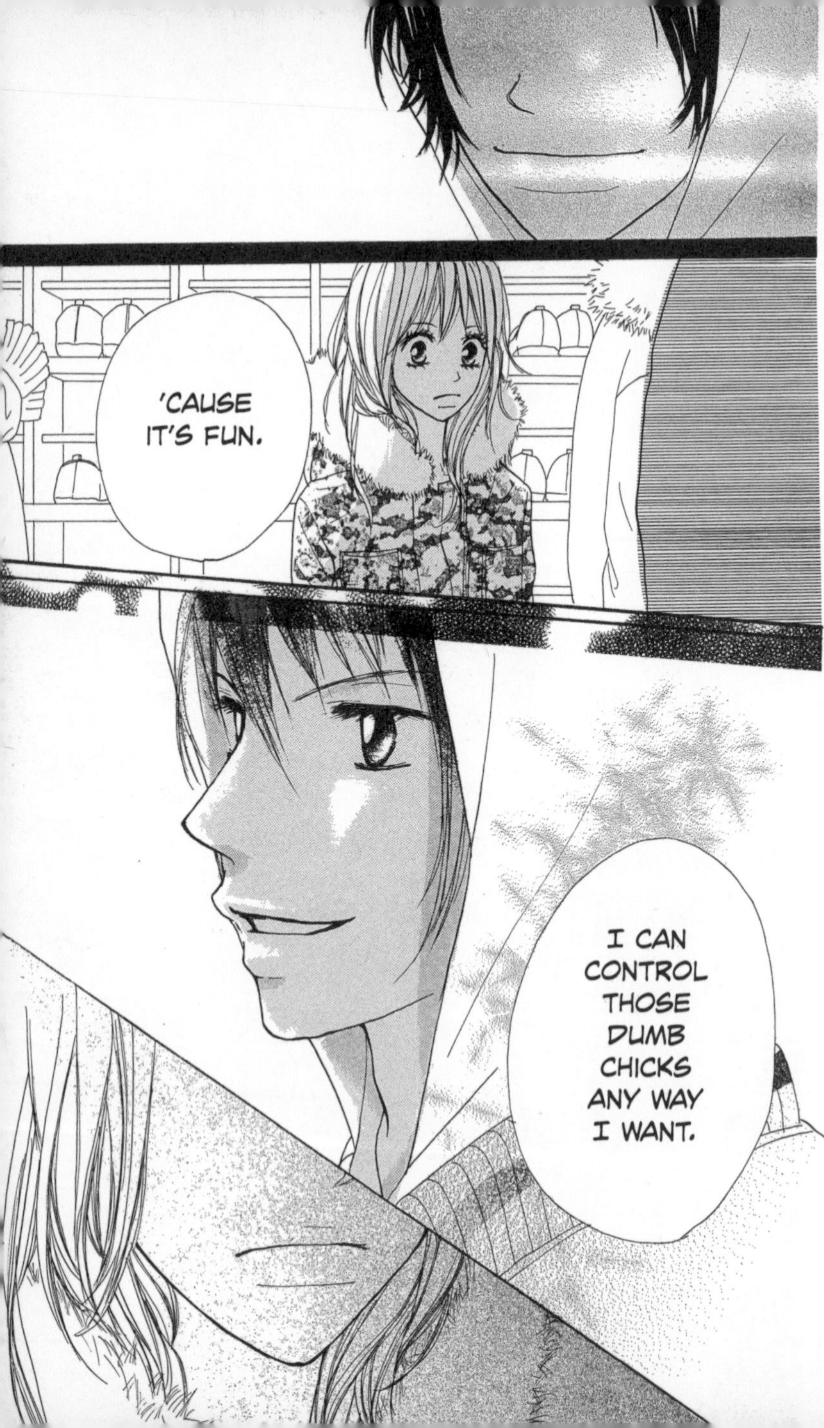
'CAUSE IT'S FUN.
I CAN CONTROL THOSE DUMB CHICKS ANY WAY I WANT.

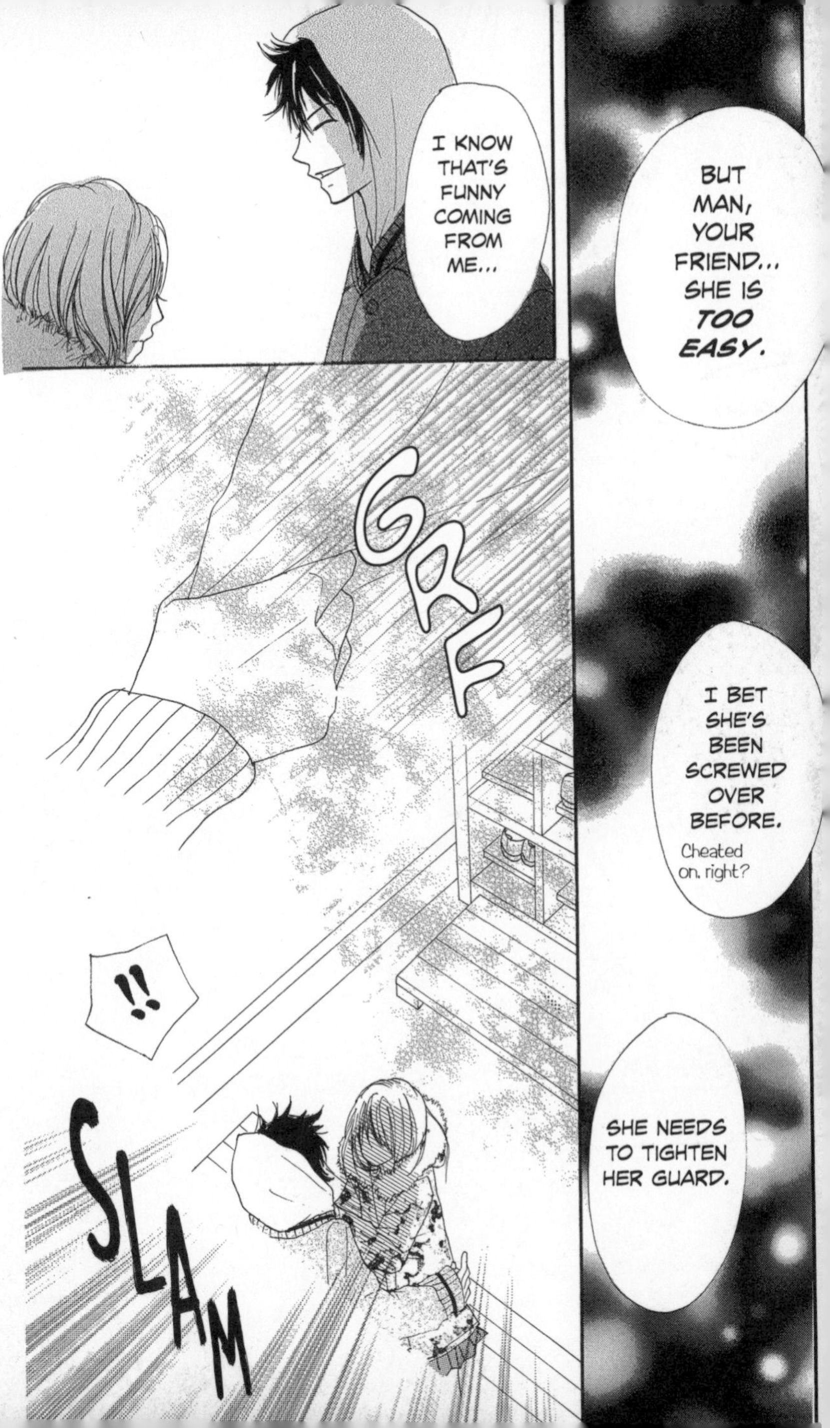
BUT MAN, YOUR FRIEND... SHE IS *TOO EASY.*
I BET SHE'S BEEN SCREWED OVER BEFORE.
Cheated on, right?
SHE NEEDS TO TIGHTEN HER GUARD.
I KNOW THAT'S FUNNY COMING FROM ME...
GRIP
!!
SLAM

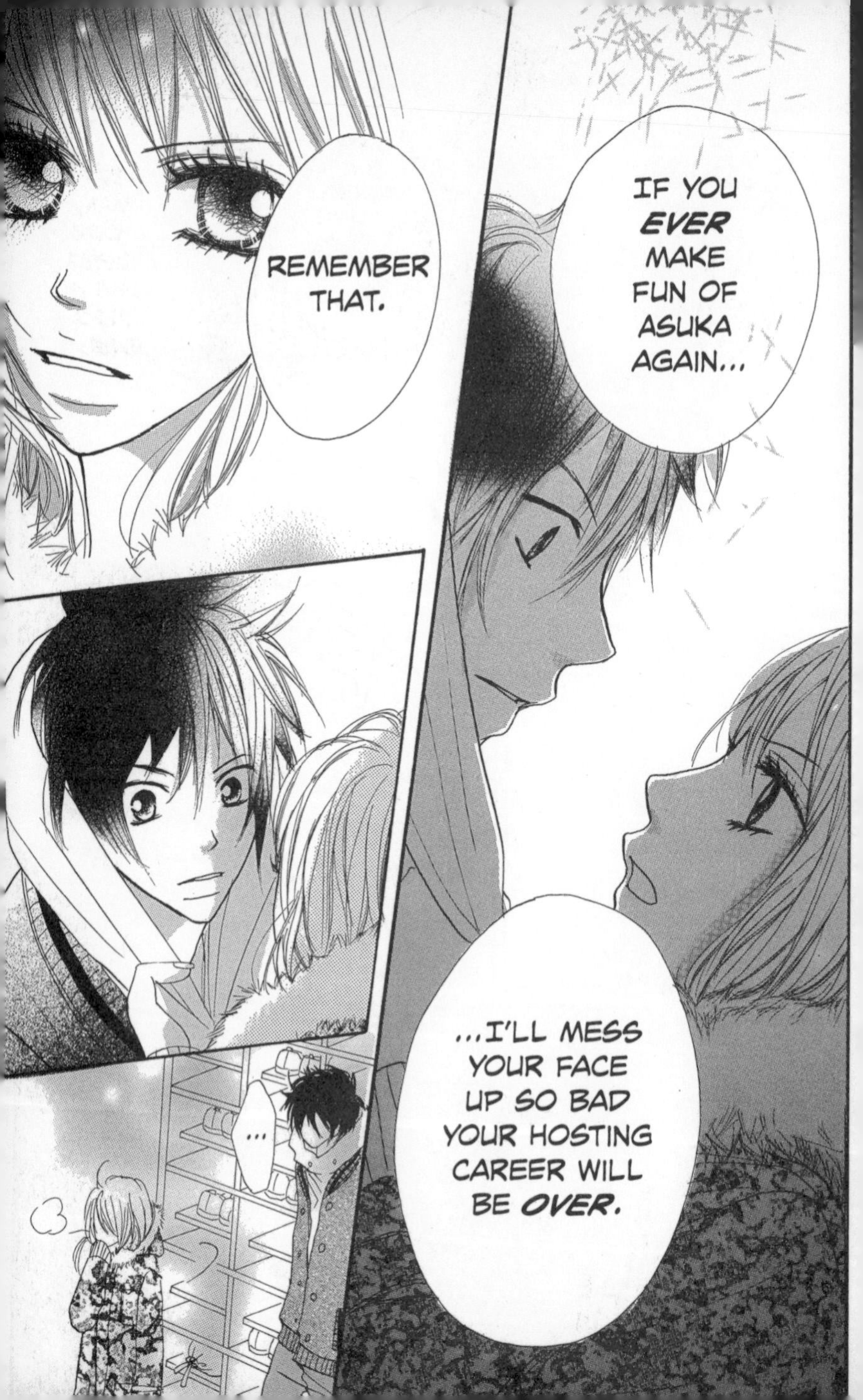
IF YOU EVER MAKE FUN OF ASUKA AGAIN...
...I'LL MESS YOUR FACE UP SO BAD YOUR HOSTING CAREER WILL BE OVER.
REMEMBER THAT.
...

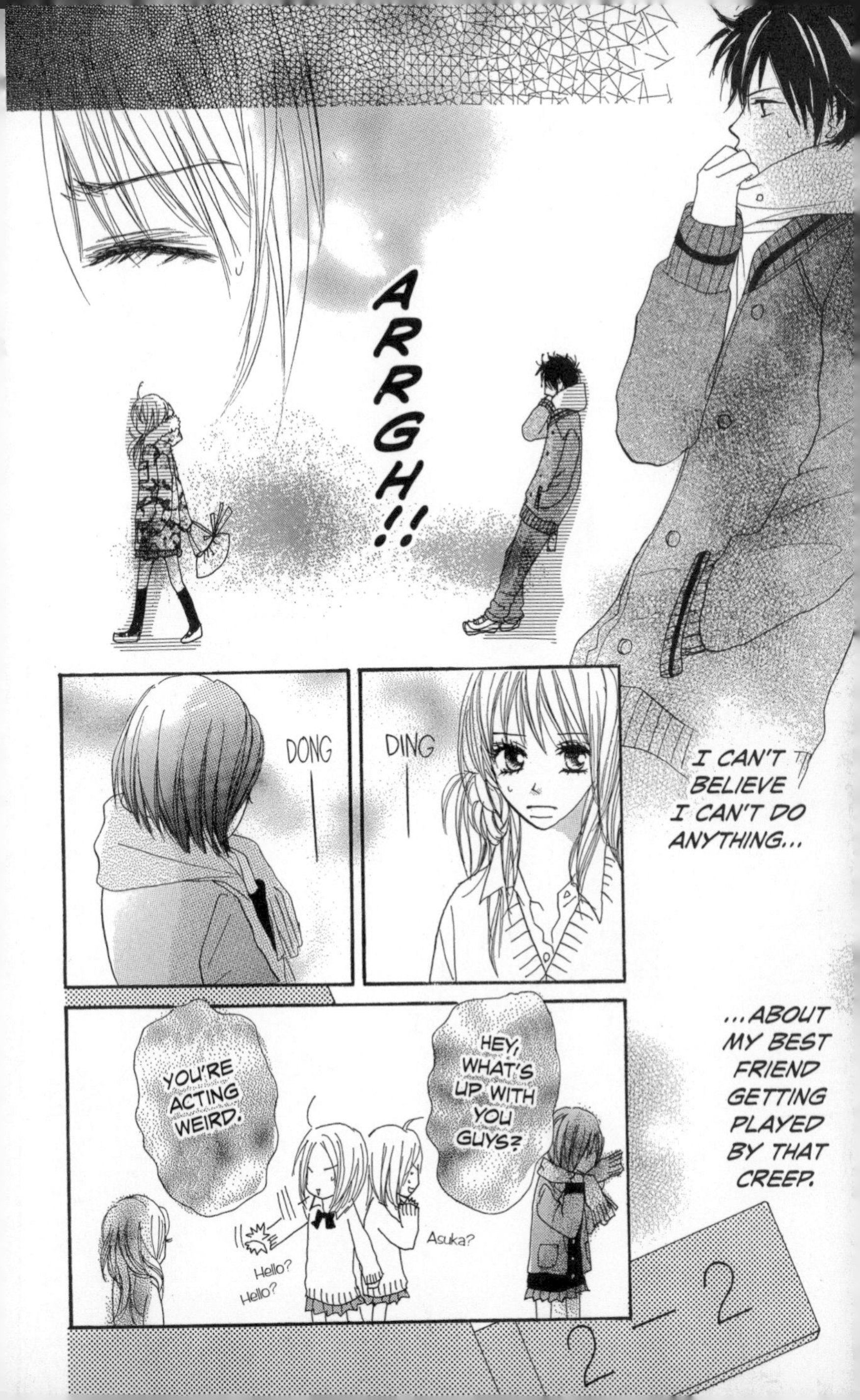
ARRGH!!
I CAN'T BELIEVE I CAN'T DO ANYTHING...
DING
DONG
...ABOUT MY BEST FRIEND GETTING PLAYED BY THAT CREEP.
HEY, WHAT'S UP WITH YOU GUYS?
Asuka?
YOU'RE ACTING WEIRD.
Hello?
Hello?

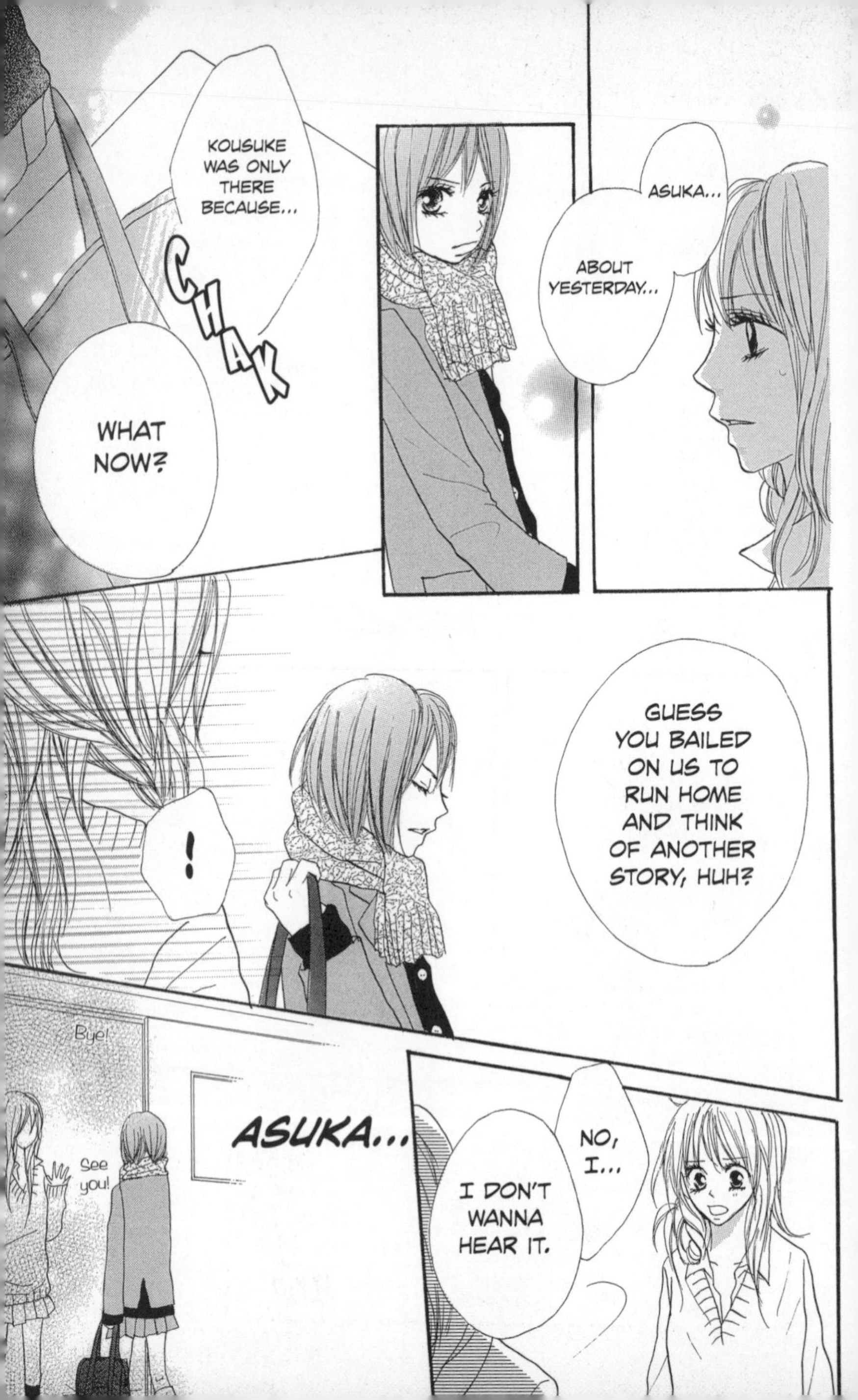
ASUKA...
ABOUT YESTERDAY...
KOUSUKE WAS ONLY THERE BECAUSE...
CHAK
WHAT NOW?
GUESS YOU BAILED ON US TO RUN HOME AND THINK OF ANOTHER STORY, HUH?
!
NO, I...
I DON'T WANNA HEAR IT.
ASUKA...
Bye!
See you!

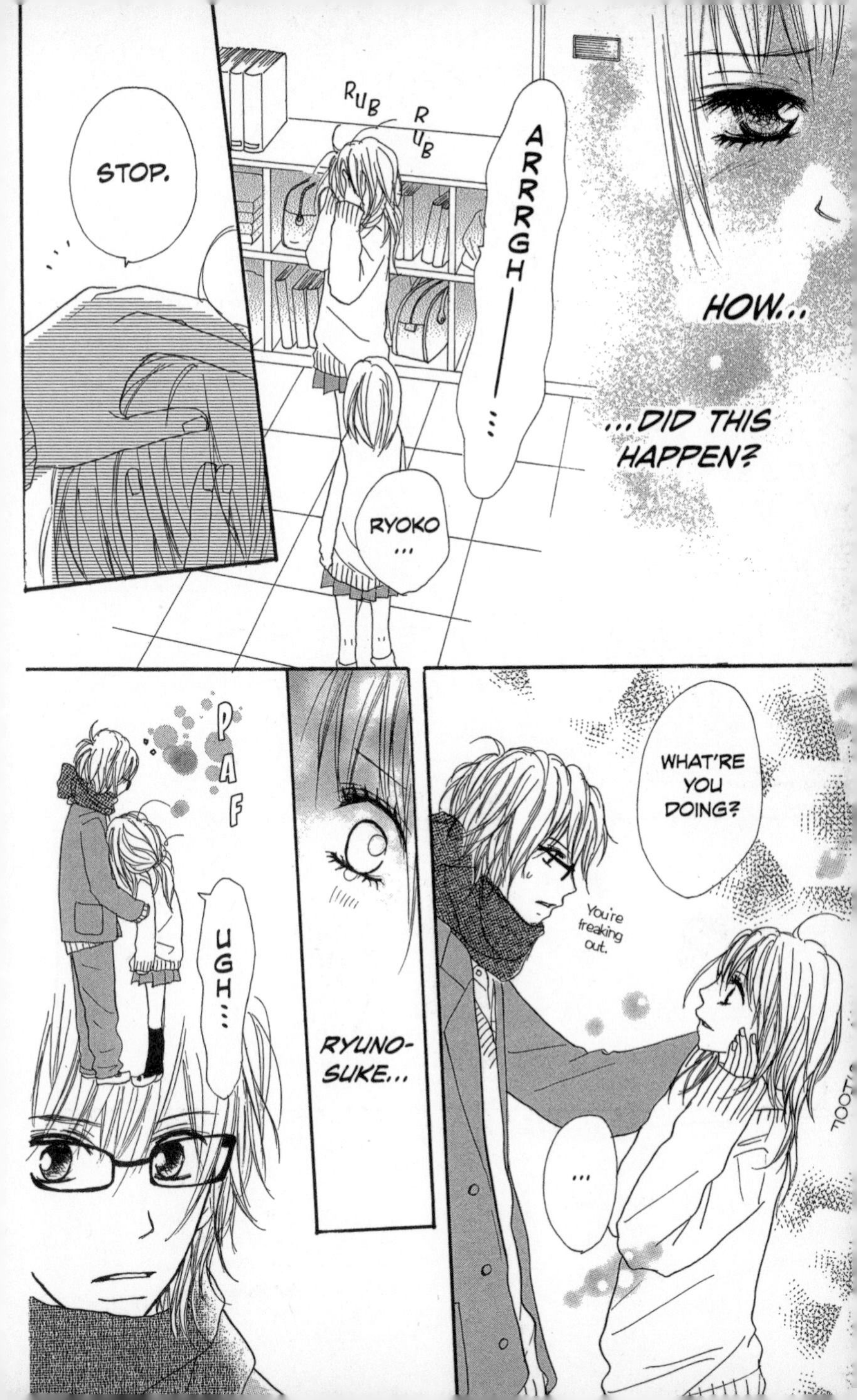
HOW...
...DID THIS HAPPEN?
ARRRGH—...
RUB RUB
RYOKO...
STOP.
...
WHAT'RE YOU DOING?
You're freaking out.
...
RYUNO-SUKE...
PAF
UGH...

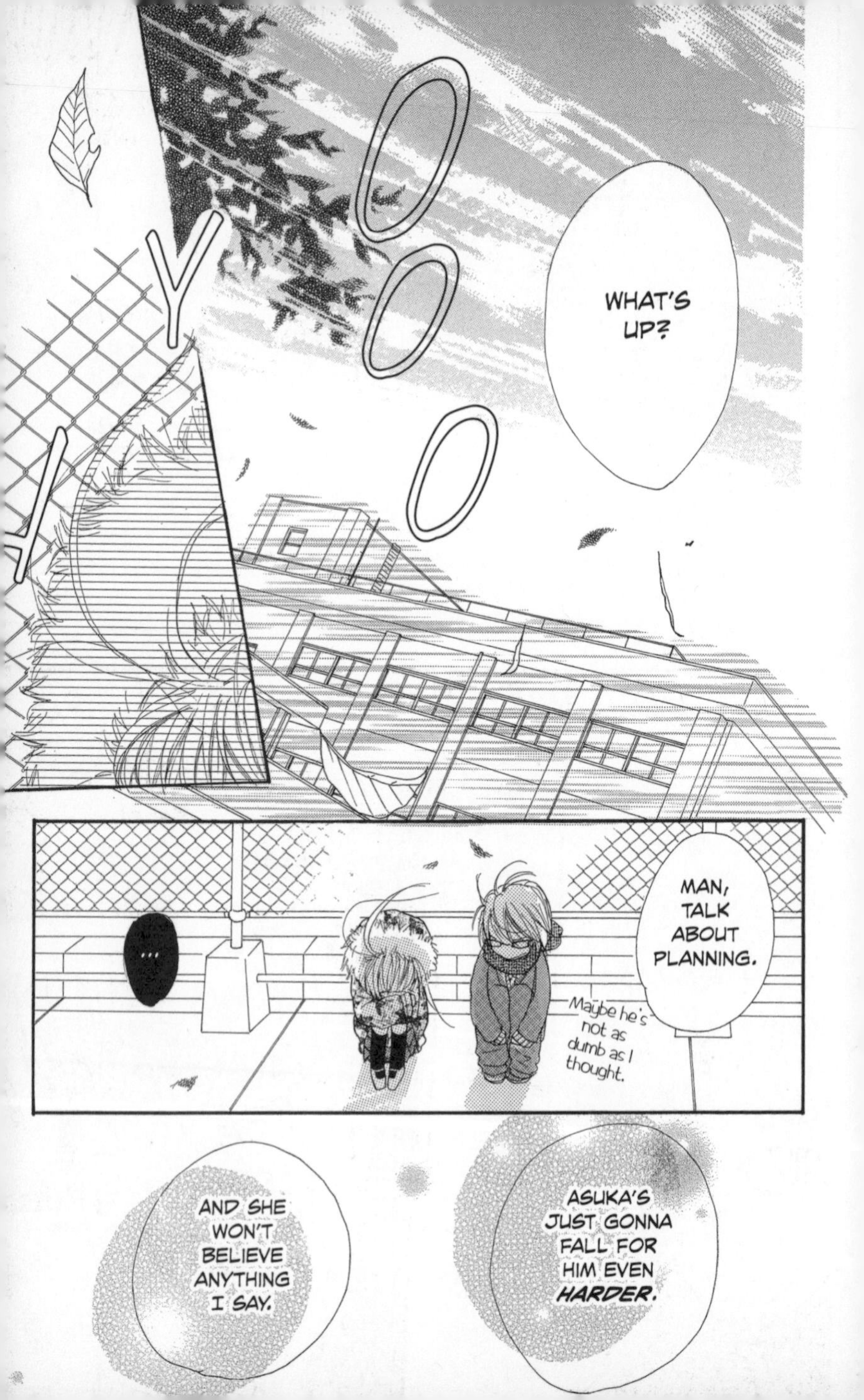
WHAT'S UP?
MAN, TALK ABOUT PLANNING.
Maybe he's not as dumb as I thought.
...
ASUKA'S JUST GONNA FALL FOR HIM EVEN *HARDER*.
AND SHE WON'T BELIEVE ANYTHING I SAY.

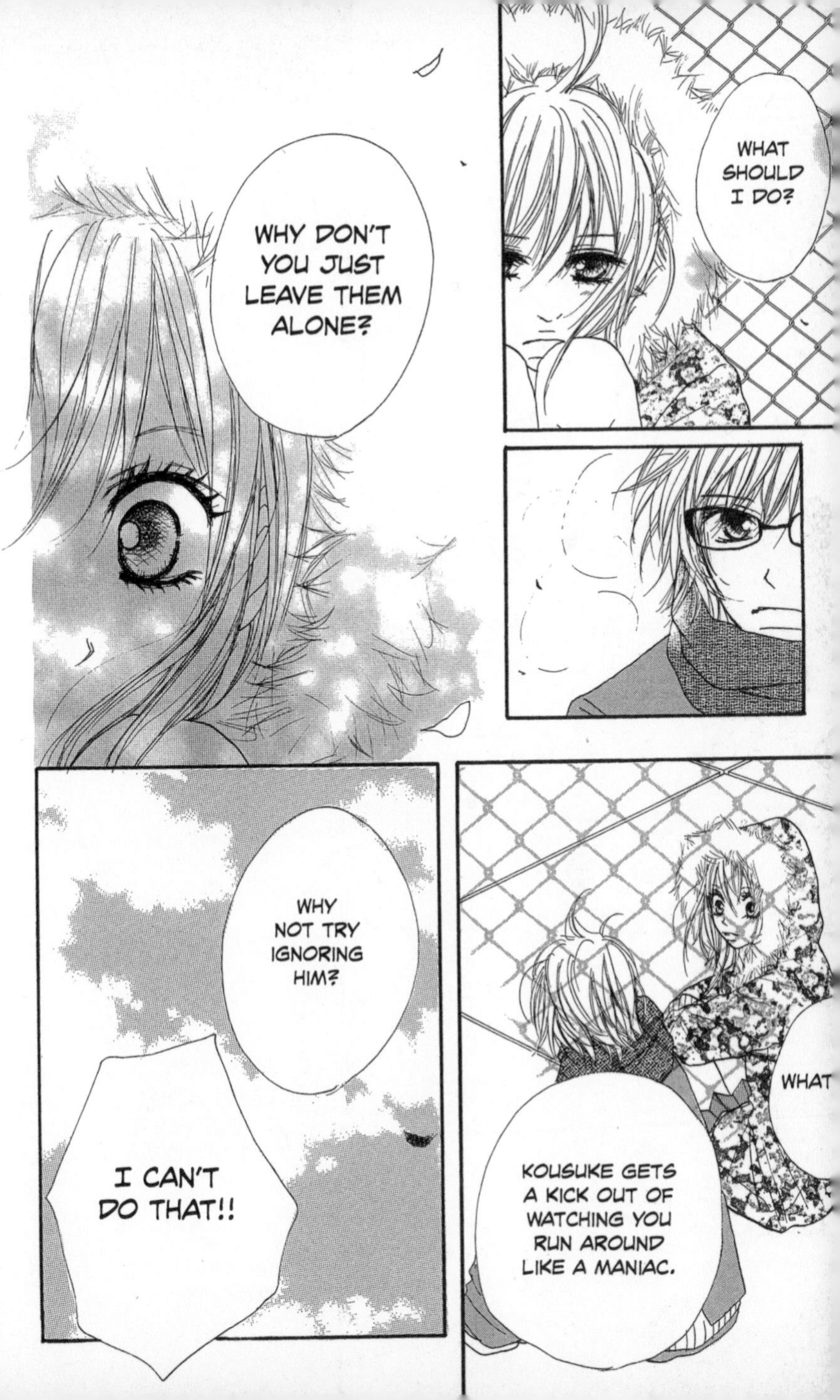
WHAT SHOULD I DO?
WHY DON'T YOU JUST LEAVE THEM ALONE?
WHAT
KOUSUKE GETS A KICK OUT OF WATCHING YOU RUN AROUND LIKE A MANIAC.
WHY NOT TRY IGNORING HIM?
I CAN'T DO THAT!!

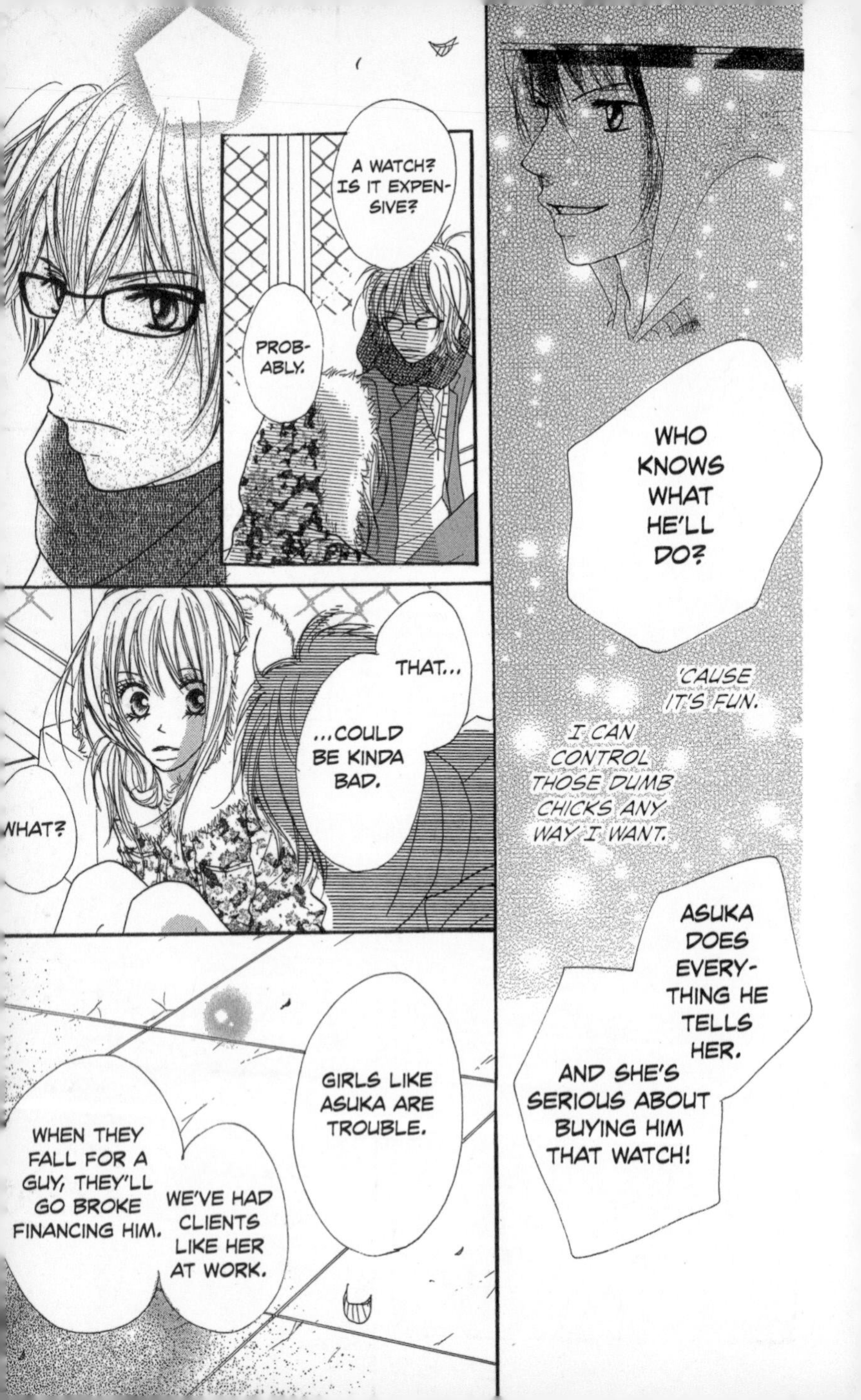
WHO KNOWS WHAT HE'LL DO?
'CAUSE IT'S FUN.
I CAN CONTROL THOSE DUMB CHICKS ANY WAY I WANT.
ASUKA DOES EVERY-THING HE TELLS HER.
AND SHE'S SERIOUS ABOUT BUYING HIM THAT WATCH!
A WATCH? IS IT EXPEN-SIVE?
PROB-ABLY.
THAT...
...COULD BE KINDA BAD.
WHAT?
GIRLS LIKE ASUKA ARE TROUBLE.
WE'VE HAD CLIENTS LIKE HER AT WORK.
WHEN THEY FALL FOR A GUY, THEY'LL GO BROKE FINANCING HIM.

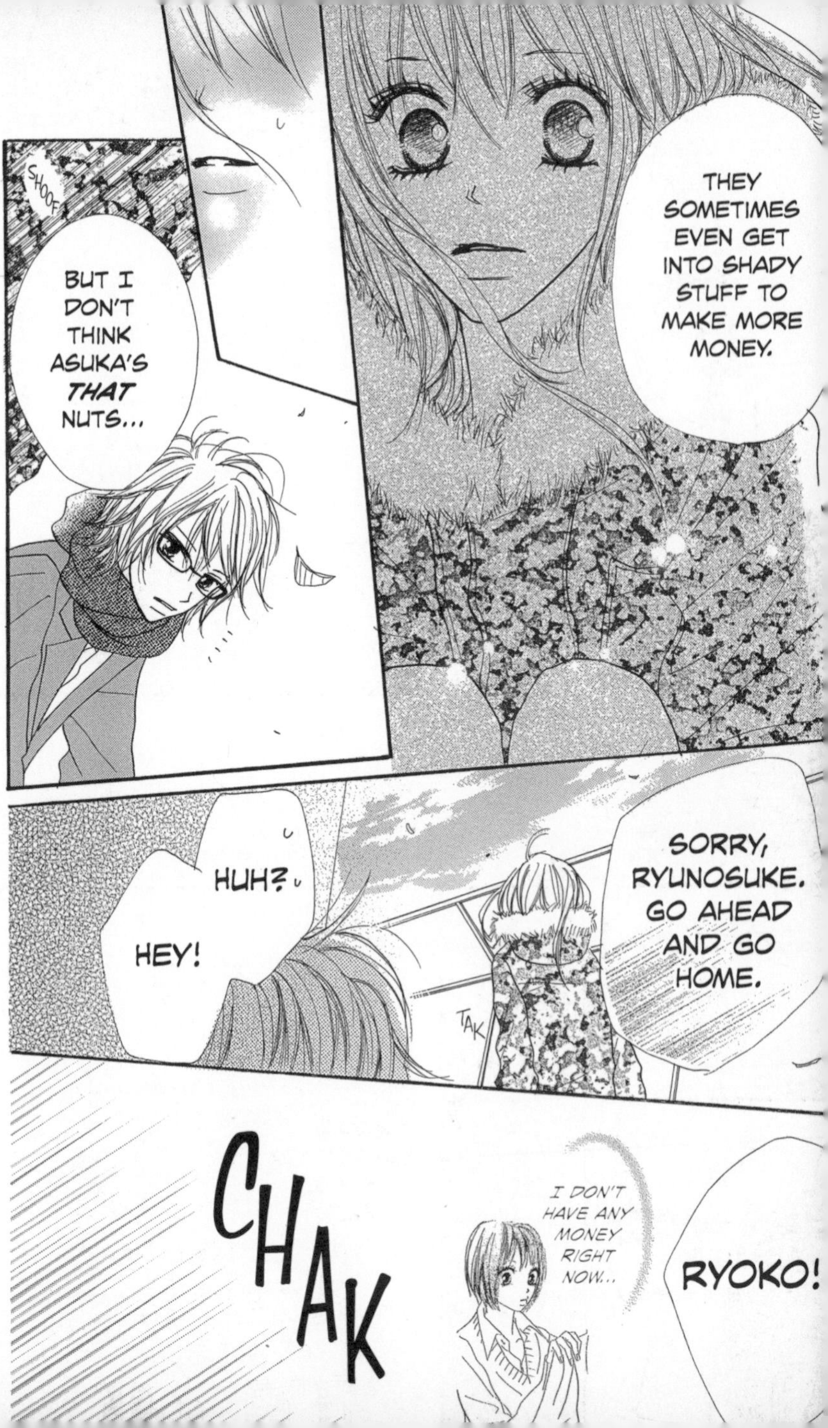
THEY SOMETIMES EVEN GET INTO SHADY STUFF TO MAKE MORE MONEY.
SHOOF
BUT I DON'T THINK ASUKA'S *THAT* NUTS...
SORRY, RYUNOSUKE. GO AHEAD AND GO HOME.
TAK
HUH?
HEY!
RYOKO!
I DON'T HAVE ANY MONEY RIGHT NOW...
CHAK

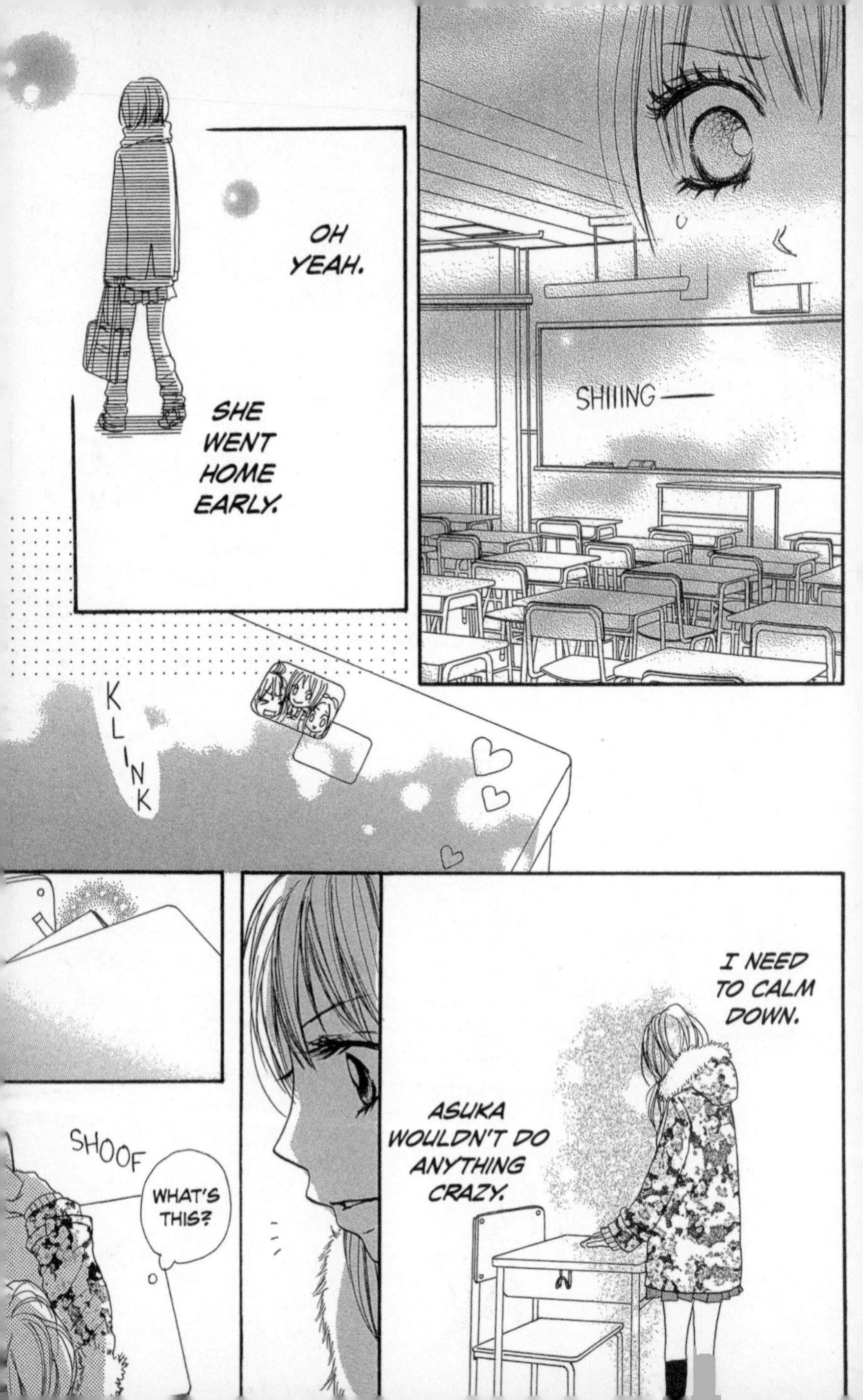
SHIIING—
OH YEAH.
SHE WENT HOME EARLY.
KLINK
I NEED TO CALM DOWN.
ASUKA WOULDN'T DO ANYTHING CRAZY.
SHOOF
WHAT'S THIS?

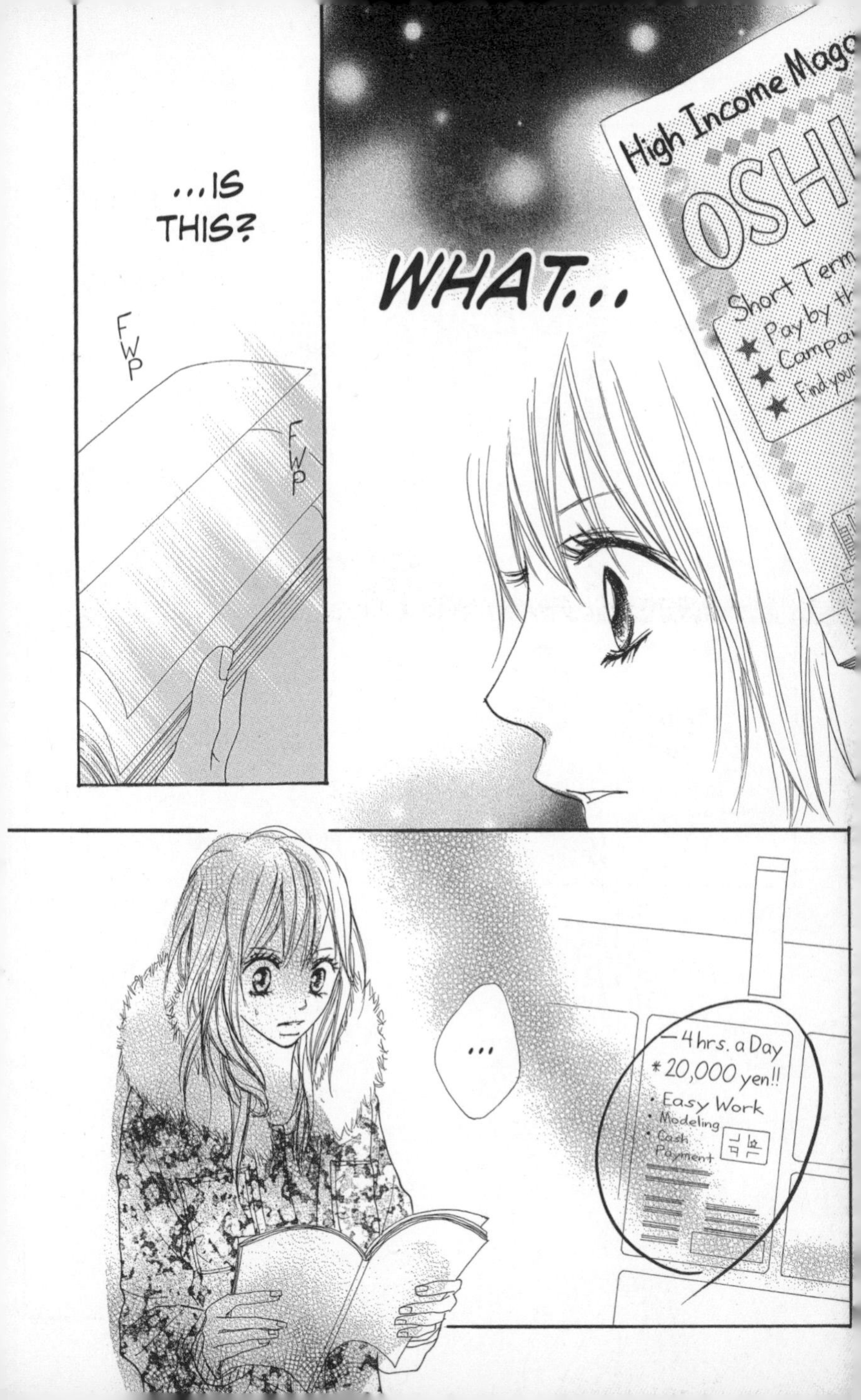

High Income Mag
OSH
Short Term
WHAT...
...IS THIS?
FWP
FWP
4 hrs. a Day
20,000 yen!!
Easy Work
Modeling
Cash Payment
...

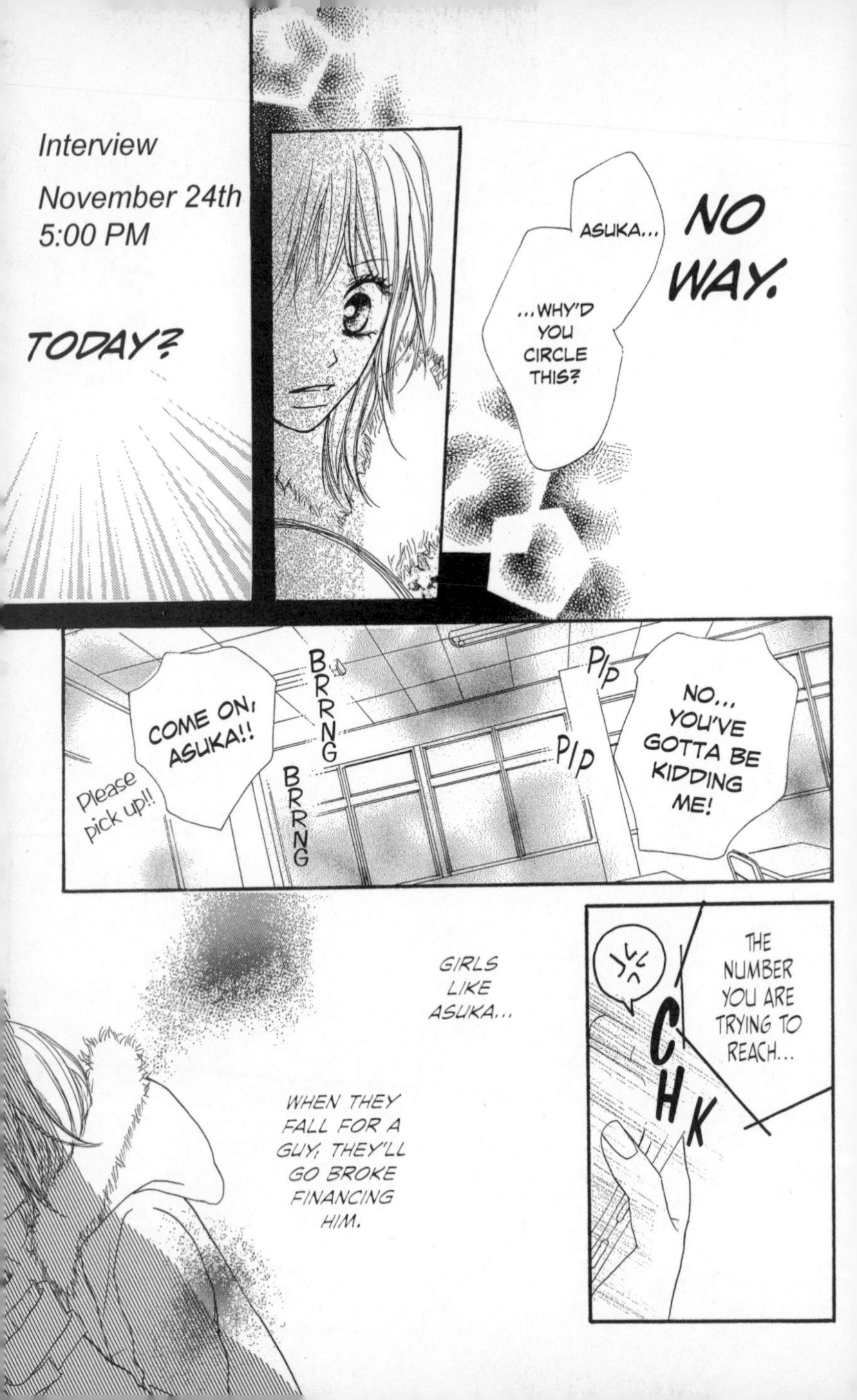
ASUKA... ...WHY'D YOU CIRCLE THIS?
NO WAY.
Interview
November 24th
5:00 PM
TODAY?
NO... YOU'VE GOTTA BE KIDDING ME!
PIP
PIP
BRRNG
BRRNG
COME ON, ASUKA!!
Please pick up!!
THE NUMBER YOU ARE TRYING TO REACH...
CHK
GIRLS LIKE ASUKA...
WHEN THEY FALL FOR A GUY, THEY'LL GO BROKE FINANCING HIM.

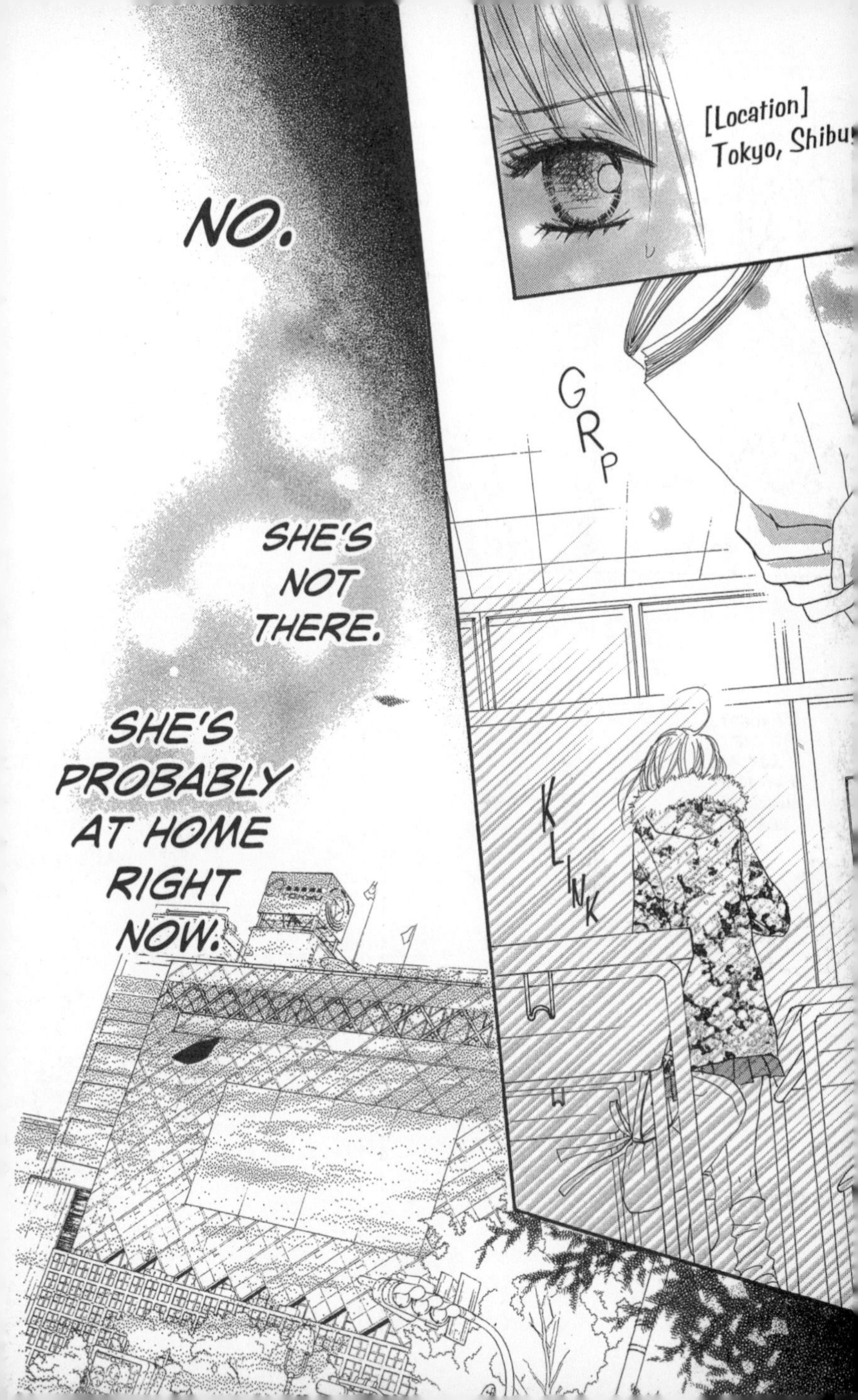
[Location]
Tokyo, Shibu
GRP
KLINK
NO.
SHE'S NOT THERE.
SHE'S PROBABLY AT HOME RIGHT NOW.

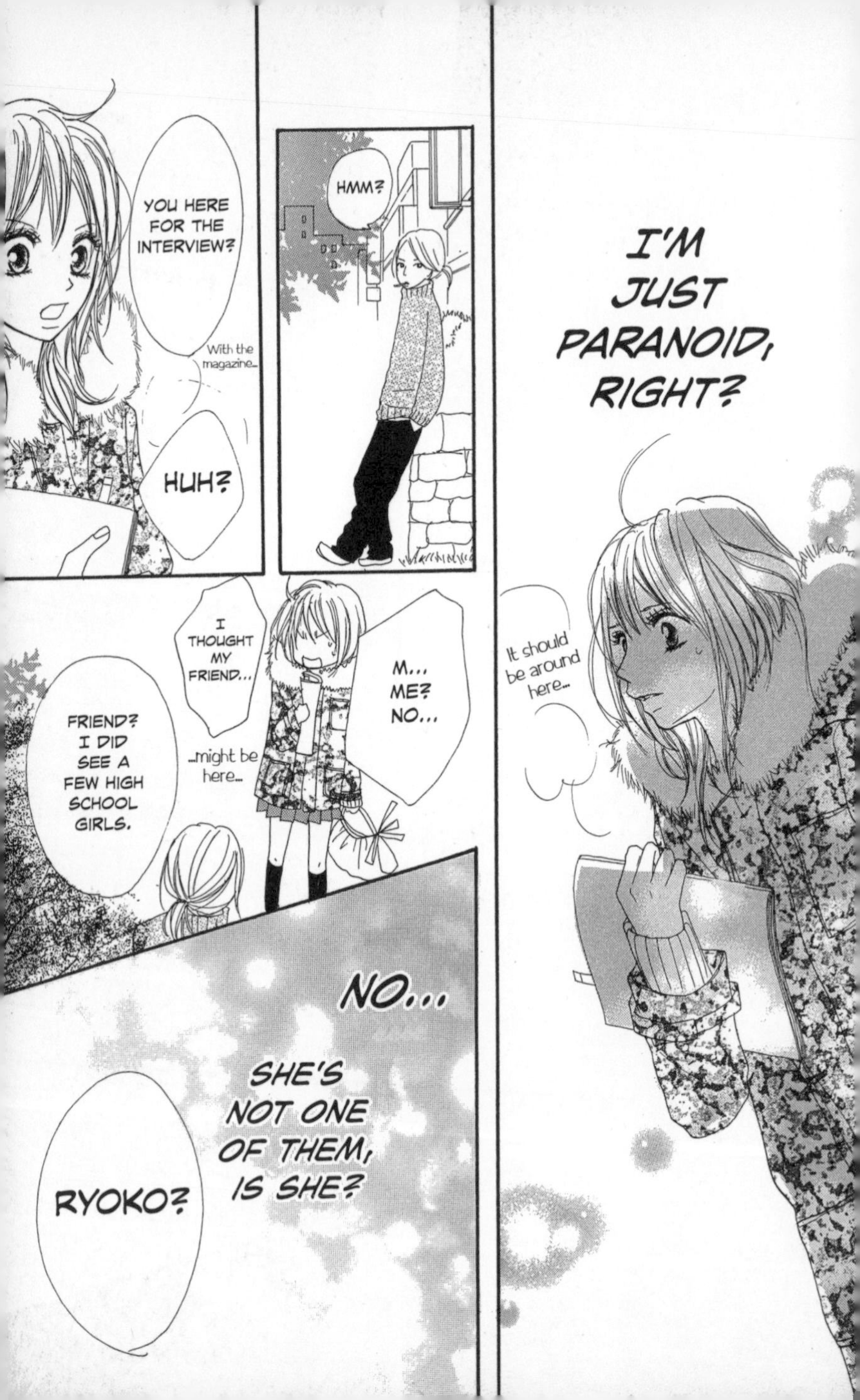
I'M JUST PARANOID, RIGHT?
It should be around here...
HMM?
YOU HERE FOR THE INTERVIEW?
With the magazine...
HUH?
M... ME? NO...
I THOUGHT MY FRIEND...
...might be here...
FRIEND? I DID SEE A FEW HIGH SCHOOL GIRLS.
NO...
SHE'S NOT ONE OF THEM, IS SHE?
RYOKO?

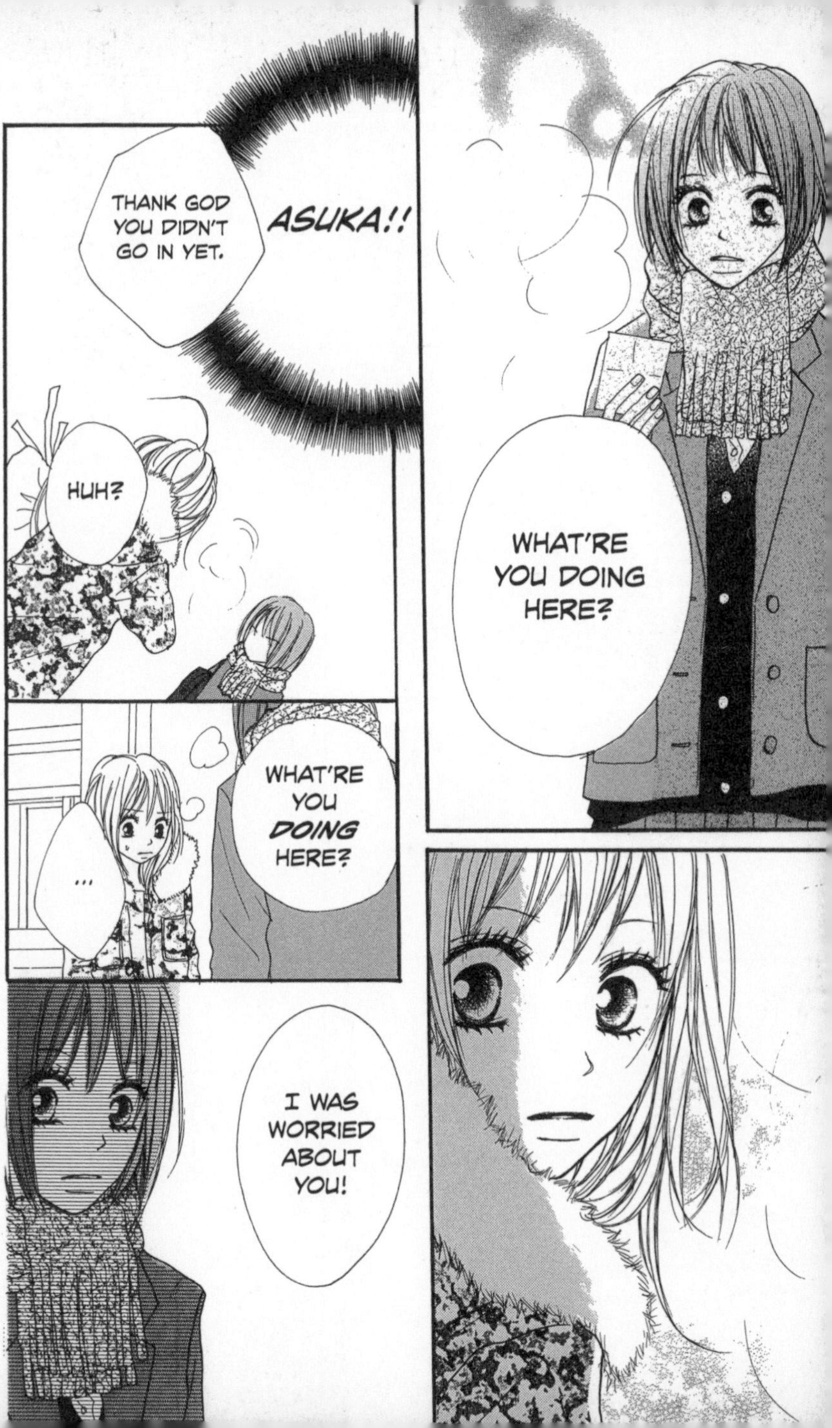
WHAT'RE YOU DOING HERE?
ASUKA!!
THANK GOD YOU DIDN'T GO IN YET.
HUH?
WHAT'RE YOU *DOING* HERE?
...
I WAS WORRIED ABOUT YOU!

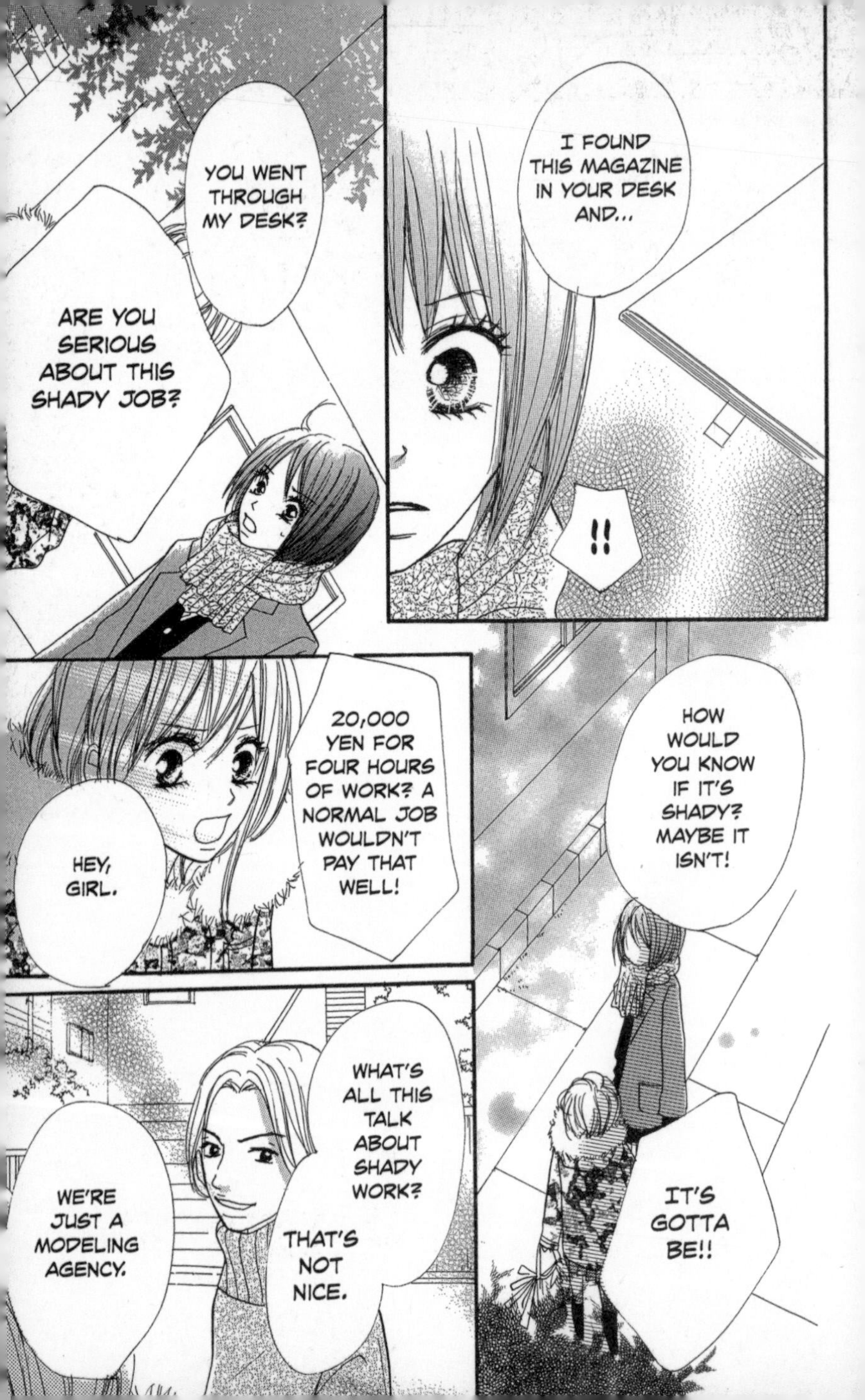
I FOUND THIS MAGAZINE IN YOUR DESK AND...
!!
YOU WENT THROUGH MY DESK?
ARE YOU SERIOUS ABOUT THIS SHADY JOB?
HOW WOULD YOU KNOW IF IT'S SHADY? MAYBE IT ISN'T!
IT'S GOTTA BE!!
20,000 YEN FOR FOUR HOURS OF WORK? A NORMAL JOB WOULDN'T PAY THAT WELL!
HEY, GIRL.
WHAT'S ALL THIS TALK ABOUT SHADY WORK?
THAT'S NOT NICE.
WE'RE JUST A MODELING AGENCY.

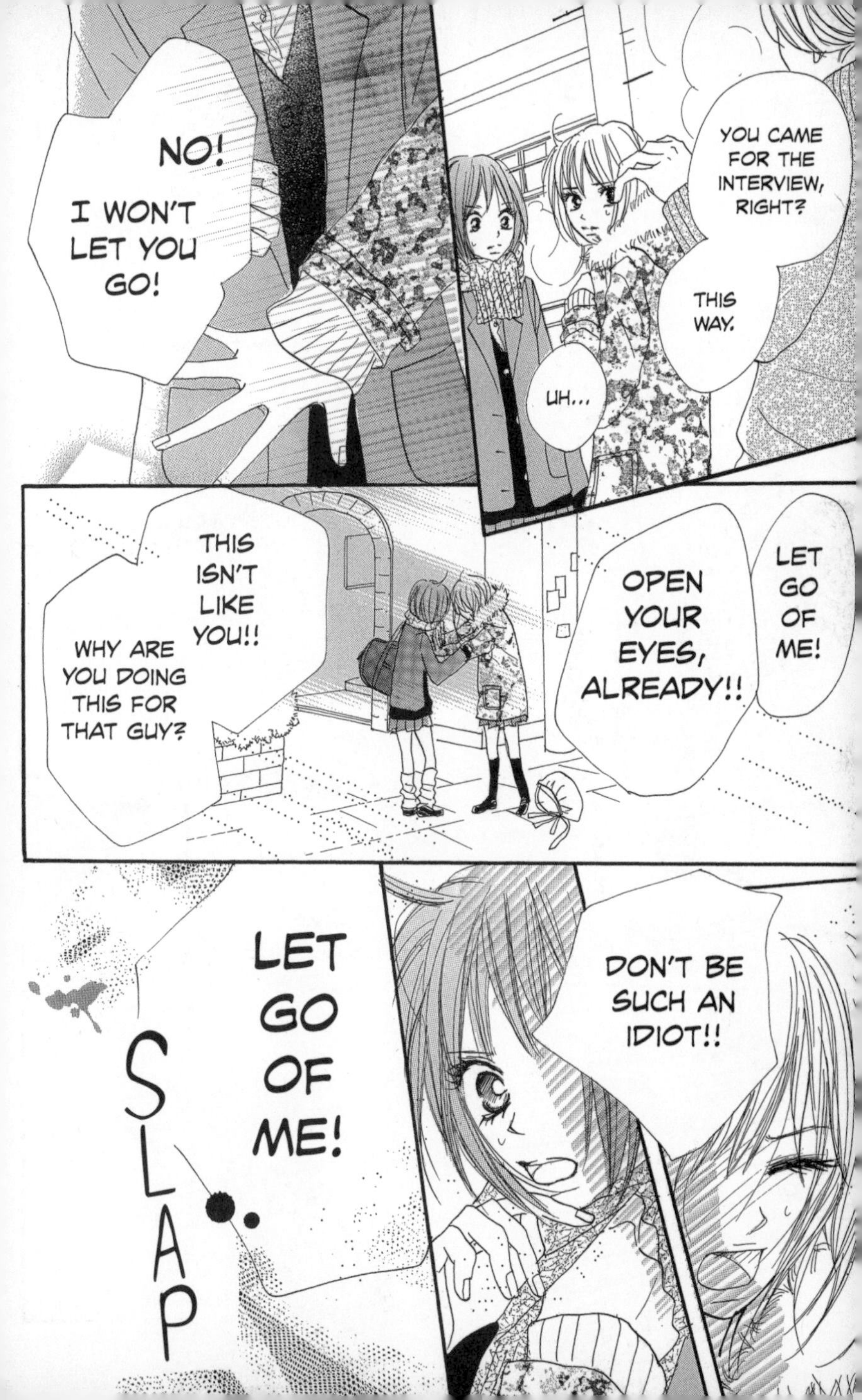
YOU CAME FOR THE INTERVIEW, RIGHT?
THIS WAY.
UH...
NO!
I WON'T LET YOU GO!
LET GO OF ME!
OPEN YOUR EYES, ALREADY!!
THIS ISN'T LIKE YOU!!
WHY ARE YOU DOING THIS FOR THAT GUY?
DON'T BE SUCH AN IDIOT!!
LET GO OF ME!
SLAP

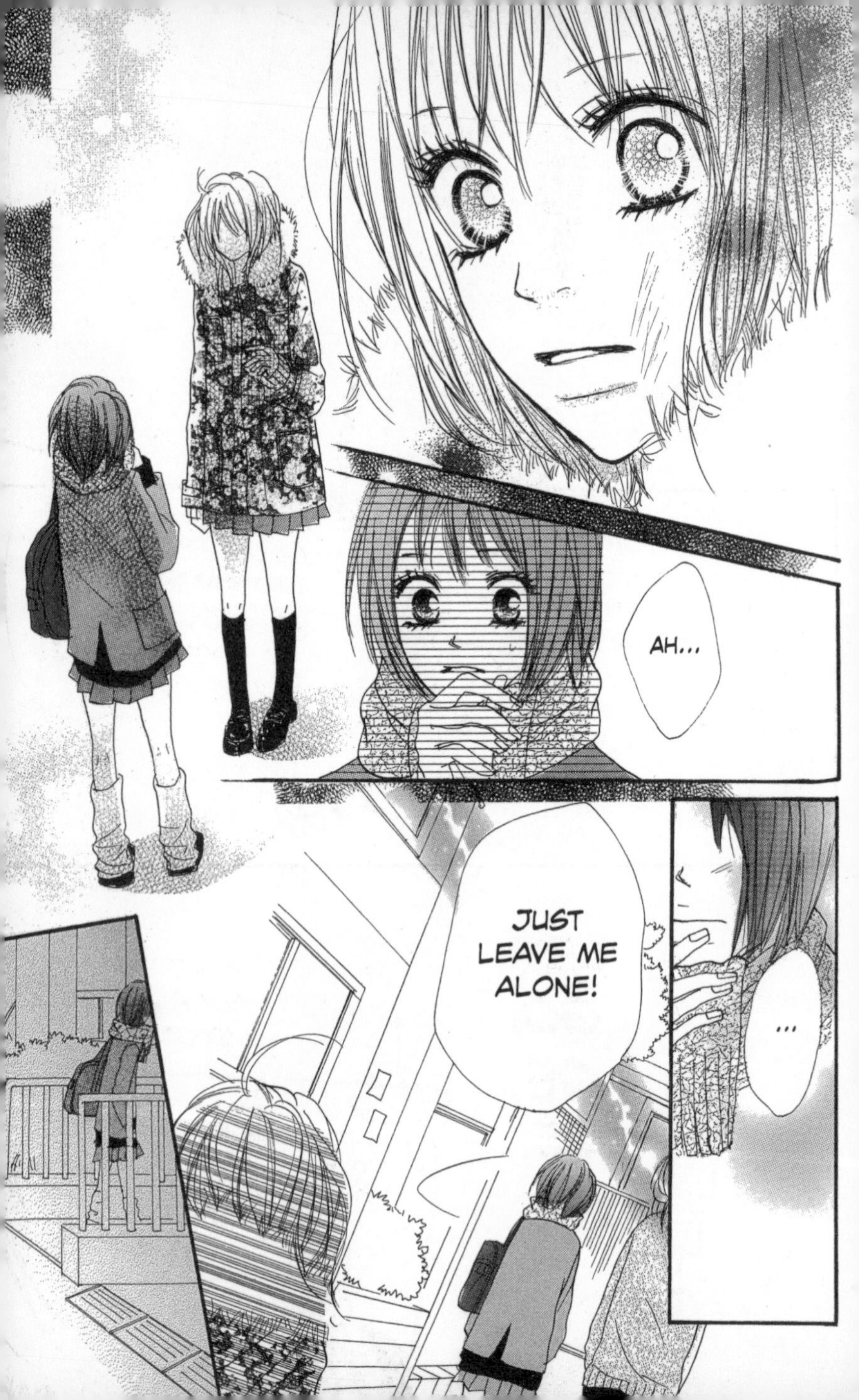
AH...
...
JUST LEAVE ME ALONE!

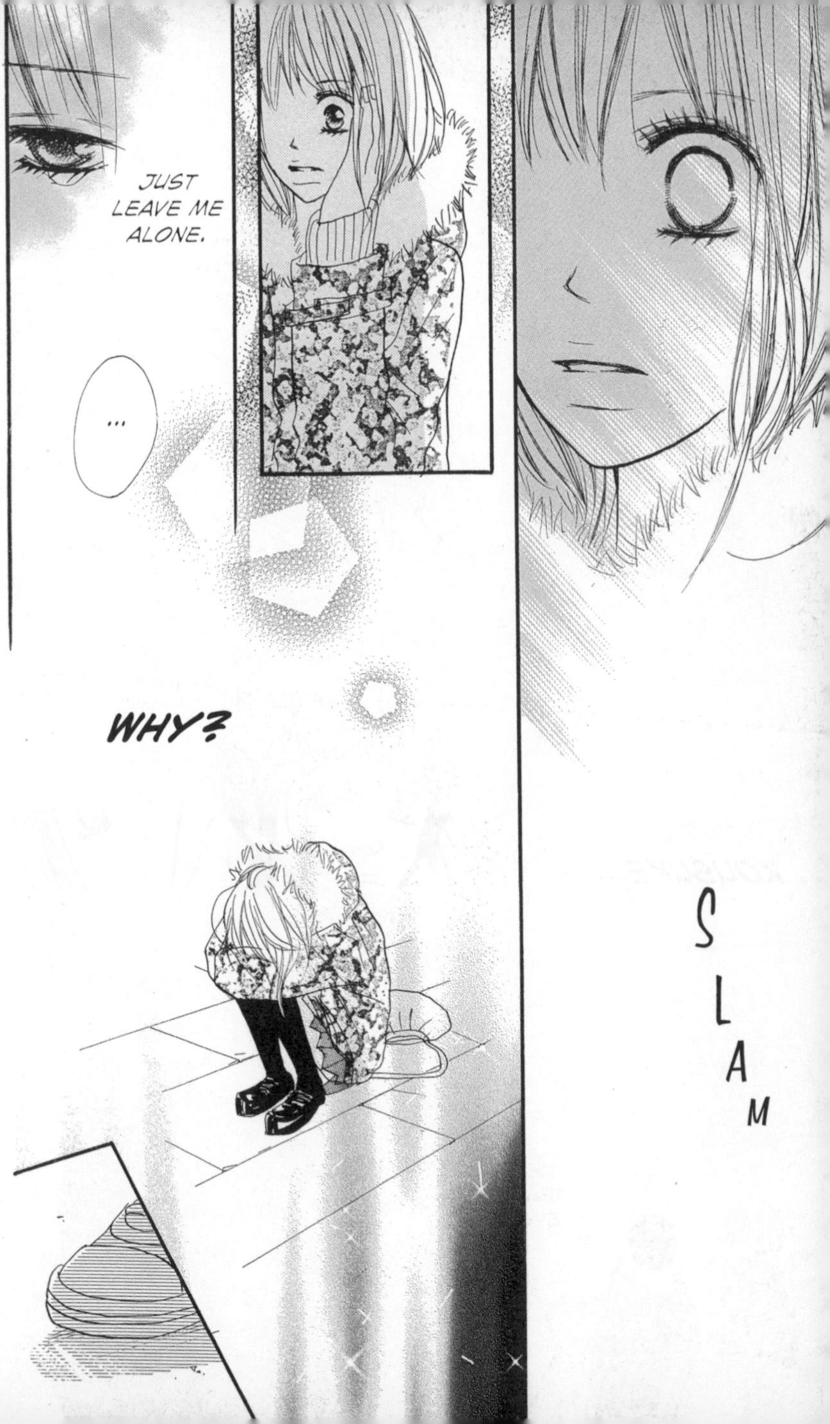
SLAM
JUST LEAVE ME ALONE.
...
WHY?

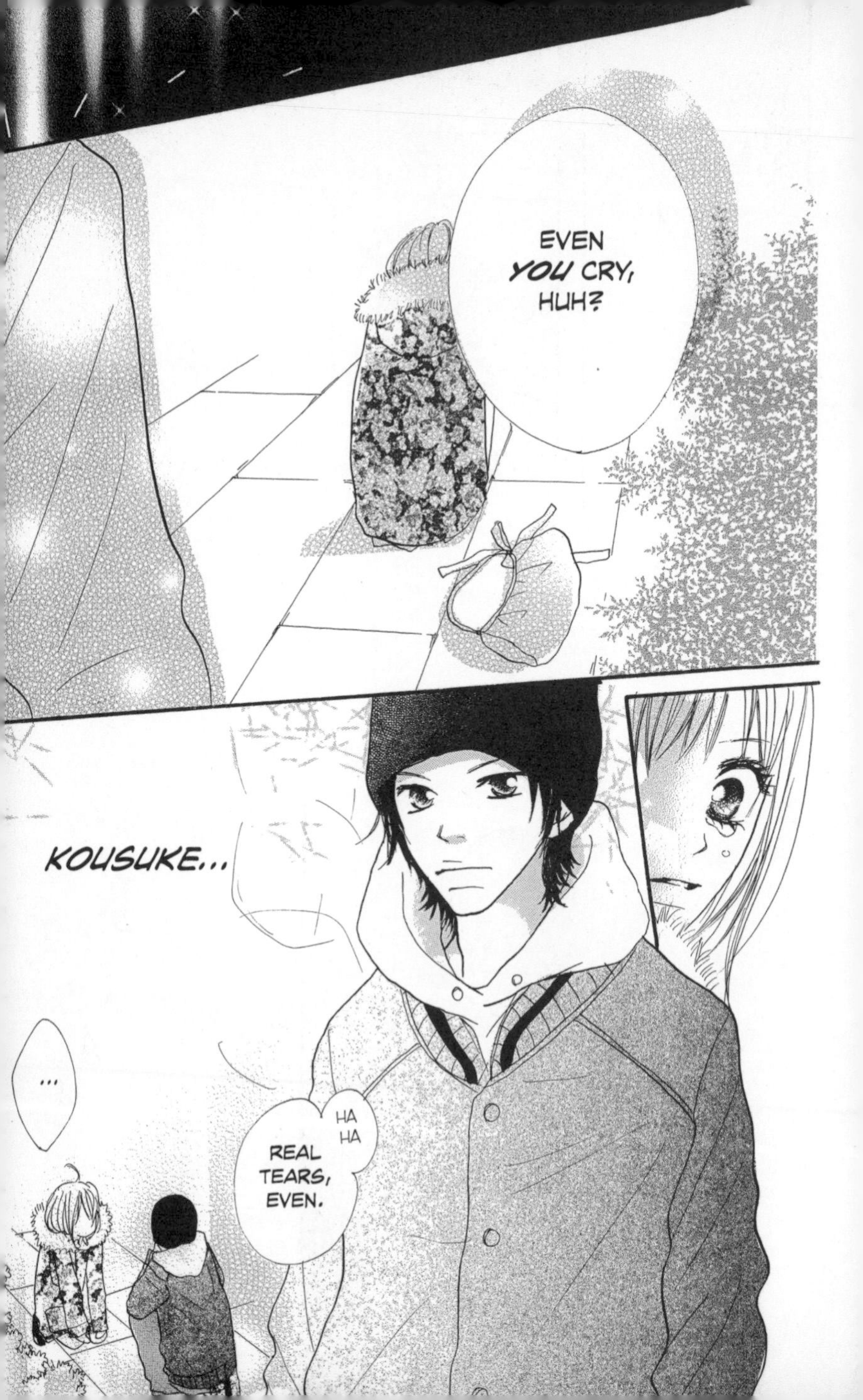
EVEN YOU CRY, HUH?
KOUSUKE...
HA HA
REAL TEARS, EVEN.
...

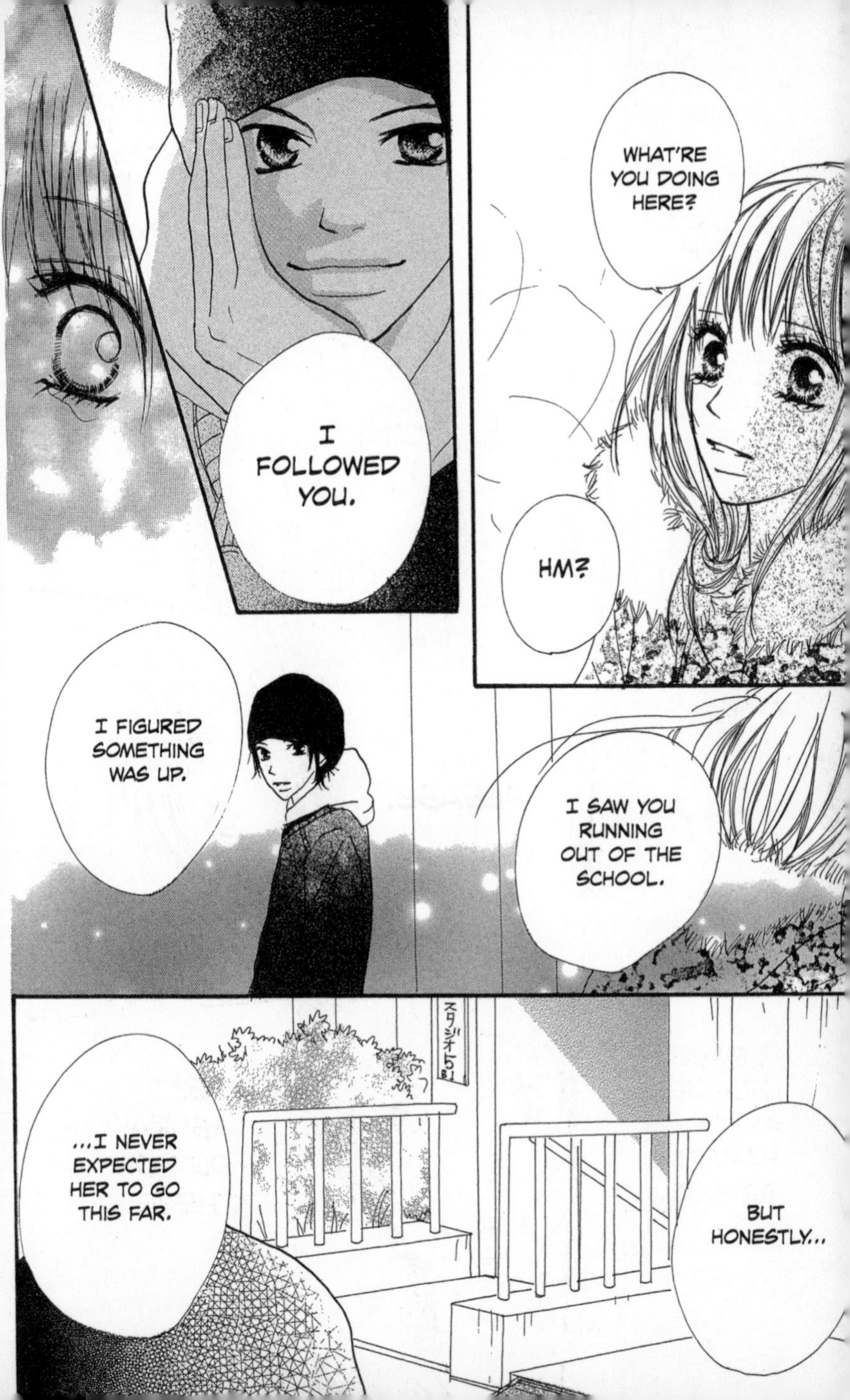
WHAT'RE YOU DOING HERE?
HM?
I FOLLOWED YOU.
I SAW YOU RUNNING OUT OF THE SCHOOL.
I FIGURED SOMETHING WAS UP.
スタジオ5 B1
BUT HONESTLY...
...I NEVER EXPECTED HER TO GO THIS FAR.

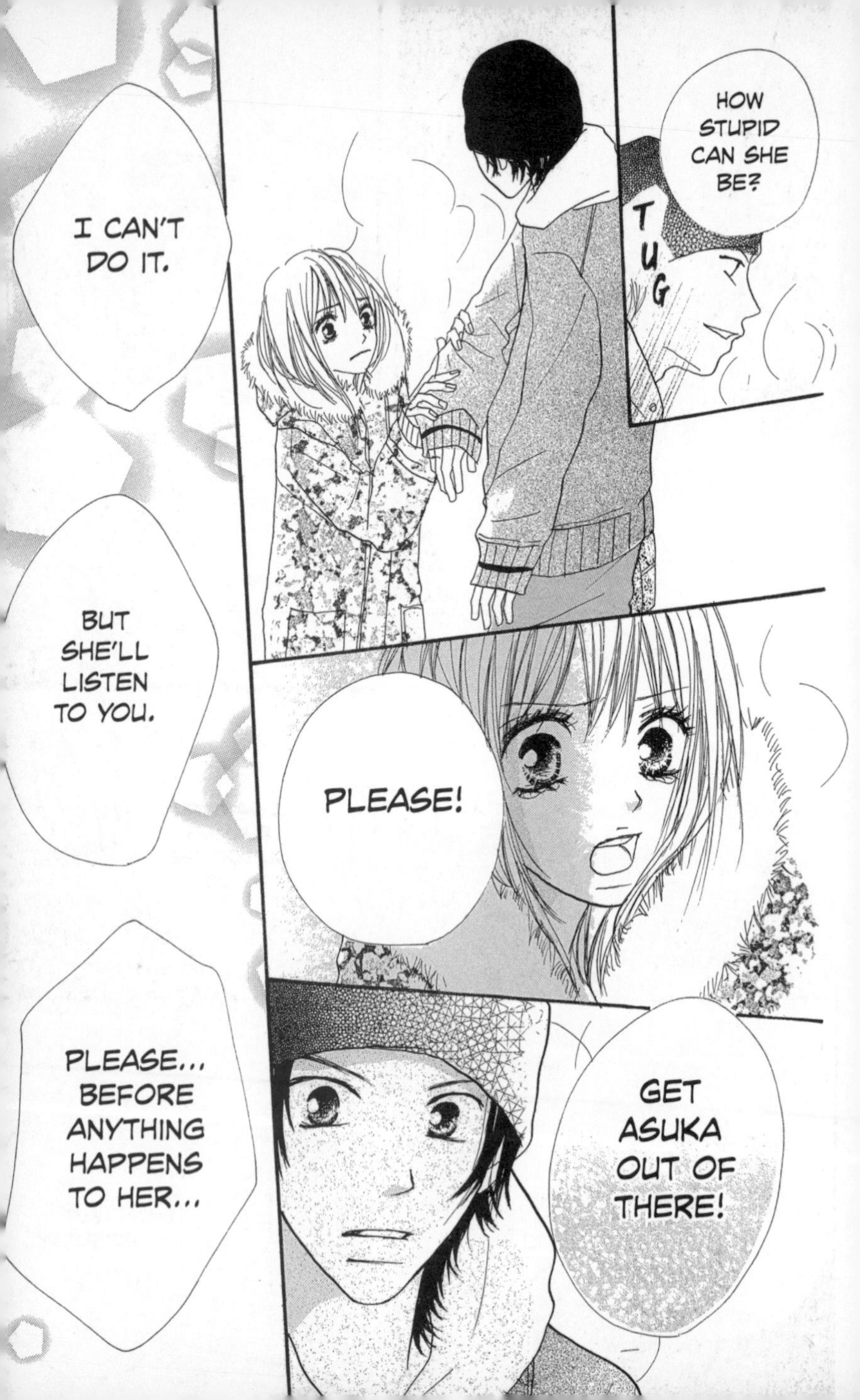
HOW STUPID CAN SHE BE?
TUG
PLEASE!
GET ASUKA OUT OF THERE!
I CAN'T DO IT.
BUT SHE'LL LISTEN TO YOU.
PLEASE... BEFORE ANYTHING HAPPENS TO HER...

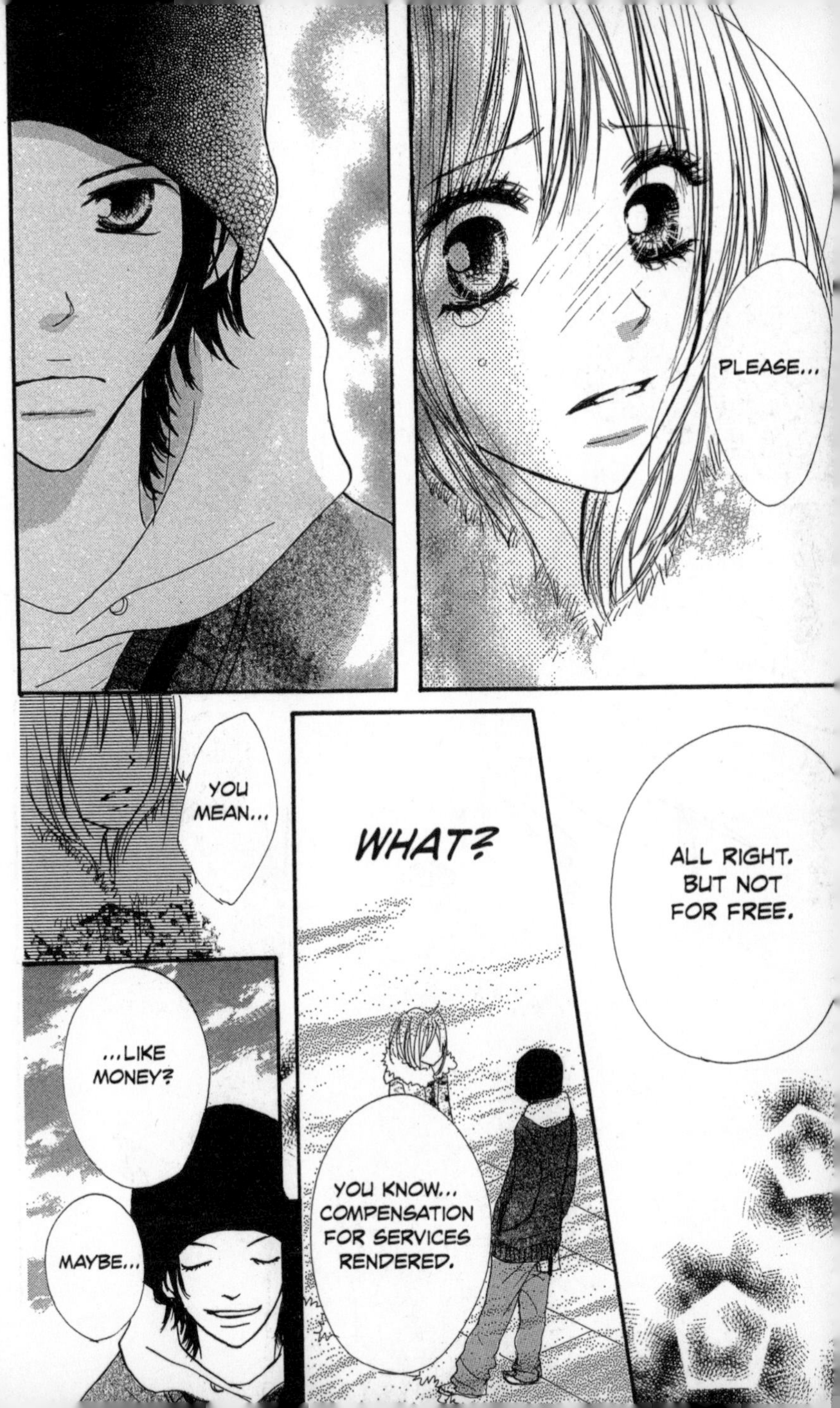
PLEASE...
ALL RIGHT. BUT NOT FOR FREE.
WHAT?
YOU KNOW... COMPENSATION FOR SERVICES RENDERED.
YOU MEAN...
...LIKE MONEY?
MAYBE...

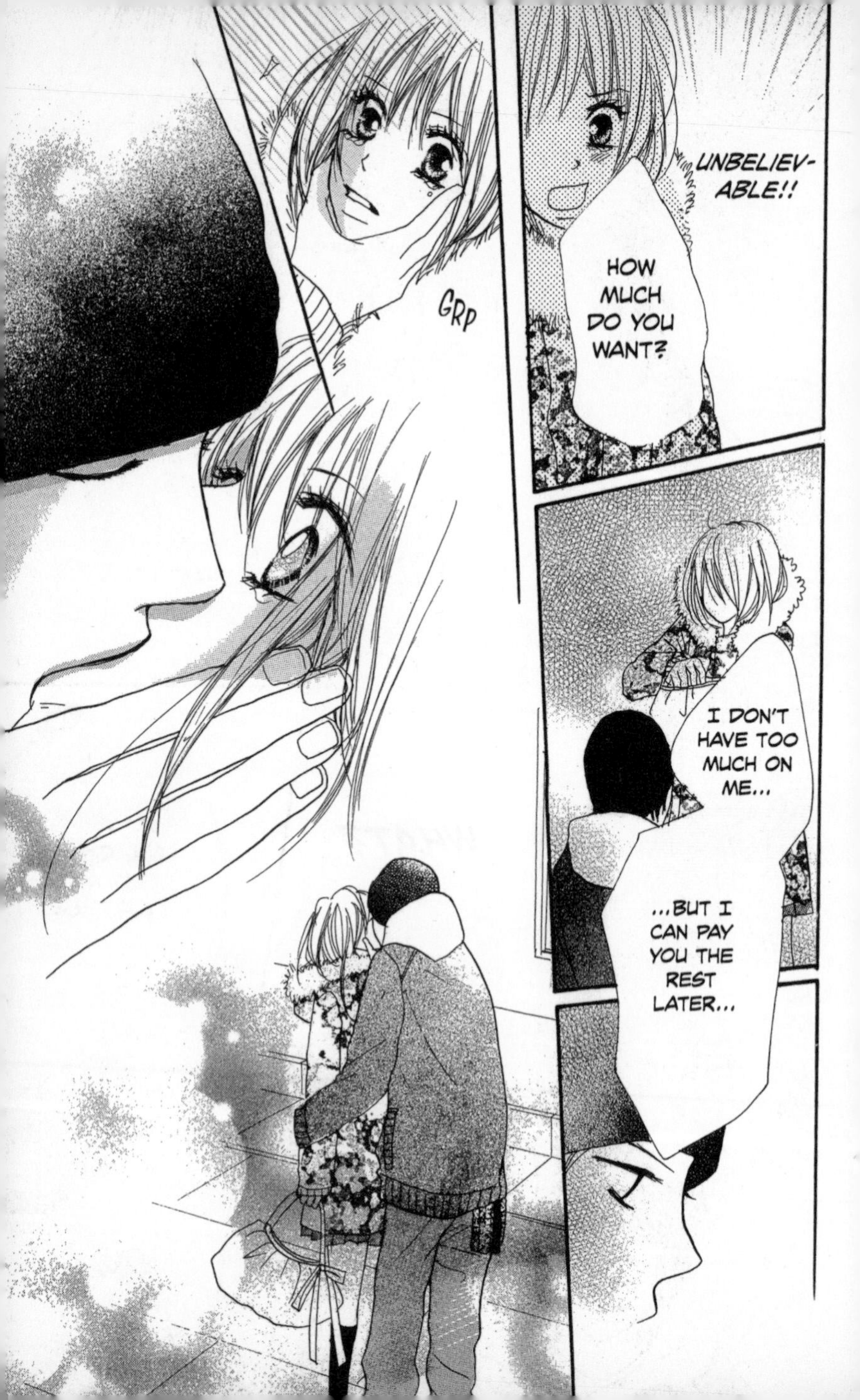
UNBELIEV-ABLE!!
HOW MUCH DO YOU WANT?
I DON'T HAVE TOO MUCH ON ME...
...BUT I CAN PAY YOU THE REST LATER...
GRP

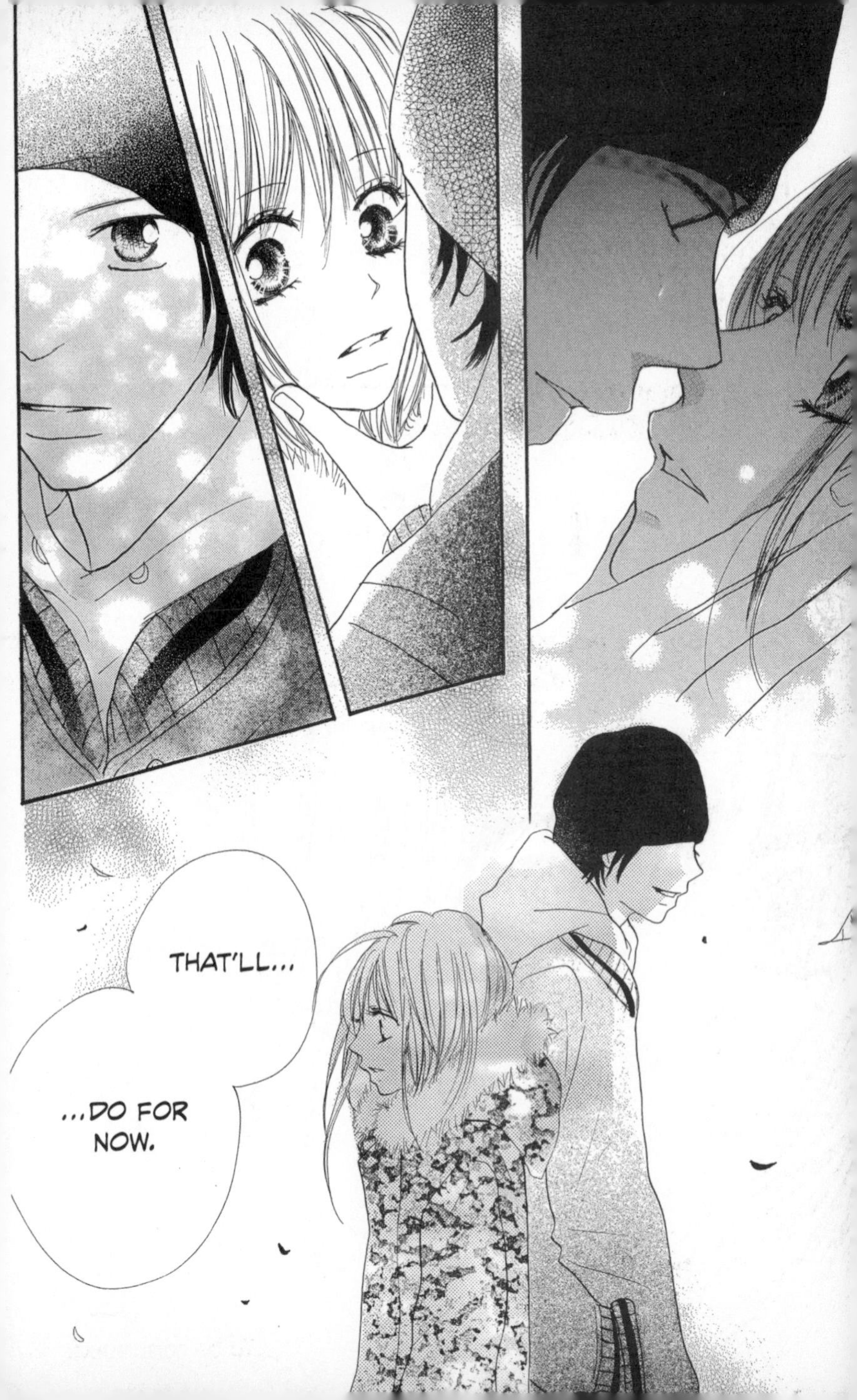
THAT'LL...
...DO FOR NOW.

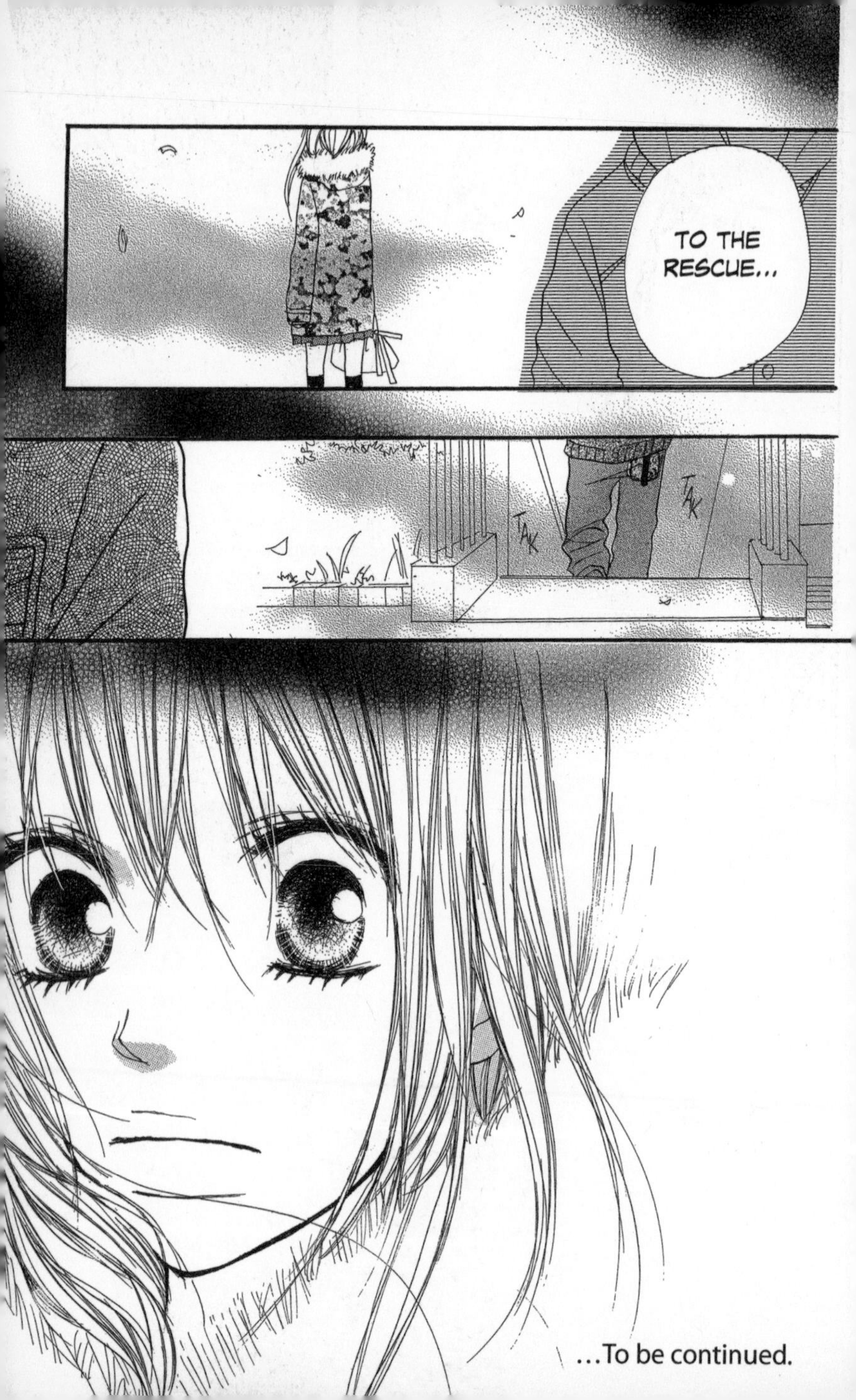
TO THE RESCUE...
TAK
TAK
...To be continued.

What'd you think——?

Did you enjoy B.O.D.Y. Volume 4? It's starting to heat up again. 'Cause you know, things happen or they don't...

What am I saying?

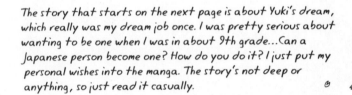

The story that starts on the next page is about Yuki's dream, which really was my dream job once. I was pretty serious about wanting to be one when I was in about 9th grade...Can a Japanese person become one? How do you do it? I just put my personal wishes into the manga. The story's not deep or anything, so just read it casually.

Well, then, I'll be waiting in Volume 5.

2005/4/14

Ao Mimori

YAY

See ya

YAY

MEW

Ochiyo

The other day I went fishing in Ichigaya with Matsu Kotô. We were both beginners, but together we caught 12 kg of fish. Our hands smelled like fish. But we'll go again...

It was fun...

How things → went

Chili Peppers

This way! Bring it over this way!!

WAAAA

Matsu

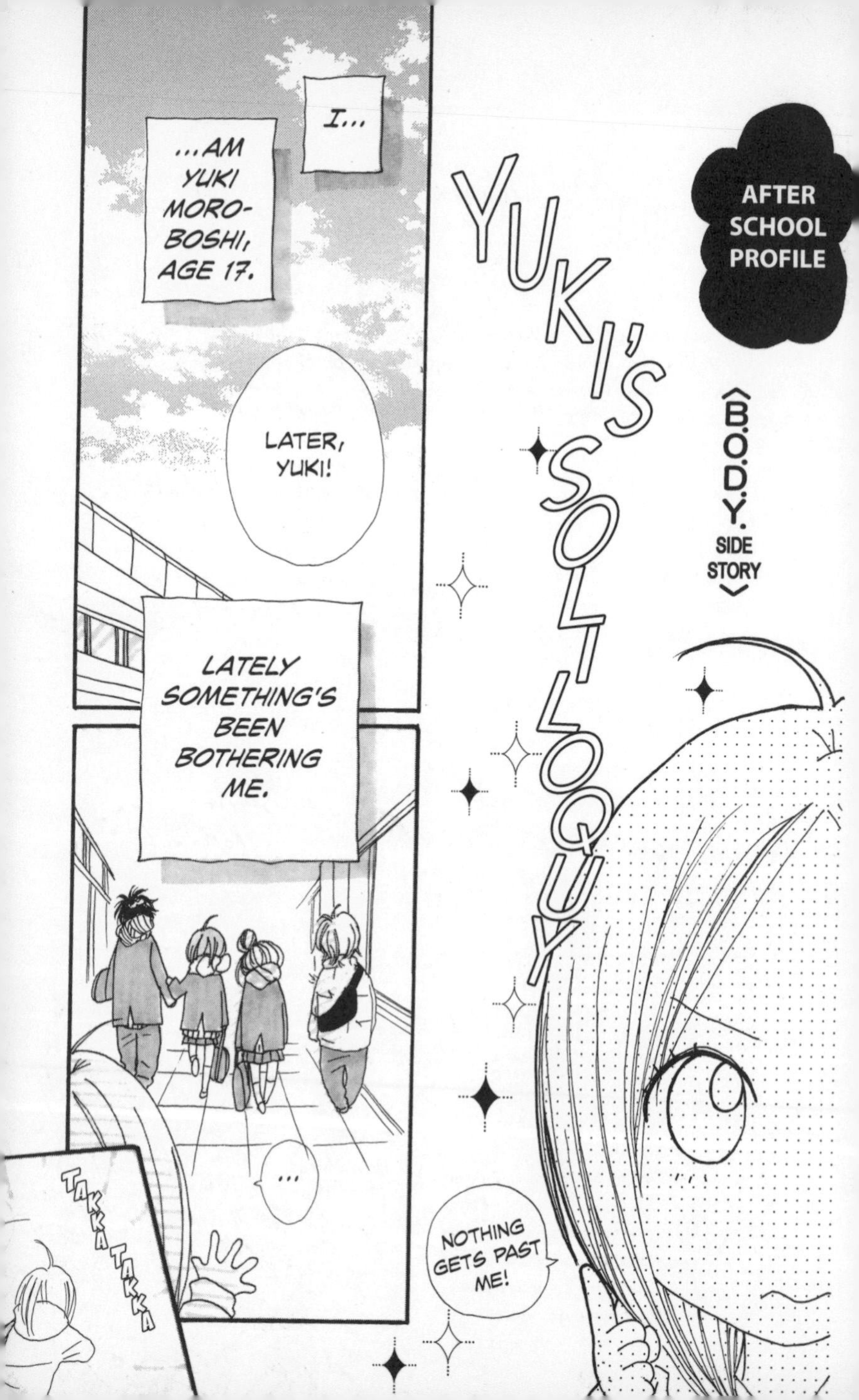
AFTER SCHOOL PROFILE
B.O.D.Y. SIDE STORY
YUKI'S SOLILOQUY
NOTHING GETS PAST ME!
I...
...AM YUKI MOROBOSHI, AGE 17.
LATER, YUKI!
LATELY SOMETHING'S BEEN BOTHERING ME.
...
TAKKA TAKKA

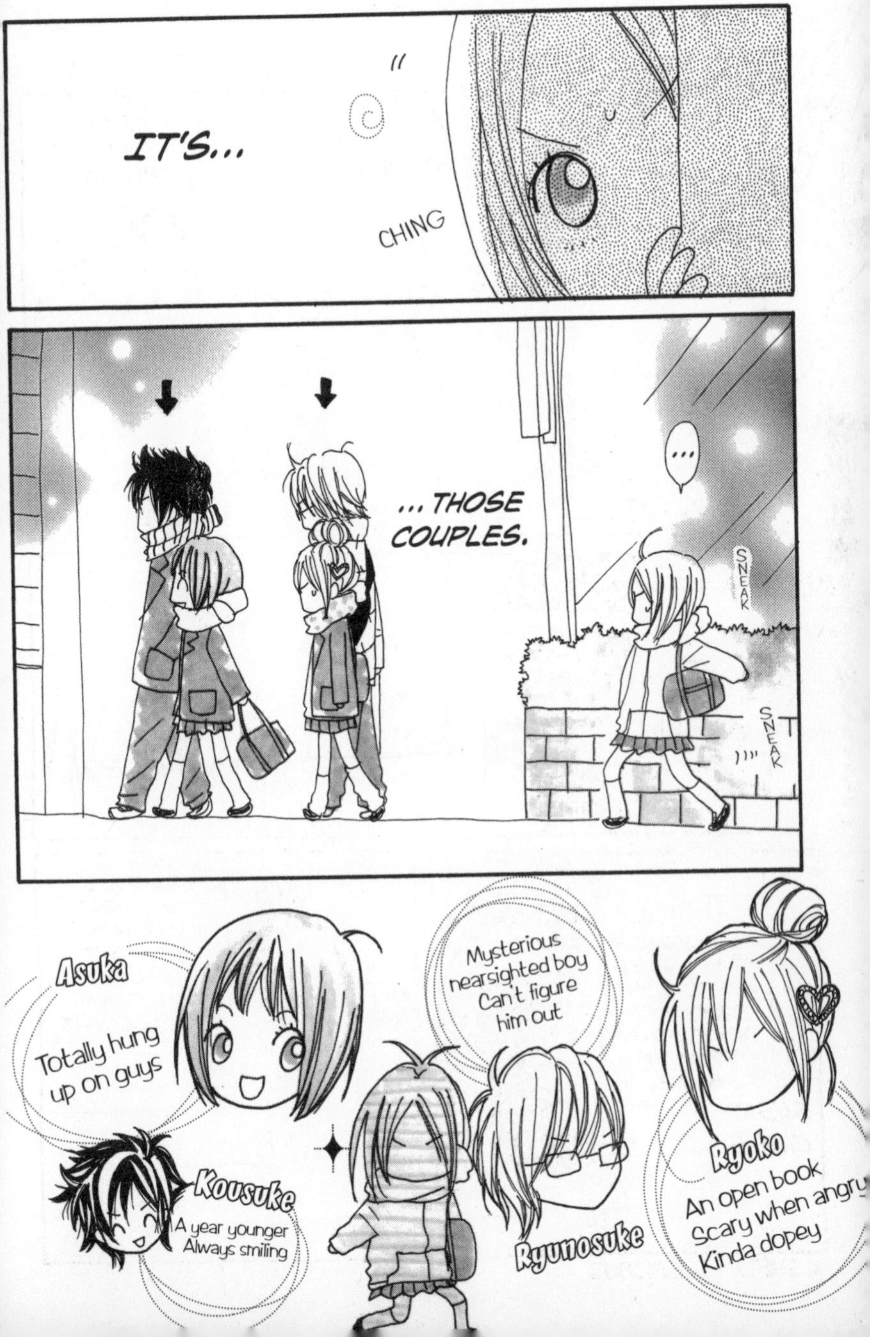
IT'S...
CHING
...
SNEAK
SNEAK
...THOSE COUPLES.
Ryoko
An open book
Scary when angry
Kinda dopey
Mysterious
nearsighted boy
Can't figure
him out
Ryunosuke
Asuka
Totally hung
up on guys
Kousuke
A year younger
Always smiling

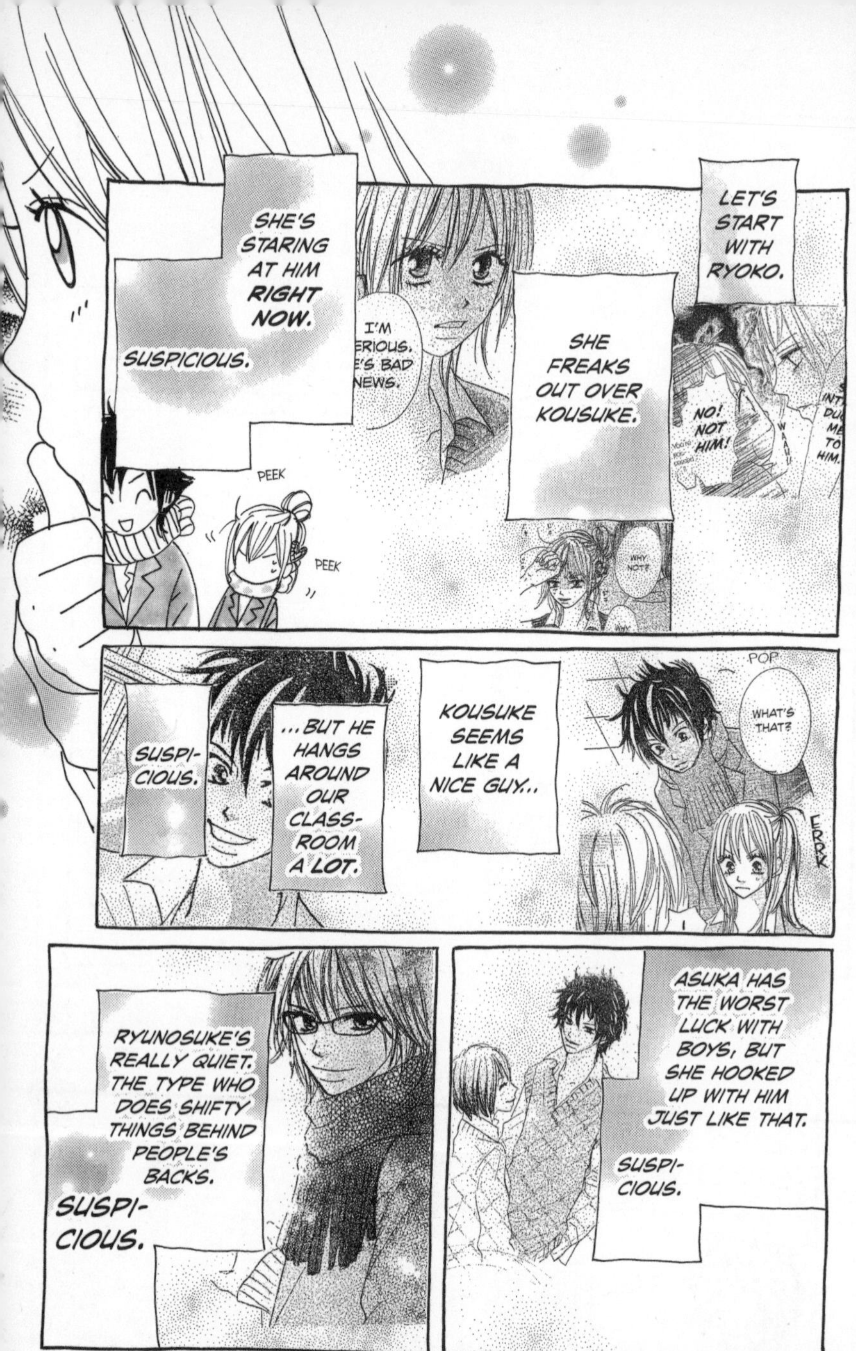
LET'S START WITH RYOKO.
NO! NOT HIM!
SHE FREAKS OUT OVER KOUSUKE.
WHY NOT?
I'M ERIOUS. E'S BAD NEWS.
SHE'S STARING AT HIM RIGHT NOW.
SUSPICIOUS.
PEEK
PEEK
POP
WHAT'S THAT?
ERRK
KOUSUKE SEEMS LIKE A NICE GUY...
...BUT HE HANGS AROUND OUR CLASSROOM A LOT.
SUSPICIOUS.
ASUKA HAS THE WORST LUCK WITH BOYS, BUT SHE HOOKED UP WITH HIM JUST LIKE THAT.
SUSPICIOUS.
RYUNOSUKE'S REALLY QUIET. THE TYPE WHO DOES SHIFTY THINGS BEHIND PEOPLE'S BACKS.
SUSPICIOUS.

※ SHIFTY = SUSPICIOUS

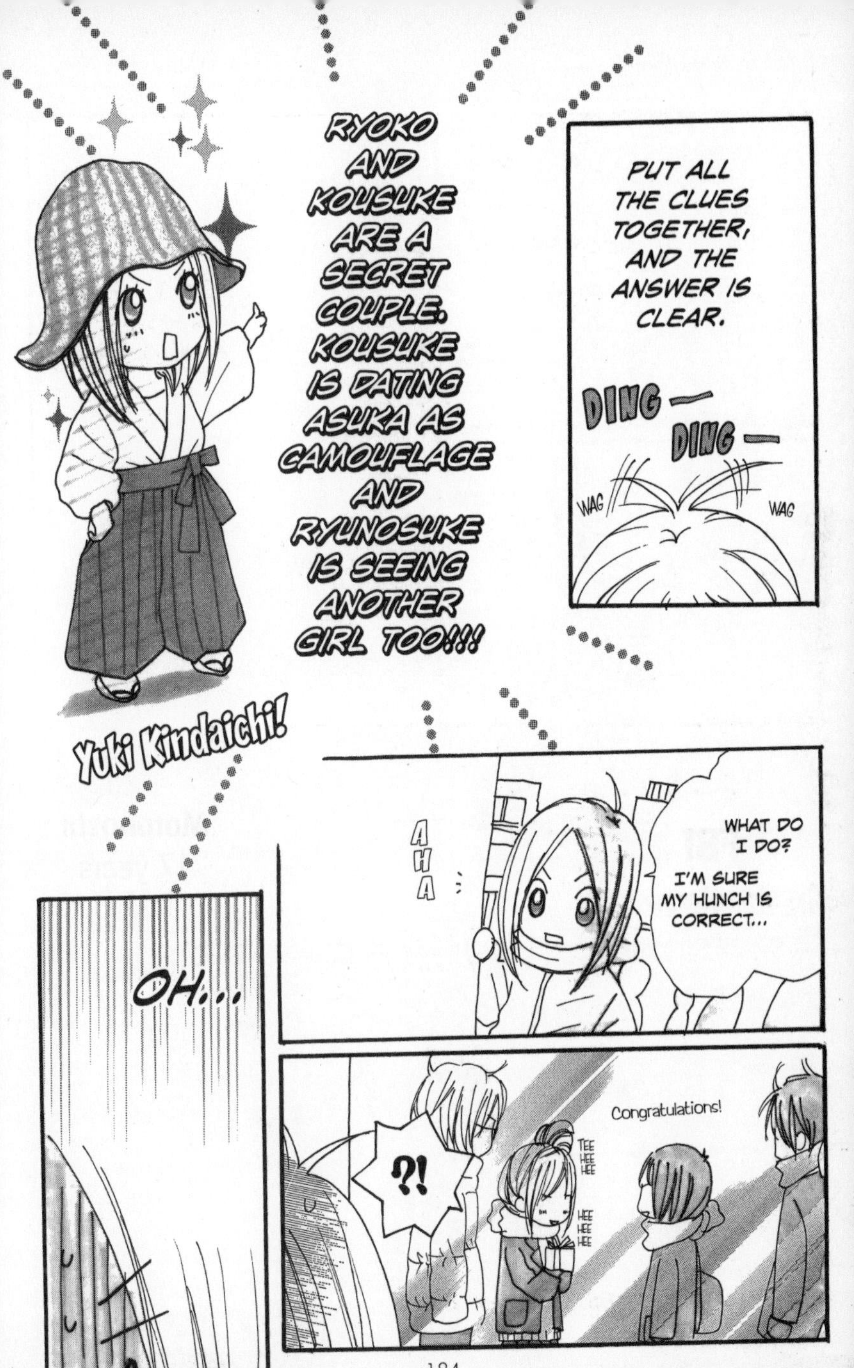
PUT ALL THE CLUES TOGETHER, AND THE ANSWER IS CLEAR.
DING—
DING—
WAG
WAG
RYOKO AND KOUSUKE ARE A SECRET COUPLE. KOUSUKE IS DATING ASUKA AS CAMOUFLAGE AND RYUNOSUKE IS SEEING ANOTHER GIRL TOO!!!
Yuki Kindaichi!
WHAT DO I DO?
I'M SURE MY HUNCH IS CORRECT...
AHA
Congratulations!
TEE HEE HEE
HEE HEE HEE
?!
OH...

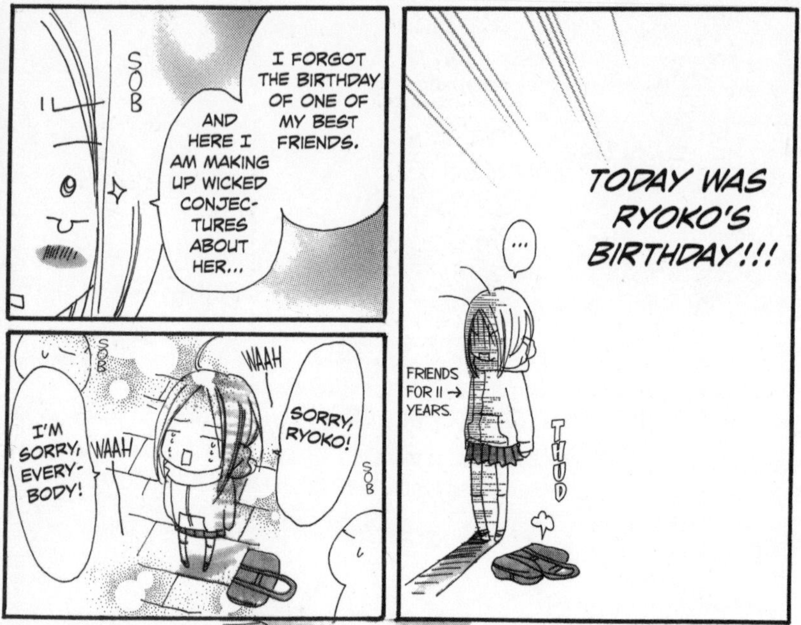
TODAY WAS RYOKO'S BIRTHDAY!!!
...
FRIENDS FOR 11 → YEARS.
THUD
I FORGOT THE BIRTHDAY OF ONE OF MY BEST FRIENDS.
AND HERE I AM MAKING UP WICKED CONJECTURES ABOUT HER...
SOB
SORRY, RYOKO!
WAAH
SOB
I'M SORRY, EVERYBODY!
WAAH
SOB

※WICKED CONJECTURES = WILD SUSPICIONS

Yuki Moroboshi
17 years old
Hobby: People Watching

Dream Job:
FBI Investigator

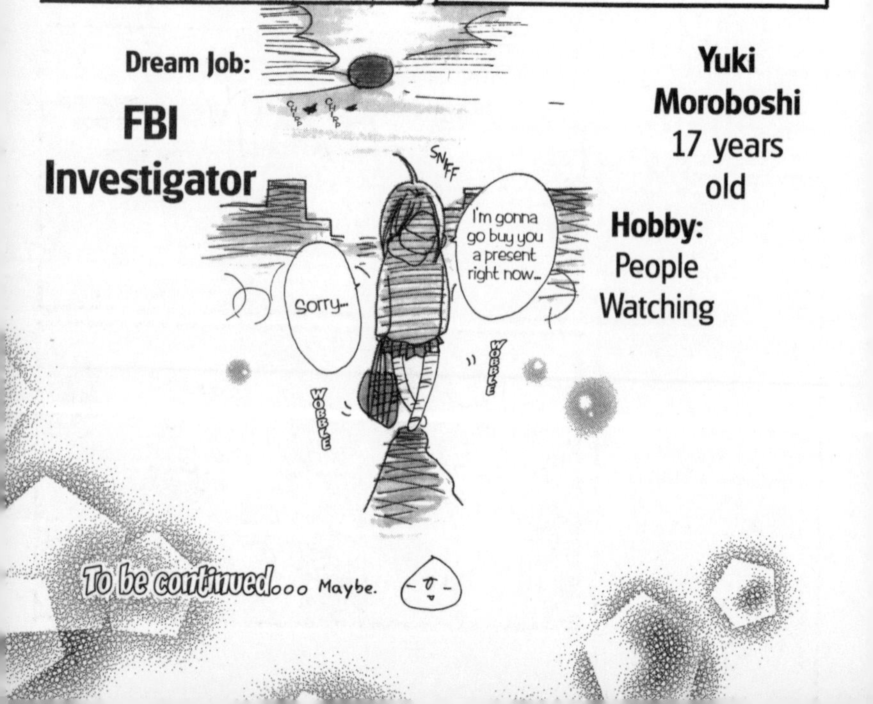
CHIRP
CHIRP
SNIFF
I'm gonna go buy you a present right now...
Sorry...
WOBBLE
WOBBLE
To be continued... Maybe.

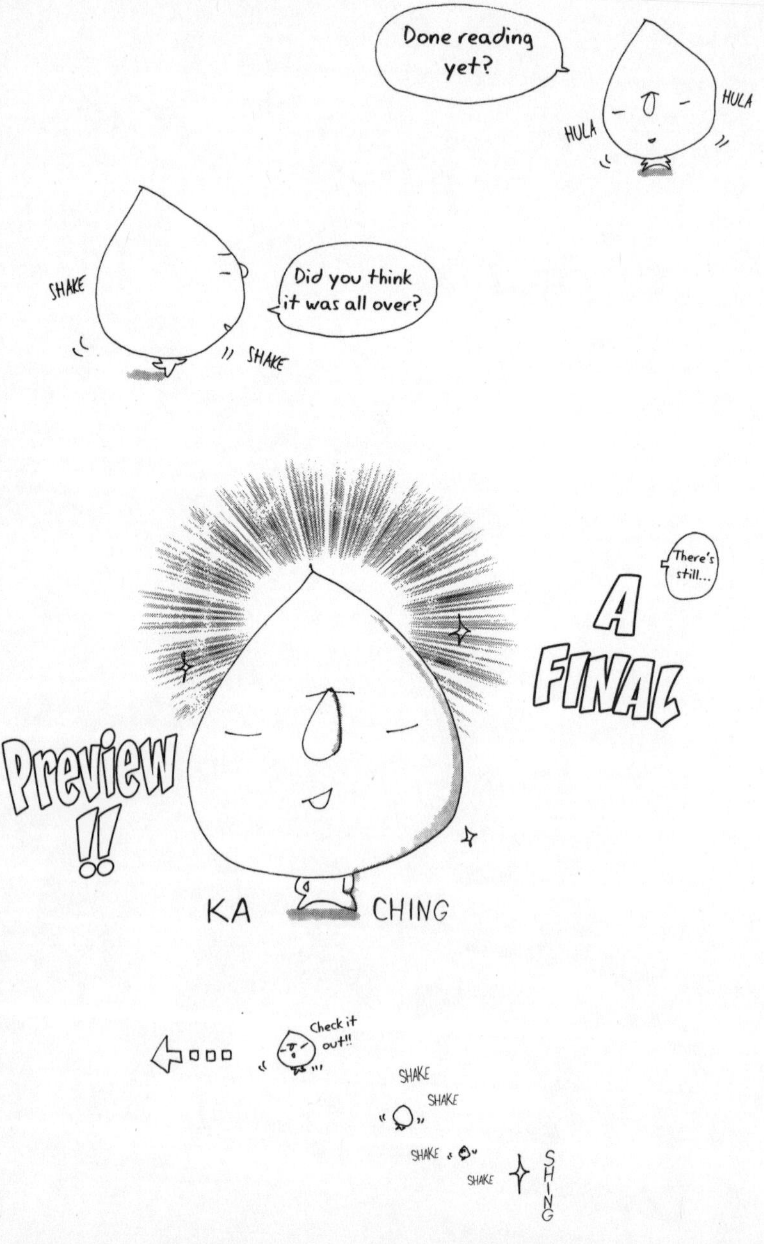
Done reading yet?
HULA
HULA
Did you think it was all over?
SHAKE
SHAKE
There's still...
A FINAL
Preview!!
KA CHING
Check it out!!
SHAKE
SHAKE
SHAKE
SHAKE
SHING

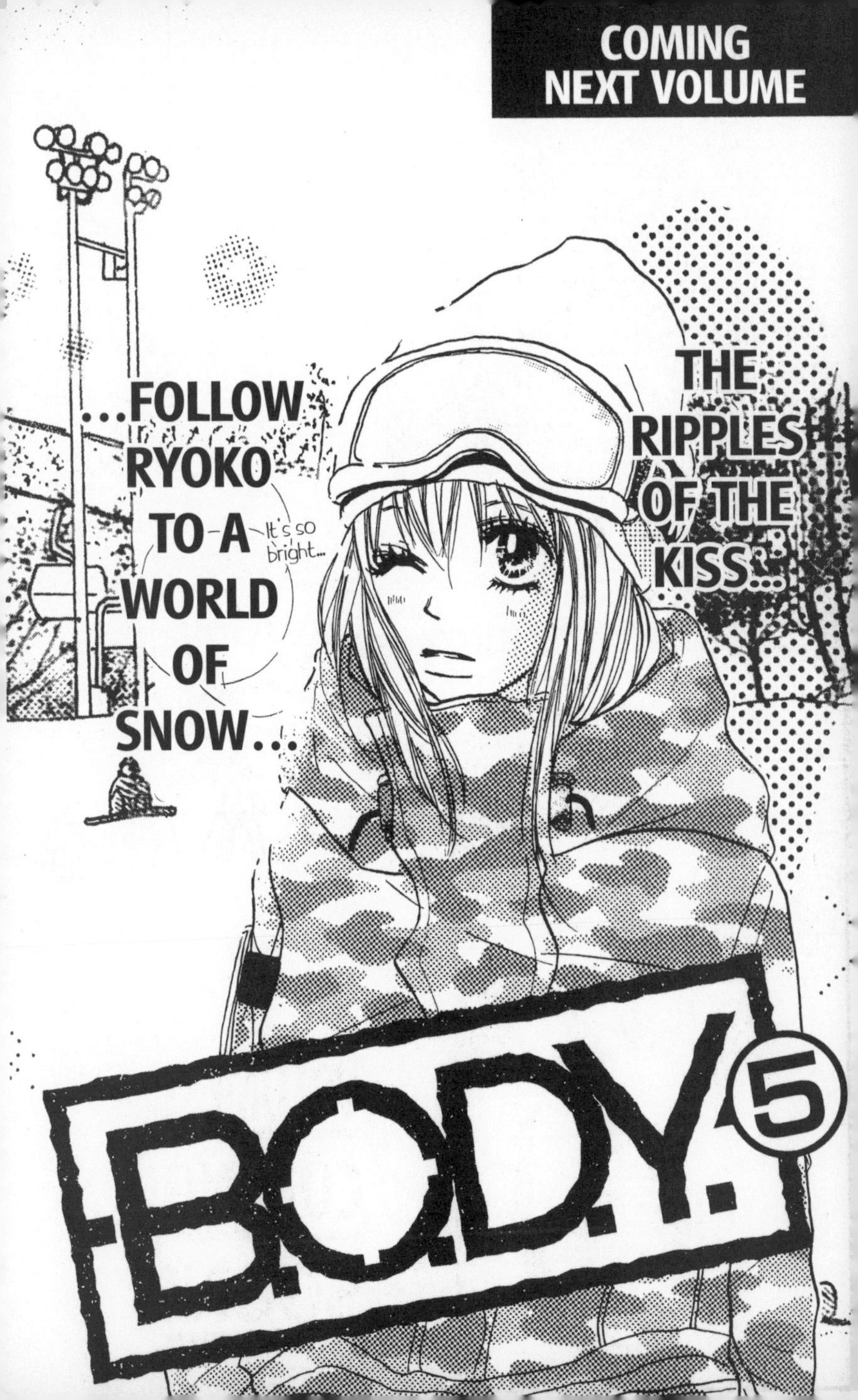
COMING NEXT VOLUME
THE RIPPLES OF THE KISS...
...FOLLOW RYOKO TO A WORLD OF SNOW...
It's so bright...
B.O.D.Y. 5

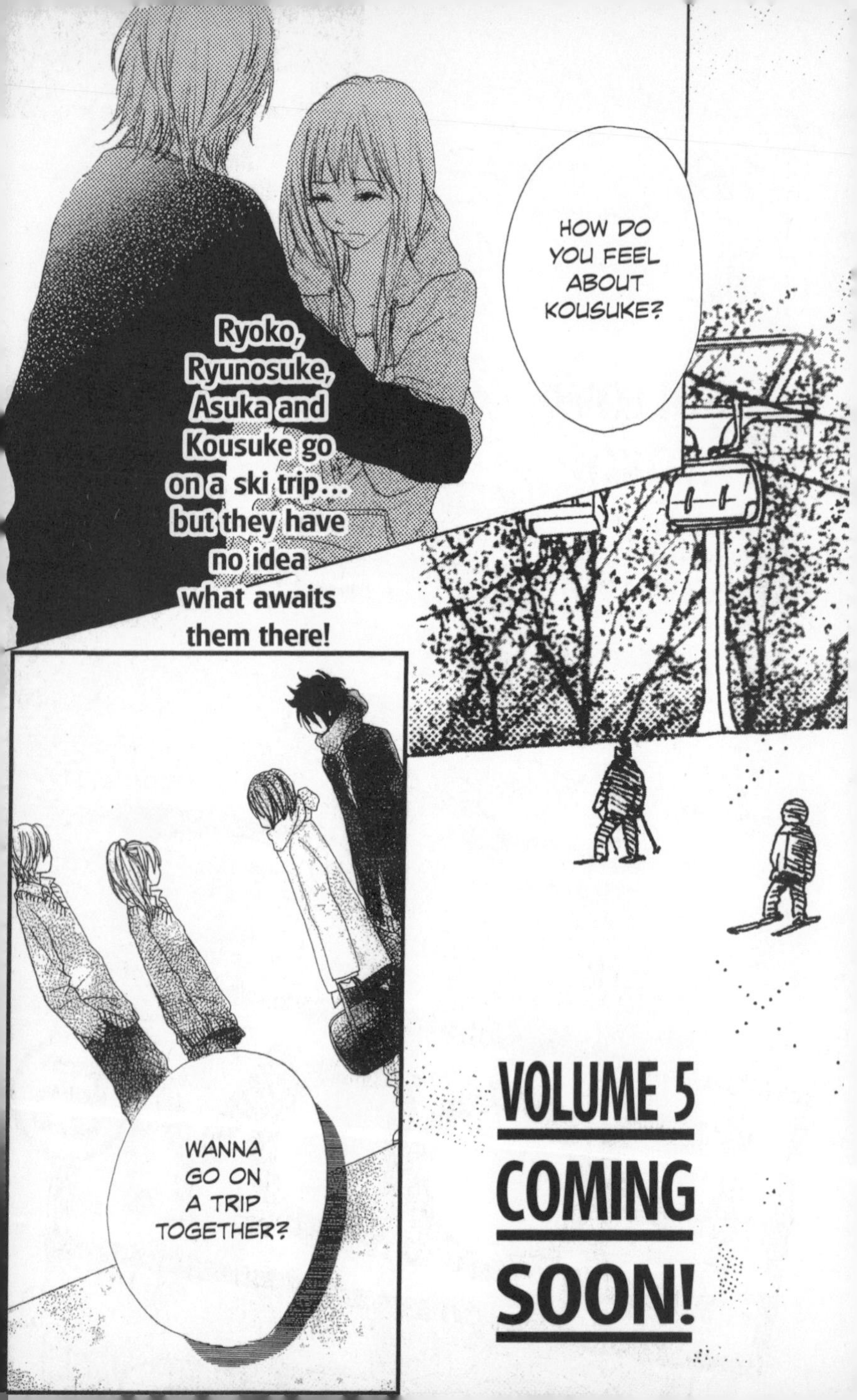
HOW DO YOU FEEL ABOUT KOUSUKE?
Ryoko, Ryunosuke, Asuka and Kousuke go on a ski trip... but they have no idea what awaits them there!
VOLUME 5 COMING SOON!
WANNA GO ON A TRIP TOGETHER?

AO MIMORI'S COMICS

Sonnano Koi Janai

Anta Nanka Iranai

Dakishimetaiyo Motto

I LOVE YOU

Kamisama no Iu Toori 2 Volumes

B.O.D.Y. ①～⑥

B.O.D.Y. Language

Page 9, panel 3: MOS Burger
A hamburger chain common throughout Japan. The name stands for "Mountain Ocean Sun."

Page 19, panel 3
The kanji on the library wall reads "stormy waves." Artistic calligraphy like this is often displayed for decoration in Japan.

Page 21, Author's Note: Donki
A Japanese discount store chain. The name is a contraction of "Don Quixote."

Page 27, panel 2: It's Sunday
Until the 1990s, most Japanese schools had six-day weeks, with a break on Sunday. Nowadays, it's usual for schools to have both Saturday and Sunday off, but many students attend supplementary "Saturday schools" or hold club meetings and events on Saturdays. Sunday may be the only day Ryoko and Ryunosuke are free to hang out with no other commitments.

Page 63, Author's Note: Karuho Shiina
A manga artist best known for *Kimi ni Todoke* (From Me to You), a shojo manga about a relationship between a cute, popular guy and a girl who has a reputation for being creepy and weird.

Page 107, Author's Note: period drama
Jidaigeki, period dramas set in feudal Japan (usually the Edo period), are staples on Japanese television. Popular *jidaigeki* can run for decades, not unlike American soap operas.

Page 107, Author's Note: *Shoten*
Anyone who grew up in Japan knows this TV comedy improv show, on the air since 1966. The structure is similar to *Whose Line Is It Anyway?*, but all the members of *Shoten* are masters of *rakugo*, a traditional form of Japanese comedy performance. As Mimori says, it's mostly popular with older people.

Page 107, Author's Note: sky fish
Also known as "solar entities" or "rods," these are said to be mysterious life forms or UFOs that move faster than the naked eye. Supposedly they can be caught only on camera; most of the evidence for sky fish consists of blurry video stills.

Page 118, panel 2: 10,000 yen
About $90.

Page 150, Author's Note: Nazca Lines
A series of enormous geoglyphs cut into rock in the Nazca Desert between 200 B.C. and 700 A.D. Because the shapes can only be seen from the air, many UFO enthusiasts believe they were made by or for ancient astronauts.

Page 150, Author's Note: 100s, Spitz, Asian Kung-Fu Generation
These are all J-pop bands.

Page 164, panel 3: 20,000 yen
About $180.

Page 180, Author's Note: Matsu Kotô
Creator of *Sakura Irony*, a shojo manga about a girl who falls for her high school teacher.

Page 184, panel 2: Kindaichi
A famous fictional detective. The hero of the manga *Kindaichi Case Files* is the grandson of the original Kindaichi.

Page 190: Ao Mimori's Comics
As of this writing, *B.O.D.Y.* is the only one of Mimori's manga available in an official English translation. Most of her early works are one-volume collections of short manga. In *Kamisama no Iu Toori* (As the God of Death Dictates), a teenage girl meets a strange boy only she can see who turns out to be a *shinigami*, or death god.

DAH DAH DA-DAH

SNIFF

10 VOLUMES!

Author's Commentary

Finally! My tenth volume!
To all my friends and family,
my editor, and you, the readers,
who pushed and pulled, soothed
and humored me to this point...
I love you.

Ao Mimori began creating manga during her junior year of college, and her work debuted when she was only 23. *B.O.D.Y.*, her third series, was first published in *Bessatsu Margaret* in 2003 and is also available in Japanese as an audio CD. Her other work includes *Sonnano Koi Iyanai* (That's Not Love), *Anta Nanka Iranai* (I Don't Need You), *Dakishimetaiyo Motto* (I Want to Hold You More), *I LOVE YOU* and *Kamisama no Iu Toori* (As the God of Death Dictates).

B.O.D.Y. VOL 4
The Shojo Beat Manga Edition

STORY & ART BY
AO MIMORI

English Adaptation/Kelly Sue DeConnick
Translation/Joe Yamazaki
Touch-up Art & Lettering/James Gaubatz
Cover Design/Izumi Hirayama
Interior Design/Sean Lee
Editor/Shaenon K. Garrity

Editor in Chief, Books/Alvin Lu
Editor in Chief, Magazines/Marc Weidenbaum
VP, Publishing Licensing/Rika Inouye
VP, Sales & Product Marketing/Gonzalo Ferreyra
VP, Creative/Linda Espinosa
Publisher/Hyoe Narita

Printed in Canada

Published by VIZ Media, LLC
P.O. Box 77010
San Francisco, CA 94107

Shojo Beat Manga Edition
10 9 8 7 6 5 4 3 2 1
First printing, February 2009

www.viz.com

store.viz.com

RATED T+ FOR OLDER TEEN

PARENTAL ADVISORY
B.O.D.Y. is rated T+ for Older Teen and is recommended for ages 16 and up. This volume contains mature themes.
ratings.viz.com

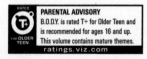

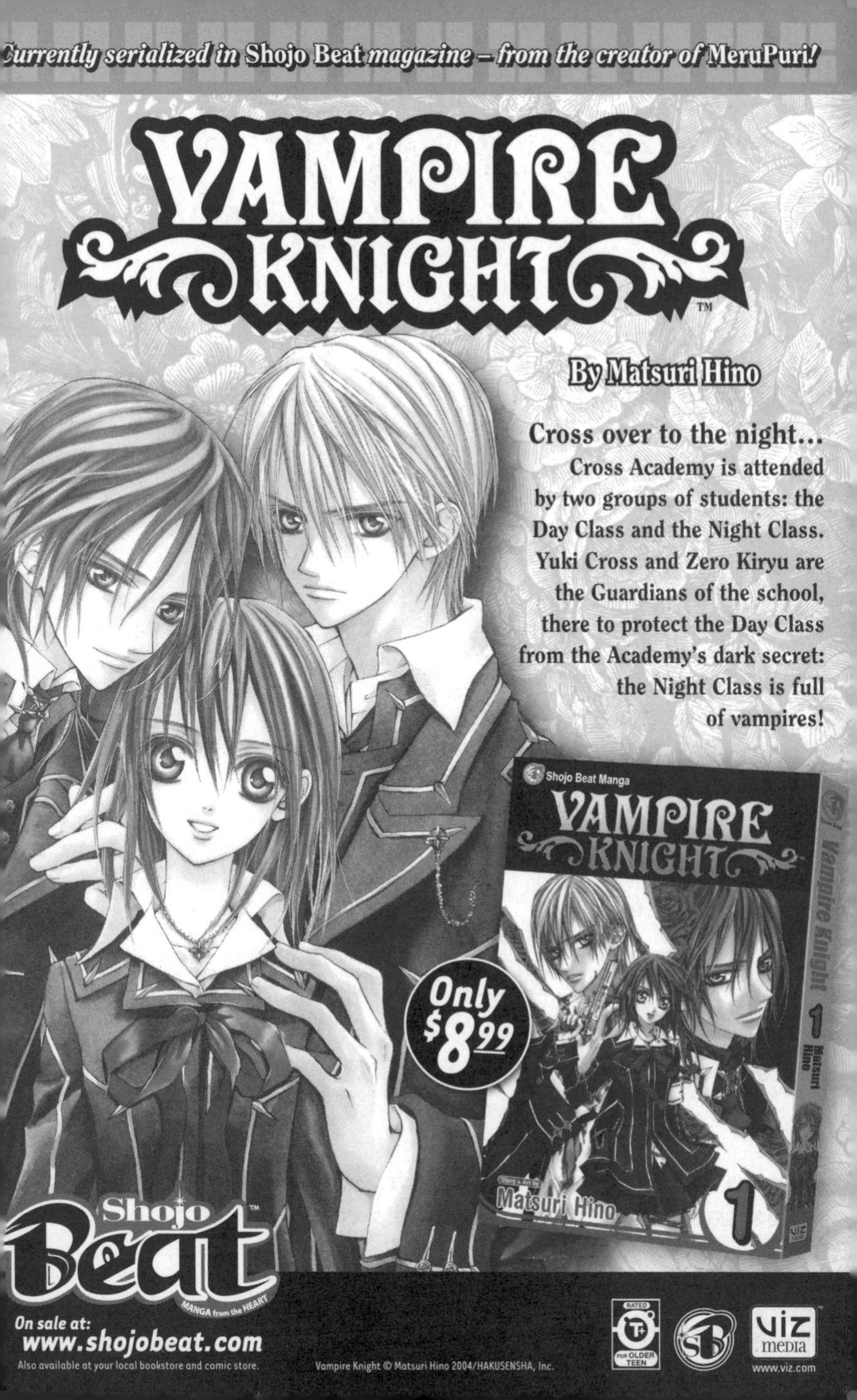